D1546237

JAMES JOYCE

GARLAND REFERENCE LIBRARY
OF THE HUMANITIES
(VOL. 328)

JAMES JOYCE
A Guide to Research

Thomas Jackson Rice

GARLAND PUBLISHING, INC. • NEW YORK & LONDON
1982

Library of Congress Cataloging in Publication Data

Rice, Thomas Jackson.
 James Joyce, a guide to research.

 (Garland reference library of the humanities ; v. 328)
 Includes indexes.
 1. Joyce, James, 1882–1941—Bibliography. I. Title.
II. Series.
Z8458.1.R5 1982   016.823′912   81-48414
[PR6019.09]
ISBN 0-8240-9383-6

Printed on acid-free, 250-year-life paper
Manufactured in the United States of America

TO
ANDREW DAVID RICE

CONTENTS

PREFACE

While James Joyce's admirers throughout the world sought various appropriate ways of celebrating the 100th anniversary of his birth, on 2 February 1982, his fellow Dubliners evidently found it easier to honor his memory by confirming his vision than by tributes. A commemorative concert, for which a number of selections from Joyce's writings had been set to music, was staggered in rehearsals when several soloists complained of indecencies in their texts. They were persuaded to perform only when told they would be paid according to the number of lines they agreed to sing. A C.B.S. evening news commentator, paraphrasing the *Irish Times'* report on the concert, suggested that Joyce himself "would have appreciated" these Dubliners in their "moral narrowness, musical meanspiritedness, and all-embracing concern for money." Knowing that critics and bibliographers are similarly vulnerable to charges of narrowness and meanspiritedness, though no one could reasonably suspect us of much concern for financial gain, I was moved to wonder what exactly Joyce might have "appreciated" in the following research guide as a centennial tribute. Certainly I might argue that there is much evidence of the breadth of moral and aesthetic values among Joyce scholars, but that just sounds pompous. Rather, I suggest that Joyce would approve the basic assumptions and intentions of this volume. Despite his often-noted delight in creating puzzles to perplex and to tantalize his readers, Joyce simultaneously encouraged various attempts to solve these puzzles and to simplify his meaning, from distributing his schema for ULYSSES and assisting Stuart Gilbert with his guide to JAMES JOYCE'S *ULYSSES*, to collaborating in the translation of "Anna Livia Plurabelle" into "basic English." The reader approaching Joyce today, and chiefly his later works, ULYSSES and FINNEGANS WAKE, initially confronts not just an apparent obscurity in the works themselves, but also a seemingly impenetrable superstructure of biographical and critical commentaries, annotations and explications, and bibliographical and textual reference works. This book attempts to guide this reader, whether neophyte or relatively experienced Joycean, through this literature *about* Joyce, to solve the puzzle of his critical reputation by pointing out the value and usefulness of each item and, occasionally, by suggesting what could or should be ignored, yet always with the final intention of equipping this reader for the vastly more important, fundamental business of returning to the literature *of* Joyce.

To be an efficient guide, this volume must necessarily be selective. I have, however, included *all* English and foreign-language books, essay collections, monographs, pamphlets, and special periodical issues concerned with Joyce and his works. These titles I have entered, *regardless of merit,* because they are conspicuous and I have always felt that one purpose of a research guide is, frankly, to tell its user that some peculiar little volume of astrological interpretations of early Joyce is worthless, not just something overlooked by the bibliographer. I have been more selective with articles and chapters appearing in periodicals or in studies not exclusively concerned with Joyce, since, while they are numerous, they tend toward considerable duplication and, at best, modest refinement of the same ideas. I have selected articles and chapters which offer original information and points of view, or which best represent certain repeated themes in Joyce criticism. I have also included a number of discussions of Joyce from standard surveys of fiction, or of the modern period (again, because they are conspicuous), since a reader with limited access to a major research library will need to rely heavily or exclusively on these titles. If I have erred in this matter of selection, I believe I have been perhaps too generous rather than too restrictive.

In my annotations throughout this guide, I have sought a balance between description and, in many cases, evaluation of a publication, feeling that a lengthy précis of a study without a judgment of its value guides the user as little as a brief and insipid evaluation which omits any mention of what the title is about. I have generally avoided an extended abstract of a book's thesis in the annotations, feeling that such condensations are comprehensible, if at all, only to someone who already knows the work and most users of this volume will know only a few of the titles included here well enough to profit from such abstracts. In the annotations throughout I have indicated various patterns among the critical responses to Joyce's works, and the relations of his critics to each other, to critical theory, or to their time. My final intention for the annotations, then, is that the user who reads through this guide should be able to trace the historical development of Joyce's critical reception and recognize the chief tendencies, concerns, and needs of contemporary Joyce criticism.

No work such as this can be completed without incurring numerous debts. For their help in translating I thank David Danow, Masako Dorrill, and Marianne Wachter. For their advice and loans of material, I thank Zack Bowen, George L. Geckle, John MacNicholas, and Joel Myerson. For their comments and suggestions on the bibliography, in its various permutations over the last several years, I thank my editors Ralph Carlson, Duane DeVries, and Theodore Grieder, and my teacher, colleague, and friend, A. Walton Litz. For assembling the index, I thank Dawn Bailey and Mary Dave Denny. For preparation of the final typescript, I thank, again, Dawn Bailey, my most able research assistant. For their forbearance, I thank my wife, Diane, and my children. And for a therapeutic lesson in the transience of uncritical adulation, I thank my son Andrew, to whom this book is dedicated, and who would far prefer that this book be about Pete Rose.

PERIODICAL ABBREVIATIONS

The following periodical abbreviations are used consistently throughout this guide, except when the periodical itself is the main entry. That is, special issues are classified as "essay collections" and entered alphabetically, by the name of the periodical.

AI	American Imago
AR	Antioch Review
ArQ	Arizona Quarterly
ASch	American Scholar
BNYPL	Bulletin of the New York Public Library
BSUF	Ball State University Forum
BuR	Bucknell Review
CE	College English
CL	Comparative Literature
CLQ	Colby Library Quarterly
CLS	Comparative Literature Studies
ConL	Contemporary Literature
ConnR	Connecticut Review
CritQ	Critical Quarterly
DR	Dalhousie Review
EA	Études Anglaises
E&S	Essays and Studies by Members of the English Association
EIC	Essays in Criticism
EJ	English Journal (College Edition)
ELH	Journal of English Literary History
ELN	English Language Notes
ELT	English Literature in Transition (1880–1920)
EM	English Miscellany
ES	English Studies
ESA	English Studies in Africa
HAB	Humanities Association Bulletin
HSL	Hartford Studies in Literature
HudR	Hudson Review

JAAC	Journal of Aesthetics and Art Criticism
JEGP	Journal of English and Germanic Philology
JGE	Journal of General Education
JJQ	James Joyce Quarterly
JML	Journal of Modern Literature
JNT	Journal of Narrative Technique
KR	Kenyon Review
L&P	Literature and Psychology
LCrit	Literary Criterion
LHY	Literary Half-Yearly
MD	Modern Drama
MFS	Modern Fiction Studies
MLN	Modern Language Notes
MLQ	Modern Language Quarterly
MLR	Modern Language Review
ModA	Modern Age
MP	Modern Philology
MQ	Midwest Quarterly
MR	Massachusetts Review
NDQ	North Dakota Quarterly
OL	Orbis Litterarum
PLL	Papers on Language and Literature
PMLA	Publications of the Modern Language Association of America
PQ	Philological Quarterly
PR	Partisan Review
PsyR	Psychoanalytic Review
PULC	Princeton University Library Chronicle
QR	Quarterly Review
REL	Review of English Literature
RLV	Revue des Langues Vivantes
RMS	Renaissance and Modern Studies
RS	Research Studies
SAQ	South Atlantic Quarterly
SatR	Saturday Review
SB	Studies in Bibliography
SEER	Slavonic and East European Review
SHR	Southern Humanities Review
SLitI	Studies in the Literary Imagination
SoR	Southern Review
SR	Sewanee Review
SSF	Studies in Short Fiction

TCL	Twentieth Century Literature
TQ	Texas Quarterly
TSLL	Texas Studies in Literature and Language
UKCR	University of Kansas City Review
UTQ	University of Toronto Quarterly
VQR	Virginia Quarterly Review
WHR	Western Humanities Review
WR	Western Review: A Journal of the Humanities
YR	Yale Review
YULG	Yale University Library Gazette

INTRODUCTION

JAMES JOYCE: A GUIDE TO RESEARCH is a selective annotated bibliography of works by and about James Joyce. It consists of three parts: (1) the primary bibliography—which includes separate bibliographies of Joyce's major works, of scholarly editions or collections of his works, of his letters, and of concordances to his works; (2) the secondary bibliography—which includes bibliographies of bibliographical, biographical, and critical works concerning Joyce generally or his individual works; and (3) major foreign-language studies—which includes, in the same format as part two, bibliographies of works on Joyce originally published in languages other than English. The balance of this introduction will explain more fully the principles of selection, arrangement, and annotation for each of these sections of the volume.

The Primary Bibliography
(Sections A through D)

Section A of the primary bibliography is a brief listing of all Joyce's major writings, with original publication data and factual annotations. The titles in Section B include a few additional minor works by Joyce, several significant collections of his published and manuscript writings, and all scholarly editions of his notes, manuscripts, typescripts, and proofs, with descriptive and evaluative annotations. Section C comprises the two major collections of Joyce's correspondence, also with descriptive and evaluative annotations. And Section D lists all the concordances of Joyce's works, with annotations describing their scope and methodology. Cross-reference numbers in the annotations, in this primary section of the bibliography, generally send the user to important textual commentaries on and introductions to a title, which are themselves entered and annotated elsewhere in the guide. Sectional headnotes likewise contain numerous cross-references to titles of related interest which are to be found in other sections of the volume (e.g., the headnote to section C, the letters, provides cross-references for other published correspondence or for commentaries on Joyce's correspondence).

The Secondary Bibliography (Sections E through P)

By far the largest part of this volume, the secondary bibliography consists of ten sections:

(1) Section E (Bibliographies) is a broad but selective listing of previous primary and secondary bibliographies concerning Joyce, as well as essay-surveys of his critical reputation. Annotations describe the nature of the bibliographies and evaluate their accuracy and usefulness.

(2) Section F (Biographies, Memoirs, Reminiscences, and Interviews) is a generous, but again selective listing of major biographical sources, published as books, articles, chapters, special journal issues, or essay collections. The annotations in this section describe and often evaluate the title and, when appropriate, provide some comment on the nature and duration of a memoirist's relationship with Joyce. For the most part, this section omits brief notes and incidental mentions in published writings or in letters, as well as essays, articles, or notes since assimilated into larger studies. For the principles followed for the occasionally difficult discrimination between biographical and critical commentaries, see the introductory headnote to section F.

Section G (Book-Length Critical Studies and Essay Collections) is a comprehensive bibliography of critical books, essay collections, monographs, and pamphlets concerned with Joyce and his works generally, or with more than *two* of his works. Studies limited to two of Joyce's works are entered in each of the two appropriate sections on the individual works (sections J through P—see below). Annotations are more detailed in this section, giving the general drift of the title's thesis, surveying its chief points, and evaluating both its contribution to Joyce's critical reputation and its practical usefulness to the student of Joyce. Dissertations are not considered published books for the purposes of this bibliography and are not included here, or elsewhere in the guide, unless subsequently published. (A complete list of dissertations on Joyce would be a useful addition to Joyce bibliography. Most American and foreign dissertations are listed by Cohn [E4] and Deming [E9], and anyone seeking such data should begin there.)

Section H (General Critical Articles or Chapters) is a generous selection of critical essays and discussions of Joyce generally, or, again, of more than *two* of his works, published in periodicals, special issues of journals, essay collections, or general studies of English, Irish, and World literatures, of modern writers, of the novel, and so on. For the most part, this listing excludes both brief notes and essays, articles, or notes later assimilated into larger studies which are entered and annotated elsewhere. It does, however, include a selection of pedestrian surveys, obviously not because they are meritorious, but because they are readily found in most general library collections and can be helpful, if the user realizes their superficial or derivative nature and has no access to a larger research library. A handful of other entries are, frankly, misguided, wrong-headed, or perverse, but are included, with warning annotations, to show the diversity of Joyce's reputation (and to provide occasional light relief). Most of the entries, however, survived the selection process by merit and their inclusion should indicate implicitly their value. Thus the majority of annotations in this section are brief, factual, and descriptive rather than evaluative.

Sections J through P are extensive checklists of studies of Joyce's individual works, DUBLINERS (Section J), A PORTRAIT OF THE ARTIST AS A YOUNG MAN (Section K), EXILES (Section L), ULYSSES (Section M), FINNEGANS WAKE (Section N), and miscellaneous writings (Section P— covering, essentially, the poetry and non-fiction prose). These checklists, in each case, consist of at least two subsections: "Book-Length Critical Studies and Essay Collections" on the given work and "General Critical Articles or Chapters" on the work. The sections for DUBLINERS (J) and ULYSSES (M), contain a third subsection, "Studies of Individual Stories/Episodes." Each of these individual-work sections opens with a lengthy introductory headnote, cross-referring the user to textual, bibliographical, biographical, or critical titles, entered and annotated in other sections of this bibliography, which comment significantly on the given work. In the DUBLINERS (J) and ULYSSES (M) sections, additional introductory headnotes appear at the beginning of the third subsection, " Studies of Individual Stories/Episodes," as well as for each story/episode division therein, referring the user to the numerous commentaries on individual stories in DUB-LINERS and episodes in ULYSSES. All of this information, of course, can also be found in the indexes and these repeated cross-reference lists take considerable space, but this multiplication of the opportunities to locate pertinent publications should simplify the task of research, which, after all, is the basic purpose of this research guide.

In parallel with sections G and H, the principles for selection and annotation vary within the subsections on Joyce's individual works. The listings of book-length studies, essay collections, monographs, and pamphlets are comprehensive, and those of articles and chapters are generous yet selective. Dissertations, again, are not considered published books or entered in the bibliographies. Most, but not all, study guides or student "cribs" on the individual works are likewise excluded, though technically they are book-length studies as defined above. (The Appendix provides a checklist of these study guides.) Annotations for books are detailed and evaluative; for articles they are concise and generally descriptive.

Major Foreign-Language Studies
(Sections Q through Z)

Part three of this guide is a ten-section, slightly annotated checklist of foreign-language studies of Joyce and his works, paralleling in arrangement and selection the the ten-section secondary bibliography described above. A great number of the titles listed here, moreover, have been entered in the secondary bibliography proper and annotated, either from their original publication, or from their subsequent whole or partial publication in English translation. In all such cases of double-entry, a cross-reference number in this part of the bibliography sends the user to the prior entry and annotation. Likewise, titles appearing in sections A through P which originally were published in a foreign language, have been given a reference number to this portion of the bibliography so that the user may locate original foreign-language publication information. These foreign-language items stand as a separate section of this guide for five basic reasons: (1) Many of the book-length studies of Joyce and his works are elementary introductions for non-English readers and are only included here to make the overall record of book-length publications in this guide more nearly complete. To an English audience they will be chiefly valuable for anyone who wishes to trace Joyce's international critical reception (about which comparatively little has been written). Individually, these works do not often contribute greatly to what has already been written in English. (2) Segregating these studies into this section will draw the user's attention to this international dimension of Joyce's reputation and, perhaps, encourage both discussion of his reception in other countries and more complete international bibliographies in the future. (3) Several of the special periodical issues and essay collections, in fact, contain a large number of articles and extracts from studies already entered in this bibliography, translated from the original English. Thus, for the predominantly English and American audience for which this guide is designed, many of these publications are as unnecessary as they are difficult to obtain. The annotations distinguish original essay collections from those containing chiefly reprinted material, in translation. (4) A number of books, moreover, are essentially unrevised, published dissertations, which are beyond the scope of this volume (see discussion of Section G, above). (5) Several of the items included here are difficult to obtain, though every attempt has been made to examine as many of the books and articles as possible and to determine whether they should be included in the secondary bibliography for fuller annotation. These unseen titles are placed here basically on speculation, because their titles are promising or because they seem to be discussions of significant length in languages which are under-represented in Joyce criticism. (Note: there is a remarkable scarcity of writings on Joyce in Russian, for reasons that are well discussed in Edgerton's bibliographical article [see E11]).

Indexes

This volume concludes with three indexes: authors, titles, and subjects. This last index should be a useful means for tracing specific figures (literary and historical), ideas, places, themes, and titles in Joyce criticism. In a way, it suggests a number of alternative topical arrangements that might have been used for organizing this bibliography and should give the user further options for research within the bibliography.

Cross-References

Cross-reference numbers are used throughout in entries to send the user to a main entry for a work or collection from which a particular title is extracted, in headnotes to refer the user to other titles which discuss a particular work or topic, and in the indexes. Cross-reference numbers found in the annotations for collections indicate the titles included in the collection which are entered and annotated elsewhere. Cross-reference numbers in the annotations throughout will also direct the user to a prior annotation for the same entry, refer the user to a title described in or relevant to the annotation, or send the user to part three of the volume for original foreign-language publication information.

Abbreviations and Reference Terms

Abbreviations are used throughout this bibliography for James Joyce's name (JJ) and for his four major works of fiction:

D   = DUBLINERS
PAYM = A PORTRAIT OF THE ARTIST AS A YOUNG
            MAN

```
U      = ULYSSES
FW     = FINNEGANS WAKE.
```
Abbreviations are not used, however, in titles, for the adjectival form of Joyce's name (e.g., Joycean, not JJ'ean), or whenever there appears to be a possibility of confusion. For journal abbreviations, see the table on p. xiii. The most frequently used, and perhaps unfamiliar reference terms are "passim" ("throughout the work" or "here and there") and "cf." (within parentheses, this indicates a comparison made by the author of the book or article annotated). Quotations within the annotations are from the work annotated unless otherwise attributed.

Dates of Coverage and Item Count

The terminal date for this bibliography was 1 January 1982. A few last-minute notes on titles appearing early in 1982 have been included, as practicable, in the last stages of the volume's preparation. The total number of entries is 1967.

PART 1. PRIMARY BIBLIOGRAPHY

A. MAJOR WORKS

This slightly annotated checklist provides basic initial publication information for JJ's principal works. It includes
first English and American editions, foreign editions (only
if first editions), and subsequent corrected or textual editions. Cross-reference numbers are also supplied here to refer the user to the most important textual studies of the
given work, to be found in the secondary section of this guide.
For posthumous collected, selected, or other textual editions
of JJ's writings, see section B below. For full bibliographical data on all publications, to 1952, see the Slocum and
Cahoon bibliography (E25).

A1 CHAMBER MUSIC. London: Elkin Mathews, 1907. Boston: Corn-
    hill, 1918. Textual edition: Ed. William York Tindall.
    New York: Columbia Univ. Press, 1954.
        Twenty-six lyric poems. For textual information
        see P32.

A2 DUBLINERS. London: Richards, 1914. New York: Huebsch,
    1916. Textual edition: Ed. Robert Scholes. New York:
    Viking, 1967.
        Fifteen short stories, including "The Sisters,"
        "An Encounter," "Araby," "Eveline," "After the
        Race," "Two Gallants," "The Boarding House," "A
        Little Cloud," "Counterparts," "Clay," "A Pain-
        ful Case," "Ivy Day in the Committee Room," "A
        Mother," "Grace," and "The Dead." For textual
        information see J51 and J182.

A3 EXILES: A PLAY IN THREE ACTS. London: Richards; New York:
    Huebsch, 1918. Rev. ed. New York: Viking Press; Harmonds-
    worth, Engl.: Penguin, 1951.
        For textual information see L1. 1951 edition
        publishes JJ's several notes for the play.

A4 FINNEGANS WAKE. London: Faber; New York: Viking, 1939.
    Corrected ed. New York: Viking, 1958.
        Pre-publication title, 1924-38: "Work in Prog-

ress." A textual edition, to appear in the
mid-1980s, is in progress, under the general
editorship of Hans Walter Gabler. For textual
information see N90, N132, and the editions of
JJ's manuscripts and notebooks, included in
section B below.

A5   POMES PENYEACH. Paris: Shakespeare and Company, 1927.
London: Harmsworth,
Princeton, N.J.: Sylvia Beach, 1931. London: Harmsworth,
1932.
     Thirteen lyric poems.

A6   A PORTRAIT OF THE ARTIST AS A YOUNG MAN. New York:
Huebsch, 1916. London: EGOIST, 1917. Textual edition:
Ed. Chester G. Anderson. New York: Viking, 1964.
     For textual information see K25, K62, and K63.

A7   STEPHEN HERO. See B21 below.

A8   ULYSSES. Paris: Shakespeare and Company, 1922. New York:
Random House, 1934. London: Lane, 1936. Corrected ed.
New York: Random House, 1961.
     A textual edition, to appear in the mid-1980s,
is in progress, under the general editorship
of Hans Walter Gabler (see M159 and M191).
For textual information see E23, M25, M114,
M146, and the editions of JJ's manuscripts and
notebooks, included in section B below.

A9   "Work in Progress." See A4 above.

B. COLLECTED AND SELECTED WORKS

JJ's manuscripts, typescripts, page proofs, and notes for vir-
tually all the works noted here are published in photo-facsim-
ile, chiefly in THE JAMES JOYCE ARCHIVE (B10). For extracts
and selections from JJ's works see Giedion-Welcker (F47), Quinn
(F126), Tindall (F150), Goldman (G33), Magalaner (G57), Baker
and Staley (J1), Scholes and Litz (J13), Moynihan (J179),
Anderson (K1), Morris and Nault (K14), Adams (L2), and Kain
(M375). Also see J181.

B1 *ANNA LIVIA PLURABELLE*: THE MAKING OF A CHAPTER. Ed. Fred
    H. Higginson. Minneapolis: Univ. of Minnesota Press, 1960.
        Reprints the six consecutive, increasingly com-
        plex drafts of the "Anna Livia Plurabelle" sec-
        tion of FW, as illustration of JJ's compositional
        techniques. Includes Higginson's editorial com-
        mentary on JJ's methods of revision ("Introduc-
        tion," pp. 3-15).

B2 THE CAT AND THE DEVIL. London: Faber, 1965.
        Wry children's story, written in 1936 by JJ for
        his grandson Stephen.

B3 COLLECTED POEMS. New York: Black Sun Press, 1936.
        Gathers the thirty-six brief lyrics previously
        published in CHAMBER MUSIC, the thirteen lyrics
        from POMES PENYEACH, and "Ecce Puer" (1932).
        Lacks several of JJ's occasional poems (see E10).

B4 THE CRITICAL WRITINGS OF JAMES JOYCE. Ed. Richard Ellmann
    and Ellsworth Mason. New York: Viking, 1959.
        Collects twenty-three reviews (published previ-
        ously, with Mason's annotations, as THE EARLY
        JOYCE [below]), together with five of his early
        student essays, his first publication ("Ibsen's
        New Drama" [1900]), two "broadsides" ("The Day
        of the Rabblement" [1901] and "The Holy Office"
        [1904-5]), plus miscellaneous prose. Includes

a brief editorial "Introduction" (pp. 7-11),
absorbed into Ellmann's JAMES JOYCE (F33).

B5 THE EARLY JOYCE: THE BOOK REVIEWS, 1902-1903. Ed. Stanislaus Joyce and Ellsworth Mason. Colorado Springs, Colo.:
Mamalujo Press, 1955.
Assimilated into THE CRITICAL WRITINGS (see
above). See P19.

B6 EPIPHANIES. Ed. Oscar A. Silverman. Buffalo, N.Y.: Lock-
wood Memorial Library of the Univ. of Buffalo, 1956.
Assimilated into the "Manuscript Materials" section of THE WORKSHOP OF DAEDALUS (see B17). See
P26.

B7 A FIRST-DRAFT VERSION OF *FINNEGANS WAKE*. Ed. David Hayman.
Austin: Univ. of Texas Press, 1963.
A "liberally defined first draft" presented as
the "complete skeleton" of FW "reduced to its
simplest language and arranged in its defini-
tive order." Compiled from over 9,000 manuscript pages. Hayman's "Draft Catalog" of the
British Library holdings of FW materials (see
E16) serves as the basis for their arrangement
in THE JAMES JOYCE ARCHIVE, vols. 44-63 (B10).
Also see N124.

B8 GIACOMO JOYCE. Ed. Richard Ellmann. New York: Viking,
1968.
Transcription and facsimile reproduction of JJ's
lyrical, sentimental, "mid-life crisis" love
diary. Includes Ellmann's discussion of the
work's biographical backgrounds ("Introduction,"
pp. xi-xxvi).

B9 INTRODUCING JAMES JOYCE: A SELECTION OF PROSE. Ed. T.S.
Eliot. London: Faber, 1942.
Includes selections from D ("The Sisters"), PAYM,
U ("Nestor," "Hades," and an extract from "Si-
rens"), and FW, with a brief introductory note
by Eliot (pp. 5-7).

B10 THE JAMES JOYCE ARCHIVE. 63 vols. Gen. ed. Michael
Groden. New York: Garland, 1977-80.
Monumental publication of photoreprints of "all
the extant prepublication materials for Joyce's
works" (i.e. notes, manuscripts, and proofs,
with some reproduction of JJ's color-coding).

Omits only the letters, the LITTLE REVIEW episodes and the Rosenbach manuscript of U (see
B22), and a few less significant items. Volume
editors are Groden, Hans Walter Gabler, David
Hayman, A. Walton Litz, and Danis Rose. Contents: verse (1 vol.), nonfiction prose (2
vols.), D (3 vols.), PAYM (4 vols.), EXILES
(1 vol.), U (16 vols.), FW (36 vols.). Also
see Groden's index volume (E15). Each major
section contains Groden's general "Introduction" and each volume has an informative but
brief "Preface" by its editor.

B11 JAMES JOYCE IN PADUA. Trans. and ed. Louis Berrone. New
York: Random House, 1977.
Photo-reproduction, transcription, and translation of JJ's correspondence with the University of Padua, his two examination essays (on
the Renaissance and on Dickens), and the offi-
cial report on his examinations. Much ado
about little. See P8. Reprinted in B14.

B12 JAMES JOYCE'S THE "INDEX MANUSCRIPT": *FINNEGANS WAKE* HOLO-
GRAPH WORKBOOK VI.B.46. Ed. Danis Rose. Colchester,
Engl.: WAKE NEWSLITTER Press, 1977.
Critical edition of JJ's most important notebooks for FW. Includes transcription of the
heavily crossed-out 1938 notebook manuscript,
arranged under fifty-seven topical headings,
with Rose's explanatory notes following each
of the sections. ˙Provides an important key
to understanding the method of JJ's composition of FW.

B13 JOYCE AND HAUPTMANN: *BEFORE SUNRISE*: JAMES JOYCE'S TRANS-
LATION. Ed. Jill Perkins. San Marino, Calif.: Huntington
Library Publications, 1978. Pp. 48-132.
Annotated edition of JJ's translation (c. 1901)
of Hauptmann's drama, VOR SONNENAUFGANG (1889).
See P20.

B14 JOYCE AS AN ITALIAN WRITER: REGARDING SCRITTI ITALIANI DI
JAMES JOYCE. Ed. Gianfranco Corsini and Giorgio Melchiori.
Milan: Mondadori, 1979.
Gathers all surviving Italian articles, essays,
and translations (of his own FW) by JJ, with
editorial commentary. Includes B11.

B15   JOYCE'S NOTES AND EARLY DRAFTS FOR *ULYSSES*: SELECTIONS
      FROM THE BUFFALO COLLECTION. Ed. Phillip F. Herring.
      Charlottesville: Univ. Press of Virginia, 1975.
           Transcriptions, with editorial introductions
           and textual notes, of two important notebooks
           for U ("Early Notes"--Buffalo VIII.A.5--and
           "Late Notes"--Buffalo V.A.2) and of the sev-
           eral draft materials for the "Cyclops" and
           "Circe" episodes (principally Buffalo V.A.6-9,
           V.A.19-20). Includes addenda for Herring's
           edition of the British Museum Notesheets (pp.
           263-69; see below).

B16   JOYCE'S *ULYSSES* NOTESHEETS IN THE BRITISH MUSEUM. Ed.
      Phillip F. Herring. Charlottesville: Univ. Press of Vir-
      ginia, 1972.
           Transcriptions of JJ's notes for the last seven
           episodes of U ("Cyclops" through "Penelope"),
           his "respository" of ideas and phrases for the
           episodes' composition, with page references for
           their eventual appearance in the published text.
           Useful for tracing the accretive development of
           the episodes, if used together with the textual
           studies by Groden (M25) and Litz (M38), and with
           Herring's "Descriptive Essays" (pp. 13-73). In-
           cludes several appendices. Also see above for
           additional transcriptions and addenda. Extract
           reprinted, in German, in M17.

B17   "Manuscript Materials." In THE WORKSHOP OF DAEDALUS. Ed.
      Robert Scholes and Richard M. Kain. Pp. 3-108. See K15.
           Reproduces JJ's "epiphanies," notebooks, and
           manuscripts (e.g., the 1904 essay-version) for
           PAYM, with annotation and editorial commentary.
           Extracts reprinted in J13 and K14.

B18   THE PORTABLE JAMES JOYCE. Ed. Harry Levin. 1947. 2nd
      rev. ed. New York: Viking, 1968.
           Includes D, PAYM, the COLLECTED POEMS, EXILES,
           two "broadsides," and excerpts from U and FW.
           Revised edition prints the corrected texts of
           D (1967) and PAYM (1964). See H123.

B19   SCRIBBLEDEHOBBLE: THE UR-WORKBOOK FOR *FINNEGANS WAKE*. Ed.
      Thomas E. Connolly. Evanston, Ill.: Northwestern Univ.
      Press, 1961.
           Error-laden transcription of one of JJ's note-
           books for FW. See N88.

B20 A SHORTER *FINNEGANS WAKE*. Ed. Anthony Burgess. New York: Viking, 1967.
>   Abridged FW which, as one reviewer perceptively notes, is rather senseless since few readers are intimidated merely by FW's length. See N77.

B21 STEPHEN HERO, BY JAMES JOYCE: EDITED FROM THE MANUSCRIPT IN THE HARVARD COLLEGE LIBRARY. Ed. Theodore Spencer. 1944. 2nd rev. ed. New York: New Directions, 1963.
>   Surviving manuscript (supplemented in 1955, 1963) of JJ's earlier, less self-critical autobiographical novel, covering matter partially retained in the fourth and fifth chapters of PAYM. See P28. Extracts reprinted in G56, J1, J13, K1, and K14.

B22 *ULYSSES*: A FACSIMILE OF THE MANUSCRIPT. Ed. Clive Driver. 3 vols. New York: Octagon, 1975.
>   Photo-offset facsimile of the 810-page handwritten Rosenbach manuscript (vols. 1-2), and reproduction of the first edition (1922)--with marginal notes comparing manuscript and the considerably altered published text (vol. 3). Includes Driver's bibliographical prefaces and notes (I, 13-38; 39-42; 43-45; III, 1-4), and a general critical "Introduction" by Harry Levin (I, 1-11). See F129.

C. LETTERS

For additional letters to or by JJ, see JAMES JOYCE IN PADUA (B11), Beckson and Munro (F7), Ellmann (F33), ENVOY (F36), Finneran (F39), Lidderdale and Nicholson (F92), Pound (F123), Quinn (F127), Richards (F130), Weaver (F157), Deming (G25), Baker and Staley (J1), Scholes and Litz (J13), Moynihan (J179), Morris and Nault (K14), and Reichert and Senn (V5). For manuscript locations of JJ's correspondence, see Scholes (E24) and Spielberg (E26). For discussion of JJ as letter writer, see Anderson (F2), Hampshire (F59), Trilling (F152), and Holthausen (R16).

C1   THE LETTERS OF JAMES JOYCE. 3 vols. Ed. Stuart Gilbert [vol. 1] and Richard Ellmann [vols. 2-3]. New York: Viking, 1957, 1966.
>   First volume includes a very incomplete collection of over 400 letters by JJ (1901-40) and several letters to JJ (slightly revised in 1966). The second and third volumes collect over 1100 additional letters by JJ (1900-40) and nearly 200 letters to JJ or "concerned with his affairs." A coherent view of JJ's correspondence will remain difficult until these collections are integrated and supplemented with the recently published additional letters. Includes general introductions by Gilbert (I, 21-38) and by Ellmann (II, xxv-liii) providing biographical and textual backgrounds, brief sectional introductions (vols. 2-3 only), F34 and K64. Extracts reprinted in J1, J3, J13, J179, K14, and below.

C2   SELECTED LETTERS OF JAMES JOYCE. Ed. Richard Ellmann. New York: Viking, 1975.
>   Excellent selection from the three-volume LETTERS, and first publication of several new or previously suppressed letters. Includes a reprint of Ellmann's "Introduction" to THE LETTERS (vol. 2, above), pp. xi-xxix.

D. CONCORDANCES

Note: A number of glossaries and lexicons for JJ's works have also been compiled. See Tysdahl (G82), Bonheim (N11), Christiani (N15), O'Hehir (N39, N40), and WAKE NEWSLITTER (N45).

D1 Anderson, Chester G., comp. A WORD INDEX TO JAMES JOYCE'S *STEPHEN HERO*. Ridgefield, Conn.: Ridgebury Press, 1958.
    Concordance to the unrevised second edition of STEPHEN HERO.

D2 Bauerle, Ruth, comp. A WORD LIST TO JAMES JOYCE'S *EXILES*. New York: Garland, 1981.
    Computer-assisted concordance for the Viking-Penguin text of the play (see A3), for its additional manuscript pages (published in L2), for its textual variants (published in L1), and for JJ's notes to EXILES (in the Viking-Penguin text). Notes page, line and speaker for each word, but does not give line context. Omits several common words.

D3 Doyle, Paul A., comp. A CONCORDANCE TO THE *COLLECTED POEMS* OF JAMES JOYCE. New York: Scarecrow Press, 1966.
    Gives complete line context.

D4 Füger, Wilhelm, comp. CONCORDANCE TO JAMES JOYCE'S *DUBLINERS*: WITH A REVERSE INDEX, A FREQUENCY LIST, AND A CONVERSION TABLE. Berlin and New York: Hildesheim, 1980.
    Unlike Lane's earlier word list (see D8), provides listings of all words in the text and their context.

D5 Hancock, Leslie, comp. WORD INDEX TO JAMES JOYCE'S *A PORTRAIT OF THE ARTIST AS A YOUNG MAN*. Carbondale: Southern Illinois Univ. Press, 1967.
    Computerized word index for the corrected 1964 edition. Lists and locates all words, by page and line. Omits common words.

D6 Hanley, Miles L., comp. WORD INDEX TO JAMES JOYCE'S
    ULYSSES. Madison: Univ. of Wisconsin Press, 1937.
        Page and line locations. Unfortunately keyed
        to the error-laden, 1934 Random House edition.
        Several appendixes.

D7 Hart, Clive, comp. A CONCORDANCE TO *FINNEGANS WAKE*. Min-
    neapolis: Univ. of Minnesota Press, 1963.
        Unique concordance, listing virtually all words
        in FW (common words omitted), JJ's "Syllabifica-
        tions" (compound-words), and "Overtones" (words
        suggested by JJ's puns, distortions, coinages).
        Page and line locations. Reprinted with cor-
        rections, 1974.

D8 Lane, Gary, comp. A WORD INDEX TO JAMES JOYCE'S *DUBLINERS*.
    New York: Haskell House, 1972.
        Computer compilation keyed to corrected 1967
        edition. Story, page, and line locations.
        Appendixes. See D4.

D9 LaPorte, Neurine W., comp. "A Word Index to GIACOMO JOYCE."
    ANALYST, No. 26 (1971), pp. 1-21.
        Questionable value.

PART 2. SECONDARY BIBLIOGRAPHY

For information on the scope and arrangement of this bibliography, see the introduction.

Note: There are a number of journals which publish bibliographical, biographical, and critical materials chiefly concerned with JJ. The most important such author-centered periodical is the JAMES JOYCE QUARTERLY (1963--; abbreviated "JJQ") which replaced the short-lived JAMES JOYCE REVIEW (1957-59; quarterly). Also published, though irregularly, are the JAMES JOYCE FOUNDATION NEWSLETTER (1967--), the JAMES JOYCE BROADSHEET (1980--), and JOYCENOTES (1969--). The WAKE NEWSLITTER [sic] (1962--; bimonthly) publishes brief notes on and explications of FW (see N45). THE ANALYST, Nos. 1-26 (1953-71), while not concerned solely with JJ, devoted fourteen of its issues (Nos. 9-10, 12, 14-17, 19-24, 26) exclusively to JJ's works, principally FW (see N1).

The vast majority of the articles appearing in JJQ and the JAMES JOYCE REVIEW have been entered and annotated in this bibliography. Furthermore, several special issues of JJQ have been listed here and treated in the same fashion as special numbers of other journals (i.e., as essay collections), with their contents summarized and with cross references provided for essays individually entered and annotated in the bibliography. However, numerous shorter notes and letters appearing in these two periodicals, as well as in the remaining journals described above, have not been included here.

E. BIBLIOGRAPHIES

Also see Aubert and Jolas (G8), Adams (H1), Stewart (H211),
Morris and Nault (K14), Ellmann (M14), Fischer-Seidel (M17),
Reichert, et al (U1), Füger (V2), and Reichert and Senn (V5).
For foreign-language bibliographical materials, see section Q.

E1 Beebe, Maurice, Phillip Herring, and A. Walton Litz, comps.
    "Criticism of James Joyce: A Selected Checklist." MFS, 15
    (1969), 105-82.
            Judicious selection of studies of JJ (biograph-
            ical, critical, and studies of individual works).
            Updates, but does not entirely assimilate ear-
            lier list in MFS, 4 (1958), 71-99. See G64 and
            G65.

E2 Benstock, Bernard. "The James Joyce Industry: A Reassess-
    ment." In YEATS, JOYCE, AND BECKETT: NEW LIGHT ON THREE
    MODERN IRISH WRITERS. Ed. Kathleen McGrory and John Unte-
    recker. Lewisburg, Pa.: Bucknell Univ. Press, 1976. Pp.
    118-32.
            Fine brief overview of the current state of JJ
            studies (comments on eighty-three books and art-
            icles by and about JJ).

E3 Cohn, Alan M. "Joyce Bibliographies: A Survey." AMERICAN
    BOOK COLLECTOR, 15, No. 10 (1965), 11-16.
            Useful comprehensive essay-review of JJ bibliog-
            raphies (1936-65). See G4.

E4 -----, comp. "Supplementary James Joyce Checklist." JJQ,
    1 (1964), and continuing.
            Primary listing and supplement to the MLA sec-
            ondary bibliography. Annual through 1976, quar-
            terly since. Especially useful for locating
            translations not indexed by MLA. Replaces ear-
            lier supplements published in THE JAMES JOYCE
            REVIEW (1958-59).

E5   Connolly, Thomas E., comp. THE PERSONAL LIBRARY OF JAMES
      JOYCE: A DESCRIPTIVE BIBLIOGRAPHY. 1955. 2nd ed. Buf-
      falo, N.Y.: University Bookstore, Univ. of Buffalo, 1957.
           Lists 468 items, in the Buffalo collection, to
           which JJ was particularly attached (he "weeded
           out" his library in 1939). Indicates all in-
           scriptions and JJ's marginalia. List also
           printed in THE JAMES JOYCE ARCHIVE, vol. 1 (see
           B10). Also see F87.

E6   Connolly, Thomas E., and K.C. Gay, comps. JAMES JOYCE: A
      DESCRIPTIVE CATALOGUE OF AN EXHIBITION OF MANUSCRIPTS,
      NOTEBOOKS, TYPESCRIPTS, PAGE PROOFS, ETC. IN THE LOCKWOOD
      MEMORIAL LIBRARY, STATE UNIVERSITY OF NEW YORK AT BUFFALO.
      Buffalo: Lockwood Library, State Univ. of New York, 1978.
           Photographs of thirty-five pages from various
           manuscripts and notebooks by JJ, in the Buffalo
           collection, with brief descriptions extracted
           from Spielberg (E26). (Pamphlet--39 pp.)

E7   Crise, Stelio, comp. AND TRIESTE, AH TRIESTE. Milan:
      All'Insegna del Pesce d'Oro, 1971.
           Exhibition catalogue, for Third International
           JJ Symposium, containing several photographs
           of JJ's Trieste.

E8   Deming, Robert H. "Introduction." In JAMES JOYCE: THE
      CRITICAL HERITAGE. Ed. Deming. Pp. 1-31. See G25.
           Useful summary of the contemporary and major
           subsequent criticisms of JJ's works.

E9   -----, ed. A BIBLIOGRAPHY OF JAMES JOYCE STUDIES. 1964.
      2nd ed. Boston: Hall, 1977.
           The "standard" secondary bibliography, an un-
           annotated listing of nearly 6,000 bibliograph-
           ical, biographical, and critical writings on
           JJ, his milieu, and his individual works. Ar-
           ranged alphabetically under several headings.
           Includes dissertations and foreign language
           studies. Admirable and daunting reference
           work, though poorly indexed.

E10   Doyle, Paul A., comp. "Joyce's Miscellaneous Verse." JJQ,
      2 (1965), 90-96.
           Lists and locates eighty poems and poem-frag-
           ments, not published in COLLECTED POEMS (B3).
           Supplemented in JJQ, 5 (1968), 71.

E11 Edgerton, William B. "Dzhoising with the Soviet Encyclo-
     pedias." JJQ, 5 (1968), 125-31.
          JJ's reputation in the Soviet Union rarely ex-
          empt from political influences.

E12 Gheerbrant, Bernard, ed. JAMES JOYCE: SA VIE, SON OEUVRE,
     SON RAYONNEMENT. Paris: La Hune, 1949.
          Catalog of the La Hune exhibition of JJ's pub-
          lications, manuscripts, related documents, and
          personal effects. Includes a listing of JJ's
          working library in Paris (202 titles). [In
          French.]

E13 Givens, Seon. "The After-Decades." In JAMES JOYCE. Ed.
     Givens. Pp. xv-xxxviii. See G30.
          Briefly describes JJ's relation to modernist
          movements and notes the major publications by
          and about JJ (1948-63).

E14 Gooch, Bryan N.S., and David S. Thatcher, comps. "Joyce,
     James Augustine Aloysius, 1882-1941." In MUSICAL SETTINGS
     OF LATE VICTORIAN AND MODERN BRITISH LITERATURE: A CATA-
     LOGUE. New York: Garland, 1976. Pp. 408-36.
          Useful listing. Includes unpublished settings
          of JJ's works.

E15 Groden, Michael, ed. JAMES JOYCE'S MANUSCRIPTS: AN INDEX
     TO *THE JAMES JOYCE ARCHIVE*. New York: Garland, 1980.
          An index to the sixty-three volumes of THE JAMES
          JOYCE ARCHIVE (see B10), plus a checklist of all
          extant JJ manuscripts, by library. Also includes
          errata list for the ARCHIVE.

E16 Hayman, David, comp. "Draft Catalogue." In A FIRST DRAFT
     VERSION OF *FINNEGANS WAKE*. Ed. Hayman. Pp. 286-330. See
     B7.
          Gives date, extent, and locations of the various
          drafts of FW in the British Museum. Incorporated
          into and superseded by Groden (above).

E17 Kain, Richard M., ed. "Portraits of James Joyce, A Pre-
     liminary Check-List." In A JAMES JOYCE MISCELLANY, SECOND
     SERIES. Ed. Marvin Magalaner. Pp. 111-17. See G56.
          Lists published photographs and drawings of JJ.
          Supplements in JJQ, 3 (1966), 205-12, and 13
          (1976), 215-17.

E18 Levine, Jennifer Schiffer. "Rejoycings in TEL QUEL." JJQ,
     16 (1979), 17–26.
         Notes the important trends in French struc-
         turalist criticism of JJ, particularly FW,
         and appends a short checklist of studies ap-
         pearing in TEL QUEL. See G44.

E19 Litz, A. Walton. "Joyce." In THE ENGLISH NOVEL: SELECT
     BIBLIOGRAPHICAL GUIDES. Ed. A.E. Dyson. London: Oxford
     Univ. Press, 1974. Pp. 349–69.
         Excellent summary and overview of the state
         of JJ studies.

E20 Magalaner, Marvin, and Richard M. Kain. "Part 3--The Rep-
     utation"; "Bibliography." In JOYCE: THE MAN, THE WORK,
     THE REPUTATION. Pp. 259–310; 351–64. See G58.
         Fine survey of the critical reputations of JJ,
         generally, and his individual works (to 1956).

E21 O'Hegarty, P.S., ed. A BIBLIOGRAPHY OF JAMES JOYCE. Dub-
     lin: Thom, 1946.
         Early descriptive primary bibliography, super-
         seded by Slocum and Cahoon (E25).

E22 Parker, Alan, ed. JAMES JOYCE: A BIBLIOGRAPHY OF HIS
     WRITINGS, CRITICAL MATERIAL, AND MISCELLANEA. Boston:
     Faxon, 1948.
         Primary bibliography, with collations, and
         secondary listing of criticism, memoirs, and
         reviews. Obsolete.

E23 Roberts, R.F. "Bibliographical Notes on James Joyce's
     ULYSSES." COLOPHON, n.s. 1 (1936), 565–79.
         Fine bibliographical comparison of various
         legitimate and pirated editions of U. Finds
         the Hamburg, Odyssey Press editions (1932,
         and subsequent impressions) most accurate.

E24 Scholes, Robert, ed. THE CORNELL JOYCE COLLECTION: A
     CATALOGUE. Ithaca, N.Y.: Cornell Univ. Press, 1961.
         Descriptive catalog of the Cornell collection
         of fifty-nine manuscripts by JJ (and four by
         Stanislaus Joyce), 324 letters by JJ, 986 let-
         ters to JJ by various correspondents, and
         seventy-seven miscellaneous documents con-
         cerning JJ.

E25 Slocum, John J., and Herbert Cahoon, eds. A BIBLIOGRAPHY
     OF JAMES JOYCE [1882-1941]. New Haven, Conn.: Yale Univ.
     Press, 1953.
         Collations, descriptions, and notes on JJ's
         books and pamphlets (56 items) and contribu-
         tions to publications (32), with a checklist
         of his periodical publications (108), and
         listings of translations (124) and musical
         settings (37) of his works. Also includes a
         miscellany of JJ materials and a discussion
         of manuscript locations (superseded by Groden;
         see E15). Still the best available primary
         bibliography.

E26 Spielberg, Peter, comp. JAMES JOYCE'S MANUSCRIPTS AND
     LETTERS AT THE UNIVERSITY OF BUFFALO: A CATALOGUE. Buf-
     falo, N.Y.: Univ. of Buffalo Press, 1962.
         Catalogs the extensive collection of manu-
         scripts at Buffalo (including JJ's "Epipha-
         nies," PAYM, EXILES, "Verses," U, FW, "Crit-
         icism," "Notebooks," and "Miscellaneous Manu-
         scripts"), and 213 letters (arranged by re-
         cipient). Includes three appendixes on the
         FW workbooks. Extracts reprinted in E6.

E27 Spoerri, James F., ed. *FINNEGANS WAKE* BY JAMES JOYCE: A
     CHECK LIST, INCLUDING PUBLICATIONS OF PORTIONS UNDER THE
     TITLE "WORK IN PROGRESS." Evanston, Ill.: Northwestern
     Univ. Library, 1953.
         Primarily useful as a checklist of the previ-
         ously published fragments of FW ("Work in
         Progress").

E28 Staley, Thomas F. "James Joyce." In ANGLO-IRISH LITERA-
     TURE: A REVIEW OF RESEARCH. Ed. Richard J. Finneran. New
     York: Modern Language Association, 1976. Pp. 366-435.
         Survey of the state of JJ research: bibliog-
         raphy, manuscripts, editions, textual studies,
         biography, background studies, and general and
         specialized criticism.

E29 Tall, Emily. "James Joyce Returns to the Soviet Union."
     JJQ, 17 (1980), 341-58.
         Opening comment on the reawakened Russian in-
         terest in JJ, principally since 1970, and in-
         terviews with three translators of U, the
         Georgian Niko Kiasaschwili (also see X92), the
         Russian Victor Khinkis, and the Lithuanian
         Tomas Venclova.

E30   Wiley, Paul L., comp. "James Joyce (1882-1941)."   In THE
      BRITISH NOVEL: CONRAD TO THE PRESENT. Northbrook, Ill.:
      AHM, 1973. Pp. 65-71.
            Brief primary and secondary checklist.

F. BIOGRAPHIES, MEMOIRS, REMINISCENCES, INTERVIEWS

Note: A writer as intensely autobiographical as JJ invites criticism which often shades into biography, and biographies and
memoirs of critical value. In this bibliography every attempt
has been made to locate writings that are primarily biographical
in matter, or value, in this subdivision, although discrimination has not always been easy. Similarly, essay collections
which devote over half their contents to biographical material
have been entered here. Many of the book-length studies and
essays entered in subsequent sections, however, do summarize
the life of JJ, apply the biography to his works, or reflect
his personal relationship with a number of his critics.

For foreign-language biographical materials, see section R.

F1 Anderson, Chester G. JAMES JOYCE AND HIS WORLD. New York:
    Viking, 1968.
          Excellent brief pictorial biography of JJ, gen-
          erously illustrated (128 photographs).

F2 -----. "Joyce's Letters and His Use of 'Place.'" JJQ, 4
    (1967), 62-74.
          The pedestrianism of his correspondence reveals
          JJ "as one of the world's worst letter-writers."

F3 Anderson, Margaret C. MY THIRTY YEARS WAR. New York:
    Covici-Friede, 1930. Pp. 244-49 and passim.
          Impression of JJ, in the twenties, as long-suf-
          fering from "irremediable facts he must accept."
          By the editor of the LITTLE REVIEW and serial
          publisher of U.

F4 Antheil, George. "James Joyce and Others." In BAD BOY OF
    MUSIC. Garden City, N.Y.: Doubleday, Doran, 1945. Pp.
    143-56 and passim.
          Composer's memories of JJ, among Eliot, Ford,
          Hemingway, Lewis, Pound, and others. (Antheil's
          apartment was in the same building as Beach's
          Shakespeare and Co.)

F5   Barnes, Djuna. "James Joyce." VANITY FAIR, 18 (Apr. 1922), 65, 104.
            Interview discussion of JJ in Paris, by a fellow novelist, stressing his simplicity, aloofness, and sanity.

F6   Beach, Sylvia. SHAKESPEARE AND COMPANY: THE STORY OF AN AMERICAN BOOKSHOP IN PARIS. New York: Harcourt, 1959. Pp. 34-76, 84-98, and passim.
            Memories of JJ in Paris and backgrounds to the publication and reception of U, by its first publisher, the proprietor of the Shakespeare and Company bookshop. Portion previously published as ULYSSES IN PARIS (1956). Extract reprinted in G25. Also see M214.

F7   Beckson, Karl, and John M. Munro. "Letters from Arthur Symons to James Joyce: 1904-1932." JJQ, 4 (1967), 91-101.
            Reprints eighteen letters to or concerning JJ, with commentary.

F8   Benco, Silvio. "James Joyce in Trieste." BOOKMAN (New York), 72 (1930), 375-80.
            Memoir of JJ's stay in Trieste (1919-20), with comment on his composition of U, by the Italian novelist, critic, and friend of JJ. Reprinted in F122 and G25 (extract). Also see R3.

F9   Borach, Georges. "Conversations with James Joyce." 1931. Trans. Joseph Prescott. In PORTRAITS OF THE ARTIST IN EXILE. Ed. Willard Potts. Pp. 69-72. See F122.
            Swiss businessman and friend's record of four conversations with JJ (1917-19), concerning U. Also see R4.

F10   Brown, Malcolm. THE POLITICS OF IRISH LITERATURE, FROM THOMAS DAVIS TO W.B. YEATS. Seattle: Univ. of Washington Press, 1972. Pp. 385-89 and passim.
            Excellent general study, with numerous specific references to JJ's reflection of Irish political issues.

F11   Budgen, Frank. FURTHER RECOLLECTIONS OF JAMES JOYCE. London: Shenval Press, 1955.
            Haphazard memories of JJ and their conversations (1918-39), supplementing his memoir (see F13). (Pamphlet--15 pp.). Reprinted in F13 and G25 (extract).

F12   -----. "James Joyce." HORIZON, 4 (1941), 104-8.
         Obituary memoir and tribute to JJ as a deserved-
         ly "self-centered man." Reprinted below, and
         in G25 (extract) and G30.

F13   -----. JAMES JOYCE AND THE MAKING OF *ULYSSES,* AND OTHER
      WRITINGS. Comp. Clive Hart. London: Oxford Univ. Press,
      1972.
         Collects Budgen's critical memoir (1934) of JJ
         during the writing of U, in Zurich and Paris
         (1918-22; see M8), with Budgen's brief preface
         to the 1960 edition (Bloomington: Indiana Univ.
         Press), three additional essays and memoirs by
         Budgen, and Hart's "Introduction" (pp. vii-xix,
         on the Joyce-Budgen relationship). Includes
         F11, F12, and N75.

F14   -----. "Mr. Joyce." In MYSELVES WHEN YOUNG. New York:
      Oxford Univ. Press, 1970. Pp. 181-204.
         Memories of his meeting and friendship with JJ
         in Zurich. Supplements above memoir.

F15   Byrne, John Francis. SILENT YEARS: AN AUTOBIOGRAPHY, WITH
      MEMOIRS OF JAMES JOYCE AND OUR IRELAND. New York: Farrar,
      Straus and Young, 1953. Pp. 35-37, 43-44, 58-66, 76-79,
      85-88, 144-71.
         Memories of JJ in Dublin, at the turn of the
         century and in 1909, and in Paris (1927), by
         his fellow student and partial model both for
         Cranly (in PAYM) and for Bloom (U). Extracts
         reprinted in F135 and F136.

F16   Carens, James F. "Joyce and Gogarty." In NEW LIGHT ON
      JOYCE. Ed. Fritz Senn. Pp. 28-45. See G73.
         Gogarty's relationship with JJ, and his role
         as Buck Mulligan in U.

F17   Chart, David A. THE STORY OF DUBLIN. London: Dent, 1907.
         History of Dublin (c. 150-1900), not concerned
         with JJ but useful for background information.
         Contains a turn-of-the-century map of Dublin.

F18   Cody, Morrill. "James Joyce in the Twenties." ConnR, 5,
      No. 2 (1972), 11-15.
         First publication of an interview with JJ in
         1923, chiefly concerning his writing of U and
         his relations with the Parisian literati.

F19 Colum, Mary, and Padraic Colum. OUR FRIEND JAMES JOYCE.
Garden City, N.Y.: Doubleday, 1958.
>Memories of JJ in Dublin and Paris by his long-
>time friends Padraic (poet and critic) and Mary
>Colum (critic and intellectual historian). Ex-
>tracts reprinted in F136 and G25. Assimilates
>N86.

F20 Corcoran, T. THE CLONGOWES RECORD: 1814 to 1932. Dublin:
Browne and Nolan, n.d. [c. 1933].
>History of JJ's and Stephen Dedalus's first
>school, in PAYM, Clongowes Wood. Contains
>useful discussion of the Jesuit "organization
>of studies."

F21 Costello, Peter. JAMES JOYCE. Dublin: Gill and Macmillan,
1980.
>Brief biography for the "popular" readership.
>Limited value.

F22 Crise, Stelio. EPIPHANIES & PHADOGRAPHS: JOYCE E TRIESTE.
Milan: All'insegna del pesce d'oro, 1967.
>Important account of JJ's Triestine sojourn
>and relationships (e.g., with Artifoni, Fran-
>cini-Bruni, Svevo). Includes an "album" of
>contemporary photographs and documents. [In
>Italian.]

F23 Crosby, Caresse. THE PASSIONATE YEARS. New York: Dial
Press, 1953. Pp. 181-87.
>The Crosbys' meetings with JJ in the late twen-
>ties, while publishing parts of "Work in Prog-
>ress" at their Black Sun Press.

F24 Curran, Constantine P. JAMES JOYCE REMEMBERED. New York:
Oxford Univ. Press, 1968.
>Memories of JJ's university years in Dublin,
>and of a few meetings with JJ in Paris in later
>years, intended partially as a corrective to
>the conscious omissions and distortions in JJ's
>own account of Dublin and his youth. Useful
>backgrounds to PAYM. Also includes brief es-
>says on JJ's interest in D'Annunzio and Ibsen.

F25 Daly, Leo. JAMES JOYCE AND THE MULLINGAR CONNECTION.
Atlantic Highlands, N.J.: Humanities Press, 1975.
>JJ's experiences of and references to the town
>of Mullingar. (Pamphlet--40 pp.)

F26   Davies, Stan Gebler. JAMES JOYCE: A PORTRAIT OF THE ART-
      IST. London: Davis-Poynter, 1975.
            Full biography, avoiding both criticism and
            scholarly documentation for the sake of "read-
            ability" and stressing JJ's excesses (drink
            and women) from the conviction that no "biog-
            raphy of a great man should be tedious." Da-
            vies too often asserts, rather than demon-
            strates, both biographical insights and crit-
            ical opinions (e.g., FW "a monument to perver-
            sity" and a waste of JJ's genius).

F27   Delaney, Frank. JAMES JOYCE'S ODYSSEY: A GUIDE TO THE
      DUBLIN OF *ULYSSES*. London: Hodder and Stoughton, 1981.
            Includes numerous photographs and illustrations,
            and eighteen maps. (Not seen--announced for
            Nov. 1981 publication.)

F28   Delimata, Bozena Berta [Schaurek]. "Reminiscences of a
      Joyce Niece." Ed. Virginia Moseley. JJQ, 19 (1981), 45-
      62.
            Memories of JJ, Nora, Stanislaus, and family,
            in Trieste in the late teens and at various
            meetings thereafter.

F29   Edel, Leon. "The Genius and the Injustice Collector: A
      Memoir of James Joyce." ASch, 49 (1980), 467-87.
            Memories of brief contacts with JJ in Paris,
            1929-31, and of a visit to Nora in Zurich, in
            1946, and observations of his paranoid, self-
            enclosed, gloomy temperament: "cut off from
            human warmth."

F30   -----. JAMES JOYCE: THE LAST JOURNEY. New York: Gotham
      Book Mart, 1947.
            Pilgrimage to JJ's grave in Zurich and visit
            with his widow Nora, in 1945, with an account
            of his return to Zurich and death (Dec. 1940-
            Jan. 1941).

F31   -----. "Joyce and the Academician." In A JAMES JOYCE
      MISCELLANY. Ed. Marvin Magalaner. Pp. 44-48. See G55.
            JJ's unique friendship with the conservative
            critic, Louis Gillet. Also published as pre-
            face for Gillet's study (G29).

F32   Ellmann, Richard. "The Hawklike Man." In EMINENT DOMAIN:
      YEATS AMONG WILDE, JOYCE, POUND, ELIOT, AND AUDEN. New
      York: Oxford Univ. Press, 1967. Pp. 29–56.
            Surveys Yeats's and JJ's few meetings, reactions
            to each other's work, mutual respect, and occa-
            sional cross-influences.

F33   -----. JAMES JOYCE. New York: Oxford Univ. Press, 1959.
            The standard biography of JJ and one of the
            outstanding modern literary biographies. Me-
            ticulously researched and documented narrative
            of the life merging, in the later years, with
            the story of JJ's art, as JJ himself comes to
            live wholly for and largely within his writings.
            Considerable critical value in Ellmann's com-
            mentaries on the biographical backgrounds to
            the fiction (e.g., the various transmutations
            of JJ's relations with his wife, father, mother,
            and brother). Assimilates Ellmann's introduc-
            tions to JJ's CRITICAL WRITINGS (B4) and Stan-
            islaus Joyce's MY BROTHER'S KEEPER (F80). Also
            includes K64. Extracts reprinted in G19, G25,
            J3, J13, J179, K1, K6, K14, and K16.

F34   -----. "James Joyce's Addresses." AMERICAN BOOK COLLEC-
      TOR, 15, No. 10 (1965), 25, 27, 29.
            List JJ's residences and travels, 1882–1941.
            See G4. Reprinted in C1.

F35   -----. JAMES JOYCE'S TOWER. Dun Laoghaire: Eastern Re-
      gional Tourism Organization, 1969.
            JJ's residence in the Sandycove Martello tower
            and his use of the tower in U.

F36   ENVOY. 5 (May 1951), 6–78. "Special Joyce Issue."
            Seven essays and memoirs, with related mate-
            rials on JJ (including several letters [pp.
            46–61] and selections from the obituary press).
            Guest editor: Brian Nolan. All but letters
            reprinted in F111. Also see F135. Includes
            F64, F86, F110, F128, H71, H102, M301, and
            N169.

F37   Fabricant, Noah D. "The Ocular History of James Joyce."
      In THIRTEEN FAMOUS PATIENTS. Philadelphia: Chilton, 1960.
      Pp. 128–38.
            Physician's account of JJ's eye problems, sug-
            gesting their relationship to his "personality
            disorders."

F38 Fallis, Richard. THE IRISH RENAISSANCE. Syracuse, N.Y.:
Syracuse Univ. Press, 1977. Pp. 141-53 and passim.
    Competent general discussion of JJ's work, in
    the context of the twentieth-century rebirth
    of Irish letters.

F39 Finneran, Richard J. "James Joyce and James Stephens:
The Record of a Friendship with Unpublished Letters from
Joyce to Stephens." JJQ, 11 (1974), 279-92.
    Amplifies Ellmann's discussion of the Joyce-
    Stephens relationship (see F33), and publishes
    six letters and cards not included in C1. See
    F71 and F143. Also see Finneran's supplemental
    note and publication of two additional letters,
    in JJQ, 13 (1976), 143-47.

F40 Flanagan, Thomas. "Yeats, Joyce, and the Matter of Ireland." CRITICAL INQUIRY, 2 (1975), 43-67.
    Comparative discussion of how each writer "came
    to accept his identity as an Irish writer."

F41 Ford, Ford Madox. IT WAS THE NIGHTINGALE. Philadelphia:
Lippincott, 1933. Pp. 290-94 and passim.
    JJ, among his adulators, in Paris.

F42 Francini-Bruni, Alessandro. "Joyce Stipped Naked in the
Piazza"; "Recollections of Joyce." 1922; 1947. Trans.
Camilla Rudolph, Lido Botti, et al. In PORTRAITS OF THE
ARTIST IN EXILE. Ed. Willard Potts. Pp. 7-39; 39-46.
See F122.
    Witty caricature of JJ, with numerous anecdotes
    of JJ in Trieste, by his friend and colleague
    at the Berlitz school, together with a later
    memoir noting their personal closeness and ideo-
    logical opposition. Both memoirs also published
    in F72. Also see R9.

F43 Frank, Nino. "The Shadow That Had Lost Its Man." 1949,
1967. Trans. Jane Carson. In PORTRAITS OF THE ARTIST IN
EXILE. Ed. Willard Potts. Pp. 74-105. See F122.
    Absorbing memoir of JJ and his circle in Paris
    (1926-38), by a Parisian journalist and writer.
    See R11 and R12.

F44 Freund, Gisele, and V.B. Carleton. JAMES JOYCE IN PARIS:
HIS FINAL YEARS. New York: Harcourt, 1965.
    Numerous photographs of JJ and his contempo-
    raries, with a brief summary of his last years
    (1938-41).

F45   Furbank, P.N. "Svevo and James Joyce." In ITALO SVEVO:
       THE MAN AND THE WRITER. Berkeley and Los Angeles: Univ.
       of California Press, 1966. Pp. 78-91.
            Excellent discussion of the complementary per-
            sonalities of Svevo and JJ, suggesting some
            sources for Bloom's character in the Triestine
            novelist.

F46   Giedion-Welcker, Carola. "Meetings with Joyce." 1948,
       1971. Trans. Wolfgang Dill. In PORTRAITS OF THE ARTIST
       IN EXILE. Ed. Willard Potts. Pp. 256-80. See F122.
            Memories of JJ's several visits to Zurich in
            the thirties and his last months in residence
            there, by an enthusiastic Swiss admirer. Ex-
            panded from previously published versions.
            Also see F99 and R13.

F47   -----, ed. IN MEMORIAM JAMES JOYCE. Zurich: Fretz and
       Wasmuth, 1941.
            Collection of memoirs and brief criticisms, in
            German, except two poems by JJ and a funeral
            address by Lord Derwent (pp. 13-15). A variant
            edition has an additional article in English,
            by the editor (see N106). Includes M274.

F48   Gluck, Barbara R. BECKETT AND JOYCE: FRIENDSHIP AND FIC-
       TION. Lewisburg, Pa.: Bucknell Univ. Press, 1979. Pp.
       19-40 and passim.
            Discussion of the Joyce-Beckett relationship
            as prologue to a full study of the "Joycean
            shadow" in Beckett's works.

F49   Gogarty, Oliver St.J. AS I WAS GOING DOWN SACKVILLE
       STREET. London: Cowan, 1937. Pp. 293-99 and passim.
            Amusing anecdotes concerning JJ, among the
            Irish Renaissance literati, by the original
            of Buck Mulligan (in U).

F50   -----. IT ISN'T THIS TIME OF YEAR AT ALL: AN UNPREMEDI-
       TATED AUTOBIOGRAPHY. Garden City, N.Y.: Doubleday, 1954.
       Pp. 45-57, 85-99, and passim.
            Memories of JJ in Dublin, 1903-4. Several in-
            cidents incorporated into U. Extracts reprinted
            in F136.

F51   -----. "James Joyce: A Portrait of the Artist." In
       MOURNING BECAME MRS. SPENDLOVE, AND OTHER PORTRAITS,

GRAVE AND GAY. New York: Creative Age Press, 1948. Pp. 41-61.
>   Memoir, recalling some events incorporated by JJ into U.

F52   -----. "James Joyce as a Tenor." In INTIMATIONS. New York: Abelard, 1950. Pp. 58-69.
>   JJ as singer and patron of singers.

F53   -----. "They Think They Know Joyce." SatR, 33 (18 Mar. 1950), 8-9, 35-37; (8 Apr. 1950), 24; (29 Apr. 1950), 10-12, 24; (13 May 1950), 22; (27 May 1950), 23-24.
>   Intemperate attack on JJ, his art ("an enormous leg-pull"), and his cultist admirers. Extract reprinted in G25. Also see F81.

F54   Goldman, Arnold. "Stanislaus, James and the Politics of Family." In ATTI DEL THIRD INTERNATIONAL JAMES JOYCE SYMPOSIUM. Pp. 60-75. See G7.
>   Comparisons between JJ and his brother in their responses to their father and family.

F55   Gorman, Herbert S. JAMES JOYCE. 1940. Rev. ed. New York: Rinehart, 1948.
>   The "authorized" biography, written with JJ's cooperation but with hardly anyone else's. Hence partial, inaccurate, and distorted. Still useful, if read with caution, but the Ellmann biography is unquestionably the primary biographical study (see F33).

F56   Graham, Rigby. "JAMES JOYCE'S TOWER," SANDYCOVE. Wymondham, Engl.: Brewhouse, 1975.
>   Brief comment (3 pp.) on the Martello tower JJ rented and later used as the opening setting for U. Includes eight prints and sketches by Graham. (Pamphlet--22 pp.)

F57   Gregory, Horace. "A Portrait of the Irish as James Joyce." 1960. In SPIRIT OF TIME AND PLACE: COLLECTED ESSAYS. New York: Norton, 1973. Pp. 250-55.
>   JJ combined within himself "all the contradictory elements of the Irish character" (here surveyed).

F58   Halper, Nathan. "How Simple: A Tale of Joyce and Pound." PR, 44 (1977), 438-46.
>   JJ's ambivalent relations with Pound.

F59   Hampshire, Stuart N.   "Letters of James Joyce."   In MODERN
      WRITERS, AND OTHER ESSAYS.   New York: Knopf, 1970.   Pp. 30-
      37.
            JJ not a great letter writer, but his corre-
            spondence sheds valuable light on his personal
            relationships and his fiction.

F60   Hayman, David.   "A Meeting in the Park and a Meeting on
      the Bridge: Joyce and Beckett."   JJQ, 8 (1971), 372-84.
            Examines JJ's influence on Beckett's stories
            in MORE PRICKS THAN KICKS (1934).   See F69.

F61   Henchy, Deidre.   "Dublin 80 Years Ago."   DUBLIN HISTORICAL
      RECORD, 26 (1972), 18-35.
            Considerable information on the population,
            economic conditions, professions, health, so-
            cial life, and other aspects of Dublin in JJ's
            youth (1892).

F62   Higgins, Aidan.   "Tired Lines, or Tales My Mother Told Me."
      In A BASH IN THE TUNNEL.   Ed. John Ryan.   Pp. 55-60.   See
      F135.
            Growing up in Ireland (1927-55), amidst the
            near-total censorship of JJ's works.

F63   Hoffmeister, Adolf.   "James Joyce"; "Portrait of Joyce."
      1961.   Trans. Norma Rudinsky.   In PORTRAITS OF THE ARTIST
      IN EXILE.   Ed. Willard Potts.   Pp. 121-27; 127-36.   See
      F122.
            Meetings and conversations with JJ in Paris,
            in the late twenties and 1930, by a Czech art-
            ist and writer.   Includes valuable comments by
            JJ on his works and a caricature of JJ by Hoff-
            meister.   See R15.

F64   Hone, Joseph.   "A Recollection of James Joyce."   ENVOY, 5
      (May 1951), 44-45.
            Brief note, by an editor's reader who read D
            for Maunsell's (1909) and subsequently met JJ.
            See F36.   Reprinted in F111, F135, and G25 (ex-
            tract).

F65   Huddleston, Sisley.   BACK TO MONTPARNASSE: GLIMPSES OF
      BROADWAY IN BOHEMIA.   Philadelphia: Lippincott, 1931.
      Pp. 192-206.
            JJ, Stuart Gilbert, and John Sullivan, the
            tenor, in Paris.   Extract reprinted in G25.

F66   -----. PARIS SALONS, CAFÉS, STUDIOS. Philadelphia: Lip-
       pincott, 1928. Pp. 208-20.
              JJ, Sylvia Beach's Shakespeare and Co., and the
              publication of U. Extract reprinted in G25.

F67   Hutchins, Patricia. JAMES JOYCE'S DUBLIN. London: Grey
       Walls Press, 1950.
              A copiously illustrated "tour" of JJ's Dublin,
              focusing on the locales, streets, and buildings
              of U.

F68   -----. JAMES JOYCE'S WORLD. London: Methuen, 1957.
              Sentimental journey through Ireland and the
              continent, describing the locales where JJ
              lived and worked.

F69   JAMES JOYCE QUARTERLY. 8 (1971), 275-424. "Beckett Is-
       sue."
              Fifteen essays, notes, and reviews concerning
              Beckett and his works. Includes two essays and
              a note on JJ's and Beckett's personal and lit-
              erary relationships by Ruby Cohn ("Joyce and
              Beckett, Irish Cosmopolitans"), David Hayman
              (F60), and Hugh B. Staples ("Beckett in the
              WAKE").

F70   JAMES JOYCE QUARTERLY. 9 (1972), 307-49. "Joyce and
       Trieste Issue."
              Includes H34, a report on the 1971 Interna-
              tional JJ Symposium by Norman Silverstein,
              and nine memoirs and essays concerning JJ's
              sojourns in Trieste (1905-15; 1919-20), by
              Claudio Antoni, Aurelia Gruber Benco, Lina
              Galli, Stelio Mattioni, Mario Nordio, Nora
              Franca Poliaghi, Niny Rocco-Bergera, Antonio
              Fonda Savio, and Letizia Fonda Savio.

F71   JAMES JOYCE QUARTERLY. 11 (1974), 187-292. "Joyce and
       the Irish Writers."
              Includes interviews with Benedict Kiely and
              Conor Cruise O'Brien, poems by Seamus Heaney,
              an article on Conor Cruise O'Brien by Darcy
              O'Brien, and the following: F39, H146, J65,
              and M19 (extract). Guest editor: Darcy O'Brien.

F72   JAMES JOYCE QUARTERLY. 14 (1977), 124-90. "Joyce Remi-
       niscences Issue."
              Publishes three memoirs of JJ (see F42 and

F154), and three articles on JJ's relations with Danish literary figures by M.S. Byram ("ULYSSES in Copenhagen: James Joyce and Tom Kristensen"), Arnold Goldman ("Ole Vinding's Writings about Joyce"), and Willard C. Potts ("Joyce and Ole Vinding"). Guest editor: Willard C. Potts. Also see F122.

F73   Jolas, Eugene. "My Friend James Joyce." PR, 8 (1941), 82–93.
      Memories of JJ in Paris (1924 and after) and remarks on his personality. Reprinted in G25 (extract) and G30. Also see N184.

F74   Jolas, Maria. "Joyce's Friend Jolas." In A JAMES JOYCE MISCELLANY. Ed. Marvin Magalaner. Pp. 62–74. See G55.
      Memoir and account of JJ's friendship with Eugene Jolas.

F75   -----. "The Little Known Paul Léon." In A JAMES JOYCE MISCELLANY, SECOND SERIES. Ed. Marvin Magalaner. Pp. 225–33. See G56.
      Several brief fragments of Léon's writing illustrate the intellect of JJ's companion; selected, translated, and discussed by Maria Jolas. See F89.

F76   -----, comp. "Documents." In A JAMES JOYCE YEARBOOK. Ed. M. Jolas. Pp. 182–91. See G45.
      Heterogeneous collection of press clippings, partisan viewpoints, and obituaries, concerning JJ and his work.

F77   [Joyce, John Stanislaus]. "Interview with Mr. John Stanislaus Joyce (1849-1931)." In A JAMES JOYCE YEARBOOK. Ed. Maria Jolas. Pp. 159–69. See G45.
      Interview with JJ's father, of doubtful authenticity. Reprinted in F136.

F78   Joyce, Stanislaus. THE COMPLETE DUBLIN DIARY OF STANISLAUS JOYCE. 1962. Ed. George H. Healy. Ithaca, N.Y.: Cornell Univ. Press, 1971.
      JJ's brother's diary, covering 1903-04, containing much material not absorbed into his autobiography, MY BROTHER'S KEEPER (F80). Revised edition restores some previously-deleted, uncomplimentary passages. Includes

brief "Preface" (pp. v-xi) and "Postscript"
(pp. 179-81) by Healy. Extracts reprinted in
F136, G25, and J3.

F79 -----. THE MEETING OF SVEVO AND JOYCE. Udine, Italy: Del
Bianco Editore, 1965.
      Describes the "spontaneous and genuine" friend-
      ship of the two authors, stressing JJ's vital
      encouragement of Svevo's writing ambitions.
      (Pamphlet--19 pp.)

F80 -----. MY BROTHER'S KEEPER: JAMES JOYCE'S EARLY YEARS.
Ed. Richard Ellmann. New York: Viking, 1958.
      Unfinished autobiography of JJ's younger broth-
      er, critic and admirer, economic mainstay, and
      antithesis ("Shaun the Post" to JJ's "Shem the
      Penman"), providing a valuable account of JJ's
      youth and adolescence (through 1903). Ellmann's
      "Introduction" (pp. x-xxii), on the brothers'
      relationship, absorbed into his biography of
      JJ (see F33). Extracts reprinted in F135 and
      F136.

F81 -----. AN OPEN LETTER TO DR. OLIVER GOGARTY. Seattle:
Univ. of Washington Press, 1954.
      Responds to distortions and inaccuracies in
      Gogarty's "They Think They Know Joyce" (see
      F53). (Pamphlet--8 pp.) Extract reprinted
      in G25.

F82 -----. RECOLLECTIONS OF JAMES JOYCE, BY HIS BROTHER. 1941.
Trans. Ellsworth Mason. New York: Gotham Book Mart, 1950.
      Brief biographical summary, with personal
      asides. (Also published in a translation by
      Felix Giovanelli, HudR, 2 [1950], 485-514.)
      Extract reprinted in J179.

F83 Kain, Richard M. DUBLIN IN THE AGE OF WILLIAM BUTLER YEATS
AND JAMES JOYCE. Norman: Univ. Of Oklahoma Press, 1962.
      Informative and witty introduction to JJ's
      (and Yeats's) cultural backgrounds and milieu.
      Excellent discussions of the Irish "Renais-
      sance," its personalities, politics, humor,
      and achievement.

F84 -----. "The Yankee-Interviewer in ULYSSES." In A JAMES
JOYCE MISCELLANY, THIRD SERIES. Ed. Marvin Magalaner. Pp.
155-57. See G57.
      American critic Cornelius Weygant, with JJ

and AE in Dublin, obliquely referred to in U.

F85 -----, ed. "An Interview with Carola Giedion-Welcker and
Maria Jolas." JJQ, 11 (1974), 94-122.
   Round-table interview discussion of JJ as art-
   ist and memoirs of JJ as friend (from the Fourth
   International JJ Symposium, Dublin, 1973).

F86 Kavanagh, Patrick. "Who Killed James Joyce?"; "Diary."
ENVOY, 5 (May 1951), 12; 70-72.
   Poem and comment. JJ "sane enough; it is his
   commentators," who have "killed" him, "who are
   mad." See F36. Reprinted in F111 and F135.

F87 Kenny, Thomas J. "James Joyce's System of Marginal Mark-
ings in the Books of His Personal Library." JML, 6 (1977),
264-76.
   Describes JJ's system for marking passages of
   interest, with marginal dots, for future reference and often for incorporation into his
   works. See E5.

F88 Kerr, Alfred. "Joyce in England." Trans. Joseph Prescott.
In A JAMES JOYCE MISCELLANY. Ed. Marvin Magalaner. Pp.
37-43. See G55.
   1936 conversation with JJ, principally concerning the censoring of U. See R17.

F89 Léon, Lucie [Lucie Noel]. JAMES JOYCE AND PAUL L. LÉON:
THE STORY OF A FRIENDSHIP. New York: Gotham Book Mart,
1950.
   Account of JJ's relationship with his "most
   devoted friend" (1928-40), unofficial secre-
   tary, and general factotum, by Léon's widow.
   (Léon, a Jew, died in a concentration camp).
   See below. Extract reprinted in G25. Also see F75.

F90 Léon, Paul. "In Memory of Joyce." 1942. Trans. Maria
Jolas. In A JAMES JOYCE YEARBOOK. Ed. Maria Jolas. Pp.
116-25. See G45.
   Affectionate memoir of JJ by his closest friend
   in his last years (see above), stressing his
   gentleness, comprehension, and love of nature.
   Reprinted in F122, G25 (extract), and R18.

F91 Lewis, Wyndham. BLASTING AND BOMBARDIERING. 1937. 2nd
ed. Berkeley and Los Angeles: Univ. of California Press,
1967. Pp. 265-70, 290-94, 298-303, and passim.
   Anecdotes about a taciturn, somewhat peculiar,

yet always generous JJ, among Eliot, Pound, and
Lewis in Paris. Extract reprinted in G25.

F92 Lidderdale, Jane, and Mary Nicholson. DEAR MISS WEAVER:
HARRIET SHAW WEAVER, 1876-1961. New York: Viking, 1970.
Passim.
    JJ's personal affairs and literary career in-
    extricably interwoven into this biography of
    his patroness, publisher, and friend.

F93 Liddy, James. ESAU, MY KINGDOM FOR A DRINK. HOMAGE TO
JAMES JOYCE ON HIS LXXX BIRTHDAY. Dublin: Dolmen Press,
1962.
    Memorial address. (Pamphlet--15 pp.)

F94 Lyons, F.S.L. "James Joyce's Dublin." TWENTIETH CENTURY
STUDIES, No. 4 (1970), pp. 6-25.
    Turn-of-the century Dublin actually politically
    and intellectually vital despite JJ's conten-
    tions otherwise.

F95 Lyons, John B. JAMES JOYCE AND MEDICINE. Dublin: Dolmen,
1973.
    Physician's thorough clinical examination of
    JJ's physical ill health ("his adult life was
    one of protracted illness") and emotional dis-
    orders (traced to childhood traumas), with
    commentaries on JJ's ineffectual attempts to
    study medicine, his medical cronies (e.g.,
    Gogarty), and his use of "medical jargon" and
    "depiction of illnesses and anatomy" in his
    writings. Assimilates JAMES JOYCE'S MILTONIC
    AFFLICTION (separately published, 1968). Ex-
    tract originally published in F135.

F96 McAlmon, Robert. BEING GENIUSES TOGETHER, 1920-1930. 1938.
Rev. ed. Garden City, N.Y.: Doubleday, 1968. Passim.
    Several comments on JJ and his family among
    the American "Lost Generation" in Paris. Ex-
    tracts reprinted in G25.

F97 MacDiarmid, Hugh. IN MEMORIAM JAMES JOYCE. Glasgow: Mac-
Lellan, 1955.
    Fine poetic tribute to JJ, by a writer sharing
    JJ's fascination with language. (Part one of
    the six-part poem, pp. 20-74, specifically con-
    cerned with JJ.)

F98   MacDonald, Dwight. "James Joyce." In AGAINST THE AMERI-
        CAN GRAIN. New York: Random House, 1962. Pp. 123-42.
                JJ, like many geniuses, a specialist with very
                narrow interests. Memoir of Paris (1932) and
                critique of Ellmann's biography (F33).

F99   McGrory, Kathleen. "Interview with Carola Giedion-Welcker,
        June 15, 1973, Burlington Hotel, Dublin." In YEATS, JOYCE,
        AND BECKETT: NEW LIGHT ON THREE MODERN IRISH WRITERS.   Ed.
        McGrory and John Unterecker. Lewisburg, Pa.: Bucknell
        Univ. Press, 1976. Pp. 110-17.
                Reminiscences of JJ in Zurich and Paris in the
                thirties, spiced with considerable comment on
                his relationship and response to contemporary
                European movements in the arts.

F100   McMillan, Dougald. *TRANSITION:* THE HISTORY OF A LITERARY
        ERA, 1927-1938. New York: Braziller, 1976. Pp. 179-231
        and passim.
                Eugene Jolas' championship of JJ's works and
                vision, and account of the part-publication
                of "Work in Progress" (FW) in Jolas' influen-
                tial journal. Also includes N140. Also see
                G81.

F101   Magalaner, Marvin, and Richard M. Kain. "Part 1--The
        Man"; "James Joyce: A Biographical Sketch." In JOYCE:
        THE MAN, THE WORK, THE REPUTATION. Pp. 3-43; 311-14.
        See G58.
                Excellent discussions of the paradoxes in JJ's
                character and the problematic relations be-
                tween his works and his biography. Includes a
                brief biography.

F102   Magee, William K. [John Eglington]. "The Beginnings of
        Joyce"; "A Glimpse of the Later Joyce." In IRISH LITER-
        ARY PORTRAITS. London: Macmillan, 1935. Pp. 131-50;
        153-58.
                Memories of JJ as a young man and of a later
                meeting with JJ in Paris. Some unperceptive
                comments on Stephen Dedalus as JJ's self-
                portrait. Extracts reprinted in F136 and G25.

F103   Markow-Totevy, Georges. "James Joyce and Louis Gillet."
        In A JAMES JOYCE MISCELLANY. Ed. Marvin Magalaner. Pp.
        49-61. See G55.
                JJ's friendship with the critic Gillet, and
                Gillet's championing of JJ's work. (Also pub-
                lished as "Introduction" in G29.)

F104   Materer, Timothy. "James Joyce and the Vortex of History." In VORTEX: POUND, ELIOT, AND LEWIS. Ithaca, N.Y.: Cornell Univ. Press, 1979. Pp. 163-97.
>JJ's personal, literary, and critical relations with the Vortex group, primarily Wyndham Lewis.

F105   Mercanton, Jacques. "The Hours of James Joyce." Trans. Lloyd C. Parks. KR, 24 (1962), 700-30; 25 (1963), 93-118.
>Valuable memoir of JJ in Paris, in the late thirties, by a French journalist and friend. Reprinted in F122. Also see R19.

F106   Mercier, Vivian. "Dublin Under the Joyces." In JAMES JOYCE. Ed. Seon Givens. Pp. 285-301. See G30.
>"What Joyce means to Dublin [and] what Dublin meant to Joyce."

F107   Meyers, Jeffrey. "James and Nora Joyce." In MARRIED TO GENIUS. New York: Barnes and Noble, 1977. Pp. 74-91.
>The course, eccentricities (JJ's anal-eroticism), and crises of the Joyces' marriage.

F108   MODERN FICTION STUDIES. 18 (1972), 3-129. "Italo Svevo."
>Special issue on JJ's Triestine associate Svevo, including numerous references to JJ among its eleven biographical and critical essays and notes, and a brief note (by Niny Rocco-Bergera) specifically concerning the Joyce-Svevo relationship.

F109   Moseley, Virginia. "Joyce and the Bible: The External Evidence." In *ULYSSES*: CINQUANTE ANS APRÈS. Ed. Louis Bonnerot. Pp. 99-110. See M7.
>Evidence of JJ's familiarity with the Bible, drawn from official curricula for Irish education and recollections of JJ's classmates.

F110   Nolan, Brian. "A Bash in the Tunnel." ENVOY, 5 (May 1951), 6-11.
>JJ's Santanism and blasphemy imply belief: he's a true "fear-shaken Irish Catholic." See F36. Reprinted below and in F135.

F111   -----, ed. JAMES JOYCE ESSAYS. Philadelphia: West, 1978.
>Reprint of ENVOY special issue (see F36). Also see F135.

F112   O'Brien, Edna. "Dear Mr. Joyce." In A BASH IN THE TUN-
       NEL. Ed. John Ryan. Pp. 43-47. See F135.
           "Dear, dirty" JJ. Affectionate character
           sketch.

F113   -----. "Joyce & Nora: A Portrait of Joyce's Marriage."
       HARPER'S, 261 (Sept. 1980), 60-64, 66, 68-73.
           Review of JJ's women and, chiefly, of his re-
           lations with Nora.

F114   O'Connor, Ulick. THE TIMES I'VE SEEN: OLIVER ST. JOHN
       GOGARTY: A BIOGRAPHY. New York: Obolensky, 1963. Pp.
       59-93.
           An objective account of JJ's and Gogarty's
           stormy relationship, seeking a middle-ground
           for comparative evaluation of the two anti-
           thetical artists. Extracts reprinted in F135
           and G25.

F115   -----, ed. THE JOYCE WE KNEW: MEMOIRS BY EUGENE SHEEHY,
       WILLIAM G. FALLON, PADRAIC COLUM, ARTHUR POWER. Cork,
       Ire.: Mercier Press, 1967.
           Collects four pleasant, anecdotal memoirs by
           JJ's friends and contemporaries.

F116   O'Mahony, Eoin. "Father Conmee and His Associates." JJQ,
       4 (1967), 263-70.
           Summarizes history of JJ's schools (chiefly
           Clongowes and Belvedere), with notes on their
           other distinguished graduates. See K12. Re-
           printed in F135.

F117   O'Neill, Michael J. "The Joyces in the Holloway Diaries."
       In A JAMES JOYCE MISCELLANY, SECOND SERIES. Ed. Marvin
       Magalaner. Pp. 103-10. See G56.
           Miscellaneous comments on JJ and his father,
           in the diary of the Dubliner Holloway.

F118   Parandowski, Jan. "Meeting with Joyce." 1959. Trans.
       Willard Potts. In PORTRAITS OF THE ARTIST IN EXILE. Ed.
       Willard Potts. Pp. 154-62. See F122.
           Polish novelist's conversation with JJ, in
           1937, chiefly concerning U. See R24.

F119   Paul, Elliot. "Farthest North: A Study of James Joyce."
       BOOKMAN (New York), 75 (1932), 156-63.
           Personal impressions of JJ by a Parisian

associate, asserting his essential convention-
ality in reaction to the assaults against his
modernism. Extract reprinted in G25.

F120   Pearl, Cyril. DUBLIN IN BLOOMTIME: THE CITY JAMES JOYCE
       KNEW. New York: Viking, 1969.
           Fascinating compilation of period photographs
           and reproduced documents (e.g., advertisements,
           the lease to the Martello Tower), with commen-
           tary on turn-of-the-century Dublin. Specifi-
           cally intended as a companion to U, but gener-
           ally valuable for biographical backgrounds.

F121   Pinker, James. "James Pinker to James Joyce, 1915-1920."
       Ed. John Firth. SB, 21 (1968), 205-24.
           Fifty-one letters from Pinker, JJ's literary
           agent (1915-22). Prefatory comments and an-
           notations by Firth.

F122   Potts, Willard, ed. PORTRAITS OF THE ARTIST IN EXILE:
       RECOLLECTIONS OF JAMES JOYCE BY EUROPEANS. Seattle: Univ.
       of Washington Press, 1979.
           Seventeen memoirs and commentaries on JJ, with
           Potts's excellent editorial introductions. All
           but one item previously published, but few a-
           vailable either in English, or in accessible
           publications. Includes two extracts from G29
           and the following: F8, F9, F42, F43, F46, F63,
           F90, F105, F118, F134, F139, F147, F154. Also
           see F72.

F123   Pound, Ezra. POUND/JOYCE: THE LETTERS OF EZRA POUND TO
       JAMES JOYCE, WITH POUND'S ESSAYS ON JOYCE. Ed. Forrest
       Read. New York: New Directions, 1967.
           Reprints, with running commentary by Read, all
           Pound's letters to JJ (1913-37), as well as
           several letters by JJ, and seven major essays
           and numerous extracts from articles by Pound
           concerning JJ's individual works, achievement,
           artistic heritage, and influence. Includes
           Read's "Introduction" on the Joyce-Pound rela-
           tionship (pp. 1-11), three documentary appen-
           dixes, and the following: H173, H174, J49,
           K119, L24, M255, and M256. Extracts reprinted
           in G25 and K1.

F124   Power, Arthur. CONVERSATIONS WITH JAMES JOYCE. Ed. Clive
       Hart. New York: Barnes and Noble, 1974.
           Irish-Parisian art critic's reconstructions

of his conversations with JJ, chiefly on literary topics, from contemporary notes (1921-
c.1940). Extract reprinted in G25.

F125   -----. "James Joyce--The Internationalist." In A BASH
IN THE TUNNEL. Ed. John Ryan. Pp. 181-88. See F135.
Recollections and impressions of JJ and Nora
(e.g., their mutual horror of provinciality).

F126   Quinn, Edward. JAMES JOYCE'S DUBLIN, WITH THE SELECTED
WRITINGS FROM JOYCE'S WORKS. London: Secker and Warburg,
1975.
Handsome collection of 131 photographs of
Dublin locales, captioned with extracts from
JJ's writings (D, FW, PAYM, STEPHEN HERO,
and U).

F127   Quinn, John. "'Quinnigan's Quake!' John Quinn's Letters
to James Joyce, 1916-1920; 1921-1924." Ed. Myron Schwartzman. BULLETIN OF RESEARCH IN THE HUMANITIES, 81 (1978),
216-60; 83 (1980), 27-66.
Describes and quotes extensively from the correspondence between JJ and his New York legal
and literary defender, concerning both U's
publication and censorship, and Quinn's pur-
chase and subsequent sale of the manuscript.

F128   "Recollections of the Man." ENVOY, 5 (May 1951), 73-78.
Four sympathetic extracts from JJ's obituaries
in the Irish papers. See F36. Reprinted as
"What the Irish Papers Said" in F111 and F135.

F129   Reid, Benjamin L. THE MAN FROM NEW YORK: JOHN QUINN AND
HIS FRIENDS. New York: Oxford Univ. Press, 1968. Pp.
273-79, 309-14, 439-58, 480-88, 529-33, and passim.
Biography of the New York lawyer and literary
patron who helped JJ in publishing U (in the
LITTLE REVIEW), in later lifting the American
ban on its publication, and in selling the U
manuscript to Rosenbach (see B22).

F130   Richards, Grant. "Grant Richards to James Joyce." Ed.
Robert Scholes. SB, 16 (1963), 139-60.
Forty-seven letters to JJ (1904-17), from
Richards, publisher of CHAMBER MUSIC and,
eventually, D. Prefatory and interspersed
commentaries by Scholes.

F131 Rocco-Bergera, Niny. "A Contribution to the Study of
Jealousy in Italo Svevo and James Joyce." In ATTI DEL
THIRD INTERNATIONAL JAMES JOYCE SYMPOSIUM. Pp. 25-30.
See G7.
> Compares and contrasts the jealous personali-
> ties of the two writers.

F132 -----. ITINERARY OF JOYCE AND SVEVO THROUGH ARTISTIC
TRIESTE. Trieste: Aziendo Autonoma Soggiorno e Turismo,
1971.
> Tourist guide to Joycean landmarks, prepared
> for the Third International JJ Symposium.
> (Pamphlet--22 pp.)

F133 Rodgers, W.R., ed. "A Portrait of Joyce as a Young Man";
"A Portrait of the Artist in Maturity." 1950. In IRISH
LITERARY PORTRAITS: W.B. YEATS: JAMES JOYCE: GEORGE MOORE:
J.M. SYNGE: GEORGE BERNARD SHAW: OLIVER ST. JOHN GOGARTY:
F.R. HIGGINS: AE (GEORGE RUSSELL). London: British Broad-
casting Corporation, 1972. Pp. 22-47; 48-74.
> Transcripts of two BBC broadcast discussions
> of JJ by his family, friends, and associates,
> including Eva and Stanislaus Joyce, Maria
> Jolas, Gogarty, Frank Budgen, Arthur Power,
> and others.

F134 Ruggiero, Paul. "James Joyce's Last Days in Zurich."
Trans. Carleton W. Carroll. In PORTRAITS OF THE ARTIST
IN EXILE. Ed. Willard Potts. Pp. 283-86. See F122.
> JJ's last days, death, and funeral, recounted
> by a long-time Swiss friend.

F135 Ryan, John, ed. A BASH IN THE TUNNEL: JAMES JOYCE BY THE
IRISH. Brighton, Engl.: Clifton Books, 1970.
> Fifteen memoirs and biographical commentaries
> and twelve critical essays, representing JJ's
> influence on, encounters with, and reception
> by his countrymen. Reprints eight selections
> from the ENVOY issue on JJ (see F36; also see
> F111). Includes F15, F62, F64, F80, F86, F95,
> F110, F112, F114, F116, F125, F128, H24, H71,
> H102, H103, H114, H196, K75, M149, M301, N53,
> N159, and N169.

F136 Scholes, Robert, and Richard M. Kain, eds. "The Artist
as a Young Man." In THE WORKSHOP OF DAEDALUS. Ed.
Scholes and Kain. Pp. 111-237. See K15.
> Accounts of JJ's family and education, discus-
> sion of Irish politics of the later nineteenth

century, and reprinted sketches of the young
JJ by ten memoirists. Includes F77 and ex-
tracts from F15, F19, F50, F78, F80, F102,
F137, and F146.

F137   Sheehy, Eugene. MAY IT PLEASE THE COURT. Dublin: Fallon,
1951. Pp. 3-10, 12-16, 21-30, and passim.
Admiring and amusing memories of JJ at Belvedere and University College. Extract reprinted
above.

F138   Sheehy, Michael. "James Joyce." In IS IRELAND DYING?
CULTURE AND THE CHURCH IN MODERN IRELAND. London: Hollis
and Carter, 1968. Pp. 88-102.
JJ condemned for his apostasy, abandonment of
Ireland, and fundamental lack of human sympathy.

F139   Soupault, Philippe. "James Joyce." 1945, 1963. Trans.
Carleton W. Carroll. In PORTRAITS OF THE ARTIST IN EXILE.
Ed. Willard Potts. Pp. 108-18. See F122.
Account of JJ and his work, by the French surrealist poet and novelist, and sometime translator of his works. Extract of earlier version
reprinted in G25 and G45. Also see R28.

F140   Staley, Thomas F. "Composition of Place: Joyce and
Trieste." MODERN BRITISH LITERATURE, 5 (1980), 3-9.
JJ's activities in and affection for Trieste.
See G63.

F141   -----. "The Irish Exile in Paris: James Joyce and George
Moore." In ULYSSES: CINQUANTE ANS APRÈS. Comp. Louis
Bonnerot. Pp. 15-22. See M7.
Parallels between JJ's and Moore's experiences
and assimilations of French culture (viz. CON-
FESSIONS OF A YOUNG MAN [1888]).

F142   Steloff, Frances. "In Touch With Genius." JML, 4 (1975),
749-882.
Memoirs of founder of Gotham Book Mart (N.Y.),
long a champion of JJ's work. (See especially
pp. 803-4, 848-56).

F143   Stephens, James. "The James Joyce I Knew"; "ULYSSES";
"FINNEGANS WAKE." 1946-1948. In JAMES, SEUMAS & JACQUES:
UNPUBLISHED WRITINGS OF JAMES STEPHENS. Ed. Lloyd Frank-
enberg. New York: Macmillan, 1964. Pp. 147-55; 156-59;
160-62.
Broadcast reminiscences of JJ, with some

general comments on U and FW, by the writer
JJ "adopted" as his symbolic "twin." Interesting defense of FW as "pure prose" (cf.
pure mathematics). Extract reprinted in G25.
Also see F39.

F144 Stern, James. "James Joyce: A First Impression." In A
JAMES JOYCE MISCELLANY, SECOND SERIES. Ed. Marvin Magalaner. Pp. 93-102. See G56.
1934 meeting with JJ and discussion of things
Irish.

F145 Straumann, Heinrich. "Last Meeting with Joyce." 1948.
Trans. Eugene Jolas and Maria Jolas. In A JAMES JOYCE
YEARBOOK. Ed. Maria Jolas. Pp. 109-15. See G45.
Recounts visit and conversation (re: Dublin,
Vico, and other matters) with JJ in late 1940.
See R30.

F146 Sullivan, Kevin. JOYCE AMONG THE JESUITS. New York:
Columbia Univ. Press, 1958.
Primarily factual and biographical study of
JJ's "actual relationships with the Jesuits,"
through the years of his education at Clongowes
Wood, Belvedere College, and University College
(1888-1902). Sullivan provides substantial
biographical backgrounds to the works and examines, with critical incisiveness, the impact
of Scholastic thought on the fiction: both JJ's
"intellectual virtues" and his "vices" (pedan-
try, arrogance), "were the product of his Jesuit training." Extracts reprinted in F136,
K1, and K14.

F147 Suter, August. "Some Reminiscences of James Joyce."
Trans. Fritz Senn. JJQ, 7 (1970), 191-97.
First publication of random memories of JJ,
in Zurich and Paris (c. 1916-22), by the
Swiss sculptor and companion of Budgen and
JJ. Reprinted in F122.

F148 Svevo, Italo. JAMES JOYCE: A LECTURE DELIVERED IN MILAN
IN 1927. Trans. Stanislaus Joyce. Norfolk, Conn.: New
Directions, 1950.
Memories of the Italo-Triestine novelist and
friend of JJ, recalling JJ's struggles to
write, to publish, and to support his family
in Trieste, with critical comment on his works.
Extract reprinted in G25. Also see R31.

F149 Thomson, Virgil. "Antheil, Joyce, and Pound." In VIRGIL
THOMSON. New York: Knopf, 1966. Pp. 73-83.
>Meetings with JJ, Antheil, and Pound in Paris
>(late twenties). Notes JJ's approval of his
>and Antheil's music.

F150 Tindall, William York. THE JOYCE COUNTRY. 1960. Rev.
ed. New York: Schocken, 1972.
>Photographs of Dublin and environs, paired
>with appropriate quotations from JJ's work.

F151 -----. "The Joyce Landscape." In YEATS, JOYCE, AND BECK-
ETT: NEW LIGHT ON THREE MODERN IRISH WRITERS. Ed. Kathleen McGrory and John Unterecker. Lewisburg, Pa.: Bucknell Univ. Press, 1976. Pp. 73-85.
>Eleven photographs of JJ and Dublin sights
>and sites.

F152 Trilling, Lionel. "James Joyce in His Letters." COMMEN-
TARY, 45 (Feb. 1968), 53-64.
>JJ's obscene letters, like his works, embrace
>"nullity," or destructive perversity, as a
>means for the transcendent affirmation of
>life. Reprinted in G19.

F153 Tuoni, Dario de. RICORDO DI JOYCE A TRIESTE. Milan:
All'insegna del pesce d'oro, 1966.
>Valuable memories of JJ, his family, and his
>literary associates and opinions, by a Tries-
>tine friend (e. 1913-15, with irregular con-
>tacts thereafter). [In Italian.]

F154 Vinding, Ole. "James Joyce in Copenhagen." 1941, 1963.
Trans. Helge Irgens-Moller. In PORTRAITS OF THE ARTIST
IN EXILE. Ed. Willard Potts. Pp. 139-52. See F122.
>Danish journalist's detailed account of the
>Joyces' visit to Denmark, in 1936, noting
>JJ's intense interest in things Scandinavian.
>Also published in F72.. Also see R33.

F155 Wagner, Geoffrey. "Master Joys and Windy Nous." In
WYNDHAM LEWIS: A PORTRAIT OF THE ARTIST AS ENEMY. New
Haven, Conn.: Yale Univ. Press, 1957. Pp. 168-88.
>Summarizes JJ's and Lewis's acquaintance
>(1920-), Lewis's criticisms of JJ (e.g., see
>H126), and JJ's rejoinders (e.g., in FW).

F156   Wain, John. "The Prophet Ezra vs. 'The Egotistical Sub-
        lime': On Pound, Eliot, Joyce." ENCOUNTER, 33 (Aug.
        1969), 63-70.
                Pound's and JJ's antithetical temperaments,
                yet similar turns toward obscurity in their
                later work (cf. Pound-Eliot).

F157   Weaver, Harriet. "Harriet Weaver's Letters to James
        Joyce, 1915-1920." Ed. John Firth. SB, 20 (1967), 151-
        88.
                Weaver's correspondence with JJ during the
                period of U's serialization in THE EGOIST,
                under her editorship. Sixty-one letters.
                Includes brief introductory note (pp. 151-
                53) and annotations by Firth.

G. BOOK-LENGTH CRITICAL STUDIES AND ESSAY COLLECTIONS

Also see the numerous books, essay collections, monographs, and
pamphlets on JJ's individual works (D, PAYM, EXILES, U, FW),
parts of works (D and U), and miscellaneous writings, listed
in sections J, K, L, M, N, and P below, as well as the foreign-
language books entered in the corresponding sections of part 3
(S, U, V, X, Y, and Z) below. This section includes studies,
monographs, and pamphlets concerned with JJ generally or with
more than *two* of his individual works. Thus, several studies
of JJ which concentrate on his early development (e.g., in D
and PAYM), on his autobiographical themes (e.g., in PAYM and
U), or on his technical experiments (e.g., in U and FW), and
which one could convincingly argue are general in their significance, are reserved for entry and annotation (with cross references), in the *two* appropriate sections on individual works
below.

Also note: PAYM and its early version, STEPHEN HERO, have been
considered as *one* work for the purposes of this classification;
so studies of PAYM and U, for example, which also touch on STE-
PHEN HERO, are entered and annotated in the PAYM section (K),
entered with a cross-reference to the PAYM annotation in the U
section (M), and noted in the headnote to the section on miscellaneous writings (P).

G1   Adams, Robert M.   AFTERJOYCE: STUDIES IN FICTION AFTER
     ULYSSES.   New York: Oxford Univ. Press, 1977.
          Perceptive summary statement of JJ's achievement
          and reputation, asserting that as a writer he
          still "lives" and only questioning "Where? and
          How?" Adams examines the impact of JJ's fic-
          tional methods, particularly structure and sym-
          bolism, and of his language on a number of more
          recent writers, including Beckett, Broch, Döblin,
          Faulkner, Gadda, Nabokov, and Woolf, among others.

G2   -----.   JAMES JOYCE: COMMON SENSE AND BEYOND.   New York:
     Random House, 1967.
          Outspoken, yet able critical overview of JJ's

works. Adams opens with a summary of "Ireland
and Joyce's Heritage from It" and a brief biographical sketch. The stories in D he finds
"of great historical importance," though several
are artistic disappointments. Adams sees PAYM
as a powerful though badly flawed novel and
views U equivocally as well, praising its epic
scope yet finding its world "dark," "brittle,"
and "hollow." Adams considers FW JJ's finest
work, provides model explications of two passages, and predicts the book's gradual accep-
tance. Extract reprinted in J1.

G3   Allt, Peter. SOME ASPECTS OF THE LIFE AND WORKS OF JAMES
AUGUSTINE JOYCE. Groningen, Neth.: Wolters, 1952.
Notes on JJ's place in the European and Gaelic-
Irish cultures and on the entertainment afforded
by his works. (Pamphlet--15 pp.)

G4   AMERICAN BOOK COLLECTOR. 15, No. 10 (1965), 6-29. "Special
James Joyce Number."
Bibliographical essay (see E3), list of JJ's addresses (see F34), and several notes and brief
reviews. Generously illustrated. Includes brief
editorial statements by the various editors of
JJ periodicals and newsletters.

G5   Appel, Alfred. JAMES JOYCE: AN APPRECIATION PUBLISHED UPON
THE OCCASION OF AN EXHIBITION. Stanford, Calif.: Stanford
Univ. Libraries, 1964.
Brief comments. (Pamphlet--5 pp.)

G6   Arnold, Armin. JAMES JOYCE. 1963. Trans. Arnold and Judy
Young. New York: Ungar, 1969.
Introduction to JJ's life and work, originally
for German students. Carelessly written, error-
laden, and distorted by Arnold's search for elements of self-martyrdom in JJ's character and
fiction. See S4.

G7   ATTI DEL THIRD INTERNATIONAL JAMES JOYCE SYMPOSIUM TRIESTE--
14-18 GIUGNO 1971. Trieste: Universita Degli Studi, 1974.
No editor specified. Collects twelve symposium
papers on JJ in English (with Italian translations), eleven papers and speeches in French
and Italian, and abstracts (most in both English and Italian) of seven panel discussions on

various Joycean topics (including an interest-
ing panel on Vico and JJ). Includes F54, F131,
G49 (extract), H109, H131, H223, K48, K73, M182,
M211, M213, and N160. Also see F71 and N27.

G8   Aubert, Jacques, and Maria Jolas, eds. JOYCE & PARIS:
      1902...1920-1940...1975. PAPERS FROM THE 5TH INTERNA-
      TIONAL JAMES JOYCE SYMPOSIUM, PARIS, 16-20 JUNE 1975.
      2 vols. Paris: Éditions du C.N.R.S., 1979.
            Publishes nine papers and abstracts, transcrip-
            tions and abstracts of thirteen panel discus-
            sions, and an exhibition catalogue (Bernard
            Gheerbrant, comp.), from the symposium. [In
            French and English.] Includes H6, H15, J55,
            M83, M423, and N200.

G9   Bates, Ronald, and Harry J. Pollock, eds. LITTERS FROM
      ALOFT: PAPERS DELIVERED AT THE SECOND CANADIAN JAMES JOYCE
      SEMINAR. MCMASTER UNIVERSITY. Tulsa, Okla.: Univ. of
      Tulsa Press, 1971.
            Gathers six original papers on JJ, his rela-
            tionships, his works, and translation of his
            works. Includes H12, H194, H197, M186, and
            extracts from G10 and N5.

G10   Benstock, Bernard. JAMES JOYCE: THE UNDISCOVER'D COUNTRY.
      New York: Barnes and Noble, 1977.
            Fine study of the sources and implications of
            JJ's treading the "thin" lines between an ob-
            session with Irish materials and a commitment
            to the world literary tradition, and between
            the antitheses of the self and the world, the
            "artist and humankind." Ranging widely among
            JJ's works "short of" FW (which he discusses
            elsewhere; see N6), Benstock shows the origins
            of the Dubliner JJ's sense of separateness
            from the Irish-Gaelic culture "beyond the Pale,"
            examines his conscious exile from his Anglo-
            Irish condition, and argues that U marks a par-
            tial return in its syntheses of pan-European
            and provincial cultures (the "undiscover'd
            country"). Extracts originally published above
            and in M60.

G11   Benstock, Shari, and Bernard Benstock, eds. WHO'S HE WHEN
      HE'S AT HOME? A JAMES JOYCE DIRECTORY. Urbana: Univ. of
      Illinois Press, 1980.
            Alphabetical directory of JJ's characters,

under two headings (named and unnamed), with
page references for their appearance in D,
EXILES, GIACOMO JOYCE, PAYM, STEPHEN HERO,
and U. Includes real and fictitious figures
present, alluded to, referred to, thought of,
and hallucinated. Also includes an appendix
on JJ's method of cataloguing characters and
references to other entries in the reference
works by Gifford and Seidman (J7, M20), Hart
and Knuth (M27), and Thornton (M64). For the
characters in FW, see Glasheen (N20).

G12 Bolt, Sydney. A PREFACE TO JAMES JOYCE. London: Longman,
1981.
General introduction for students, surveying
JJ's life, discussing the impact of Ireland,
the Church, and the literary tradition on his
development as an artist, and commenting on
the major works (principally PAYM and U). Includes a brief "Reference Section." (Not
seen--paraphrased from publisher's announce-
ment.)

G13 Bowen, Zack. MUSICAL ALLUSIONS IN THE WORKS OF JAMES
JOYCE: EARLY POETRY THROUGH *ULYSSES*. Albany: State Univ.
of New York Press, 1974.
Brief essays on JJ's use of musical allusions
in his works, followed by identifications of
and often extended "remarks" on each such allusion. Four-fifths of Bowen's text is concerned with U. For identification of song
elements in FW, see Hodgart and Worthington
(G41).

G14 -----, ed. IRISH RENAISSANCE ANNUAL II. Newark: Univ.
of Delaware Press, 1981.
Special JJ volume, containing six articles on
D, PAYM, and U. Includes J42, K43, K45, K47,
M402, and M441.

G15 Boyle, Robert, S.J. JAMES JOYCE'S PAULINE VISION: A CATHO-
LIC EXPOSITION. Carbondale: Southern Illinois Univ. Press,
1978.
Wide-ranging traversal of JJ's works to demon-
strate his fundamental concurrence with St.
Paul's vision of the Infinite Being's "embrace
[of] so crass an animal as man" (viz. I Cor.
2:9), and to argue JJ's "most rare epiphanic

vision" of God's infinite love. Avoiding sim-
ple-minded theological exegesis, Boyle shows
"a Catholic alertness to the religious profun-
dities of the text [and] a philosopher's sensitivity to its metaphysical implications" in
demonstrating JJ's "constantly deeper use, and
his decreasingly acrimonious toleration, of religious and specifically Catholic doctrines and
attitudes to express his own literary theory
and practice." Includes frequent comparisons
of JJ's views with the Pauline visions of Shakespeare and Hopkins, and chapters on his aesthetic and on his Jesuit training. Assimilates
M88, M89, and M90.

G16   Brivic, Sheldon R. JOYCE BETWEEN FREUD AND JUNG. Port
      Washington, N.Y.: Kennikat Press, 1980.
            Three-part study, comprising an intensive Freud-
      ian exploration of the origins and Oedipal na-
      ture of JJ's "mental life" in PAYM, a pyschoana-
      lytic investigation of the "unconscious deter-
      minants of Joyce's personality" (e.g., ambiva-
      lence), and their connections to his "conscious
      systems of meaning and value" in "The Dead" and
      EXILES (e.g., ambiguity), and a Jungian analysis
      of JJ's search for value in life through his ob-
      sessively "personal mythology" in U and FW. Bri-
      vic parallels JJ's development, from naturalist
      to symbolist; to the evolution of psychology
      from the "materialist" Freud to the "spiritual-
      ist" Jung. While surpassed in parts, Brivic's
      is a balanced and informed psychoanalytic study.
      Assimilates articles previously published in
      PSYCHOANALYSIS AND LITERARY PROCESS (ed. Fred-
      erick C. Crews, 1970), and in G43.

G17   Burgess, Anthony. RE JOYCE. New York: Norton, 1965. Pub-
      lished as HERE COMES EVERYBODY: AN INTRODUCTION TO JAMES
      JOYCE FOR THE ORDINARY READER. London: Faber, 1965.
            Useful condensation and consolidation of much
      recent critical discussion of JJ. Unfortunately
      Burgess both refuses to acknowledge his debts
      and dyspeptically attacks the very "Joyce indus-
      try" from which he has so directly benefitted.
      He has, nevertheless, produced an engaging in-
      troduction, with some good insights into JJ's
      use of language. Extract reprinted in J3. Also
      see H63.

G17a CAHIERS VICTORIENS & ÉDOUARDIENS. No. 14 (1981), pp. 1-
121. "Studies in the Early Joyce."
Collects ten essays, seven in French, principal-
ly but not exclusively on D and PAYM, by Alain
Blayac ("'After the Race' ou les Avatars d'un
Texte Polysémique"), Jean Fuzier ("Cape Horn Re-
visited: An Exploration of James Joyce's Use of
Some Limericks"), Fabienne Garcier ("James Joyce
et la Nouvelle"), Claude Jacquet ("James Joyce:
Quelques Épiphanies du Monde Extérieur"), Fran-
çois Laroque ("Hallowe'en Customs in 'Clay'--a
Study of James Joyce's Use of Folklore in DUB-
LINERS"), Jean-Marie Maguin ("Le Fonctionnement
Symbolique de 'Ivy Day in the Committee Room'"),
Jacky Martin ("'Paralysie,' 'Simonie,' 'Gnomon':
Les Conditions de Représentation du Désir dans
DUBLINERS"), Jean-Michel Rabaté ("Le Silence
dans DUBLINERS"), Fritz Senn ("Gogarty and Joyce:
Verbal Intimacy"), and Pierre Vitoux ("L'Esthé-
tique de Joyce: de l'Épiphanie à la Déconstruc-
tion de l'Objet"). Received too late for each
article's individual entry and annotation in
this bibliography.

G18 CEA CRITIC. 14, No. 2 (1952), 1-8.
Six brief notes on JJ's academic reception and
the problems of teaching his works. Most items
slight. Includes M123 and H102 (extract).

G19 Chace, William M., ed. JOYCE: A COLLECTION OF CRITICAL
ESSAYS. Englewood Cliffs, N.J.: Prentice-Hall, 1974.
Extracts from nine previously published commentaries on the four works of fiction, and two
general essays on JJ's character and critical
reputation. Chace's "Introduction" (pp. 1-10)
surveys the contents of the collection. Includes F152, H1, and extracts from F33, G21,
G47, G52, H237, M15, M22, M110, and N21.

G20 Chatterjee, Sisir [also Sisir Chattopadhyaya]. JAMES
JOYCE: A STUDY IN TECHNIQUE. 1957. 2nd ed. Calcutta:
Orient Longmans, 1970.
Pedestrian study of JJ's narrative technique,
from D to FW, and "detailed examination of his
aesthetic theory of epiphany with which he
started" (but rejected, as Chatterjee fails to
observe). Second edition adds an irrelevant
chapter on Stephen's Shakespeare theory in U.

G21 Cixous, Hélène. THE EXILE OF JAMES JOYCE. 1968. Trans.
     Sally A.J. Purcell. New York: David Lewis, 1972.
         A diffuse, 'loose baggy monster' of subjective
     literary criticism. Cixous proposes to examine
     the art of JJ through his life (resulting in
     some strenuously biographical readings and mis-
     readings), yet frequently shifts grounds to
     speculate on the "inner life" of the artist as
     revealed in his works. There are a number of
     appealing insights here and an equal number of
     appalling gaffes. For the better biography see
     Ellmann (F33) and for the better critical over-
     view see any number of other general studies.
     Extract reprinted in G19.

G22 Cope, Jackson I. JOYCE'S CITIES: ARCHAEOLOGIES OF THE
     SOUL. Baltimore: Johns Hopkins Univ. Press, 1981.
         Essentially a study of JJ's assimilation of sev-
     eral sources and literary influences, detect-
     able in his developing vision of the city in his
     works. Cope argues that, in D, JJ began as a
     Victorian, primarily concerned with the family
     unit and the hostile forces of the "Dantesque [sic]
     cities of the dreadful night" (cf. James Thomp-
     son). While this vision of the dead metropolis
     also functions as background to U, JJ's growing
     sense of the city's "histerico-mythic" dimen-
     sion, under the principal influence of D'Annunzio
     (cf. EXILES and PAYM and LA CITTÀ MORTA [1897],
     LE VERGINI DELLE ROCCE [1895], and IL FUOCO
     [1909]), is further vitalized by his study of
     Kabbalistic lore (influences of MacGregor Ma-
     thers and A.E. Waite), and finally matures as
     the dynamic, universal "heliopolis" of FW (cf.
     Marinetti and THE BOOK OF THE DEAD).

G23 CRANE BAG (Dublin). 2 (1978), 5-56.
         Includes, among other materials, six articles
     on mythic dimensions of JJ's works, by Bernard
     Benstock ("A Setdown Secular Phoenish: The Finn
     of FINNEGANS WAKE"), Mark Patrick Hederman
     ("'The Dead' Revisited"), John Jordan ("Amor
     Fati sive Contemptus Mundi"), Vivian Mercier
     ("James Joyce as Medieval Artist"), Joseph Ste-
     phen O'Leary ("Joyce and the Myth of the Fall"),
     and Bruce Stewart ("Adamology"). Not seen.

G24 Cross, Richard K. FLAUBERT AND JOYCE: THE RITE OF FICTION.
Princeton, N.J.: Princeton Univ. Press, 1971.
  Counterpointed readings of the two dedicated
'priests' of art, comparing works by Flaubert
and JJ which are similar in theme (L'EDUCATION
SENTIMENTALE [1869] and PAYM) and technique
(TROIS CONTES [1877] and D; MADAME BOVARY [1857]
and "Proteus"and "Nausicaa"; LE TENTATION DE
SAINT ANTOINE [1874] and "Circe"; BOUVARD ET
PÉCUCHET [1881] and "Ithaca"). Some interest-
ing observations, but goes little beyond ampli-
fying correspondences between the two writers,
argued early and energetically by Pound (see
F123).

G25 Deming, Robert H., ed. JAMES JOYCE: THE CRITICAL HERITAGE.
2 vols. London: Routledge, 1970.
  Massive compilation of 344 extracts from reviews, commentaries, and assessments chiefly
published during JJ's lifetime. Extremely use-
ful guide to JJ's reputation, although unfairly
maligned by reviewers for its fragmentariness
(many of the extracts are very brief) and oc-
casionally inept translations. Excellent index.
Includes E8 and extracts from F6, F8, F11, F12,
F19, F33, F53, F64, F65, F66, F73, F78, F81,
F89, F90, F91, F96, F102, F114, F119, F123,
F124, F139, F143, F148, G29, G36, G52, G77, G84,
H36, H37, H51, H57, H60, H126, H142, H150, H157,
H173, H174, H178, H215, H221, H232, H237, H238,
J34, J49, K64, K119, K136, K146, L5, L12, L14,
L18, L24, M67, M74, M101, M102, M106, M107, M112,
M115, M116, M132, M136, M138, M142, M150, M180,
M206, M207, M234, M236, M242, M255, M266, M274,
M283, M309, N64, N65, N75, N86, N87, N97, N106,
N140, N142, N178, N189, N195, N205, N210, N221,
P3, and P35.

G26 DUBLIN MAGAZINE. 10, No. 2 (1973), 21-32, 42-76, 106-12.
"A James Joyce Number."
  Contains, among other miscellaneous items, four
essays and a review concerning JJ. Includes
H18, J35, J71, and M273.

G27 Duff, Charles. JAMES JOYCE AND THE PLAIN READER: AN ESSAY.
London: Harmsworth, 1932.
  Early monograph attempting to unlock the "mys-
teries" of JJ to the "plain reader," based,

however, on the assumption that such a reader
is "more intelligent...than he suspects himself." The reader is thus brought to JJ, rather than the reverse. Some good insights and
strong emphasis on U and FW.

G27a   Epstein, Edmund L., ed. A STARCHAMBER QUIRY: A JAMES
JOYCE CENTENNIAL VOLUME, 1882-1982. London: Methuen,
1982.
Collects five essays, by Robert Boyle, S.J.
("Worshipper of the Word: James Joyce and the
Trinity"), Epstein ("James Joyce and the Body"),
Clive Hart ("Afterword: Reading FINNEGANS
WAKE"), Hugh Kenner ("Notes Toward an Anatomy
of 'Modernism'"), and Fritz Senn ("James Joyce
and his Style: Weaving, Unweaving"), together
with the editor's introduction. (Announced
for publication in Feb. 1982--not seen.)

G28   Eruvbetine, A.E. INTELLECTUALIZED EMOTIONS AND THE ART
OF JAMES JOYCE. Hicksville, N.Y.: Exposition Press, 1980.
Based on the debatable assumption that JJ's
writings are generally viewed both as lacking
"normal human emotion" and as "extremely bor-
ing," Eruvbetine argues that JJ's art effectively portrays "human feelings," explores the
"reality of feelings," embodies the aesthetic
theory that art advocates "sane feelings," employs his notorious devices to structure "universal and particular emotions," and affirms
the "emotional resilience" of the human spirit.
Several good points, but neither original nor
unorthodox in finding JJ an affirmative and
humane author.

G29   Gillet, Louis. CLAYBOOK FOR JAMES JOYCE. 1941. Trans.
Georges Markow-Totevy. New York: Abelard-Schuman, 1958.
Collects Gillet's five admiring essays on JJ
and his works: on U (1925); on FW (1931 [from
G81], 1940 [review]); an obituary critique
(1941); and an affectionate memoir (1941).
Documents Gillet's important role in the French
reception of JJ. Also includes prefatory essays by the translator (see F103) and by Leon
Edel (F31), and an essay by Gide (H72). Extracts reprinted in F122, G25, and G45. Also
see S17.

G30 Givens, Seon, ed. JAMES JOYCE: TWO DECADES OF CRITICISM.
     1948. Rev. ed. New York: Vanguard Press, 1963.
          Outstanding collection of five original and fif-
          teen previously published essays and memoirs.
          The 1963, "augmented" edition adds an essay by
          the editor on JJ's critical reputation (see E13)
          and a few new items to the bibliography. In-
          cludes F12, F73, F106, G47 (extract), H32, H51,
          H73, H86, H93, J41, K58, K89, L13, M115, M132,
          M323, N75, N80, N210, N224, and P11.

G31 Goldberg, S.L. JAMES JOYCE. New York: Grove Press, 1962.
          Competent general survey of JJ's work, tracing his
          development from the "kinetic" early stories,
          verse, and fragments, composed under the influ-
          ence of his Romantic precursors, to the mature,
          "static" art of the classically disciplined
          "The Dead," PAYM, and U. FW is dismissed as
          not "worth detailed exegesis." Extracts re-
          printed in J1 and J6.

G32 Golding, Louis. JAMES JOYCE. London: Butterworth, 1933.
          Still useful study of JJ, though dated in some
          opinions. Golding pursues several threads
          through the works, arguing the overall unity
          of JJ's career-in-progress, among them the
          "theme" of Stephen Dedalus: the "pitiful lit-
          tle" poet of the "mawkish" and "derivative"
          verse, the boy of the early stories in D, the
          central figure in PAYM and EXILES (though named
          Richard Rowan), a major protagonist in U, and
          a voice in FW. Includes a strong appreciation
          of the Aristotelian design of U, in response
          to early attacks on its formlessness, and a per-
          ceptive analysis of FW in progress.

G33 Goldman, Arnold. JAMES JOYCE. London: Routledge, 1968.
          Introduction to JJ's works, consisting of fifty-
          six extracts from D, PAYM, U, and FW, with Gold-
          man's running commentary on JJ's chief themes
          and techniques.

G34 -----. THE JOYCE PARADOX: FORM AND FREEDOM IN HIS FICTION.
     Evanston, Ill.: Northwestern Univ. Press, 1966.
          Cogent and persuasive analysis of the sources
          and implications of paradox in JJ's works (chief-
          ly the first four stories of D, PAYM, and U).

Goldman sees the strongest evidence for JJ's
'negative capability' in the decisively op-
posed views of his work current in academic
criticism and attributes his radical ambiguity
to JJ's study of Ibsen. Through the Norwegian
dramatist, Goldman contends, JJ assimilated
Søren Kierkegaard's "either/or" principle, so
influential for the irresolvable conflicts
among ethics, aesthetics, and religion in Ibsen.
The burden of Goldman's book applies Kierkegaard
to the interpretation of the "paradoxes" of
style, symbolism, and theme in U.

G35   Gordon, John. JAMES JOYCE'S METAMORPHOSES. New York:
      Barnes and Noble, 1981.
            Study of the fiction based on the assumption
            that JJ's writings can best be approached as
            metamorphoses of his biography, or transmuta-
            tions of his own experiences into art. Gordon
            "explores the radical changes in literary style
            that distinguish all of Joyce's writings and
            examines in detail the creative use that Joyce
            made of his own life story." Includes numerous
            identifications of JJ's literary and personal
            allusions. Presumably assimilates M417. Not
            seen. (Quoted and paraphrased from publisher's
            announcement.)

G36   Gorman, Herbert S. JAMES JOYCE: HIS FIRST FORTY YEARS.
      New York: Huebsch, 1924.
            Influential, first book-length study of JJ's
            works (through U), establishing several of the
            touchstones of later criticism: the progressive,
            organic development of JJ's style, the "man-
            nered" quality of the early verse, the "photo-
            graphic" realism of D, the autobiographical
            dimensions of PAYM and EXILES, the relation
            of Stephen's aesthetics to JJ's practice, the
            interplay of realism and symbolism in U, the
            amorality of U, and the extrinsic nature of
            the Homeric analogies in U ("scaffolding").
            (Note: JJ was sufficiently impressed by Gorman
            to name him his authorized biographer--in the
            end a dubious reward; see F55). Extracts re-
            printed in G25.

G37   Grose, Kenneth. JAMES JOYCE. London: Evans, 1975.
            Introduction to JJ's fiction, drama, and verse,

concentrating on PAYM and U, the works through
which "most people will approach" JJ. Grose's
critiques are balanced, finding PAYM fruitfully
equivocal and U a "humane revelation" of what
Stephen must learn, "'what the heart is and what
it feels.'"

G38 Gross, John. JAMES JOYCE. New York: Viking Press, 1970.
Survey of JJ's fiction, concentrating on D, U,
and FW, which has value, though it fails "to
relate Joyce, however loosely, to the intellectual climate of the age." Gross summarizes the
biographical ghosts JJ 'exorcises' in his works
(e.g., his father), treats D as the most important early work (PAYM and EXILES lightly touched
on), gives U a cautiously negative reading ("a
book that strains after the status of myth but
that can never fully attain it"), and dismisses
FW as a "dazzling failure," after some impartial
but superficial discussion. Extract reprinted
in J3.

G39 Harmon, Maurice, ed. THE CELTIC MASTER: CONTRIBUTIONS TO
THE FIRST JAMES JOYCE SYMPOSIUM HELD IN DUBLIN, 1967.
Dublin: Dolmen, 1969.
Five papers, of variable quality, on JJ and
selected works ("The Dead," FW, and U). Includes Harmon's cursory "Introduction" (p. 7),
and H151, H214, J176, M434, and N41 (extract).

G40 Hodgart, Matthew J.C. JAMES JOYCE: A STUDENT'S GUIDE.
London: Routledge, 1978.
Weakly-argued interpretations of D, PAYM, U,
and FW, for the most part concentrating on
Christian symbols and patterns and, in FW, dis-
proportionately emphasizing the significance of
opera. Hodgart, unlike Tindall in his more balanced, yet similar guide, also provides capsule
summaries of Irish art, history, and politics,
as well as a brief biography of JJ.

G41 Hodgart, Matthew J.C., and Mabel P. Worthington. SONG IN
THE WORK OF JAMES JOYCE. New York: Columbia Univ. Press,
1959.
Introductory essays on JJ's knowledge of music
and his use of musical allusions and on the
structural and thematic significance of song

in FW, followed by unannotated lists of song
references in the poems, EXILES, D, STEPHEN
HERO, PAYM, U, and FW. Three-quarters of the
references are traced in FW (for fuller information on the earlier works see Bowen [G13]).

G42   JAMES JOYCE QUARTERLY. 4 (1967), 163-246. "Translation
      Issue."
      Fourteen essays and notes on translating JJ and
      on translations of and by JJ, by Jacques Aubert
      (Y10), Mogens Boisen ("Translating ULYSSES"),
      Michel Butor ("La Traduction, Dimension Fonda-
      mentale de Notre Temps"), Alan M. Cohn (M416),
      Jack P. Dalton ("'Stately, Plumb Buck Mulligan'
      in Djoytsch"), Péter Egri ("James Joyce's Work
      in Hungarian Translation"), Nathan Halper ("Joyce
      and 'Anna Livia'"), Breon Mitchell ("On the Sta-
      tus of the Authorized Translation"), Fritz Senn
      ("The Tellings of the Taling," three brief notes,
      and an earlier version of M288), and Bjørn J.
      Tysdahl ("Two Translations by Joyce"). Also in-
      cludes two examples of JJ's U ("Proteus") in
      translation (by John Vandenbergh [Dutch] and
      Maciej Slomczynski [Polish]), and an essay on
      Stuart Gilbert's translation of Dujardin's LES
      LAURIERS SONT COUPÉS (1887), by Vivian Mercier
      ("Justice for Édouard Dujardin"). Guest editor:
      Fritz Senn.

G43   JAMES JOYCE QUARTERLY. 13 (1976), 266-384. "Joyce and
      Modern Psychology."
      Introductory note on and concluding brief check-
      list of psychoanalytic studies of JJ, by the
      guest editor Mark Shechner, and six psycholog-
      ical interpretations of JJ and his works: G16
      (extract), H4, H163, K91, M200, and N202. A
      supplement to this issue, in JJQ, 14 (1977), 416-
      49, includes two additional essays, by Jeanne
      McKnight ("Unlocking the Word-Hoard: Madness,
      Identity and Creativity in James Joyce") and Jane
      Ford (see M143).

G44   JAMES JOYCE QUARTERLY. 16 (1978-79), 5-149. "Structural-
      ist/Reader Reponse Issue."
      Contains eleven essays on structuralist criti-
      cism, on the texts of JJ's fiction, and on read-
      er responses to his works, "which reflect the

many recent developments in literary theory,"
by Suzanne Ferguson ("A Sherlook at DUBLINERS"),
David Hayman (see N125), Joseph A. Kestner ("Vir-
tual Text/Virtual Reader"), Jennifer Schiffer
Levine (see E18), Jean Ricardou ("Time of the
Narration, Time of the Fiction," trans. Kest-
ner), Herbert Schneidau and David Hayman (see
M405), Robert Scholes (see J91), Fritz Senn
("The Challenge: '*ignotas animum*'" [PAYM]),
James J. Sosnowski ("Reading Acts and Reading
Warrants" [PAYM]), and Brook Thomas ("Not a
Reading of, but the Act of Reading ULYSSES"--
similar to M313).

G45 Jolas, Maria, ed. A JAMES JOYCE YEARBOOK. Paris: Transition Press, 1949.
   Heterogeneous collection of original and reprinted critical articles (six), memoirs (four),
   and notes. Includes F76, F77, F90, F139, F145,
   G29 (extract), H230, L26, M93, N108, and N187.

G46 Jones, William Powell. JAMES JOYCE AND THE COMMON READER.
Norman: Univ. of Oklahoma Press, 1955.
   General survey of JJ's four major works. Jones
   usefully describes the structural patterns of
   the "realistic" D and the interplay between realism and poetry in PAYM. U, to which he devotes four chapters, he views as an accessible,
   ambitious experiment, with special stress on
   its comedy and language (Jones is a linguist by
   training). Jones briefly considers FW as the
   logical culmination and *reductio ad absurdam* of
   the linguistic experiments of U. Good, solid
   introduction. Extract reprinted in K14.

G47 Kenner, Hugh. DUBLIN'S JOYCE. Bloomington: Indiana Univ.
Press, 1956.
   Generally brilliant, often idiosyncratic reading of JJ's works, by one of the most respected
   critics of modern letters. As a protégé of both
   Wyndham Lewis and Marshall McLuhan and as a distinguished critic of Pound, Kenner responds to
   Lewis's attacks on JJ (see H126), by suggesting
   that JJ was as severe a critic of himself, ex-
   tends several of the insights of McLuhan's analyses of JJ's scholasticism (see H139), and reaffirms Pound's recognition of JJ's essential

realism (see M255). Kenner's emphatically ironic reading of PAYM ("THE PORTRAIT in Perspective") has been his most influential as well as
his most controversial contribution (see K89).
Includes detailed, occasionally eccentric analyses of all the major works. Extract originally
published in G30. Extracts reprinted in G19,
J3, J6, K1, K6, K14, and K16.

G48   -----. JOYCE'S VOICES. Berkeley and Los Angeles: Univ.
of California Press, 1978.
Four clever, witty, interrelated lectures on
JJ's manipulations of traditional narrative objectivity in "Grace" (in D; cf. Swift, Dickens,
and Flaubert), on the "characterizing vocabulary" of JJ's supposedly detached narrative
voice (in PAYM and U, especially "Eumaeus"), on
JJ's "Pyrrhonism," which would deny such abso-
lutes as objectivity, and on his ultimate ex-
plosion of traditional conceptions of narrative
detachment in the multiple voices of U. Par-
tially assimilates N146.

G49   Knuth, A.M. Leo. THE WINK OF THE WORD: A STUDY OF JAMES
JOYCE'S PHATIC COMMUNICATION. Amsterdam: Rodopi, 1976.
Seeing JJ's verbal acrobatics and comedy (found
chiefly in his allusions, jokes, puns, and puzzles) as his "jocoserious" attempt to "get
through" to the ideal reader, rather than "'hon-
est communication,'" Knuth examines the special
"bond" JJ creates between himself and his readers, the "knowing wink" that results when the
message has been received. Less a critical
overview than a discussion and appreciation of
the serious "social activity" in the "game" of
reading JJ. Includes an excellent analysis of
the "Wandering Rocks" episode of U (originally
published in G7), and an extended explication
of Shem's riddle in FW.

G50   Kopper, Edward A., ed. JAMES JOYCE: NEW GLANCES. Butler,
Pa.: MODERN BRITISH LITERATURE, 1980.
Separate monograph publication of G63.

G51   Kronegger, Maria Elisabeth. JAMES JOYCE AND ASSOCIATED
IMAGE MAKERS. New Haven, Conn.: College and Univ. Press,
1968.
Intensive comparisons of JJ's "imagistic" tech-

niques with those of Edgar Allan Poe and "representative impressionist, post-impressionist,
and metaphysical painters" (however, only De-
Chirico is mentioned more than briefly), who
alike "dislocate and recombine elements of visual experience" to create "symbolic revelations
of transcendental reality." Involves more free
association between Poe's stories and JJ's D,
PAYM, and U, than plausible criticism, and provides little substantive evidence of JJ being
influenced by the contemporary visual arts.

G52 Levin, Harry. JAMES JOYCE: A CRITICAL INTRODUCTION. 1941.
2nd ed. New York: New Directions, 1960.
Superior general introduction to JJ's works and
to his place in the European literary tradition.
Levin briefly surveys the early work, D, EXILES,
and PAYM, tracing JJ's movement toward "a dialectical synthesis of the naturalistic tradition
and the symbolistic reaction." This synthesis
is achieved principally in U, where JJ holds in
tension naturalism and symbolism, the "map" of
Dublin and the "myth" of the Odyssey, life and
art, the citizen and the artist, the kinesis
and stasis of the "motion-picture." (Levin is
among the first to note JJ's cinematographic,
montage techniques.) FW, an almost purely symbolic narrative, counterbalances the early, naturalistic works. Levin's revised edition adds
a chapter reviewing JJ's growing critical reputation and modifying his earlier portrait of JJ
as too detached to portray human emotion profoundly. Extracts reprinted in G19, G25, J3,
K1, K6, K13, K14, and K16.

G53 Litz, A. Walton. JAMES JOYCE. 1966. Rev. ed. New York:
Twayne, 1972.
Excellent general introduction to JJ's works,
major and minor, touching on their biographical backgrounds and on critical problems in
their interpretation, but concentrating on providing sane, balanced critical overviews of
JJ's purposes and achievement (e.g., Litz's
chapter of U surveys the novel's action, characters, and techniques, analyzes one exemplary
motif [keys], and evaluates the usefulness of
the novel's Homeric parallels.) Unlike most

introductions, Litz's includes a discussion of
FW, a "supremely serious," "supremely rational"
novel. Later edition includes a revised annotated primary and secondary bibliography. Extract reprinted in Jl.

G54   MacCabe, Colin. JAMES JOYCE AND THE REVOLUTION OF THE
WORD. London: Macmillan, 1978.
Theoretical defense for an "original," practical approach to JJ's radical use of language
to revolutionize both the literary text and the
act of reading ("passive consumption" becomes
"active metamorphosis"). MacCabe surveys JJ's
development from the "banal" discourse in D and
"the end of the story" in PAYM, to the "radical
separation" of form and meaning in U. In FW he
sees the end of referential language for JJ as
his literary creation becomes a politically revolutionary act. MacCabe concludes with vague
chapters on FW as a political novel and on JJ's
politics. Neither an engaging nor a persuasive
study.

G55   Magalaner, Marvin, ed. A JAMES JOYCE MISCELLANY. New
York: James Joyce Society, 1957.
Miscellaneous collection of six memoirs and crit-
ical essays, with a brief "Foreword" by Padraic
Colum (pp. 9-10) and two slight letters concern-
ing JJ. Includes F31, F74, F88, F103, H106, and
H236.

G56   -----. A JAMES JOYCE MISCELLANY, SECOND SERIES. Carbondale: Southern Illinois Univ. Press, 1959.
Fifteen original papers on JJ, with newly discovered fragments of STEPHEN HERO (incorporated
into B21). Includes E17, F75, F117, F144, H76,
H98, H224, J130, M109, M190, M217, M239, N190,
and extracts from K30, M38, and M50.

G57   -----. A JAMES JOYCE MISCELLANY, THIRD SERIES. Carbon-
dale: Southern Illinois Univ. Press, 1962.
Transcriptions, with commentary, of JJ's story
fragment "Christmas Eve" (by John J. Slocum and
Herbert Cahoon) and his two broadsides: "The
Holy Office" and "Gas from a Burner" (by Robert
Scholes), plus eight original and three reprint-
ed essays on the individual works. Includes
F84, J15, K140, M50 (extract), M133, M378, M431,
N112, N126, N165, and N215.

G58 Magalaner, Marvin, and Richard M. Kain. JOYCE: THE MAN,
THE WORK, THE REPUTATION. New York: New York Univ. Press,
1956.
> Still quite useful survey of the status and
> problems of JJ's biography (see F101), with
> generous critical introductions to his works
> (pp. 47-255), and a summary of his critical
> reputation (see E20). Extracts reprinted in
> J1, K5, K13, and K14.

G59 Majault, Joseph. JAMES JOYCE. 1963. Trans. Jean Stewart.
London: Merlin, 1971.
> Half routine biography (pp. 1-41), half routine
> critical commentary on the major works (pp. 45-
> 81), suitable for an undergraduate introduction.
> See S29.

G60 Manganiello, Dominic. JOYCE'S POLITICS. London: Routledge, 1980.
> Argues the centrality of "political issues and
> discussions" in JJ's fiction and examines the
> evolution of JJ's political "attitudes," from
> his views of the Irish quest for home rule and
> national identity and his awareness of the Euro-
> pean political situation during his years of
> exile, to his responses to socialism, national-
> ism, anarchism, and fascism. Manganiello con-
> cludes by linking JJ's political views to his
> literary experimentation ("literary politics").

G61 Martin, Violet F. [Martin Ross]. MUSIC AND JAMES JOYCE.
Chicago: Argus Book Shop, 1936.
> JJ's musical training and musical qualities in
> his style, particularly in FW. (Pamphlet--10
> pp.)

G62 Misra, B.P. THE INDIAN INSPIRATION OF JAMES JOYCE. Agra,
India: Prasad, n.d. [c. 1963].
> Not seen.

G63 MODERN BRITISH LITERATURE. 5 (1980), 1-79. "Special
James Joyce Combined Volume."
> Publishes nine essays on JJ and his works, to-
> gether with a brief editorial "Introduction"
> (pp. 1-2), by Edward A. Kopper. Includes F140,
> K36, L17, M287, M314, M426, M443, N54, and P14.
> Also see G50.

G64 MODERN FICTION STUDIES. 4 (1958), 3-99. "James Joyce
     Special Number."

G65 MODERN FICTION STUDIES. 15 (1969), 3-182. "James Joyce
     Special Number."
          Two special issues, containing six and eight
          original articles respectively, plus biblio-
          graphical checklists (see E1). Includes H101,
          J45, J73, K65, K123, L4, M171, M271, M336,
          M374, N59, N63, and extracts from M38 and M61.

G66 Morse, J. Mitchell. THE SYMPATHETIC ALIEN: JAMES JOYCE
     AND CATHOLICISM. New York: New York Univ. Press, 1959.
          Examines the extent of JJ's immersion in the
          teachings of the Church fathers and medieval
          commentators, with too frequently forced illus-
          tration of their impact on his works (chiefly
          PAYM, U, and FW). Much interesting commentary
          on the backgrounds to JJ's thought (e.g., Eri-
          gen's heresy and JJ's theory of androgyny, var-
          ious reflections of Loyola, Aquinas, and Augus-
          tine). Extract reprinted in K6.

G67 Moseley, Virginia. JOYCE AND THE BIBLE. DeKalb: Northern
     Illinois Univ. Press, 1967.
          Enthusiastic, emphatic, and at times eccentric
          pursuit of JJ's allusions to the Bible and, by
          association, to Dante and to religious ritual,
          traced through STEPHEN HERO, the poetry, "The
          Dead," PAYM, EXILES, U (extensively), and FW
          (opening lines). Moseley overemphasizes the
          significance of the Bible and Biblical patterns
          (e.g., the Martha-Mary contrast is considered
          central in U) and frequently notes references
          for their own sake, yet she does track down a
          wealth of information that could be valuable
          to a better critic.

G68 Murillo, L.A. THE CYCLICAL NIGHT: IRONY IN JAMES JOYCE
     AND JORGE LUIS BORGES. Cambridge, Mass.: Harvard Univ.
     Press, 1968.
          Theoretical investigation of JJ's use of irony,
          not as a rhetorical device or a tone of voice,
          but as a structural principle in his development
          of the "art of the novel," through FW, "into the
          realm of myth." Defining irony in the most gen-
          eral terms as the writer's expression of "two

meanings simultaneously, one of them explicitly
stated, the other implied or concealed," which
he expands to include the multiple meanings in
simultaneous expression in JJ's later works,
Murillo demonstrates the increasing ironic complexity of JJ's fiction. While some comparisons are made, Murillo's discussion of Borges
in the second half of the book is separate.

G69 Noon, William T., S.J. JOYCE AND AQUINAS. New Haven,
Conn.: Yale Univ. Press, 1957.
Excellent analysis of the overt and implicit
Thomism of JJ, from the "applied Aquinas" of
the aesthetic in STEPHEN HERO and PAYM and the
idea of the "epiphany" in D, to the indirect
reflection of Thomistic conceptions of comedy,
the trinity, and creation in U and FW. Noon
summarizes JJ's probable familiarity with Aquinas, through his Jesuit schooling and personal
reading, and his scholastic cast of mind, yet
he also documents JJ's considerable distortion
and misconstruction of Aquinas. One of the
few indispensible books on JJ's intellectual
formation. Extracts reprinted in J1, J179,
and K14.

G70 O'Brien, Darcy. THE CONSCIENCE OF JAMES JOYCE. Princeton,
N.J.: Princeton Univ. Press, 1967.
Study of JJ's works, arguing that JJ was, like
Stephen in PAYM, "supersaturated" by the ethi-
cal bias against the flesh inculcated by the
Irish Catholicism in which he disbelieved. JJ's
art rejects the ideal of stasis, posited by
Stephen in PAYM, showing the warring contraries of human nature where the sordid, the flesh-
ly, and the real too often undermine the sublime, the spiritual, and the ideal. The ki-
netic art of D contradicts, as does PAYM, the
aesthetics of Stephen. Yet the very existence
of JJ's own conscience, particularly manifested
in his "intellectual aversion to sex," shows
that in U and FW he "himself harbored" Stephen's
ideal of "spiritual innocence." Polemical, controversial, and dangerously facile thesis.

G71 Peake, C.H. JAMES JOYCE: THE CITIZEN AND THE ARTIST.
Stanford, Calif.: Stanford Univ. Press, 1977.
Thirty-eight unpretentious, detailed critical

commentaries on JJ's fiction, work-by-work and
part-by-part, through U, with a brief treatment
of FW. Peake makes a number of worthwhile observations, particularly in his discussion of
the styles in U.

G72   Ryf, Robert S. A NEW APPROACH TO JOYCE: THE *PORTRAIT OF
THE ARTIST* AS A GUIDEBOOK. Berkeley and Los Angeles:
Univ. of California Press, 1962.
Introduction to CHAMBER MUSIC, D, FW, PAYM, STE-
PHEN HERO, and U. Applying the theory of the
"organic inter-relationship" of JJ's works, Ryf
has chosen PAYM as his central achievement, his
"best-written" work, and uses it as a "guidebook" for pedestrian analyses of the themes,
techniques, and "artistic method" upon which
"all his works are based." Systematic comparisons of PAYM with the major works are supple-
mented by essays on JJ's aesthetic theory,
irony, "visual imagination," and place in modern letters. Extract reprinted in K13.

G73   Senn, Fritz, ed. NEW LIGHT ON JOYCE FROM THE DUBLIN SYM-
POSIUM. Bloomington: Indiana Univ. Press, 1972.
Thirteen original papers from the 1969 Dublin
symposium: four general critical commentaries
and nine studies of individual works (U and FW
exclusively). Includes a brief "Preface" by
Senn (pp. vii-xi) and the following: F16, H25,
H88, H164, M61 (extract), M87, M114, M137, M209,
N120, N132, N185, and N227.

G74   Smidt, Kristian. JAMES JOYCE AND THE CULTIC USE OF FIC-
TION. 1955. Rev. ed. New York: Humanities Press, 1959.
Intensive study of the implications of JJ's
substitution of a religion of art for the or-
thodox Catholicism in which he was raised.
This "extremely individualistic" cult of art
required "his own doctrines" (the aesthetic
in PAYM and U), and "his own language and rit-
ual" (style and symbolism in U and FW). Even
JJ's persistent theme of exile is the surrogate
of the soul's "longing for his lost religious
home." Several penetrating insights, despite
the dubious fundamental assumption that Stephen
is JJ's "alter-ego."

G75   Staley, Thomas F., ed. JAMES JOYCE TODAY: ESSAYS ON THE
      MAJOR WORKS. Bloomington: Indiana Univ. Press, 1966.
         Seven original essays, many of them distin-
         guished, on JJ and his works (CHAMBER MUSIC,
         D, FW, PAYM, and U). A good view of the crit-
         ical and textual status of the major works.
         Includes H20, H107, J14, K110, M184, N118, and
         P16.

G76   Stewart, J.I.M. JAMES JOYCE. London: Longmans, 1957.
         Notes the "scrupulous meanness" of JJ's style
         in the early fiction and briefly comments on
         PAYM (an "apologia"), U (ends affirmatively),
         and FW ("undigestible"). (Pamphlet--37 pp.)
         Assimilated into Stewart's fuller survey; see
         H211. Extract reprinted in K16.

G77   Strong, Leonard A.G. THE SACRED RIVER: AN APPROACH TO
      JAMES JOYCE. London: Methuen, 1949.
         The first book-length study of JJ by a fellow
         Irishman (and professional novelist). Strong
         briefly summarizes JJ's early "external" works
         (D and PAYM), discusses the literary influences
         on JJ (Shakespeare, Swift, and Blake--with ap-
         pended notes on JJ's references to these writ-
         ers in FW), examines JJ's conception of the un-
         conscious in light of literary tradition (e.g.,
         Dostoevsky) and modern psychology, and describes
         his experiments with narrative technique and
         symbolism (with intriguing reference to modern
         science). Enthusiastic, yet perceptive and
         balanced. Extracts reprinted in G25.

G78   STUDIES IN THE LITERARY IMAGINATION. 3, No. 2 (1970),
      1-96. "James Joyce in the Seventies: The Expanding Di-
      mensions of His Art."
         Unsatisfactory collection of eight original es-
         says on JJ and his works. Includes a brief
         "Comment" by the issue editor, Ted. R. Spivey
         (pp. 1-2), and the following essays: H85, H104,
         H202, J26, K148, M99, M135, and N163.

G79   Tindall, William York. JAMES JOYCE: HIS WAY OF INTERPRE-
      TING THE MODERN WORLD. New York: Scribner's, 1950.
         Often excellent and still influential survey
         of JJ, finding him the heir to Dante for form,
         to Rimbaud and the symbolistes for symbolic

techniques and ironic detachment in presenta-
tion. Further, Tindall suggests that JJ's impact on modern art has been as profound as that
of his true contemporaries: Einstein in physics
and Freud in psychology. Despite some mislead-
ing simplifications (e.g., U is a novel of
Stephen's "adolescence"; he "goes away" at the
end "to write ULYSSES"), Tindall writes pro-
vocatively on JJ's treatment of the artist and
humanity, on his use of cyclic patterns, and
on his adaptations of myth and symbol.

G80   -----. A READER'S GUIDE TO JAMES JOYCE. New York: Noonday, 1959.
        Work-by-work and part-by-part commentaries on
        D, PAYM, STEPHEN HERO, EXILES, U, and FW, for
        the "general reader." Tindall's disproportion-
        ate stress upon symbols and image patterns, how-
        ever, makes JJ seem more suited for the initiate
        into the sacred mysteries than for the common
        man. Extracts reprinted in J1 and J179.

G81   TRANSITION. No. 21 (1932), pp. 245-82. "Homage to James
Joyce."
        Special issue celebrating JJ's fiftieth birth-
        day. Includes Cesar Abin's often-reproduced
        caricature of JJ, a number of brief notes and
        tributes, and a "translation" of the "Anna Liv-
        ia Plurabelle" section of FW into "basic Eng-
        lish." Also includes G29 (extract) and H221.
        Extracts reprinted in G25. Also see F100.

G82   Tysdahl, Bjørn J. JOYCE AND IBSEN: A STUDY IN LITERARY
INFLUENCE. New York: Humanities Press, 1968.
        An inevitable comparative study of JJ and Ibsen,
        one of the most important and "most enduring"
        literary influences on JJ's work. Fortunately
        Tysdahl is cautious of facile correspondences,
        perceptively assessing the impact of JJ's early
        enthusiasm for Ibsen on his conception of art
        (particularly his high valuation of drama) and
        on his "early realism." Tysdahl ranges far be-
        yond EXILES, JJ's most consciously Ibsenite
        work, to note the traces of influence in the
        themes, structures, and characters in D, PAYM,
        and U ("a Dublin PEER GYNT?"). His longest
        chapter, on FW, examines both Ibsen's various

influences and JJ's numerous references to the
Norwegian dramatist and his plays. Includes an
appendix of Norwegian words in one section of
FW (compiled with Clive Hart).

G83 Waldron, Philip. THE NOVELS OF JAMES JOYCE. Wellington,
N.Z.: Wai-te-ata Press, 1962.
JJ's emerging comic spirit in his works culmin-
ates in U and FW. (Pamphlet--16 pp.)

G84 Wilder, Thornton. JAMES JOYCE, 1882-1941. Aurora, N.Y.:
Wells College Press, 1944.
Obituary praising JJ's works, his "comic genius," and the "imcomparable musicality" of
his style. (Pamphlet--8 pp.) Extract reprinted in G25.

G85 Zyla, Wolodymyr T., ed. JAMES JOYCE: HIS PLACE IN WORLD
LITERATURE: PROCEEDINGS OF THE COMPARATIVE LITERATURE SYM-
POSIUM, II, FEBRUARY 7 AND 8, 1969. Lubbock: Interdepart-
mental Committee on Comparative Literature, Texas Technical
College, 1969.
Contains six original papers on JJ, his work,
his influence, and his critics, with the edi-
tor's brief "Preface" (pp. 1-5). Includes H117,
H162, J168, M246, M300, and N84.

H. GENERAL CRITICAL ARTICLES OR CHAPTERS ON JOYCE

Many "general" studies of JJ in reality concentrate on one or
two of the major-works of fiction. In most cases such items
have been placed, with cross-references, in the appropriate
section or sections following this (i.e., sections J, K, L, M,
and N, studies of D, PAYM, EXILES, U, and FW, respectively);
however, several articles which are truly "general" in their
significance have been placed in the section below though they
may draw their illustration from a narrow base in the works
(e.g., discussions of JJ's aesthetics, frequently derived from
PAYM, or studies concentrated on "phases" of JJ's career and
resulting interrelationships between his works [D and PAYM,
PAYM and U, U and FW]).

For foreign-language articles on JJ, see section T.

H1   Adams, Robert M. "The Bent Knife-Blade: Joyce in the 1960s."
     PR, 29 (1962), 507-18.
          Speculations on JJ's shifting reputation "as a
          result of changes in our cultural and intellec-
          tual weather." Also argues that JJ's mind "buck-
          led" after U and surrendered to accident. Re-
          printed in G19.

H2   Allen, Walter. THE MODERN NOVEL IN BRITAIN AND THE UNITED
     STATES. New York: Dutton, 1964. Pp. 2-14 and passim.
          JJ's works will "stand" (PAYM, U) or "fall" (FW)
          insofar as they are "rooted in the actual and
          the specific."

H3   Allott, Miriam. "James Joyce: The Hedgehog and the Fox."
     In ON THE NOVEL: A PRESENT FOR WALTER ALLEN ON HIS 60TH
     BIRTHDAY FROM HIS FRIENDS AND COLLEAGUES. Ed.B.S. Benedikz.
     London: Dent, 1971. Pp. 161-77.
          JJ's search for a synthesizing vision (cf. Dante--
          the "hedgehog") to order the "vast variety of ex-
          periences" (cf. Shakespeare--the "fox").

H4   Anderson, Chester G.   "James Joyce as Sunny Jim: A Tale
      of a Tub." JJQ, 13 (1976), 328–49.
            Freudian implications of JJ's coprophilia.   See
            G43.

H5   -----.   "On the Sublime and its Anal–Urethral Sources in
      Pope, Eliot, and Joyce."   In MODERN IRISH LITERATURE: ES-
      SAYS IN HONOR OF WILLIAM YORK TINDALL.   Ed. Raymond J.
      Porter and James D. Brophy.   New York: Iona College Press
      and Twayne, 1972.   Pp. 235–49.
            'Healthy'incorporation of anal–urethral func-
            tions into art.

H6   Anglès, Auguste, et al.   "Accueils français à Joyce entre
      les deux guerres."   In JOYCE & PARIS.   Ed. Jacques Aubert
      and Maria Jolas.   I, 37–58.   See G8.
            Round-table discussion of the French critical
            reception of JJ's works during the twenties
            and thirties.   [In French.]

H7   Aronson, Alex.   "The Musical Unconscious."   In MUSIC AND
      THE NOVEL: A STUDY IN TWENTIETH CENTURY FICTION.   Totowa,
      N.J.: Rowman and Littlefield, 1980.   Pp. 37–64.
            Musical imagery in D, GIACOMO JOYCE, and PAYM,
            and analogies between the composition of U and
            that of the "musical score."

H8   Baker, James R.   "James Joyce: Esthetic Freedom and Drama-
      tic Art."   WHR, 5 (1950–51), 29–40.
            JJ's aesthetic, derived from PAYM, STEPHEN HERO,
            and the early notebooks.   Reprinted in K14.

H9   Bates, Ronald.   "The Tradition of the Marketplace: Joyce's
      Nice Use of Diction."   ENGLISH STUDIES IN CANADA, 1 (1975),
      203–16.
            Discriminating discussion of JJ's use of indi-
            rect and oblique discourse.

H10   Beach, Joseph Warren.   "Post-Impressionism: Joyce."   In
      THE TWENTIETH–CENTURY NOVEL: STUDIES IN TECHNIQUE.   New
      York: Appleton, 1932.   Pp. 403–24.
            JJ's radical break with the traditions of well-
            made fiction (cf. post-impressionist art).

H11   Beebe, Maurice.   "Joyce and Aquinas: The Theory of Aesthe-
      tics."   PQ, 36 (1957), 20–35.
            JJ's secularization of Aquinas and distortion
            of the scholastic argument in his aesthetic

theories (chiefly re: STEPHEN HERO and PAYM).
Reprinted in J3 and K6.

H12   -----. "Joyce and the Meanings of Modernism." In LITTERS
FROM ALOFT. Ed. Ronald Bates and Harry J. Pollock. Pp.
15-25. See G9.
    Defines the chief characteristics of the Mod-
    ernist movement, as distinguished from Post-
    Modernism, and argues JJ's central position
    therein.

H13   Beja, Morris. "James Joyce: The Bread of Everyday Life."
In EPIPHANY IN THE MODERN NOVEL. Seattle: Univ. of Washington Press, 1971. Pp. 71-111.
    Stephen's definition of the "epiphany" in STE-
    PHEN HERO applied to JJ's fictional strategies.

H14   -----. "The Wooden Sword: Threatener and Threatened in
the Fiction of James Joyce." 1964. In JAMES JOYCE: *DUB-
LINERS* AND *A PORTRAIT*. Ed. Beja. Pp. 208-23. See J3.
    Basic affinities between victim and antagonist
    in JJ. Revised from original publication in
    JJQ, 2 (1964), 33-41.

H15   Beja, Morris, et al. "Political Perspectives on Joyce's
Work." In JOYCE & PARIS. Ed. Jacques Aubert and Maria
Jolas. II, 101-23. See G8.
    Panel discussion of political themes and ef-
    fects of JJ's writings.

H16   Bennett, Linda. "George Moore and James Joyce: Story-Tel-
ler versus Stylist." STUDIES, 66 (1977), 275-91.
    Comparisons between the two Irish authors, with
    comment on their views of each other ("controlled
    animosity") and of each other's work.

H17   Benstock, Bernard. "A Covey of Clerics in Joyce and O'Casey." JJQ, 2 (1964), 18-32.
    Compares JJ's generally unflattering and O'Ca-
    sey's more objective portraits of priests.

H18   -----. "Joyce's Swift: Synthetical but not Serene." DUB-
LIN MAGAZINE, 10, No. 2 (1973), 21-32.
    JJ's references to Swift culminate in the major
    pattern of allusion in FW. See G26.

H19   Bickerton, Derek. "James Joyce and the Development of Interior Monologue." EIC, 18 (1968), 32-46.
    Despite Dujardin's example, JJ's technique in

U independently evolved through D and PAYM.

H20 Blissett, William. "James Joyce in the Smithy of His Soul." In JAMES JOYCE TODAY. Ed. Thomas F. Staley. Pp. 96–134. See G75.
> Technical and thematic relationships between Wagner and JJ (e.g., Stephen=Seigfried).

H21 Block, Haskell M. "The Critical Theory of James Joyce." JAAC, 8 (1950), 172–84.
> JJ's search within scholastic thought for validation of his radically original art. Reprinted in K6.

H22 -----. "Theory of Language in Gustave Flaubert and Joyce." REVUE DE LITTÉRATURE COMPARÉE, 35 (1961), 197–206.
> JJ and Flaubert establish the novel as "equal or superior to other modes of literary expression."

H23 Bowen, Elizabeth. "James Joyce." THE BELL, 1 (Mar. 1941), 40–49.
> Non-adulatory, perceptive obituary critique.

H24 Boyle, Patrick. "Drums and Guns, and Guns and Drums. Hurrah! Hurrah!" In A BASH IN THE TUNNEL. Ed. John Ryan. Pp. 157–61. See F135.
> Insensitive commentary on JJ's weaknesses in language and style.

H25 Boyle, Robert, S.J. "Astroglodynamologos." In NEW LIGHT ON JOYCE. Ed. Fritz Senn. Pp. 131–40. See G73.
> JJ's view of the artist as priest, transubstantiating the "eucharistic and life-giving word."

H26 Bredin, Hugh. "Applied Aquinas: James Joyce's Aesthetics." EIRE, 3, No. 1 (1968), 61–78.
> JJ's metaphysics Thomistic, but not his "psychology."

H27 Brennan, Joseph Gerard. THREE PHILOSOPHICAL NOVELISTS: JAMES JOYCE, ANDRÉ GIDE, THOMAS MANN. New York: Macmillan, 1964. Pp. 3–55.
> General examination of JJ's assimilation and reflection of both various schools of philosophy and individual philosophers in his works.

H28 Byrd, Don. "Joyce's Method of Philosophic Fiction." JJQ, 5 (1967), 9–21.
> Seeks the fundamental, philosophic method of

JJ's fiction, as distinguished from the more
superficially philosophic subject matter found
in the novels.

H29 Campbell, Joseph. THE MASKS OF GOD: CREATIVE MYTHOLOGY.
New York: Viking, 1968. Passim.
Numerous comments on mythic archetypes and mo-
tifs in JJ.

H30 Carver, Craig. "James Joyce and the Theory of Magic."
JJQ, 15 (1978), 201-14.
JJ's interest in magic, particularly the oc-
cultist idea of the cosmic memory.

H31 Chattopadhyaya, Sisir [also Sisir Chatterjee]. "James
Joyce and the Epiphany of Experience." In THE TECHNIQUE
OF THE MODERN ENGLISH NOVEL. Calcutta: Mukhopadhyay, 1959.
Pp. 110-67.
JJ's epiphany technique and experiments with
language and style. Survey.

H32 Chayes, Irene Hendry. "Joyce's Epiphanies." SR, 54 (1946),
449-67.
Frequently-reprinted, balanced survey of JJ's
epiphanic technique. Reprinted in G30, K1, K6,
K14, and K16.

H33 Church, Margaret. "James Joyce: Time and Time Again." In
TIME AND REALITY: STUDIES IN CONTEMPORARY FICTION. Chapel
Hill: Univ. of North Carolina Press, 1963. Pp. 27-66.
Linear, cyclical, durational, and racial time
in JJ's works.

H34 -----. "Joyce and Vico Panel." JJQ, 9 (1972), 311-17.
Summarizes discussion of JJ's debts to Vico,
among Church, Attila Faj, Ellsworth Mason, .
Giorgio Tagliacozzo, and Patrick White, from
the 1971 International JJ Symposium. See
F70 and G7.

H35 Collins, Arthur S. ENGLISH LITERATURE OF THE TWENTIETH
CENTURY. 1951. 4th ed. London: University Tutorial
Press, 1961. Pp. 211-17.
General overview of JJ's career (cf. Woolf).

H36 Colum, Mary. "The Revolt." In FROM THESE ROOTS: THE
IDEAS THAT HAVE MADE MODERN LITERATURE. New York: Scrib-
ner's, 1937. Pp. 312-60 passim.
JJ's revolutionary experiments with language

and time, within the larger context of the literary and intellectual revolts of the modern
era. Extract reprinted in G25.

H37 Connolly, Cyril. "James Joyce." In PREVIOUS CONVICTIONS:
SELECTED WRITINGS OF A DECADE. New York: Harper, 1963.
Pp. 269-81.
Obituary tribute to JJ as "literary anti-Pope"
(1941), with later comments on the pathos of
JJ's life (late 1950s--review essays). Extracts
of obituary reprinted in G25.

H38 Connolly, Thomas E. "Joyce's Aesthetic Theory." UKCR, 23
(1956), 47-50.
Summary, drawn from STEPHEN HERO, PAYM, and Gorman's biography (F55). Reprinted in K6.

H39 Cope, Jackson I. "James Joyce: Test Case for a Theory of
Style." ELH, 21 (1954), 221-36.
Theoretical attempt to define the static-dynamic
qualities of JJ's style.

H40 Costello, Peter. THE HEART GROWN BRUTAL: THE IRISH REVOLU-
TION IN LITERATURE, FROM PARNELL TO THE DEATH OF YEATS,
1891-1939. London: Gill and Macmillan, 1977. Pp. 51-58
and passim.
Comparisons (isolation and exile) and contrasts
(rural vs. urban) between George Moore and JJ.

H41 Coveny, Peter. THE IMAGE OF CHILDHOOD: THE INDIVIDUAL
AND SOCIETY: A STUDY OF THE THEME IN ENGLISH LITERATURE.
1957. Rev. ed. Baltimore: Penguin, 1967. Pp. 306-12.
JJ's excellent approximation of the consciousness of the young child in his fiction.

H42 Dahl, Liisa. LINGUISTIC FEATURES OF THE STREAM-OF-CON-
SCIOUSNESS TECHNIQUES OF JAMES JOYCE, VIRGINIA WOOLF AND
EUGENE O'NEILL. Turku, Finland: Turun Yliopisto, 1970.
Pp. 16-17, 21-41.
Describes JJ's varied uses of vocabulary and
syntax in his fiction.

H43 Dahlberg, Edward, and Herbert Read. TRUTH IS MORE SACRED:
A CRITICAL EXCHANGE ON MODERN LITERATURE. New York: Hori-
zon Press, 1961. Pp. 11-65.
Debate. Dahlberg: JJ "an epicure of the toilet."
Read: "I end by joining you in condemning Joyce."

H44 Daiches, David. "James Joyce: The Artist as Exile." CE,
     2 (1940), 197-206.
         JJ's realization that only in exile could he
         "look objectively on the world of men and re-
         cord their doings with the disinterested crafts-
         manship of the artist."

H45 -----. THE NOVEL AND THE MODERN WORLD. 1939. Rev. ed.
     Chicago: Univ. of Chicago Press, 1960. Pp. 63-137.
         JJ's progressive "renunciation of any share in
         the world he portrays," already emerging through
         the stories in D, the source of the "ideal com-
         edy" of U and FW. Extract reprinted in J6.

H46 Deakin, William. "D.H. Lawrence's Attacks on Proust and
     Joyce." EIC, 7 (1957), 383-403.
         Lawrence's "untenable" indictment of JJ and
         Proust for their self-conscious artistry.

H47 DiGaetani, John Louis. "Comic Uses of Myth: Richard Wag-
     ner and James Joyce." In RICHARD WAGNER AND THE MODERN
     BRITISH NOVEL. Rutherford, N.J.: Fairleigh Dickinson Univ.
     Press, 1978. Pp. 130-57.
         Wagnerian patterns, allusions, and techniques
         (e.g., leitmotif) in JJ's fiction.

H48 Durant, Will, and Ariel Durant. "James Joyce." In INTER-
     PRETATIONS OF LIFE: A SURVEY OF CONTEMPORARY LITERATURE.
     New York: Simon and Schuster, 1970. Pp. 77-89.
         Popular and appreciative brief introduction,
         concentrating on the later fiction.

H49 Eagleton, Mary, and David Pierce. "James Joyce." In AT-
     TITUDES TO CLASS IN THE ENGLISH NOVEL, FROM WALTER SCOTT
     TO DAVID STOREY. London: Thames and Hudson, 1979. Pp.
     108-18.
         JJ's extrication of himself from the social at-
         titudes of the Irish Catholic middle-class.

H50 Eliot, T.S. AFTER STRANGE GODS. London: Faber, 1933. Pp.
     35-38 and passim.
         JJ the "most ethically [and literarily] ortho-
         dox of the more eminent writers" of modern times
         (cf. Lawrence, the "heretic").

H51 -----. "A Message to the Fish." HORIZON, 3 (1941), 173-7:
         Vigorous praise of JJ and his work, in response
         to the London TIMES' lukewarm obituary. Reprint-
         ed in G25 and G30.

H52 Empson, William. "Joyce's Intentions." TWENTIETH CEN-
TURY STUDIES, No. 4 (1970), pp. 26-36.
Survey of career, emphasizing JJ's Luciferian
stance.

H53 Engstrom, Alfred G. "A Few Comparisons and Contrasts in
the Word-Craft of Rabelais and James Joyce." In RENAIS-
SANCE AND OTHER STUDIES IN HONOR OF WILLIAM LEON WILEY.
Ed. George B. Daniel. Chapel Hill: Univ. of North Carolina Press, 1968. Pp. 65-82.
Useful paralleling of the attitudes "shown
toward language" by JJ and Rabelais, two "comic geniuses."

H54 Enroth, C.A. "Introduction." In JOYCE AND LAWRENCE. New
York: Holt, 1969. Pp. 1-6.
The Apollonian JJ contrasted to the Dionysian
Lawrence. Introduces a school-text anthology
of their shorter works.

H55 Evans, B. Ifor. "James Joyce." In ENGLISH LITERATURE
BETWEEN THE WARS. London: Methuen, 1948. Pp. 40-48.
Strange and "bewildering" genius of JJ's works.

H56 Fanger, Donald. "Joyce and Meredith: A Question of Influence and Tradition." MFS, 6 (1960), 125-30.
Several general similarities between the authors.

H57 Farrell, James T. A NOTE ON LITERARY CRITICISM. New York:
Vanguard, 1936. Pp. 83-85, 97-106.
Responses to the simplifications and attacks of
Marxist critics of JJ (e.g., Mirsky, see H150).
Extract reprinted in G25.

H58 Faulkner, Peter. HUMANISM IN THE ENGLISH NOVEL. London:
Elek, 1976. Pp. 134-45.
JJ, despite his rejection of such labels, es-
sentially a humanist "in his defense of the
ordinary man as a private individual" (D through
U).

H59 Fleming, Rudd. "*Quidditas* in the Tragi-Comedy of Joyce."
UKCR, 15 (1949), 288-96.
Exposition of the aesthetic discussion in PAYM,
identifying Stephen's views with JJ's. Reprinted
in K14.

H60   Ford, Ford Madox. "A Haughty and Proud Generation." YR,
      11 (1922), 703-17.
          JJ seen as the most accomplished among the new
          generation of writers. Extract reprinted in G25.

H61   Forster, Leonard W. "James Joyce, Dadism, Surrealism, and
      After." In THE POET'S TONGUES: MULTILINGUALISM IN LITERA-
      TURE. London: Cambridge Univ. Press in association with the
      Univ. of Otago Press, 1970. Pp. 74-96.
          JJ's relation to modernist literary movements,
          especially in his linguistic experimentation.

H62   Freund, Philip. THE ART OF READING THE NOVEL. 1947. Rev.
      ed. New York: Macmillan, 1965. Pp. 181-91 and passim.
          JJ and Woolf as popularizers and most accom-
          plished practitioners of the stream-of-con-
          sciousness technique.

H63   Friedman, Melvin J. "Anthony Burgess and James Joyce: A
      Literary Confrontation." LCrit, 9, No. 4 (1971), 71-83.
          A solid, favorable study of Burgess's criticism
          of JJ (see G17 and N77) and of JJ's influence
          on Burgess's fiction.

H64   -----. "James Joyce: The Full Development of the Method."
      In STREAM OF CONSCIOUSNESS: A STUDY IN LITERARY METHOD.
      New Haven, Conn.: Yale Univ. Press, 1955. Pp. 210-43.
          JJ both brings stream of consciousness to full
          maturity as a literary technique and demonstrates
          its self-destructive possibilities (in FW). Ex-
          tracts reprinted in K5 and K14.

H65   Frierson, William C. THE ENGLISH NOVEL IN TRANSITION,
      1885-1940. Norman: Univ. of Oklahoma Press, 1942. Pp.
      200-03, 234-36.
          JJ's fiction surveyed, with emphasis on PAYM
          (a painful "life-novel") and U ("willfully
          dadaistic").

H66   Fritz, Helen M. "Joyce and Existentialism." JAMES JOYCE
      REVIEW, 2, Nos. 1-2 (1958), 13-21.
          Existentialist overtones in JJ's work.

H67   Füger, Wilhelm. "Joyce's Use of the MAYNOOTH CATECHISM."
      JJQ, 13 (1976), 407-14.
          Finds several passages in JJ's works reminiscent
          of the MAYNOOTH CATECHISM. Also see H204.

H68 Furst, Lilian R. "Thomas Mann's Interest in James Joyce."
     MLR, 64 (1970), 605-13.
          Cites Mann's comments on and interest in JJ
          (provoked by Levin's comparison of the two,
          see G52), although Mann "never read any of
          Joyce's works."

H69 Garcia-Ponce, Juan. "Musil and Joyce." Trans. Boyd and
     Eileen Carter. JJQ, 5 (1968), 75-85.
          Compares the parallel, yet divergent careers
          and works of JJ and the Austrian novelist,
          Robert Musil. See T21.

H70 Garrett, Peter K. "James Joyce: The Artifice of Reality."
     In SCENE AND SYMBOL FROM GEORGE ELIOT TO JAMES JOYCE:
     STUDIES IN CHANGING FICTIONAL MODE. New Haven, Conn.:
     Yale Univ. Press, 1969. Pp. 214-71.
          The relationship between realism and symbolism
          (reality and art), a dominant characteristic of
          and theme in JJ's fiction. JJ's career a para-
          digm for the modern movement from realistic
          (e.g., D) to symbolic modes (e.g., FW).

H71 Garvin, John [Andrew Cass]. "Childe Horrid's Pilgrimace."
     ENVOY, 5 (May 1951), 19-30.
          Autobiographical implications of the works,
          with cautions against too facile and injudi-
          cious use of the biography. See F36. Reprint-
          ed in F111 and F135.

H72 Gide, André. "Desperate Words Call for Desperate Little
     Remedies." 1942. Trans. Georges Markow-Totevy. In Louis
     Gillet's CLAYBOOK FOR JAMES JOYCE. Pp. 123-27. See G29.
          Dialogue with himself, debating the pros and
          cons of JJ's work. See T23.

H73 Gilbert, Stuart. "James Joyce." In WRITERS OF TODAY.
     Ed. Denys Val Baker. London: Sidgwick and Jackson, 1946.
     Pp. 43-57.
          JJ's command of language, attitude of detach-
          ment, and "gift of imposing order" in his art.
          Reprinted in G30.

H74 -----. "The Latin Background of James Joyce's Art." HORI-
     ZON, 10 (1944), 178-89.
          Influence of the Greek and Roman classics on
          JJ's work.

H75 Gillie, Christopher. "James Joyce." In MOVEMENTS IN ENG-
LISH LITERATURE, 1900-1940. Cambridge: Cambridge Univ.
Press, 1975. Pp. 92-101.
Motifs of estrangement and "recovery into strong
affirmation" in the works.

H76 Glasheen, Adaline. "Joyce and the Three Ages of Charles
Stewart Parnell." In A JAMES JOYCE MISCELLANY, SECOND
SERIES. Ed. Marvin Magalaner. Pp. 151-78. See G56.
Parnell symbolically developed in JJ's work
through the cycle of god ("Ivy day in the Com-
mittee Room"), hero (PAYM), and human (U).

H77 Glicksburg, Charles I. "Eros and Agape in James Joyce."
In THE SEXUAL REVOLUTION IN MODERN ENGLISH LITERATURE. The
Hague: Martinus Nijhoff, 1973. Pp. 73-87.
JJ's anti-romantic, anti-metaphysical desancti-
fication of human love.

H78 Goldman, Arnold. "James Joyce." In THE TWENTIETH CENTURY.
Ed. Bernard Bergonzi. London: Barrie and Jenkins, 1970.
Pp. 75-105.
JJ, the unique culmination of the European lit-
erary tradition. Competent historical and crit-
ical survey.

H79 Goodheart, Eugene. "Joyce and the Career of the Artist-
Hero." In THE CULT OF THE EGO: THE SELF IN MODERN LITER-
ATURE. Chicago: Univ. of Chicago Press, 1968. Pp. 183-
200.
Traces the artist-ego's attempt to escape the
paralyzing community (D and PAYM), his inevi-
table failure (U), and his consequent escape
into art (FW).

H80 Gould, Gerald. "Mr. Lawrence and Mr. Joyce." In THE ENG-
LISH NOVEL OF TODAY. London: Castle, 1924. Pp. 19-27.
JJ's "bitter" realism and "sinister" descent
into the unconscious (cf. Lawrence).

H81 Gregor, Ian, and Mark Kinkead-Weekes. "Lawrence and Joyce:
A Critical Comparison." In THE ENGLISH NOVEL. Ed. Cedric
Watts. London: Sussex Books, 1976. Pp. 135-52.
Illuminating comparisons and contrasts by two
distinguished critics, presented in dialogue
form.

H82 Grossvogel, David I. "Joyce and Robbe-Grillet." In LIMITS
OF THE NOVEL: EVOLUTIONS OF A FORM FROM CHAUCER TO ROBBE-
GRILLET. Ithaca, N.Y.: Cornell Univ. Press, 1968. Pp.
256-99.
    JJ's role in the evolution of the objective,
    detached novel (e.g., the nouveau roman).

H83 Halper, Nathan. "Marshall McLuhan and Joyce." In MCLUHAN:
PRO & CON. Ed. Raymond Rosenthal. New York: Funk and Wag-
nalls, 1968. Pp. 58-81.
    Severe attack on the carelessness, distortions,
    and fabrications of McLuhan's criticism of JJ
    (see H139, H140, and H141).

H84 Hart, Clive. "James Joyce's Sentimentality." PQ, 46
(1967), 516-26.
    Deflates the myth of JJ's myriad-minded genius,
    noting his tendency toward sentimentality and
    his strategies (chiefly irony) to mask it.

H85 Hartley, Lodwick. "'Swiftly-Sterneward': The Question of
Sterne's Influence on Joyce." SLitI, 3, No. 2 (1970),
37-47.
    Unlike the case with Swift, the connections be-
    tween Sterne and JJ merely "superficial." See
    G78.

H86 Hendry, J.F. "The Element of Myth in James Joyce." SCOT-
TISH ARTS AND LETTERS, No. 1 (1945), pp. 16-20.
    JJ's works, especially U and FW, lyrical myths
    of our time. Reprinted in G30.

H87 Heppenstall, Rayner. "Streams of Consciousness." In THE
FOURFOLD TRADITION: NOTES ON THE FRENCH AND ENGLISH LITER-
ATURES. New York: New Directions, 1961. Pp. 132-59.
    Comparisons and contrasts between JJ and Law-
    rence (their backgrounds and views of art), and
    between JJ and Dujardin (JJ's "symbiosis" with
    the continental literary traditions and tech-
    niques).

H88 Herring, Phillip F. "Joyce's Politics." In NEW LIGHT ON
JOYCE. Ed. Fritz Senn. Pp. 3-14. See G73.
    JJ as partisan and politically nearsighted as
    the "citizen" (in U).

H89 Highet, Gilbert. THE CLASSICAL TRADITION: GREEK AND ROMAN

INFLUENCES ON WESTERN LITERATURE. New York: Oxford Univ. Press, 1949. Pp. 501-19.
On the persistence of classical themes in the symbolist movement, with JJ and Eliot as prime examples.

H90 Hoare, Dorothy M. "Moore and Joyce: A Contrast." In SOME STUDIES IN THE MODERN NOVEL. London: Chatto and Windus, 1938. Pp. 133-47.
Moore's flippancy and shallowness appear acute in contrast with the "serious moralist" JJ.

H91 Hoffman, Frederick J. "'The Book of Himself': Joyce and Lawrence." In THE MORTAL NO: DEATH AND THE MODERN IMAGIN-ATION. Princeton, N.J.: Princeton Univ. Press, 1964. Pp. 393-423.
Death and rebirth secular metaphors for self-realization in both authors as they adapt Christian myth and traditional views of mortality to their personal ideologies. (JJ: pp. 393-408).

H92 -----. "The Hardness of Reality: Joyce's Stephen Dedalus." In THE IMAGINATION'S NEW BEGINNING: THEOLOGY AND MODERN LITERATURE. Notre Dame, Ind.: Univ. of Notre Dame Press, 1967. Pp. 21-47.
JJ's progressive abandonment of Stephen Dedalus through his works seen as his rejection of Stephen's "elaborate formulas of explanation," his naive attempts to control rather than to understand reality.

H93 -----. "Infroyce." In FREUDIANISM AND THE LITERARY MIND. 1945. 2nd ed. Baton Rouge: Louisiana State Univ. Press, 1957. Pp. 116-50.
JJ's exposure to psychoanalytic theory, between PAYM and U, judicially related to his development as a novelist. Reprinted in G30.

H94 Honig, Edwin. DARK CONCEIT: THE MAKING OF ALLEGORY. Evanston, Ill.: Northwestern Univ. Press, 1959. Pp. 174-76 and passim.
Epic and allegory in Spenser and JJ.

H95 Hope, A.D. "The Esthetic Theory of James Joyce." AUSTRA-LASIAN JOURNAL OF PSYCHOLOGY AND PHILOSOPHY, 21 (1943), 93-114.
Explicates theory (via notebooks and PAYM), as systematically derived from the scholastic philosophy of Aquinas. Reprinted in K6.

H96   Houdebine, Jean-Louis, and Philippe Sollers. "La Trinité
      de Joyce." TEL QUEL, 83 (1980), 36-88.
            Extended interview-discussion of JJ's Cathol-
            icism and Catholic imagination. [In French.]
            See S46.

H97   Howarth, Herbert. "James Augustine Joyce, 1882-1941."
      In THE IRISH WRITERS, 1880-1940: LITERATURE UNDER PAR-
      NELL'S STAR. London: Rockliff, 1958. Pp. 243-87.
            Discusses the political backgrounds to JJ's
            works (e.g., his continued Irish concerns and
            his messiah-Parnell theme).

H98   -----. "The Joycean Comedy: Wilde, Jonson, and Others."
      In A JAMES JOYCE MISCELLANY, SECOND SERIES. Ed. Marvin
      Magalaner. Pp. 179-94. See G56.
            JJ's movement from Jonson's comedy of judgment,
            or satire, to Wilde's serio-comic mixture of
            the ridiculous and beautiful.

H99   Isaak, Jo-Anna. "James Joyce and the Cubist Esthetic."
      MOSAIC, 14, No. 1 (1981), 61-90.
            Major characteristics of Cubist and Futurist
            reactions against representational art corre-
            spond closely to JJ's literary techniques.
            (Illustrations).

H100 Iser, Wolfgang. THE ACT OF READING: A THEORY OF AESTHETIC
      RESPONSE. Baltimore: Johns Hopkins Univ. Press, 1978. Pp.
      207-11 and passim.
            Turgid theoretical discussion of the relation-
            ships among narrator, character, and reader in
            JJ's works.

H101 Jenkins, William D. "It Seems There Were Two Irishmen..."
      MFS, 15 (1969), 63-71.
            Correspondences between Arthur Conan Doyle and
            JJ. See G65.

H102 Johnston, Denis. "A Short View of the Progress of Joyce-
      anity." ENVOY, 5 (May 1951), 13-18.
            Chides American academics for taking JJ so
            seriously. See F36. Reprinted in F111, F135,
            and G18 (extract).

H103 Jordan, John. "Joyce Without Fears: A Personal Journey."
      In A BASH IN THE TUNNEL. Ed. John Ryan. Pp. 135-46. See
      F135.
            Ease of reading and general accessibility

of JJ's works, to a native Dubliner.

H104   Kain, Richard M. "James Joyce and the Game of Language."
SLitI, 3, No. 2 (1970), 19-25.
   Light introduction to JJ's games with words
   (puns, acrostics, palindromes). See G78.

H105   -----. "Problems of Interpreting Joycean Symbolism."
JGE, 17 (1965), 227-35.
   Warns against the perils of the "delightful
   game" of symbol-hunting in JJ.

H106   Kaye, Julian B. "Simony, the Three Simons, and Joycean
Myth." In A JAMES JOYCE MISCELLANY. Ed. Marvin Magala-
ner. Pp. 20-36. See G55.
   Simony theme and symbolism in D, PAYM, and U.

H107   Kelly, Robert G. "Introduction: Joyce Hero." In JAMES
JOYCE TODAY. Ed. Thomas F. Staley. Pp. 3-10. See G75.
   JJ's "perfectionism" renders the "least aspect
   of his work critically significant."

H108   Kenner, Hugh. "The Counterfeiters." VQR, 42 (1966), 72-
88.
   Modern artists (JJ, Pound, Warhol) as forgers,
   not "poet-legislators."

H109   -----. "Joyce and the 19th Century Linguistics Explo-
sion." In ATTI DEL THIRD INTERNATIONAL JAMES JOYCE SYM-
POSIUM. Pp. 45-52. See G7.
   JJ's assimilation and reflection of new research in linguistics.

H110   -----. THE POUND ERA. Berkeley and Los Angeles: Univ.
of California Press, 1971. Pp. 34-39, 44-50, 271-74;
and passim.
   Comments on JJ's works, in the general context
   of the major modern movements in the arts. Assimilates M193.

H111   Kermode, Frank. "Puzzles and Epiphanies." In PUZZLES
AND EPIPHANIES: ESSAYS AND REVIEWS, 1958-1961. New York:
Chilmark, 1962. Pp. 86-90.
   JJ's work matures while he himself failed to,
   progressively losing what hold on reality he
   had.

H112 Kestner, Joseph A. THE SPATIALITY OF THE NOVEL. Detroit:
Wayne State Univ. Press, 1978. Pp. 139-46 and passim.
Transformation of JJ's narrative from the temp-
oral mode (STEPHEN HERO) to the spatial mode
(PAYM), the prelude to the interplay of space
and time in U.

H113 Kettle, Arnold. "The Consistency of James Joyce." In
THE MODERN AGE. Ed. Boris Ford. 1961. 3rd ed. Baltimore: Penguin, 1973. Pp. 301-14.
Argues a developmental, organic "coherence"
and "completeness" in JJ's life and work.

H114 Kiely, Benedict. "The Artist on the Giant's Grave." In
A BASH IN THE TUNNEL. Ed. John Ryan. Pp. 235-41. See
F135.
JJ, though too long unacknowledged in Ireland,
the one Irish writer who "could shake the world."

H115 -----. MODERN IRISH FICTION: A CRITIQUE. Dublin: Golden
Eagle Books, 1950. Pp. 6-9, 44-47, 102-07, 132-36, and
passim.
JJ's reflection of quintessentially Irish pos-
tures (revolt, exile) and themes (the city,
fantasy, belief) in his works.

H116 Kiely, Robert. BEYOND EGOTISM: THE FICTION OF JAMES
JOYCE, VIRGINIA WOOLF, AND D.H. LAWRENCE. Cambridge,
Mass.: Harvard Univ. Press, 1980. Pp. 18-23, 26-29,
51-61, 87-103, 136-49, 191-208, and passim.
Distinguished study of the three novelists who,
despite numerous particular differences, both
share similar backgrounds and basic assumptions
and reflect comparable thematic and technical
concerns.

H117 Kimpel, Ben D. "James Joyce in Contemporary World Literature." In JAMES JOYCE: HIS PLACE IN WORLD LITERATURE.
Ed. Wolodymyr T. Zyla. Pp. 93-101. See G85.
JJ's typical modernity (e.g., use of myth, rebellion against convention).

H118 Klawitter, Robert. "Henri Bergson and James Joyce's Fictional World." CLS, 3 (1966), 429-37.
JJ's debts to Bergson (use of time) and ultimate parody of his world view (in FW).

H119 Knight, G. Wilson. "Lawrence, Joyce, and Powys." EIC,
      11 (1961), 403-17.
          Sadism and anal eroticism in the works of the
          three novelists.

H120 Korg, Jacob. "Joyce." In LANGUAGE IN MODERN LITERATURE:
      INNOVATION AND EXPERIMENT. New York: Barnes and Noble,
      1979. Pp. 95-111.
          JJ's various experiments with "verbal imita-
          tions of mental processes," from PAYM through
          FW. Also see N150.

H121 Kumar, Shiv K. "James Joyce." In BERGSON AND THE STREAM
      OF CONSCIOUSNESS NOVEL. New York: New York Univ. Press,
      1963. Pp. 103-38.
          "Interesting and illuminating parallels be-
          tween Bergsonism and some significant aspects
          of Joyce's technique and attitude." Extract
          reprinted in K14.

H122 Lawrence, D.H. "Surgery for the Novel--Or a Bomb." In
      PHOENIX. Ed. Edward D. McDonald. New York: Viking, 1936.
      Pp. 517-20.
          Joyce, with Dorothy Richardson and Proust, ex-
          coriated for his "senile-precocious" preoccupa-
          tion with self-consciousness.

H123 Levin, Harry. "Editor's Introduction." In THE PORTABLE
      JAMES JOYCE. Ed. Levin. Pp. 1-16. See B18.
          Surveys the "irreducible substances out of
          which" JJ created his art: "nationality, re-
          ligion, and language."

H124 -----. "Joyce's Sentimental Journey through France and
      Italy." In CONTEXTS OF CRITICISM. Cambridge, Mass.:
      Harvard Univ. Press, 1957. Pp. 131-39.
          JJ's debt to French and Italian literature,
          particularly Flaubert and Dante.

H125 Levitt, Morton P. "Shalt be Accurst? The Martyr in James
      Joyce." JJQ, 5 (1968), 285-96.
          Traces the "progressively more important" theme
          of the "tortured artist" in JJ's works.

H126 Lewis, Wyndham. "An Analysis of the Mind of James Joyce.'
      In TIME AND WESTERN MAN. London: Chatto and Windus, 1927.
      Pp. 91-130.
          JJ's extremely conventional mind. JJ a "crafts-

man rather than a creator," despite the tech-
nical triumph of the "Bergson-Einstein, Stein-
Proust" school of "time-philosophy" in his U.
Extract reprinted in G25. Also see F155 and
G47.

H127   Lindsay, Jack. "James Joyce." In SCRUTINIES. Comp.
Edgell Rickword. London: Wishart, 1931. II, 100-22.
JJ's "profound creative potentialities" limited
and diluted by his self-consciousness.

H128   Litz, A. Walton. "Vico and Joyce." In GIAMBATTISTA VICO:
AN INTERNATIONAL SYMPOSIUM. Ed. Giorgio Tagliacozzo and
Hayden V. White. Baltimore: Johns Hopkins Univ. Press,
1969. Pp. 245-55.
JJ demonstrates the "special vitality and rel-
evance" of Vico's ideas for the modern artist.

H129   Lodge, David. "James Joyce." In THE MODES OF MODERN
WRITING: METAPHOR, METONYMY, AND THE TYPOLOGY OF MODERN
LITERATURE. London: Arnold, 1977. Pp. 125-44.
JJ's works mirror his artistic development
from "realism to mythopoeia," from "metonymy
to metaphor."

H130   Loss, Archie K. "Interior and Exterior Imagery in the
Earlier Work of Joyce and in Symbolist Art." JML, 8
(1980), 99-117.
Imagery of "chamber and forest, of interior
and exterior worlds" in symbolist artists
(eighteen illustrations) and in JJ (through
PAYM).

H131   -----. "The Pre-Raphaelite Woman, the Symbolist *Femme-
Enfant,* and the Girl with Long Flowing Hair in the Earlier Work of Joyce." JML, 3 (1973), 3-23.
Parallels between JJ's visual images and the
art of the 1890s. Earlier version published
in G7.

H132   -----. "Presences and Visions in EXILES, A PORTRAIT OF
THE ARTIST, and ULYSSES." JJQ, 13 (1976), 148-62.
JJ's use of characteristic sensory techniques
of the French Symboliste writers.

H133   Lovett, Robert M. "Post-Realistic Novel." In PREFACE
TO FICTION: A DISCUSSION OF GREAT MODERN NOVELS. Chicago:

Rockwell, 1931. Pp. 113-27.
JJ, Proust, and others, as major modern experi-
mentalists.

H134　Lovett, Robert M., and Helen S. Hughes. "James Joyce
(1882-)." In THE HISTORY OF THE NOVEL IN ENGLAND. Boston: Houghton Mifflin, 1932. Pp. 455-62.
Surveys JJ's "somewhat bewildering experimentations."

H135　Lynd, Robert. "James Joyce and a New Kind of Fiction."
1935. In BOOKS AND WRITERS. London: Dent, 1952. Pp.
147-56.
JJ a bewildering "born experimenter of genius."

H136　Lyons, F.S.L. "The Parnell Theme in Literature." In
PLACE, PERSONALITY AND THE IRISH WRITER. Ed. Andrew
Carpenter. New York: Barnes and Noble, 1977. Pp. 69-
95.
Parnell as a Mosaic figure, in JJ and other
Irish writers.

H137　MacCarthy, Desmond. "James Joyce." 1941. In MEMORIES.
New York: Oxford Univ. Press, 1953. Pp. 113-20.
Obituary praise of JJ's "extraordinary virtuosity and originality"; yet his influence is
"chiefly confined to writers or potential
writers."

H138　MacGregor, Geddes. "Artistic Theory in James Joyce."
LIFE AND LETTERS, 54 (July 1947), 18-27.
JJ no aesthetician, but consistently follows
in his fiction the main tenets of the theory
presented in PAYM, especially the "idea of
artistic arrest," or stasis. Reprinted in K6.

H139　McLuhan, H. Marshall. "James Joyce: Trivial and Quad-
rivial." THOUGHT, 28 (1953), 75-98.
Excellent analysis of JJ's symbolism, relating
his techniques to the exegetical methods of
the Scholastics (chiefly St. Augustine). See
G47 and H83.

H140　-----. "Joyce, Aquinas, and the Poetic Process." RENA-
SCENCE, 4 (1951), 3-11.
JJ makes explicit in his theory and practice
Aquinas's relationship of the stages of appre-

hension ("negotiating the labyrinth") and the
creative process. Reprinted in K6. Also see
H83.

H141   -----. "Joyce, Mallarmé, and the Press." SR, 62 (1954),
38-55.
       "Spatial manipulation of mental states" in JJ,
       Mallarmé, and the press. See H83.

H142   Macy, John A. "James Joyce." In THE CRITICAL GAME. New
York: Boni and Liveright, 1922. Pp. 317-22.
       JJ's work "outspoken, vigorous, original, beau-
       tiful." Good early appreciation. Extract re-
       printed in G25.

H143   Magalaner, Marvin. "James Joyce and Marie Corelli." In
MODERN IRISH LITERATURE: ESSAYS IN HONOR OF WILLIAM YORK
TINDALL. Ed. Raymond J. Porter and James D. Brophy. New
York: Iona College Press and Twayne, 1972. Pp. 185-93.
       Corelli's influence on Stephen's Satanism (cf.
       SORROWS OF SATAN [1895]) and on JJ's sentimen-
       tal style (cf. ZISKA [1897]).

H144   Markovic, Vida E. "Stephen Dedalus." In THE CHANGING
FACE: DISINTEGRATION OF PERSONALITY IN THE TWENTIETH-
CENTURY BRITISH NOVEL, 1900-1950. Carbondale: Southern
Illinois Univ. Press, 1970. Pp. 38-53.
       The development (PAYM) and ultimate disintegra-
       tion (U and FW) of the inward-turning "isolated
       consciousness" (Stephen and Shem) in JJ's work.

H145   Mason, Ellsworth. "Joyce's Categories." SR, 51 (1953),
427-32.
       JJ's refusal to subscribe to Stephen's "cate-
       gories" (PAYM) in his own art. Valuably dis-
       tinguishes between Stephen's and JJ's views.
       Reprinted in K14.

H146   Mays, J.C.C. "Brian O'Nolan and Joyce on Art and on
Life." JJQ, 11 (1974), 238-56.
       O'Nolan (i.e. Brian Nolan) indebted in several
       respects to JJ's example. See F71.

H147   Melchiori, Giorgio. "Joyce and the Tradition of the
Novel"; "Echoes in 'The Waste Land.'" In THE TIGHTROPE
WALKERS: STUDIES OF MANNERISM IN MODERN ENGLISH LITERA-
TURE. London: Routledge, 1956. Pp. 34-52; 53-88.
       JJ's influences upon the development of the
       novel and upon Eliot's poetry.

H148   Mercier, Vivian. "The Greatest Precursor: Joyce." In
        THE NEW NOVEL: FROM QUENEAU TO PINGET. New York: Farrar,
        Straus and Giroux, 1971. Pp. 23-40.
            Novelists' experiments with time and language.

H149   -----. "Joyce and the Irish Tradition of Parody." In
        THE IRISH COMIC TRADITION. Oxford: Clarendon Press,
        1962. Pp. 210-36.
            Influences of Gaelic forms of parody and blar-
            ney, and of the "innately destructive" Irish
            cast of mind on JJ's comedy.

H150   Mirsky, Dmitri P. "Joyce and Irish Literature." Trans.
        D. Kinkead. NEW MASSES, Nos. 10-22 (3 Apr. 1934), pp.
        31-34.
            JJ a decadent artist and no "social realist,"
            despite his use of realistic conventions. Ex-
            tract reprinted in G25. Also see H57 and T36.

H151   Montgomery, Niall. "A Context for Mr. Joyce's Work." In
        THE CELTIC MASTER. Ed. Maurice Harmon. Pp. 9-15. See
        G39.
            JJ's "obsession with form" the culmination of
            the Celtic literary tradition.

H152   Moore, John Rees. "Artifices for Eternity: Joyce and
        Yeats." EIRE, 3, No. 4 (1968), 66-73.
            Contrasts the lives and temperaments of the
            two writers.

H153   More, Paul Elmer. "James Joyce." In ON BEING HUMAN.
        Princeton, N.J.: Princeton Univ. Press, 1936. Pp. 69-
        96.
            Traces JJ's artistic decline from "The Dead,"
            through the aestheticism of PAYM to the "moral
            slough" of U. Influential.

H154   Morin, Edward. "Joyce as Thomist." RENASCENCE, 9 (1957),
        127-31.
            Similarities between Joyce's aesthetic and the
            SUMMA.

H155   Morse, J. Mitchell. "Baudelaire, Stephen Dedalus, and
        Shem the Penman." BuR, 7 (1958), 187-98.
            Elements from the life and work of Baudelaire
            inform JJ's three successive portraits of the
            artist (PAYM, U, FW).

H156   -----. "Joyce and the Early Thomas Mann." REVUE DE
        LITTÉRATURE COMPARÉE, 36 (1962), 377-85.
        Correspondences between Mann and JJ (e.g., Tonio
        Kroger and Stephen), asserting Mann's influence
        on JJ.

H157   Muir, Edwin. "James Joyce." In TRANSITION: ESSAYS ON
        CONTEMPORARY LITERATURE. New York: Viking, 1926. Pp.
        19-45.
        JJ's humor and "mastery" of language, with spe-
        cial praise for U. Extract reprinted in G25.

H158   Muller, Herbert J. "James Joyce." In MODERN FICTION:
        A STUDY OF VALUES. New York: Funk and Wagnalls, 1937.
        Pp. 288-316.
        JJ a "genius," but for specialists only (PAYM,
        U, and FW flawed works).

H159   Neill, S. Diana. A SHORT HISTORY OF THE ENGLISH NOVEL.
        1951. Rev. ed. New York: Collier, 1964. Pp. 312-24.
        Undistinguished, readable survey.

H160   Nicholson, Norman. MAN AND LITERATURE. London: Macmil-
        lan, 1943. Pp. 144-51.
        JJ's moral orthodoxy and his fundamentally
        Christian conception of man as an "Imperfect"
        being.

H161   Noon, William T., S.J. "James Joyce: Unfacts, Fiction,
        and Facts." PMLA, 76 (1961), 254-76.
        Important emphasis on the distance between JJ's
        fiction and what has been assumed to be auto-
        biographical fact.

H162   -----. "The Religious Position of James Joyce." In
        JAMES JOYCE: HIS PLACE IN WORLD LITERATURE. Ed. Wolo-
        dymyr T. Zyla. Pp. 7-21. See G85.
        JJ's developing humanistic response to Irish
        Jansenism, in his works, ultimately affirms
        essentially religious values.

H163   O'Brien, Darcy. "A Critique of Psychoanalytic Criticism,
        Or What Joyce Did and Did Not Do." JJQ, 13 (1976), 275-
        92.
        Reasonable cautionary statement of the limita-
        tions of psychoanalytic criticism of JJ. See
        G43.

H164   -----. "Some Psychological Determinants of Joyce's View
        of Love and Sex." In NEW LIGHT ON JOYCE. Ed. Fritz Senn.
        Pp. 15-27. See G73.
            JJ's personal sexual confusion and Oedipal dis-
            tress reflected in the dissociation of sensu-
            ality and affection in his work.

H165   O'Connor, Frank. "Antithesis--I, II." In A SHORT HIST-
        ORY OF IRISH LITERATURE: A BACKWARD LOOK. New York: Put-
        nam's, 1967. Pp. 194-202, 203-11.
            JJ's international, Catholic, urban, and mod-
            ernist orientation distinct from the largely
            nationalist, Protestant, rural traditionalism
            of the Irish literary revival (e.g., Yeats).

H166   -----. "Joyce and Dissociated Metaphor." In THE MIRROR
        IN THE ROADWAY: A STUDY OF THE MODERN NOVEL. New York:
        Knopf, 1956. Pp. 295-312.
            JJ violates the relationship between author
            and audience in his use of dissociating meta-
            phors: like "dreams," they "baffle and de-
            ceive the conscious mind." Reprinted in J3,
            J179, and K1.

H167   O'Faolain, Sean. "Virginia Woolf and James Joyce, or
        'Narcissa and Lucifer.'" In THE VANISHING HERO: STUDIES
        IN NOVELISTS OF THE TWENTIES. London: Eyre and Spottis-
        woode, 1956. Pp. 193-222.
            JJ actually intensely subjective, despite the
            illusion of objective detachment (cf. Woolf).

H168   Orel, Harold. "The Two Attitudes of James Joyce." In
        IRISH HISTORY AND CULTURE: ASPECTS OF A PEOPLE'S HERITAGE.
        Ed. Orel. Lawrence: Univ. Press of Kansas, 1976. Pp.
        309-27.
            JJ's love-hate for Ireland lightly traced
            through the works.

H169   Palomo, Dolores. "Alpha and Omega: of Chaucer and Joyce."
        MOSAIC, 8, No. 2 (1975), 19-31.
            Several parallels between the two writers'
            contemporary situations, their techniques,
            and their achievements.

H170   Paterson, John. "James Joyce: It's All Won." In THE
        NOVEL AS FAITH: THE GOSPEL ACCORDING TO JAMES, HARDY,
        CONRAD, JOYCE, LAWRENCE AND VIRGINA WOOLF. Boston:
        Gambit, 1973. Pp. 107-42.
            JJ repudiates all traditional approaches to

life and conventions for art, while maintain-
ing an "almost traditional" view of the "artist's moral and social mission."

H171 Poirier, Richard. "The Literature of Waste: Eliot, Joyce,
and Others." In THE PERFORMING SELF. New York: Oxford
Univ. Press, 1971. Pp. 45-61.
Eliot and JJ as skeptics who despaired "at giving any kind of order" to their fragmented world.

H172 Porter, Raymond J. "The Cracked Lookingglass." In YEATS,
JOYCE, AND BECKETT: NEW LIGHT ON THREE MODERN IRISH WRIT-
ERS. Ed. Kathleen McGrory and John Unterecker. Lewisburg, Pa.: Bucknell Univ. Press, 1976. Pp. 87-91.
JJ's important place in Irish culture as the
writer who liberated the Irish literary tradition from the past.

H173 Pound, Ezra. "Joyce." THE FUTURE, 2, No. 6 (1916), 161-
63.
Notes the "bass and treble" of JJ's method:
the "swift alteration of subjective beauty
and external shabbiness, squalor, and sordid-
ness." Reprinted in F123 and G25.

H174 -----. "Past History." EJ, 22 (1933), 349-58.
The "quality" of JJ's works (D, PAYM, U praised,
FW dismissed), his literary heritage (Flaubert
and Ibsen), and his "contribution and influence"
("almost exclusively Flaubert's influence, extended"). Reprinted in F123 and G25.

H175 Powys, John Cowper. "Modern Fiction." In SEX IN THE
ARTS: A SYMPOSIUM. Ed. John F. McDermott and Kendall B.
Taft. New York: Harper, 1932. Pp. 34-63.
Hails JJ's view of sex as "the grand panacea
for the ills of modern life" (pp. 43-52).

H176 Praz, Mario. "Notes on James Joyce." Trans. Wallace
Sillanpoa. MOSAIC, 6, No. 1 (1972), 85-100.
General critique of JJ as a major modernist,
by a distinguished Italian critic. See M45
and T40.

H177 Raisor, Philip. "Grist for the Mill: James Joyce and
the Naturalists." ConL, 15 (1974), 457-73.
Continental Naturalism an important "shaping

force in Joyce's art" (e.g., Ibsen, Tolstoy,
and Zola).

H178 Read, Herbert. "James Joyce." 1930. In A COAT OF MANY
COLOURS. 1945. Rev. ed. London: Routledge, 1956. Pp.
145-49.
JJ a "Romantic," rather than a "classical" author, who has "reduced his egocentricity to
its last refinement." Extract reprinted in G25.

H179 Robson, W.W. MODERN ENGLISH LITERATURE. London: Oxford
Univ. Press, 1970. Pp. 73-82 and passim.
JJ's "best work rests not on virtuosity but on
something deeply humane." Survey.

H180 Rodway, Allan. "Expanding Images in the Joycian [sic]
Universe." RMS, 15 (1971), 63-69.
JJ's imagery expands, through his career, as
his subject matter contracts.

H181 Rosenfeld, Paul. "James Joyce." In MEN SEEN. New York:
Dial Press, 1925. Pp. 23-42.
JJ's *comedie intellectuelle* supplants the
"old divine and human comedies." Ambivalent
survey.

H182 Rothman, Nathan L. "Thomas Wolfe and James Joyce: A Study
in Literary Influence." In A SOUTHERN VANGUARD: THE JOHN
PEALE BISHOP MEMORIAL VOLUME. Ed. Allen Tate. New York:
Prentice-Hall, 1947. Pp. 52-77.
Influences of JJ's fictional techniques gener-
ally and particularly of his characterization of
Stephen, on Wolfe's LOOK HOMEWARD, ANGEL (1929).

H183 Russell, Francis. "Joyce and Alexandria." 1951. In
THREE STUDIES IN TWENTIETH CENTURY OSBSCURITY. Aldington, Engl.: Hand and Flower Press, 1954. Pp. 7-44.
JJ's "nihilistic achievement" both a natural
product of "our cultural void" and reminiscent
of the long-lost obscurantist literature that
arose out of a similar era of chaos, in third-
century B.C. Alexandria.

H184 Savage, Derek S. "James Joyce." In THE WITHERED BRANCH:
SIX STUDIES IN THE MODERN NOVEL. London: Eyre and Spot-
tiswoode, 1950. Pp. 156-99.
Traces the "main strands" of solitude, religion,
and art in JJ's ultimately "perverse and destruc-
tive" works. (FW ignored.)

H185 Schneidau, Herbert N. "Pound and Joyce: The Universal
in the Particular." In EZRA POUND: THE IMAGE AND THE
REAL. Baton Rouge: Louisiana State Univ. Press, 1969.
Pp. 74-109.
Pound's early and continuous appreciation of
JJ's works related to his literary and criti-
cal development.

H186 Scholes, Robert. "Joyce and the Epiphany: The Key to
the Labyrinth?" SR, 72 (1964), 65-77.
Important caution against applying the "epiphany" idea, defined in STEPHEN HERO, to the
interpretation of JJ's works, since he himself
abandoned the notion.

H187 Scholes, Robert, and Robert Kellogg. THE NATURE OF NAR-
RATIVE. London: Oxford Univ. Press, 1966. Pp. 199-203,
268-72, and passim.
JJ's experimentation with characterization and
point of view (cf. James).

H188 Scott, Bonnie K. "Joyce and the Dublin Theosophists:
'Vegetable Verse' and Story." EIRE, 13, No. 2 (1978),
54-70.
JJ's debts to and fascination with Theosophis-
tic lore, despite sharp differences with and
considerable hostility toward Theosophists
(e.g., AE, Eglington, and Yeats).

H189 -----. "Joyce's Schooling in the Field of George Moore."
EIRE, 9, No. 4 (1974), 117-41.
JJ's rejection of and borrowing from his Irish
precursor, Moore.

H190 Scott, Nathan A. THE BROKEN CENTER: STUDIES IN THE THEO-
LOGICAL HORIZON OF MODERN LITERATURE. New Haven, Conn.:
Yale Univ. Press, 1966. Passim.
JJ's works frequently cited to illustrate the
relation between the religious and the liter-
ary imagination.

H191 Scott-James, Rolfe A. FIFTY YEARS OF ENGLISH LITERATURE,
1900-1950; WITH A POSTSCRIPT 1951-1955. London: Longmans,
1956. Pp. 131-37.
JJ's reaction to literary realism in his fiction of "interior vision" (cf. Lawrence, Dorothy Richardson, and Woolf).

H192   Semmler, Clement. FOR THE UNCANNY MAN: ESSAYS, MAINLY
        LITERARY. London: Angus and Robertson, 1963. Pp. 12-
        132.
               Collects six previously published essays (1952-
               60): on JJ's judicial, popular, and critical
               reception in Australia (pp. 12-92); on themes
               and language in FW (pp. 93-108); on JJ's comic
               gift (pp. 109-11); on his years in Zurich (pp.
               112-20); on his love of radio and radio allu-
               sions in FW (pp. 121-26); and on Molly Bloom
               as the "entirely feminine" woman (pp. 127-32).

H193   Senn, Fritz. "Dogmad or Dubliboused." JJQ, 17 (1980),
        237-61.
               Quite sanely wonders why JJ's critics tend
               toward dogmatic positions when his works de-
               velop, from D through FW, a warning against
               the traps of certainty.

H194   -----. "Joycean Translatitudes: Aspects of Translation."
        In LITTERS FROM ALOFT. Ed. Ronald Bates and Harry J. Pol-
        lock. Pp. 26-49. See G9.
               A general consideration of the multiple
               perils of translating JJ, from D to FW.

H195   Seward, Barbara. "Joyce and Synthesis." In THE SYMBOLIC
        ROSE. New York: Columbia Univ. Press, 1960. Pp. 187-221.
               JJ's use of "affirmative" rose symbolism, both
               for its traditional, liturgical significance
               and for its more contemporary mystical and sen-
               sual connotations. Extracts reprinted in K6
               and K16.

H196   Share, Bernard. "Downes's Cakeshop and Williams's Jam."
        In A BASH IN THE TUNNEL. Ed. John Ryan. Pp. 189-92.
        See F135.
               Confused defense of Dublin against the dis-
               torted picture presented in JJ's early works.

H197   Sidnell, M.J. "A Daintical Pair of Accomplasses: Joyce
        and Yeats." In LITTERS FROM ALOFT. Ed. Ronald Bates
        and Harry J. Pollock. Pp. 50-73. See G9.
               Correspondences between JJ and Yeats, and
               their reactions to each other.

H198   Slochower, Harry. "In Quest of Everyman: James Joyce."
        In NO VOICE IS WHOLLY LOST...: WRITERS AND THINKERS IN

WAR AND PEACE. New York: Creative Age Press, 1945. Pp. 243-48.
> JJ's incomplete revolt against his heritage seen from a Marxist political and cultural perspective.

H199 Solberg, Sara M. "On Comparing Apples and Oranges: James Joyce and Thomas Pynchon." CLS, 16 (1979), 33-40.
> Two authors share common "preoccupations" in their works which provide fruitful comparisons, if not proof of influence.

H200 Spears, Monroe K. DIONYSUS AND THE CITY: MODERNISM IN TWENTIETH-CENTURY POETRY. New York: Oxford Univ. Press, 1970. Pp. 93-99 and passim.
> JJ's distinctively modern treatment of the city in English fiction.

H201 Spiegel, Alan. FICTION AND THE CAMERA EYE: VISUAL CONSCIOUSNESS IN FILM AND THE MODERN NOVEL. Charlottesville: Univ. Press of Virginia, 1976. Pp. 63-68, 71-82, 90-97, 109-15, 136-50, 164-74.
> Striking use of intensely visualized scenes ("cinematographic form"), in JJ (cf. James, Conrad, and others.)

H202 Spivey, Ted R. "The Reintegration of Modern Man: An Essay on James Joyce and Hermann Hesse." SLitI, 3, No. 2 (1970), 49-64.
> Superficial comparison of the "quest" for reintegration in the two authors' works. See G78. Reprinted in his JOURNEY BEYOND TRAGEDY (Orlando: Univ. Presses of Florida, 1980), pp. 109-25.

H203 Splitter, Randolph. "Proust, Joyce, and the Theory of Metaphor." L&P, 29 (1979), 4-18.
> Proust's and JJ's similar uses of flower metaphors, in light of the theories of the French psychoanalyst, Jacques Lacan.

H204 Staley, Harry C. "Joyce's Cathechisms." JJQ, 6 (1968), 137-53.
> Shows influence of the DEHARBE CATECHISM, principally, and the MAYNOOTH CATECHISM on JJ's style and ideas. Also see H67.

H205 Staley, Thomas F. "James Joyce and the Dilemma of American Academic Criticism." DUBLIN MAGAZINE, 6, No. 1 (1967), 38-45.
      JJ's hold on American popular and critical imagination.

H206 Stanford, William B. IRELAND AND THE CLASSICAL TRADITION. Totowa, N.J.: Rowman and Littlefield, 1976. Pp. 102-09 and passim.
      JJ's systematic classical education and its impact on his work.

H207 Starkie, Enid. FROM GAUTIER TO ELIOT: THE INFLUENCE OF FRANCE ON ENGLISH LITERATURE, 1851-1939. London: Hutchinson, 1960. Pp. 186-97.
      Influence of Proust and the *monologue intérieur* on JJ and Woolf.

H208 Steinberg, Erwin R. "The Sources of the Stream." In IN HONOR OF AUSTIN WRIGHT. Ed. Joseph Baim, et al. Pittsburgh: Carnegie Mellon Univ. Press, 1972. Pp. 87-101.
      Relates JJ's aesthetic and practice to contemporary views of art.

H209 Stevenson, Lionel. THE HISTORY OF THE ENGLISH NOVEL. Vol. 11. YESTERDAY AND AFTER. New York: Barnes and Noble, 1967. Pp. 208-30 and passim.
      JJ the chief proponent of the "turn inwards" in modern fiction. Survey.

H210 Stewart, Douglas H. "James Joyce--Apocalypticism." In THE ARK OF GOD: STUDIES IN FIVE MODERN NOVELISTS. London: Carey Kingsgate Press, 1961. Pp. 17-43.
      JJ's assertions that "man is without God" compel us to reexamine our spiritual situation.

H211 Stewart, J.I.M. "Joyce." In EIGHT MODERN WRITERS. Oxford: Clarendon Press, 1963. Pp. 422-83; 680-86.
      Assimilates and expands Stewart's pamphlet survey of JJ and his work (see G76). Good brief bibliography. Extract reprinted in J3.

H212 Stoll, Elmer E. "Psychoanalysis in Criticism: Dickens, Kipling, Joyce." In FROM SHAKESPEARE TO JOYCE: AUTHORS AND CRITICS; LITERATURE AND LIFE. Garden City, N.Y.: Doubleday, Doran, 1944. Pp. 339-88.
      JJ (pp. 350-88), an eccentric, self-consciously psychoanalytic writer of dubious merit.

H213 Strong, Leonard A.G. "James Joyce." In THE ENGLISH
      NOVELISTS: A SURVEY OF THE NOVEL BY TWENTY CONTEMPORARY
      NOVELISTS. Ed. Derek Verschoyle. London: Chatto and
      Windus, 1936. Pp. 279-93.
          Conflict between originality and tradition
          both provoked and found at the heart of JJ's
          achievement.

H214 Sultan, Stanley. "A Joycean Look at THE PLAYBOY OF THE
      WESTERN WORLD." In THE CELTIC MASTER. Ed. Maurice Har-
      mon. Pp. 45-55. See G39.
          The Irishman's betrayal of his saviors a theme
          common to JJ and Synge.

H215 Swinnerton, Frank. "James Joyce." In THE GEORGIAN LIT-
      ERARY SCENE, 1910-1935. 1934. 2nd ed. London: Hutch-
      inson, 1969. Pp. 324-27.
          JJ a brilliant "master of extravagant inven-
          tion," with traits of the sophisticated jour-
          nalistic entrepreneur. Extract reprinted in
          G25.

H216 Taylor, Estella R. THE MODERN IRISH WRITERS. Lawrence:
      Univ. of Kansas Press, 1954. Pp. 97-100, 140-44, and
      passim.
          JJ among Gogarty, Lady Gregory, and Yeats, and
          his influence on Irish letters.

H217 Thornton, Weldon. "James Joyce and the Power of the
      Word." In THE CLASSIC BRITISH NOVEL. Ed. Howard M.
      Harper and Charles Edge. Athens: Univ. of Georgia Press,
      1972. Pp. 183-201.
          JJ's fascination with language both for tech-
          nical experimentation and for theme: the tran-
          substantiation of reality into art.

H218 Tindall, William York. FORCES IN MODERN BRITISH LITERA-
      TURE, 1885-1956. New York: Knopf, 1956. Passim.
          Copious references to JJ in relation to modern
          literary themes and movements.

H219 -----. THE LITERARY SYMBOL. New York: Columbia Univ.
      Press, 1955. Pp. 56-60, 76-86, 195-202, 224-29, 239-
      42, and passim.
          Comments on JJ's debts to occult literature
          and the "Hermetic tradition" and on JJ's sym-
          bolic techniques in his works. Extracts re-
          printed in K1, K5, and K14.

H220   Ussher, Arland. "James Joyce: Doubting Thomist and Jok-
       ing Jesuit." In THREE GREAT IRISHMEN: SHAW, YEATS, AND
       JOYCE. London: Gollancz, 1952. Pp. 115-60.
              Stresses JJ's comedy, finding FW, however, the
              Icarus-fall of the over-extended artist.

H221   "The Veritable James Joyce, According to Stuart Gilbert
       and Oliver St. J. Gogarty." TRANSITION, No. 21 (1932),
       pp. 273-82.
              Supports Gogarty's deflation of JJ's art and
              learning, despite Gilbert's adulation. Signed:
              "A Fellow Dubliner." See G81. Extract re-
              printed in G25.

H222   Vickery, John B. "James Joyce: From the Beginnings to
       A PORTRAIT OF THE ARTIST AS A YOUNG MAN." In THE LITER-
       ARY IMPACT OF *THE GOLDEN BOUGH*. Princeton, N.J.: Prince-
       ton Univ. Press, 1973. Pp. 326-45.
              Frazer's work an "instructive locus of meta-
              phoric possibilities" for JJ in his early
              works. Also see M325 and N212.

H223   Vidan, Ivo. "Joyce and the South Slaves [sic]." In ATTI
       DEL THIRD INTERNATIONAL JAMES JOYCE SYMPOSIUM. Pp. 116-
       23. See G7.
              JJ's familiarity with Slavic language and lit-
              erature.

H224   Von Phul, Ruth. "Joyce and the Strabismal Apologia." In
       A JAMES JOYCE MISCELLANY, SECOND SERIES. Ed. Marvin Maga-
       laner. Pp. 119-32. See G56.
              Vision and literal, emotional, and spiritual
              blindness provide patterns and symbols in JJ's
              work.

H225   -----. "The Last Word in Stolentelling." MODERN BRITISH
       LITERATURE, 1 (1976), 3-21.
              Influence of Kierkegaard on JJ's developing
              view of ethics.

H226   Wagenknecht, Edward. "Below the Stream: James Joyce."
       In CAVALCADE OF THE ENGLISH NOVEL. New York: Holt, 1954.
       Pp. 512-21.
              Skeptical survey of JJ's fiction, through U,
              as a logical extension of the stream-of-con-
              sciousness movement. (FW dismissed.)

H227 Wall, Richard. "Joyce's Use of the Anglo-Irish Dialect
of English." In PLACE, PERSONALITY AND THE IRISH WRITER.
Ed. Andrew Carpenter. New York: Barnes and Noble, 1977.
Pp. 121-35.
> Surveys JJ's careful, precise, and often comic
> use of Anglo-Irish dialect.

H228 Watson, G.J. "James Joyce: From Inside to Outside and
Back Again." In IRISH IDENTITY AND THE LITERARY REVIVAL:
SYNGE, YEATS, JOYCE AND O'CASEY. New York: Barnes and
Noble, 1979. Pp. 151-244.
> Extended discussion of JJ's relation to the
> emerging Irish national consciousness, in his
> reflection of the political, religious, and
> social condition of Ireland, and in his cen-
> tral theme of the quest for identity (D, PAYM,
> and U).

H229 Webb, Eugene. "A Darkness Shining in Brightness: James
Joyce and the Obscure Soul of the World." In THE DARK
DOVE: THE SACRED AND SECULAR IN MODERN LITERATURE. Se-
attle: Univ. of Washington Press, 1975. Pp. 111-56.
> JJ's use of "traditional imagery of the sacred
> to resacralize the secular."

H230 Weidlé, Wladimir. "On the Present State of Poetic Language." 1947. Trans. Maria Jolas. In A JAMES JOYCE YEAR-
BOOK. Ed. Maria Jolas. Pp. 20-31. See G45.
> Breakdown of distinct literary modes and pure
> referential language in modern writing partic-
> ularly well illustrated in JJ's works.

H231 Weir, Lorraine. "Joyce, Myth and Memory: On His Blindness." IRISH UNIVERSITY REVIEW, 2 (1972), 172-88.
> Disputes the overly-literal correlation be-
> tween JJ's eye problems and his opaque later
> writing, but suggests JJ himself encouraged
> the analogy.

H232 West, Rebecca. "The Strange Necessity." In THE STRANGE
NECESSITY. Garden City, N.Y.: Doubleday, Doran, 1928.
Pp. 1-213.
> JJ a chief example, along with Constant, Pavlov
> (!), Proust, Shaw, and Yeats, of the debilitat-
> ing effect of false emotion in art: JJ's radi-
> cal originality undermined by his "reactionary
> sentimentality." See N222. Extract reprinted
> in G25.

H233   White, David A. "Joyce and Wittgenstein." JJQ, 12
       (1975), 294-304.
              Exposition of Wittgenstein's developing ideas
              of the limitations of language, "as a basis
              for appreciating Joyce's linguistic develop-
              ment," from PAYM through FW.

H234   White, William. "Irish Antitheses: Shaw and Joyce."
       SHAVIAN, 2, No. 3 (1961), 24-34.
              Various points of contact between the two art-
              ists, who never met, and their generally cool
              views of one another.

H235   Wicker, Brian. "Joyce and the Sense of an Ending." In
       THE STORY-SHAPED WORLD: FICTION AND METAPHYSICS: SOME
       VARIATIONS ON A THEME. Notre Dame, Ind.: Univ. of Notre
       Dame Press, 1975. Pp. 134-50.
              JJ's attempt to "secularize," in his highly
              metaphoric fiction, "an overreligious, indeed
              neurotically religious culture."

H236   Wilder, Thornton. "Joyce and the Modern Novel." In A
       JAMES JOYCE MISCELLANY. Ed. Marvin Magalaner. Pp. 11-
       19. See G55.
              JJ's simplicity within complexity a reflection
              of the ultimately archetypal dimensions of unique
              individual experience.

H237   Wilson, Edmund. "James Joyce." In AXEL'S CASTLE: A
       STUDY OF THE IMAGINATIVE LITERATURE OF 1870-1930. New
       York: Scribner's, 1931. Pp. 191-236.
              Critical overview, with an excellent, extended,
              insightful, pre-Stuart Gilbert analysis of U (a
              masterpiece, though overly "elaborated"), and
              comments on the earlier fiction and FW ("Work
              in Progress"). Extracts reprinted in G19 and
              G25.

H238   Woolf, Virginia. "Modern Fiction." 1919. In her COL-
       LECTED ESSAYS. Ed. L. Woolf. London: Hogarth, 1966-67.
       II, 103-10 passim.
              Enlists JJ, the "most notable" younger writer,
              in her campaign against Edwardian realism. Ex-
              tract reprinted in G25.

H239   Worthington, Mabel P. "Gilbert and Sullivan Songs in
       the Works of James Joyce." HSL, 1 (1969), 209-18.
              Catalog of JJ's Gilbert and Sullivan allusions,

with comments on their contextual appropriateness.

H240   -----. "Maundy, Thursday, Good Friday, the Sorrowing
       Mother, and the Day of Judgement." In MODERN IRISH LIT-
       ERATURE: ESSAYS IN HONOR OF WILLIAM YORK TINDALL. Ed.
       Raymond J. Porter and James D. Brophy. New York: Iona
       College Press and Twayne, 1972. Pp. 143-51.
         JJ's allusions to Catholic hymns.

J. STUDIES OF *DUBLINERS* (1914)

The following section is subdivided into three parts: i. Books
and Essay Collections on D; ii. General Critical Articles, or
Chapters on D; and iii. Studies of Individual Stories (in order
of their appearance in the collection).

For facsimiles of JJ's surviving manuscripts and of the print-
ers' proofs for the 1910 (cancelled) and the 1914 editions of
D, see vols. 4-6 of THE JAMES JOYCE ARCHIVE (B10). For concordances to D, see Füger (D4) and Lane (D8).

For biographical backgrounds to D, see, in section F above,
Ellmann (F33), Hone (F64), S. Joyce (F80), Lyons (F95), Pound
(F123), and Richards (F130).

For additional critical commentaries and information on D as
a whole, see the following books, in section G above: Adams
(G2), Benstock and Benstock (G11), Bowen (G13), CAHIERS VIC-
TORIENS (G17a), Cope (G22), Cross (G24), Goldberg (G31), Gold-
ing (G32), Goldman (G34), Gorman (G36), Grose (G37), Gross
(G38), Hodgart (G40), Hodgart and Worthington (G41), JAMES
JOYCE QUARTERLY (G44), Jones (G46), Kenner (G47), Kronegger
(G51), Levin (G52), Litz (G53), MacCabe (G54), Magalaner and
Kain (G58), Majault (G59), Moseley (G67), Murillo (G68), Noon
(G69), O'Brien (G70), Peake (G71), Ryf (G72), Smidt (G74),
Stewart (G76), Strong (G77), Tindall (G80), Tysdahl (G82);
the following critical articles, in section H above: Aronson
(H7), Chayes (H32), Daiches (H45), Garrett (H70), Goodheart
(H79), Kaye (H106), O'Connor (H166), Raisor (H177), Scott
(H189), Vickery (H222), Watson (H228); and the following stud-
ies, entered in other sections of this bibliography: Lawrence
(M37), Reynolds (M42), and Sorensen (P5). For additional crit-
ical commentary and information on the individual stories in
D, see the headnotes for section J, iii below and for each of
the stories within section J, iii.

For foreign-language studies of D, see section U. See item
U1, in particular, for an international bibliography of criticism on D.

J, i. Books and Essay Collections on DUBLINERS

Also see the following books, essay collections, and pamphlets
on individual stories: on "Araby": JAMES JOYCE QUARTERLY (J82);
on "Eveline": Scholes (J91); on "The Dead": Hedberg (J169) and
Moynihan (J179). Also see U1, U6, and the appendix.

J1 Baker, James R., and Thomas F. Staley, eds. JAMES JOYCE'S
    DUBLINERS: A CRITICAL HANDBOOK. Belmont, Calif.: Wads-
    worth, 1969.
            Casebook. Gathers several miscellaneous writings
        by JJ pertinent to the themes and techniques of
        D, three JJ letters concerning D's publication,
        four general essays on the volume, and sixteen
        commentaries on the individual stories. Chronol-
        ogy, study questions, and brief bibliography. In-
        cludes J15, J30, J32, J60, J73, J80, J89, J107,
        J110, J128, J137, J152, J174, J186, and extracts
        from B21, C1, G2, G31, G53, G58, G69, G80, and
        P28.

J2 Beck, Warren. JOYCE'S *DUBLINERS:* SUBSTANCE, VISION, AND
    ART. Durham, N.C.: Duke Univ. Press, 1969.
            Distended readings of the stories, lacking in-
        sight or ingenuity. Beck's contempt for symbol-
        hunting, which he uses as justification for ig-
        noring virtually all substantial criticism on
        D, is not countered by any demonstrated capacity
        to say much of significance about the stories.

J3 Beja, Morris, ed. JAMES JOYCE: *DUBLINERS* AND *A PORTRAIT
    OF THE ARTIST AS A YOUNG MAN:* A CASEBOOK. London: Macmil-
    lan, 1973.
            Useful collection. Reprints selected letters
        and manuscript materials by JJ, six contempo-
        rary reviews of the two works, and thirteen
        biographical and critical commentaries, with
        Beja's "Introduction" (pp. 15-32), on the works'
        critical receptions. Includes H11, H14, J32,
        J34, K35, K64, and extracts from C1, F33, F78,
        G17, G38, G47, G52, H166, and H211.

J4 Brandabur, Edward. A SCRUPULOUS MEANNESS: A STUDY OF
    JOYCE'S EARLY WORK. Urbana: Univ. of Illinois Press, 1971.
            Free-wheeling psychoanalytic analyses of D and
        EXILES, seeing JJ attributing the paralysis of

Dublin to the "sadomasochistic neuroses" of the
Dubliners who fail to live, seeking their fulfillment through vicarious identification with
"the experience of others." Brandabur provides
some good insights into individual works (e.g.,
"Ivy Day in the Committee Room," "The Dead," and
EXILES), and useful commentary on the masochism
implicit in several of JJ's themes (e.g., celi-
bacy, humiliation, hypocrisy), yet his critiques
are too often methodologically unsound, facile,
or forced. Includes a superficial concluding
note on PAYM and U. Extracts originally published in J13 and J179.

J5   Brown, Homer O. JAMES JOYCE'S EARLY FICTION: THE BIOGRAPHY
     OF A FORM. Cleveland, Ohio: The Press of Case Western Re-
     serve Univ., 1972.
          Study of the relationship between fictional form
          and the "meaning of the world" that form presents
          in JJ's early fiction. Brown traces JJ's evolv-
          ing view of the nature of reality as "other" than
          the perceiver, implicit in his realistic tech-
          niques in the early stories, through his transi-
          tional stages of vision in "The Dead" and STE-
          PHEN HERO, to his ultimate view of reality as
          created by the perceiver, implicit in his sym-
          bolic techniques in PAYM. This development, com-
          pleted in PAYM, is the basis for JJ's highly sub-
          jective techniques in U and FW, which are not
          discussed here.

J6   Garrett, Peter K., ed. TWENTIETH CENTURY INTERPRETATIONS
     OF *DUBLINERS:* A COLLECTION OF CRITICAL ESSAYS. Englewood
     Cliffs, N.J.: Prentice-Hall, 1968.
          Good collection of nine previously published es-
          says, plus Garrett's "Introduction" (pp. 1-17),
          a general summary of themes and techniques in
          the stories. Includes J32, J46, J81, J98, J125,
          J173, and extracts from G31, G47, and H45.

J7   Gifford, Don, and Robert J. Seidman. NOTES FOR JOYCE:
     DUBLINERS AND *A PORTRAIT OF THE ARTIST AS A YOUNG MAN.*
     New York: Dutton, 1967.
          Often excellent annotations for the story col-
          lection and novel, keyed to the pagination of
          the most available editions, with general pre-
          fatory discussions of JJ's biography, Irish

politics, monetary values, and such. Despite
some duplication, also useful in conjunction
with the critical editions of both works, which
are also annotated (see J13 and K1). A second,
revised and enlarged edition has been announced
for 1982 publication, by the Univ. of California Press.

J8   Halper, Nathan. THE EARLY JAMES JOYCE. New York: Columbia Univ. Press, 1973.
Genial and informative introductory monograph
for students, on JJ's early life and works, concentrating almost entirely on D and PAYM.

J9   Hart, Clive, ed. JAMES JOYCE'S *DUBLINERS*: CRITICAL ESSAYS.
London: Faber, 1969.
Fifteen original essays, several very good, de-
voted to close reading and interpretation of
each of the stories in D. Includes J61, J75,
J77, J90, J96, J100, J103, J105, J111, J118,
J127, J139, J142, J148, and J154.

J10   JAMES JOYCE QUARTERLY. 2 (1965), 66-89. "DUBLINERS Number."
Disappointingly slight "special issue," in fact
containing only three essays, by Sidney Feshbach (J72), Fritz Senn (J67), and Florence L.
Walzl (J102).

J11   Magalaner, Marvin. TIME OF APPRENTICESHIP: THE FICTION
OF YOUNG JAMES JOYCE. New York: Abelard-Schuman, 1959.
Essentially a study of the backgrounds to and
composition of D, with considerable reference
to JJ's later works as well. Magalaner summarizes JJ's years of preparation for the publication of D, the influence of his reading (particularly Hauptmann, Nietzsche, and Taxil), the
texual evolution of D, aspects of STEPHEN HERO
and PAYM relevant to D, and the place of D in
his artistic development. Includes several useful appendixes, but is weakened by questionable
emphasis on the weaker stories and by digres-
sions (e.g., his previously published essay on
JJ's "Léo Taxil motif" in U).

J12   San Juan, Epifanio. JAMES JOYCE AND THE CRAFT OF FICTION:
AN INTERPRETATION OF *DUBLINERS*. Rutherford, N.J.: Fair-
leigh Dickinson Univ. Press, 1972.
Uninspired explications and critiques, tracing

some general patterns of relationship among the
stories but offering little of interest to the
experienced reader.

J13 Scholes, Robert, and A. Walton Litz, eds. *DUBLINERS:*
TEXT, CRITICISM, AND NOTES. New York: Viking, 1969.
Reprints Scholes's corrected text of D (1968),
relevant selections from JJ's manuscripts, letters, and other writings, and eleven critical
essays on the collection and on individual stories. Includes topics for discussion, an editorial "Introduction to the Criticism Section"
(pp. 297-303), excellent annotations for the
stories (pp. 462-504), the following essays:
J32, J46, J87, J100, J111, J158, J173, J184,
J187, and extracts from B17, B21, C1, F33, and
J4.

J, ii. General Critical Articles or Chapters on DUBLINERS

J14 Atherton, James S. "The Joyce of DUBLINERS." In JAMES
JOYCE TODAY. Ed. Thomas F. Staley. Pp. 28-53. See G75.
General survey of the stories' compositional and
publication history, techniques, and sources.

J15 Baker, James R. "Ibsen, Joyce, and the Living-Dead: A
Study of DUBLINERS." In A JAMES JOYCE MISCELLANY, THIRD
SERIES. Ed. Marvin Magalaner. Pp. 19-32. See G57.
JJ's views of Ibsen and Ibsen's several influ-
ences on D. Reprinted in J1 and J179.

J16 Bates, Herbert E. THE MODERN SHORT STORY: A CRITICAL
SURVEY. New York: Nelson, 1943. Pp. 153-57.
JJ's originality lies in his "power to trans-
mute ordinary life...to render it naturally and
compassionately, objectively and yet with rare
beauty."

J17 Beckson, Karl. "Moore's THE UNTILLED FIELD and Joyce's
DUBLINERS: The Short Story's Intricate Maze." ELT, 15
(1972), 291-304.
Similarities (paralysis theme, labyrinth symbols, integrated structure) and differences
(negation vs. affirmation) between D and Moore's
story collection (1903).

J18   Benstock, Bernard. "Joyce's Rheumatics: The Holy Ghost
       in DUBLINERS." SoR, 14 (1978), 1-15.
           The "Holy Spirit" as a central symbol pattern
           within the stories.

J19   Berkman, Sylvia. KATHERINE MANSFIELD: A CRITICAL STUDY.
       New Haven, Conn.: Yale Univ. Press, 1951. Pp. 159-77 and
       passim.
           Broad and specific parallels between JJ's and
           Mansfield's themes and story techniques.

J20   Carrier, Warren. "DUBLINERS: Joyce's Dantean Vision."
       RENASCENCE, 17 (1965), 211-15.
           Traces of Dante, especially Canto 33 of the IN-
           FERNO, in D and in JJ's synecdochic method.

J21   Chesnutt, Margaret. "Joyce's DUBLINERS: History, Ideology,
       and Social Reality." EIRE, 14, No. 2 (1979), 93-105.
           Useful summary of the "historical and ideologi-
           cal context" of D.

J22   Church, Margaret. "DUBLINERS and Vico." JJQ, 5 (1968),
       150-56.
           Finds a Viconian, four-fold structure in the
           story collection.

J23   Colum, Padraic. "Introduction." In JJ's DUBLINERS. New
       York: Modern Library, 1926. Pp. v-xiii.
           Summarizes JJ's difficulties in getting D pub-
           lished and notes the insight of his views of
           Dubliners.

J24   Cronin, Edward J. "James Joyce's Trilogy and Epilogue:
       'The Sisters,' 'An Encounter,' 'Araby,' and 'The Dead.'"
       RENASCENCE, 31 (1979), 229-48.
           The boys' lessons in language, action, and emo-
           tion, in the opening stories of D, coalesce in
           the final story of the collection.

J25   Curry, Sister Martha. "Sherwood Anderson and James Joyce."
       AMERICAN LITERATURE, 52 (1980), 236-49.
           Discounts theories of D's influence on WINES-
           BURG, OHIO (1919), despite the remarkable sim-
           ilarities between the story collections.

J26   Davis, Joseph K. "The City as Radical Order: James Joyce's
       DUBLINERS." SLitI, 3, No. 2 (1970), 79-96.
           Dublin as microcosm of the "world-city which

has come in this century to dominate, perhaps
to tyrannize over, our lives." See G78.

J27   Delany, Paul. "Joyce's Political Development and the Aesthetic of DUBLINERS." CE, 34 (1972), 256-66.
Argues importance of JJ's social and political
analyses of Dublin's lower middle class.

J28   Engel, Monroe. "DUBLINERS and Erotic Expectation." In
TWENTIETH CENTURY LITERATURE IN RETROSPECT. Ed. Reuben
A. Brower. Cambridge, Mass.: Harvard Univ. Press, 1971.
Pp. 3-26.
Autobiographical elements in D's first three
stories, particularly in the ironic counter-
point between the boys' erotic expectations
and the impossibility of their fulfillment.

J29   French, Marilyn. "Missing Pieces in Joyce's DUBLINERS."
TCL, 24 (1978), 443-72.
Gaps in thinking and "masking language," symp-
tomatic of the Dubliners' blindness, traced
through the stories as JJ's chief theme and
technical approach.

J30   Friedrich, Gerhard. "The Perspective of Joyce's DUBLIN-
ERS." CE, 24 (1965), 421-26.
Continuity and progressive interrelationship
of the stories. Reprinted in J1.

J31   Garrison, Joseph M. "DUBLINERS: Portraits of the Artist
as a Narrator." NOVEL, 8 (1975), 226-40.
Collection read as a chronicle of JJ's developing narrative voice.

J32   Ghiselin, Brewster. "The Unity of Joyce's DUBLINERS."
ACCENT, 16 (1956), 75-88; 196-231.
The unifying symbolic patterns within the collection (e.g., movement, color, liturgy). Reprinted in J1, J3, J6, and J13.

J33   Gibbons, T.H. "DUBLINERS and the Critics." CritQ, 9
(1967), 179-87.
Examines "the tendency toward speculative ana-
logizing, based on Joyce's guessed intentions,"
in symbol-criticism of D.

J34   Gould, Gerald. "New Novels." NEW STATESMAN, 3 (1914),
374-75.
Perceptive, admiring early review. Reprinted
in G25, J3, and J179.

J35 Hart, John Raymond. "Moore on Joyce: The Influence of
     THE UNTILLED FIELD on DUBLINERS." DUBLIN MAGAZINE, 10,
     No. 2 (1973), 61-76.
          Traces of Moore's "stories about Irish life"
          (1903) in the collection. See G26.

J36 Jordan, Richard D. "The Trouble with DUBLINERS." DURHAM
     UNIVERSITY JOURNAL, 39, No. 1 (1977), 35-40.
          Ambiguities and varieties of interpretations
          of the stories are a flaw in the collection,
          caused by the "unresolved conflict" between
          JJ's realism and symbolism.

J37 Keen, William P. "The Rhetoric of Spatial Focus in Joyce's
     DUBLINERS." SSF, 16 (1979), 195-203.
          Spatial qualities and planes of meaning in the
          stories.

J38 Lachtman, Howard. "The Magic-Lantern Business: James
     Joyce's Ecclesiastical Satire in DUBLINERS." JJQ, 7 (1970),
     82-92.
          Finds JJ's views of clerics uniformly negative.

J39 LaValley, Albert J. "'Doublin Their Mumper': Some Thoughts
     on the Symbolist Drama of Joyce's DUBLINERS." In LITERARY
     STUDIES: ESSAYS IN MEMORY OF FRANCIS A. DRUMM. Ed. John H.
     Dorenkamp. Worcester, Mass.: College of the Holy Cross,
     1973. Pp. 172-90.
          Patterns of symbolism within the "realistic
          drama" of D.

J40 Lester, John A. "Joyce, Yeats, and the Short Story." ELT,
     15 (1972), 305-14.
          Finds JJ the better story teller.

J41 Levin, Richard, and Charles Shattuck. "First Flight to
     Ithaca: A New Reading of Joyce's DUBLINERS." ACCENT, 4
     (1944), 75-99.
          Ingenious, if not entirely convincing, explor-
          ation of parallels to the Homeric ODYSSEY in D.
          Reprinted in G30.

J42 Lyons, John B. "Diseases in DUBLINERS: Tokens of Disaf-
     fection." In IRISH RENAISSANCE ANNUAL II. Ed. Zack Bowen.
     Pp. 185-94. See G14.
          Physician's discussion of the relations between
          the characters' illnesses and alcoholism in D,
          and JJ's pervasive paralysis theme.

J43   McGuinness, Arthur E. "The Ambience of Space in Joyce's
      DUBLINERS." SSF, 11 (1974), 343-51.
           Man's "lack of connection with the spaces that
           surround him" defines and illuminates character
           in the collection.

J44   Montgomery, Judith. "The Artist as Silent Dubliner." JJQ,
      6 (1969), 306-20.
           Progressive withdrawal of personality implicit
           in the shift away from first-person narration,
           after the first three stories in the collection.

J45   Murphy, Michael W. "Darkness in DUBLINERS." MFS, 15
      (1969), 97-104.
           Pervasive, unifying darkness symbolism in D.
           See G65.

J46   O'Connor, Frank. "Work in Progress." In THE LONELY VOICE:
      A STUDY OF THE SHORT STORY. Cleveland: World, 1963. Pp.
      113-27.
           JJ's concern for language and form in D and the
           developing complexity of the stories through
           the collection. Reprinted in J6 and J13.

J47   Ostroff, Anthony. "The Moral Vision in DUBLINERS." WEST-
      ERN SPEECH, 20 (1956), 196-209.
           "Taking the line of least resistance," the fail-
           ure to act, or "to *act morally,*" JJ's unifying
           definition of moral paralysis in the collection.

J48   Peterson, Richard F. "Joyce's Use of Time in DUBLINERS."
      BSUF, 14, No. 1 (1973), 43-51.
           Structural and thematic use of chronometric and
           durational time in the stories.

J49   Pound, Ezra. "DUBLINERS and Mr. James Joyce." EGOIST,
      1 (1914), 267.
           Early recognition of JJ's "clear hard prose."
           Reprinted in F123 and G25 (extract).

J50   Russell, John. "James Joyce: DUBLINERS." In STYLE IN
      MODERN BRITISH FICTION: STUDIES IN JOYCE, LAWRENCE, FOR-
      STER, LEWIS, AND GREEN. Baltimore: Johns Hopkins Univ.
      Press, 1978. Pp. 17-42.
           "Lexical and syntactic analysis" of the collec-
           tion, noting JJ's significant use of punctua-
           tion (semicolon and colon especially).

J51   Scholes, Robert. "Further Observations of the Text of
      DUBLINERS." SB, 17 (1964), 107-22.
            Comments on the variations among various proofs
            and published texts of the first fourteen sto-
            ries. Also see J182.

J52   Somerville, Jane. "Money in DUBLINERS." SSF, 12 (1975),
      109-16.
            Symbolic and thematic significance of money and
            the exchange of money in several stories.

J53   Thorn, Eric P. "James Joyce: Early Imitations of Struc-
      tural Unity." COSTERUS, 9 (1973), 229-39.
            Argues necessity of reading D as an integrated
            whole.

J54   Walsh, Ruth M. "That Pervasive Mass--In DUBLINERS and A
      PORTRAIT OF THE ARTIST AS A YOUNG MAN." JJQ, 8 (1971),
      205-20.
            Clarifies JJ's references to the Mass in the
            two books and, again (see M331), discusses "the
            fallacy of trying to establish *exact structural*
            parallels" between JJ's works and religious rit-
            uals.

J55   Walzl, Florence L. "The Life Chronology of DUBLINERS."
      JJQ, 14 (1977), 408-15.
            Clarifies the age-of-characters scheme in JJ's
            original plan for D's structure. Summary ver-
            sion published in G8.

J56   -----. "The Liturgy of the Epiphany Season and the Epiph-
      anies of Joyce." PMLA, 80 (1965), 436-50.
            JJ's use of the liturgical year, Christ's life
            cycle, and the epiphany season for structure
            and symbolism in D. (See subsequent discus-
            sions by Robert Scholes and Walzl, PMLA, 82
            [1967], 152-54). Extract reprinted in K16.

J57   -----. "Pattern of Paralysis in Joyce's DUBLINERS: A
      Study of the Original Framework." CE, 22 (1961), 221-28.
            Progressive use of paralysis symbolism in the
            first fourteen stories.

J58   West, Michael. "George Moore and the Hermeneutics of
      Joyce's DUBLINERS." HARVARD LIBRARY BULLETIN, 26 (1978),
      212-35.
            Intensive exploration of the parallels between

D and Moore's THE UNTILLED FIELD (1903), its
"main literary source."

J59   Wigginton, B. Eliot. "DUBLINERS in Order." JJQ, 7 (1970),
      297-314.
         Describes numerous patterns of relationships
         among the stories in the collection.

J, iii.   Studies of Individual Stories

Since JJ placed great emphasis on the arrangement of the fifteen stories in D and since much criticism since has focused
on the patterns of relationship among the stories as well as
on the architecture of the collection as a whole, this subsection on the criticism of the individual stories follows the
order of the stories *within* D: "The Sisters," "An Encounter,"
"Araby," "Eveline," "After the Race," "Two Gallants," "The
Boarding House," "A Little Cloud," "Counterparts," "Clay," "A
Painful Case," "Ivy Day in the Committee Room," "A Mother,"
"Grace," and "The Dead."

Several of the books and essay collections in sections G and
J above contain story-by-story commentaries. See Bowen (G13),
Hodgart (G40), Peake (G71), Tindall (G80), Baker and Staley
(J1), Beck (J2), Brandabur (J4), Gifford and Seidman (J7),
Hart (J9), and San Juan (J12). Also see, among the articles
in section J, ii above: French (J29), Ghiselin (J32), Levin
and Shattuck (J41), and Wigginton (J59).

"The Sisters"

For additional important commentaries and information on this
story, see the following studies: Adams (G2), Bowen (G13),
Cixous (G21), Goldman (G34), Hodgart (G40), Kenner (G47), Ma-
galaner and Kain (G58), Peake (G71), Tindall (G80), Kaye (H106),
Beck (J2), Brandabur (J4), Gifford and Seidman (J7), San Juan
(J12), Cronin (J24), Engel (J28), French (J29), Ghiselin (J32),
Levin and Shattuck (J41), Scholes (J51), and Wigginton (J59).
Also see U4.

J60   Connolly, Thomas E. "Joyce's 'The Sisters': A Pennyworth
      of Snuff." CE, 27 (1965), 189-95.
         Literal-minded attempt at a "straightforward"
         reading. Reprinted in J1.

J61 Corrington, John W. "'The Sisters.'" In JAMES JOYCE'S
DUBLINERS. Ed. Clive Hart. Pp. 13-25. See J9.
Frustration and dreams of escape in the story.

J62 Fischer [-Seidel], Therese. "From Reliable to Unreliable
Narrator: Rhetorical Changes in Joyce's 'The Sisters.'"
JJQ, 9 (1971), 85-92.
Developing sophistication of JJ's narrative
technique in the story, from its earliest to
its final versions.

J63 Kennedy, Eileen. "'Lying Still': Another Look at 'The
Sisters.'" JJQ, 12 (1975), 362-70.
Priest a false teacher and maleficent influence.

J64 Korninger, Siefried. "Artistic Integration in Joyce's
DUBLINERS." In FESTSCHRIFT PROF. DR. HERBERT KOZIOL. Ed.
Gero Bauer, Franz K. Stanzl, and Franz Zaic. Vienna:
Bramuller, 1973. Pp. 147-68.
Intensive study of the story's style, symbolism,
technique, and theme to determine JJ's princi-
ples of artistic integration for the collection.

J65 Lyons, John B. "Animadversions on Paralysis as a Symbol
in 'The Sisters.'" JJQ, 11 (1974), 257-65.
Attack on over-zealous symbol-hunting in criticism of the story and corrective comments on
its medical backgrounds.

J66 Newell, Kenneth B. "The Sin of Knowledge in Joyce's 'The
Sisters.'" BSUF, 20, No. 3 (1979), 44-53.
New light on the story achieved through clari-
fication of the terms "gnomon" and "simony."

J67 Senn, Fritz. "'He Was Too Scrupulous Always': Joyce's
'The Sisters.'" JJQ, 2 (1965), 66-72.
Finds a suggestive play with language in the
story, characteristic of JJ's later works. See
J10.

J68 Spielberg, Peter. "'The Sisters': No Christ at Bethany."
JJQ, 3 (1966), 192-95.
Eliza and Nannie as Mary and Martha figures.

J69 Staley, Thomas F. "A Beginning: Signification, Story,
and Discourse in Joyce's 'The Sisters.'" GENRE, 12 (1979),
533-49.
Intensive analysis of the story's opening para-

      graph, finding therein the embryo of JJ's art
      (a "radical restatement of the nature of art
      and language").

J70   Walzl, Florence L. "Joyce's 'The Sisters': A Development."
      JJQ, 10 (1973), 375-421.
        Extended study of five states of the text of
        "The Sisters," showing both its transformation
        into a fitting "introduction" to D's themes,
        images, and techniques, and its characters'
        evolution into types.

"An Encounter"

For additional important commentaries and information on this
story, see the following studies: Bowen (G13), Cixous (G21),
Goldman (G34), Hodgart (G40), Magalaner and Kain (G58), Peake
(G71), Tindall (G80), Beck (J2), Brandabur (J4), Gifford and
Seidman (J7), San Juan (J12), Cronin (J24), Engel (J28), French
(J29), Ghiselin (J32), Levin and Shattuck (J41), Scholes (J51),
and Wigginton (J59).

J71   Bluefarb, Sam. "Quest, Initiation and Escape: 'American'
      Themes in James Joyce's 'An Encounter.'" DUBLIN MAGAZINE,
      10, No. 2 (1973), 53-60.
        Possible influence of American adventure lit-
        erature on the story. See G26.

J72   Feshbach, Sidney. "Death in 'An Encounter.'" JJQ, 2 (1965)
      82-89.
        Story describes the "spiritual death" of its
        young-boy narrator. See J10.

J73   Kaye, Julian B. "The Wings of Daedalus: Two Stories in
      DUBLINERS." MFS, 4 (1958), 31-41.
        Symbolic readings of "An Encounter" and "The
        Dead." See G64. Reprinted in J1.

J74   Leatherwood, A.M. "Joyce's Mythic Method: Structure and
      Unity in 'An Encounter.'" SSF, 13 (1976), 71-78.
        Unity of story found in the initiation quest
        and color symbolism (green).

J75   Senn, Fritz. "'An Encounter.'" In JAMES JOYCE'S *DUBLI-*
      NERS. Ed. Clive Hart. Pp. 26-38. See J9.
           Despite the partially successful escape, shades
           of the prison house of Dublin affect the boys
           and the story itself (style and theme).

"Araby"

For additional important commentaries and information on this
story, see the following studies: Bowen (G13), Hodgart (G40),
Magalaner and Kain (G58), Peake (G71), Tindall (G80), Loss
(H131), Beck (J2), Brandabur (J4), Gifford and Seidman (J7),
San Juan (J12), Cronin (J24), Engel (J28), French (J29), Ghiselin (J32), Levin and Shattuck (J41), Scholes (J51), and Wigginton (J59).

J76   apRoberts, Robert P. "'Araby' and the Palimpsest of Crit-
      icism; or, Through a Glass Eye Darkly." AR, 26 (1966-67),
      469-89.
           Attack on symbol-mongering criticism of liter-
           ature generally, of JJ's works especially, of
           "Araby" specifically, and by Harry Stone par-
           ticularly (see J87). Also see J78.

J77   Atherton, James S. "'Araby.'" In JAMES JOYCE'S *DUBLINERS*.
      Ed. Clive Hart. Pp. 39-47. See J9.
           Story's autobiographical elements and precise,
           symbolic style.

J78   Benstock, Bernard. "Arabesques: Third Position of Con-
      cord." JJQ, 5 (1967), 30-39.
           Comments on the interpretive problems in the
           story, epitomized in the controversy between
           apRoberts and Stone (see J76 and J87).

J79   Booth, Wayne C. "Pluralism and Its Rivals." In NOW DON'T
      TRY TO REASON WITH ME. Chicago: Univ. of Chicago Press,
      1970. Pp. 131-49.
           The story's malleability permits numerous val-
           id interpretations.

J80   Brooks, Cleanth, and Robert Penn Warren. "Discussion [of
      'Araby']." In UNDERSTANDING FICTION. Ed. Brooks and War-
      ren. 1943. 3rd ed. Englewood Cliffs, N.J.: Prentice-
      Hall, 1979. Pp. 125-28.
           Story is both an account of "the psychology of

growing up" and "a symbolic reordering of a central conflict in mature experience" (i.e., the
real and the ideal). Reprinted in Jl.

J81   Collins, Ben L. "Joyce's 'Araby' and the 'Extended Sim-
      ile.'" JJQ, 4 (1967), 84-90.
      JJ's use of symbolic suggestion, especially in
      his portrayal of Mangan's sister. Reprinted
      in J6.

J82   JAMES JOYCE QUARTERLY. 18 (1981), 237-99. "THE MURGE
      PROJECT: 'Araby' as Story and Discourse."
      Report of group analysis of the story, in light
      of Seymour Chatman's theories of interpretation
      (from STORY AND DISCOURSE, 1978). Includes a
      summary of findings, four related papers by Jon-
      athan Culler ("The Application of Theory"), Ger-
      ald Prince ("What's the Story in Narratology?"),
      and James J. Sosnowski ("STORY AND DISCOURSE and
      the Practice of Literary Criticism: 'Araby,' A
      Test Case" and "On the Anvil of Theoretical De-
      bate: STORY AND DISCOURSE as Literary Theory"),
      and a concluding comment by Chatman ("Analgo-
      rithm").

J83   Lyons, John O. "James Joyce and Chaucer's Prioress." ELN,
      2 (1964), 127-32.
      Parallels between "Araby" and the "Prioress'
      Tale" as stories of initiation.

J84   Peters, Margot. "The Phonological Structure of James
      Joyce's 'Araby.'" LANGUAGE AND STYLE, 6 (1973), 135-44.
      Thematic and structural significance of "sound
      patterns" in the story.

J85   Rosowski, Susan J. "Joyce's 'Araby' and Imaginative Free-
      dom." RS, 44 (1976), 183-88.
      Boy merely adopts a "new romantic role" at the
      story's end.

J86   Stein, William B. "Joyce's 'Araby': Paradise Lost." PER-
      SPECTIVE, 12 (1962), 215-22.
      Eden myth in the story.

J87   Stone, Harry. "'Araby' and the Writings of James Joyce."
      AR, 25 (1965), 375-410.
      Intensive reading of "Araby" as an autobiograph-
      ical "portrait of the artist as a young boy."
      Extract reprinted in J13. Also see J76 and J78.

"Eveline"

For additional important commentaries and information on this
story, see the following studies: Bowen (G13), Goldman (G34),
Hodgart (G40), Peake (G71), Tindall (G80), Beck (J2), Brandabur
(J4), Gifford and Seidman (J7), San Juan (J12), French (J29),
Ghiselin (J32), Levin and Shattuck (J41), Scholes (J51), and
Wigginton (J59). Also see Connolly (J115).

J88   Chatman, Seymour. "New Ways of Analyzing Narrative Struc-
      ture, with an Example from Joyce's DUBLINERS." LANGUAGE
      AND STYLE, 2 (1969), 3-36.
          Theoretical structuralist analysis of "Eveline."

J89   Dolch, Martin. "'Eveline.'" In INSIGHT II: ANALYSES OF
      MODERN BRITISH LITERATURE. Ed. John V. Hagopian and Dolch.
      Frankfurt, Germany: Hirschgraben, 1964. Pp. 193-200.
          Surveys the multiple conflicts of story. Re-
          printed in J1.

J90   Hart, Clive. "'Eveline.'" In JAMES JOYCE'S *DUBLINERS*.
      Ed. Hart. Pp. 48-52. See J9.
          Eveline's feelings, life, and capacity for love
          all "shallow."

J91   Scholes, Robert. SEMIOTIC APPROACHES TO A FICTIONAL TEXT:
      JOYCE'S "EVELINE." Moscow: Univ. of Idaho, 1976.
          Three structuralist theories of criticism ap-
          plied to JJ's story. (Pamphlet--11 pp.) Re-
          printed in G44 and in Scholes' SEMIOTICS AND
          INTERPRETATION (New Haven, Conn.: Yale Univ.
          Press, 1982).

J92   Solomon, Albert J. "The Background of 'Eveline.'" EIRE,
      6, No. 3 (1971), 23-38.
          Parallels to the story in George Moore's EVE-
          LYN INNES (1898) and its sequel, SISTER TERESA
          (1901).

J93   -----. "The Sound of Music in 'Eveline': A Long Note on
      a Barrel-Organ." COSTERUS, 9 (1973), 187-94.
          Historical note on street-organs and comment
          on George Moore's similar use of the barrel-
          organ image (in CONFESSIONS OF A YOUNG MAN
          [1888]).

J94   Stein, William B.   "The Effects of Eden in Joyce's 'Eve-
      line.'" RENASCENCE, 15 (1963), 124-26.
         Frank a "false redeemer" for the spiritually
         paralyzed Eveline.

J95   Torchiana, Donald T.   "Joyce's 'Eveline' and the Blessed
      Margaret Mary Alacoque." JJQ, 6 (1968), 22-28.
         Appropriateness and significance of JJ's iden-
         tification of Eveline with the (since canon-
         ized) saint.

"After the Race"

For additional important commentaries and information on this
story, see the following studies: Adams (G2), Bowen (G13),
Blayac (in G17a), Hodgart (G40), Peake (G71), Tindall (G80),
Beck (J2), Brandabur (J4), Gifford and Seidman (J7), San Juan
(J12), French (J29), Ghiselin (J32), Levin and Shattuck (J41),
Scholes (J51), and Wigginton (J59).

J96   Bowen, Zack.   "'After the Race.'"   In JAMES JOYCE'S *DUB-
      LINERS*. Ed. Clive Hart. Pp. 53-61. See J9.
         Doyle's self-betrayal through "misguided social
         values."

J97   Torchiana, Donald T.   "Joyce's 'After the Race,' the Races
      of Castlebar, and Dun Laoghaire." EIRE, 6, No. 3 (1971),
      119-28.
         Motifs from Irish history and international pol-
         itics in the story.

"Two Gallants"

For additional important commentaries and information on this
story, see the following studies: Adams (G2), Bowen (G13),
Hodgart (G40), Noon (G69), Peake (G71), Tindall (G80), Beck
(J2), Brandabur (J4), Gifford and Seidman (J7), San Juan (J12),
French (J29), Ghiselin (J32), Levin and Shattuck (J41), Scholes
(J51), and Wigginton (J59).

J98   Boyle, Robert, S.J.   "'Two Gallants' and 'Ivy Day in the

Committee Room.'" JJQ, 1, No. 1 (1963), 3-9.
    Symbolic interpretations, stressing the sto-
    ries' national themes. Reprinted in J6.

J99   Day, Robert Adams. "Joyce's Gnomons, Lenehan, and the
       Persistence of an Image." NOVEL, 14 (1980), 5-19.
           Lenehan, JJ's pseudo-betrayer figure, with
           "sexual overtones," unsuccessful in action
           and incomplete in characterization ("a gno-
           mon") in D and U.

J100   Litz, A. Walton. "'Two Gallants.'" In JAMES JOYCE'S
       DUBLINERS. Ed. Clive Hart. Pp. 62-76. See J9.
           History of story's composition and close read-
           ing of JJ's betrayal theme and ironic tech-
           nique. Reprinted in J13.

J101   Torchiana, Donald T. "Joyce's 'Two Gallants': A Walk
       through the Ascendancy." JJQ, 6 (1968), 115-27.
           JJ's allusions to late-eighteenth-century
           Irish political treacheries.

J102   Walzl, Florence L. "Symbolism in Joyce's 'Two Gallants.'"
       JJQ, 2 (1965), 73-81.
           Story "a study of betrayal, social, political,
           and religious," incorporating significant
           Christian symbolism. See J10.

"The Boarding House"

For additional important commentaries and information on this
story, see the following studies: Bowen (G13), Hodgart (G40),
Peake (G71), Tindall (G80), Beck (J2), Brandabur (J4), Gifford
and Seidman (J7), San Juan (J12), French (J29), Ghiselin (J32),
Levin and Shattuck (J41), Scholes (J51), and Wigginton (J59).

J103   Halper, Nathan. "'The Boarding House.'" In JAMES JOYCE'S
       DUBLINERS. Ed. Clive Hart. Pp. 72-83. See J9.
           Doran a fictional projection of JJ's view of
           himself, had he remained in Dublin. Good ana-
           lysis of the story's ironically vulgar style.

J104   Rosenberg, Bruce A. "The Crucifixion in 'The Boarding
       House.'" SSF, 5 (1967), 44-53.
           Bob Doran a "diminished Jesus...debased and
           trivialized" by the modern world.

"A Little Cloud"

For additional important commentaries and information on this
story, see the following studies: Bowen (G13), Cixous (G21),
Hodgart (G40), Peake (G71), Tindall (G80), Beck (J2), Brandabur (J4), Gifford and Seidman (J7), San Juan (J12), French
(J29), Ghiselin (J32), Levin and Shattuck (J41), Scholes (J51),
and Wigginton (J59).

J105   Boyle, Robert, S.J.   "'A Little Cloud.'"   In JAMES JOYCE'S
       DUBLINERS. Ed. Clive Hart. Pp. 84-92. See J9.
            Story a study of the self-pitying, sterile,
            inartistic soul.

J106   Brodbar, Harold.   "A Religious Allegory: Joyce's 'A Lit-
       tle Cloud.'"   MQ, 2 (1961), 221-27.
            Chandler inprobably viewed as a Christ-figure.

J107   Ruoff, James.   "'A Little Cloud': Joyce's Portrait of
       the Would-Be Artist."   RS, 25 (1957), 256-71.
            The puerile Chandler's arrested development as
            artist. Reprinted in J1.

J108   Short, Clarice.   "Joyce's 'A Little Cloud.'"   MLN, 72
       (1957), 275-78.
            Parallel between Chandler and Byron's prisoner
            of Chillon.

"Counterparts"

For additional important commentaries and information on this
story, see the following studies: Bowen (G13), Cixous (G21),
Hodgart (G40), Peake (G71), Tindall (G80), Beck (J2), Brandabur (J4), Gifford and Seidman (J7), San Juan (J12), French
(J29), Ghiselin (J32), Levin and Shattuck (J41), Scholes (J51),
and Wigginton (J59).

J109   Davis, William V.   "The Loss of Time in 'Counterparts.'"
       JJQ, 10 (1973), 336-39.
            Time symbolism in the story.

J110   Hagopian, John V.   "'Counterparts.'"   In INSIGHT II:
       ANALYSES OF MODERN BRITISH LITERATURE.   Ed. Hagopian

and Martin Dolch. Frankfurt, Germany: Hirschgraben, 1964. Pp. 201-06.
> Story's theme of "wrath." Reprinted in J1.

J111 Scholes, Robert. "'Counterparts.'" In JAMES JOYCE'S *DUBLINERS*. Ed. Clive Hart. Pp. 93-99. See J9.
> JJ's contrapuntal techniques, in the story and in the collection, and his control of the reader's sympathies. Reprinted in J13.

J112 Stein, William B. "'Counterparts': A Swine Song." JJQ, 1, No. 2 (1964), 30-32.
> JJ's use of animal imagery in his portrait of Farrington.

"Clay"

For additional important commentaries and information on this story, see the following studies: Bowen (G13), Cross (G24), Laroque (in G17a), Goldman (G34), Hodgart (G40), Magalaner and Kain (G58), Peake (G71), Tindall (G80), Beck (J2), Brandabur (J4), Gifford and Seidman (J7), San Juan (J12), French (J29), Ghiselin (J32), Levin and Shattuck (J41), Scholes (J51), and Wigginton (J59). Also see U5 and U6.

J113 Booth, Wayne C. "How to Use Aristotle." In NOW DON'T TRY TO REASON WITH ME. Chicago: Univ. of Chicago Press, 1970. Pp. 117-29.
> How to approach JJ's story *"as it is,"* avoiding the "juggling" of "abstractions" that characterizes dialectical criticism.

J114 Carpenter, Richard, and Daniel Leary. "The Witch Maria." JAMES JOYCE REVIEW, 3 (1959), 3-7.
> Explication of JJ's witch symbolism and its significance.

J115 Connolly, Thomas E. "Marriage Divination in Joyce's 'Clay.'" SSF, 3 (1966), 293-99.
> The symbolism of divination games in the story (and Maria's symbolic kinship to Eveline).

J116 Deneau, Daniel P. "Joyce's 'Minute' Maria." JNT, 2 (1972), 26-45.
> Argues against overly ingenious, positive

views of Maria, a pathetic, simple, indecisive character.

J117 Easson, Angus. "Parody as Comment in James Joyce's 'Clay.'" JJQ, 7 (1970), 75-81.
> Maria not as blind as she appears, adopting a "cheerful front" in the face of a mean and small-minded Dublin of which she is, herself, a part.

J118 Glasheen, Adaline. "'Clay.'" In JAMES JOYCE'S *DUBLINERS*. Ed. Clive Hart. Pp. 100-06. See J9.
> Explication, asserting Maria's "scarcely conscious" awareness of her plight.

J119 Kloss, Robert J. "The Function of Forgetting in Joyce's 'Clay.'" HSL, 6 (1974), 167-79.
> Suppressed hostility and sexuality in Maria's character.

J120 Mathews, F.X. "Punchestime: A New Look at 'Clay.'" JJQ, 4 (1967), 102-06.
> Maria both a Punch and a Judy figure.

J121 Nebeker, H.E. "James Joyce's 'Clay': The Well-Wrought Urn." RENASCENCE, 28 (1976), 123-38.
> Manhandles story to show Maria a transcendent figure, symbolic of the Church triumphant.

J122 Noon, William T., S.J. "Joyce's 'Clay': An Interpretation." CE, 17 (1955), 93-95.
> Maria one of the work-a-day saints in honor of which All Saints Day is reserved.

J123 Scholes, Robert. "A Commentary on 'Clay.'" In ELEMENTS OF FICTION. New York: Oxford Univ. Press, 1968. Pp. 66-77.
> Illustrative critique of the story's plot, character, structure, and symbolism.

J124 Staley, Thomas F. "Moral Responsibility in Joyce's 'Clay.'" RENASCENCE, 18 (1966), 124-28.
> The dominance of the "theme of disintegration of human understanding and love" in the story, and in JJ generally.

J125 Walzl, Florence L. "Joyce's 'Clay.'" EXPLICATOR, 20
      (Feb. 1962), Item 46.
            Prominent death symbols in the story. Reprint-
            ed in J6.

J126 Weber, Robert. "'Clay.'" In INSIGHT II: ANALYSES OF MOD-
      ERN BRITISH LITERATURE. Ed. John V. Hagopian and Martin
      Dolch. Frankfurt, Germany: Hirschgraben, 1964. Pp. 206-12.
            Story summary, critique, and study questions.

"A Painful Case"

For additional important commentaries and information on this
story, see the following studies: Bowen (G13), Cixous (G21),
Hodgart (G40), Kenner (G47), Peake (G71), Tindall (G80), Beck
(J2), Brandabur (J4), Gifford and Seidman (J7), Magalaner (J11),
San Juan (J12), French (J29), Ghiselin (J32), Levin and Shat-
tuck (J41), Scholes (J51), and Wigginton (J59).

J127 Connolly, Thomas E. "'A Painful Case.'" In JAMES JOYCE'S
      DUBLINERS. Ed. Clive Hart. Pp. 107-14. See J9.
            Stresses complexity of Duffy's character and
            of his responses to the "frustration of love
            that ends in death."

J128 Corrington, John W. "Isolation as Motif in 'A Painful
      Case.'" JJQ, 3 (1966), 182-91.
            Duffy damned to an isolated, death-in-life (cf.
            Gabriel in "The Dead"). Reprinted in J1.

J129 Delaney, Paul, and Dorothy E. Young. "Turgenev and the
      Genesis of 'A Painful Case.'" MFS, 20 (1974), 217-21.
            Parallels to Turgenev's story "Clara Militch"
            (1882).

J130 Lyons, John O. "The Man in the Macintosh." In A JAMES
      JOYCE MISCELLANY, SECOND SERIES. Ed. Marvin Magalaner.
      Pp. 133-38. See G56.
            Identifies Mr. Duffy as "M'Intosh," the mystery
            man in U. Also see below.

J131 Raleigh, John Henry. "Who Was M'Intosh?" JAMES JOYCE
      REVIEW, 3 (1959), 59-62.
            Suggests that Mr. Duffy is the man in the mack-
            intosh at Glasnevin cemetery, in U. Also see
            above.

J132   Sloan, Barbara L. "The D'Annunzian Narrator in 'A Pain-
       ful Case': Silent, Exiled and Cunning." JJQ, 9 (1971),
       26-36.
              D'Annunzio's "concept of the poet as a super-
              man" influences the story's narrator, central
              characters, and author.

J133   Voelker, Joseph C. "'He Lumped the Emancipates Together':
       More Analogues for Joyce's Mr. Duffy." JJQ, 18 (1980),
       23-34.
              Finds Yeats's Owen Aherne and Joachim of Flora
              two additional prototypes for Duffy's character.

J134   West, Michael, and William Hendricks. "The Genesis and
       Significance of Joyce's Irony in 'A Painful Case.'" ELH,
       44 (1977), 701-27.
              Duffy's false epiphany and the story's ironic
              ending strongly influenced by George Moore's
              "John Norton" (in CELIBATES [1895]).

J135   Wright, Charles D. "Melancholy Duffy and Sanguine Sinico:
       Humors in 'A Painful Case.'" JJQ, 3 (1966), 171-81.
              JJ's "almost clinical" analysis of Duffy, in
              terms of the medieval theory of the humors.

J136   Zlotnik, Joan. "Influence or Coincidence: A Comparative
       Study of 'The Beast in the Jungle' and 'A Painful Case.'"
       CLQ, 11 (1975), 132-35.
              Argues direct influence of James's story (1903),
              on JJ's.

"Ivy Day in the Committee Room"

For additional important commentaries and information on this
story, see the following studies: Adams (G2), Bowen (G13),
Maguin (in G17a), Cixous (G21), Hodgart (G40), Magalaner and
Kain (G58), Peake (G71), Tindall (G80), Daiches (H45), Glasheen
(H76), O'Connor (H166), Beck (J2), Brandabur (J4), Gifford and
Seidman (J7), San Juan (J12), French (J29), Ghiselin (J32),
Levin and Shattuck (J41), Scholes (J51), and Wigginton (J59).

J137   Blotner, Joseph L. "'Ivy Day in the Committee Room': Death
       without Resurrection." PERSPECTIVE, 9 (1957), 210-17.
              Story's ironic allusions to the Last Supper and
              the Pentecost, with Parnell as Christ. Reprint-
              ed in J1.

J138 Boyle, Robert, S.J. "'Two Gallants' and 'Ivy Day in t.
Committee Room.'" JJQ, 1, No. 1 (1963), 3-9.
See J98.

J139 Hodgart, Matthew J.C. "'Ivy Day in the Committee Room.'"
In JAMES JOYCE'S *DUBLINERS*. Ed. Clive Hart. Pp. 115-21.
See J9.
> Surveys the history of the story's composition
> and clarifies its political and archetypal back-
> grounds.

J140 Ormsby, Frank, and John Cronin. "'A Very Fine Piece of
Writing': 'Ivy Day in the Committee Room.'" EIRE, 7, No.
1 (1972), 84-94.
> Story's dispassionate surface and apparent in-
> consequentiality mask its intensity.

J141 Stern, Frederick C. "'Parnell is Dead': 'Ivy Day in the
Committee Room.'" JJQ, 10 (1973), 228-39.
> Historical, political, and symbolic signifi-
> cances of Parnell for the story.

"A Mother"

For additional important commentaries and information on this
story, see the following studies: Bowen (G13), Hodgart (G40),
Peake (G71), Tindall (G80), Beck (J2), Brandabur (J4), Gifford
and Seidman (J7), San Juan (J12), French (J29), Ghiselin (J32),
Levin and Shattuck (J41), Scholes (J51), and Wigginton (J59).

J142 Hayman, David. "'A Mother.'" In JAMES JOYCE'S *DUBLINERS*.
Ed. Clive Hart. Pp. 122-33. See J9.
> Story a "brutally ironic" indictment both of
> provincial life and of the dominant female
> character JJ feared and despised.

J143 O'Neill, Michael J. "Joyce's Use of Memory in 'A Mother.'"
MLN, 74 (1959), 226-30.
> JJ's adaptation and transposition of his own
> concert experiences in the story.

"Grace"

For additional important commentaries and information on this
story, see the following studies: S. Joyce (F80), Bowen (G13),
Cixous (G21), Hodgart (G40), Kenner (G48), Knuth (G49), Peake
(G71), Tindall (G80), Kaye (H106), Beck (J2), Brandabur (J4),
Gifford and Seidman (J7), San Juan (J12), French (J29), Ghiselin (J32), Levin and Shattuck (J41), Scholes (J51), and Wigginton (J59). Also see U7.

J144   Baker, Joseph E. "The Trinity in Joyce's 'Grace.'" JJQ,
        2 (1965), 299-303.
                Associates Power, Cunningham, and McCoy with
                the trinity.

J145   Boyle, Robert, S.J. "Swiftian Allegory and Dantean Par-
        ody in Joyce's 'Grace.'" JJQ, 7 (1969), 11-21.
                Clarifies story's parodies of Christian sectar-
                ianism and offers an allegorical reading.

J146   Cunningham, Frank R. "Joyce's 'Grace': Gracelessness in
        a Lost Paradise." JJQ, 6 (1969), 219-23.
                Argues the Dubliners' lack of grace is presented
                by JJ more as an "emotional and cultural dearth"
                than a "moral deficiency."

J147   Jackson, Robert S. "A Parabolic Reading of James Joyce's
        'Grace.'" MLN, 76 (1961), 719-24.
                Appropriateness of the parable of the "unjust
                steward," quoted as the text for Fr. Purdon's
                sermon, for interpreting the story.

J148   Kain, Richard M. "'Grace.'" In JAMES JOYCE'S DUBLINERS.
        Ed. Clive Hart. Pp. 134-52. See J9.
                Fine analysis of the story's comedy, content,
                and style.

J149   Kauvar, Elaine M. "Swift's Clothing Philosophy in A TALE
        OF A TUB and Joyce's 'Grace.'" JJQ, 5 (1968), 162-65.
                JJ's clothing imagery influenced by Swift.

J150   Moseley, Virginia. "The 'Coincidence' of 'Contraries' in
        'Grace.'" JJQ, 6 (1968), 3-21.
                Reads story as if it were FW.

J151   Newman, Francis X. "The Land of Ooze: Joyce's 'Grace'
        and THE BOOK OF JOB." SSF, 4 (1966), 70-79.
                Actual source for story's structure "and much

of its narrative" THE BOOK OF JOB (rather than
Dante's COMMEDIA).

J152 Niemeyer, Carl. "'Grace' and Joyce's Method of Parody."
CE, 27 (1965), 196-201.
JJ's manipulation of the story's parallels
with Dante. Reprinted in J1.

J153 Senn, Fritz. "A Rhetorical Account of James Joyce's
'Grace.'" MODERNA SPRAK, 74 (1980), 121-28.
Not seen.

"The Dead"

For additional important commentaries and information on this
story, see the following studies: Ellmann (F33), Adams (G2),
Benstock (G10), Bowen (G13), Brivic (G16), Cixous (G21), CRANE
BAG (G23), Cross (G24), Goldberg (G31), Goldman (G33), Hodgart
(G40), Kenner (G47), Levin (G52), Magalaner and Kain (G58),
Moseley (G67), Noon (G69), O'Brien (G70), Peake (G71), Tindall
(G80), Daiches (H45), Kaye (H106), More (H153), O'Connor (H166),
Tindall (H219), Beck (J2), Brandabur (J4), Brown (J5), Gifford
and Seidman (J7), San Juan (J12), Baker (J15), Cronin (J24),
French (J29), Ghiselin (J32), Levin and Shattuck (J41), and
Wigginton (J59). Also see Corrington (J128).

J154 Benstock, Bernard. "'The Dead.'" In JAMES JOYCE'S *DUB-
LINERS*. Ed. Clive Hart. Pp. 153-69. See J9.
Consolidating discussion of symbols, techniques,
and interpretive questions in the story.

J155 Bierman, Robert. "Structural Elements in 'The Dead.'"
JJQ, 4 (1966), 42-45.
Ironic juxtaposition of motifs JJ's "structural
strategy" in the story.

J156 Bogorad, Samuel N. "Gabriel Conroy as 'Whited Sepulchre':
Prefiguring Imagery in 'The Dead.'" BSUF, 14, No. 1
(1973), 52-58.
Images of death, rigidity (paralysis), and en-
tombment (hypocrisy) in the story.

J157 Boyd, John D., and Ruth A. Boyd. "The Love Triangle in
Joyce's 'The Dead.'" UTQ, 42 (1973), 202-17.
Distortions created by taking Gabriel's limited,
but very human vision as the story's vision.

J158   Burke, Kenneth. "Three Definitions." KR, 13 (1951),
        173-92.
                Rhetorical strategies in fiction (includes
                "The Dead" and PAYM). Reprinted in J13, J179,
                and K1.

J159   Chapple, J.A.V. DOCUMENTARY AND IMAGINATIVE LITERATURE,
        1880-1920. New York: Barnes and Noble, 1970. Pp. 353-64.
                JJ's sense of political and moral tragedy in
                "The Dead" and PAYM related to the contempo-
                rary vision of society in decline.

J160   Cox, Roger L. "Johnny the Horse in Joyce's 'The Dead.'"
        JJQ, 4 (1966), 36-41.
                Gabriel's "ideal aloofness from human life"
                paralleled with the horse's subservience to a
                monument.

J161   Deane, Paul. "Motion Picture Techniques in James Joyce's
        'The Dead.'" JJQ, 6 (1969), 231-36.
                Film-style analysis of the scenic and visual
                qualities of "The Dead."

J162   Eggers, Tilly. "What Is a Woman...a Symbol of?" JJQ, 18
        (1981), 379-95.
                "The Dead" shows the maturation of JJ's atti-
                tudes toward women in his displacement of the
                virgin-ideal to the unreliable perspective of
                Gabriel.

J163   Foster, John W. "Passage Through 'The Dead.'" CRITICISM,
        15 (1973), 91-108.
                Gabriel's transcendent recognition of death-
                in-life and life-in-death.

J164   Friedrich, Gerhard. "Bret Harte as a Source for James
        Joyce's 'The Dead.'" PQ, 33 (1954), 442-44.
                Sources for names and snow symbolism in Harte's
                GABRIEL CONROY (1876).

J165   Gandolfo, Anita. "A Portrait of the Artist as Critic:
        Joyce, Moore, and the Background of 'The Dead.'" ELT, 22
        (1979), 239-50.
                JJ's admiration for Moore's VAIN FORTUNE (1891)
                and resemblances between the novel and JJ's
                story.

J166 Geckle, George L. "The Dead Lass of Aughrim." EIRE, 9,
No. 3 (1974), 86-96.
Appropriateness of JJ's allusion to the Irish
ballad, sung by D'Arcy in the story.

J167 Going, William T. "Joyce's Gabriel Conroy and Robert
Browning: The Cult of 'Broad Cloth.'" PLL, 13 (1977),
202-07.
Speculates on the sources of Gabriel's unused
Browning quote, and their appropriateness.

J168 Handy, William J. "Joyce's 'The Dead.'" In MODERN FIC-
TION: A FORMALIST APPROACH. Carbondale: Southern Illinois
Univ. Press, 1971. Pp. 29-61.
Theoretical problems posed by the criticism of
JJ's works, illustrated in interpreting "The
Dead." Originally published in G85.

J169 Hedberg, Johannes, ed. JAMES JOYCE: "THE DEAD." 2 vols.
Stockholm: Almqvist and Wiksell, 1968.
Introduction, text, and textual companion, intended primarily for non English-speaking students.

J170 Kaye, Julian B. "The Wings of Daedalus: Two Stories in
DUBLINERS." MFS, 4 (1958), 31-41.
See J73.

J171 Kelleher, John V. "Irish History and Mythology in James
Joyce's 'The Dead.'" REVIEW OF POLITICS, 27 (1965), 414-
33.
Comments on archetypal Irish figures (e.g.,
Conaire), in the story's background.

J172 Knox, George. "Michael Furey: Symbol-Name in Joyce's 'The
Dead.'" WHR, 13 (1959), 221-22.
Note on JJ's name symbolism. Reprinted in J179.

J173 Loomis, C.C. "Structure and Sympathy in Joyce's 'The
Dead.'" PMLA, 75 (1960), 149-51.
JJ's manipulation of the reader's sympathy and
detachment. Reprinted in J6, J13, and J179.

J174 Ludwig, Jack Barry. "James Joyce's DUBLINERS." In STO-
RIES: BRITISH AND AMERICAN. Ed. Ludwig and Richard Poir-
ier. Boston: Houghton Mifflin, 1953. Pp. 384-91.
Symbols in the collection, chiefly illustrated

by an analysis of snow as a death symbol in
"The Dead." Reprinted in J1.

J175 Lytle, Andrew. "A Reading of Joyce's 'The Dead.'" SR,
77 (1969), 193-216.
    Explication, tracing various Christian arche-
    types in the story. More appreciation than
    insight.

J176 MacDonagh, Donagh. "'The Lass of Aughrim' or the Betrayal
of James Joyce." In THE CELTIC MASTER. Ed. Maurice Harmon. Pp. 17-25. See G39.
    JJ's attraction to ballad themes of betrayal
    seen in story.

J177 MacNicholas, John. "Comic Design in Joyce's 'The Dead.'"
MODERN BRITISH LITERATURE, 1 (1976), 56-65.
    Story's "basic movement" and conclusion comic.

J178 Miller, Milton. "Definition by Comparison: Chaucer, Lawrence, and Joyce." EIC, 3 (1953), 369-81.
    Shared vitalism of Lawrence and Chaucer; the
    shared sense of the past in JJ and Chaucer
    (Lawrence's "The Man Who Died" and "The Dead").

J179 Moynihan, William T., ed. JOYCE'S "THE DEAD." Boston:
Allyn and Bacon, 1965.
    Collects the story's text, a related letter
    and a poem by JJ, Ellmann's "chronology" of
    JJ's life (from THE LETTERS, vol. 1; see C1),
    twelve biographical and critical essays (all
    but one previously published), with the edi-
    tor's suggestions for discussion and further
    study. Includes J15, J34, J172, J173, J180, and ex-
    tracts from F33, F82, G69, G80, H166, J4, and
    J158.

J180 O'Hehir, Brendan. "Structural Symbol in Joyce's 'The
Dead.'" TCL, 3 (1957), 3-13.
    Story as three-act, tragic morality play. Re-
    printed above.

J181 Schmidt, Hugo. "Hauptmann's MICHAEL KRAMER and Joyce's
'The Dead.'" PMLA, 80 (1965), 141-42.
    Theme of spiritual death in the two works (MICH-
    AEL KRAMER [1900] was translated by JJ in 1901
    [manuscript location unknown]).

J182 Scholes, Robert. "Some Observations of the Text of DUB-
LINERS: 'The Dead.'" SB, 15 (1962), 191-205.
Variations among the various proofs and published texts of the story; by the editor of
the textual edition (see J13). Also see J51.

J183 Smith, Thomas F. "Color and Light in 'The Dead.'" JJQ,
2 (1965), 304-09.
Color and light imagery in "The Dead" associated with its snow symbolism.

J184 Tate, Allen. THE HOUSE OF FICTION. Ed. Caroline Gordon
and Allen Tate. New York: Scribner's, 1950. Pp. 279-82.
JJ's synthesis of naturalistic detail and symbolic meaning in "The Dead." Reprinted in J13
and in Tate's MEMOIRS AND OPINIONS, 1926-1974
(Chicago: Swallow, 1975), pp. 164-69.

J185 Torchiana, Donald T. "The Ending of 'The Dead': I Follow
Saint Patrick." JJQ, 18 (1981), 123-32.
Speculations on Gabriel's Browning quote and
his ironic associations with St. Patrick.

J186 Trilling, Lionel. "Commentary." In THE EXPERIENCE OF
LITERATURE. Ed. Trilling. New York: Holt, 1967. Pp. 652-
55.
The "subtlety and diversity" of JJ's literary
techniques. Reprinted in J1.

J187 Walzl, Florence L. "Gabriel and Michael: The Conclusion
of 'The Dead.'" JJQ, 4 (1966), 17-31.
The intentional doubleness of JJ's symbolism
throughout "The Dead" encourages two logical,
yet directly contradictory interpretations.
Reprinted in J13.

K. STUDIES OF *A PORTRAIT OF THE ARTIST AS A YOUNG MAN* (1916)

The following section is subdivided into two parts: i. Books
and Essay Collections on PAYM; and ii. General Critical Articles,
or Chapters on PAYM.

For facsimiles of JJ's surviving notes, early manuscript mate-
rials, and typescripts for PAYM, see vols. 7-10 of THE JAMES
JOYCE ARCHIVE (B10). For a concordance to PAYM, see Hancock
(D5).

For biographical backgrounds to PAYM, see, in section F above,
Byrne (F15), Corcoran (F20), Curran (F24), Ellmann (F33), Henchy
(F61), J.S. Joyce (F77), S. Joyce (F78, F80), Kain (F83), F.S.L.
Lyons (F94), J.B. Lyons (F95), Magee (F102), Nolan (F110), Pink-
er (F121), Pound (F123), Rogers (F133), Sheehy (F137), and Sul-
livan (F146).

For additional critical commentaries and information on PAYM,
see the following books, in section G above: Adams (G2), Ben-
stock (G10), Benstock and Benstock (G11), Bolt (G12), Bowen
(G13), Boyle (G15), Brivic (G16), Burgess (G17), CAHIERS VIC-
TORIENS (G17a), Chatterjee (G20), Cixous (G21), Cope (G22),
Cross (G24), Eruvbetine (G28), Goldberg (G31), Golding (G32),
Goldman (G33, G34), Gorman (G36), Grose (G37), Gross (G38),
Hodgart (G40), Hodgart and Worthington (G41), JAMES JOYCE QUAR-
TERLY (G44), Jones (G46), Kenner (G47, G48), Knuth (G49), Kron-
egger (G51), Levin (G52), Litz (G53), MacCabe (G54), Magalaner
and Kain (G58), Majault (G59), Morse (G66), Moseley (G67), Mu-
rillo (G68), Noon (G69), O'Brien (G70), Peake (G71), Ryf (G72),
Smidt (G74), Stewart (G76), Strong (G77), Tindall (G79, G80),
Tysdahl (G82); the following critical articles, in section H
above: Aronson (H7), Beja (H14), Blissett (H20), Boyle (H25),
Chayes (H32), Coveny (H41), Daiches (H45), Friedman (H64), Frierson (H65), Garrett (H70), Glasheen (H76), Goodheart (H79), Hoffman (H92, H93), Honig (H94), Kaye (H106), Kestner (H112), Korg
(H120), Kumar (H121), Loss (H130, H132), Magalaner (H143), Mark-
ovic (H144), More (H153), Morse (H155), O'Connor (H166), Savage
(H184), Seward (H195), Thornton (H217), Tindall (H219), Vickery
(H222), Von Phul (H224), Watson (H228), White (H233), Woolf

(H238); and the following studies, entered in other sections of this bibliography: Brandabur (J4), Magalaner (J11), Goldberg (M22), Litz (M38), Prescott (M50), Reynolds (M52), Schoonbroodt (M54), Schutte (M55), Shechner (M57), Roberts (M266), Von Phul (N215), Jackson (P4), and Tobin (P33).

Note: Several studies of JJ's aesthetics and of STEPHEN HERO, the fragmentary early version of PAYM, rely principally on PAYM for their illustration. See, among the general commentaries in section H above, Baker (H8), Beebe (H11), Beja (H13), Block (H21), Boyle (H25), Bredin (H26), Connolly (H38), Fleming (H59), Hope (H95), MacGregor (H138), McLuhan (H140), Mason (H145), Morin (H154), Scholes (H186); and among the commentaries on JJ's miscellaneous writings, in section P below, Aubert (P1), Sorensen (P5), Connolly (P10), Farrell (P11), Scholes (P22), and Spencer (P28).

For foreign-language studies of PAYM, see section V. See items V2 and V5, particularly, for international bibliographies of criticism on PAYM.

K, i. Books and Essay Collections on A PORTRAIT OF THE ARTIST AS A YOUNG MAN

Also see V1 through V5, and the appendix.

K1   Anderson, Chester G., ed. *A PORTRAIT OF THE ARTIST AS A YOUNG MAN:* TEXT, CRITICISM, AND NOTES. New York: Viking, 1968.
       Reprints Anderson's corrected text of the novel (1964--see K25), a number of selections from "related texts" by JJ (e.g., his "Epiphanies," and extracts from STEPHEN HERO, U, and FW), several early reviews and comments, and ten major critical essays on PAYM. Includes Anderson's "Introduction" to the problem of esthetic distance in PAYM (pp. 446-54), other brief editorial notes, excellent, detailed annotations for the novel (pp. 481-550), topics for discussion, selected bibliography by Kevin Sullivan (from F146), the following essays: H32, H166, K35, K64, K119, K131, K146, and extracts from B21, F33, F123, G47, G52, H219, J158, and K30.

K2   Beja, Morris, ed. JAMES JOYCE: *DUBLINERS* AND *A PORTRAIT*
     OF THE ARTIST AS A YOUNG MAN: A CASEBOOK. London: Macmil-
     lan, 1973.
          See J3.

K3   Brown, Homer O. JAMES JOYCE'S EARLY FICTION: THE BIOGRAPHY
     OF A FORM. Cleveland, Ohio: The Press of Case Western Re-
     serve Univ., 1972.
          See J5.

K4   Campbell, John W. *A PORTRAIT OF THE ARTIST AS A YOUNG MAN:*
     AN APPRECIATION. Sydney: Sydney Univ. Literary Society,
     1933.
          Slight lecture on PAYM. (Pamphlet--14 pp.)

K5   Collingwood, Frank, ed. *PORTRAIT:* NOTES. Toronto: Coles
     Notes, 1970.
          Gathers eight important, previously published es-
          says, together with the editor's extended bio-
          graphical and critical "Introduction" (pp. 5-48).
          Includes K24, K37, K86, K103, and extracts from
          G58, H64, H219, and M50.

K6   Connolly, Thomas E., ed. JOYCE'S *PORTRAIT:* CRITICISMS AND
     CRITIQUES. New York: Appleton-Century-Crofts, 1962.
          Good casebook. Collects twenty essays on PAYM
          (all but one previously published), grouped as
          "general studies," "special studies," and com-
          mentaries on the "aesthetic theory," together
          with "problems for study and discussion" and Con-
          nolly's "Introduction" (pp. 1-6), a general crit-
          ical overview of PAYM. Includes H11, H21, H32,
          H38, H95, H138, H140, K24, K68, K82, K123, K134,
          K141, K143, and extracts from F33, G47, G52, G66,
          H195, and M50.

K7   Epstein, Edmund L. THE ORDEAL OF STEPHEN DEDALUS: THE CON-
     FLICT OF THE GENERATIONS IN JAMES JOYCE'S *A PORTRAIT OF THE*
     ARTIST AS A YOUNG MAN. Carbondale: Southern Illinois Univ.
     Press, 1971.
          Detailed, chapter-by-chapter analysis of PAYM.
          Finding all JJ's "lifework as a piece" and the
          dominant pattern therein the tensions of growth
          (sonhood), maturation, and achievement of father-
          hood within the family, Epstein traces JJ's pre-
          dominantly naturalistic treatment of the "real
          and symbolic father-son relationships" in PAYM,

with frequent references to the theme's presen-
tation in "'fable' form" in FW. He concludes
by examining the Nighttown chapter of U ("Circe"),
the "natural climax to the double development
of the artist and the son to fatherhood," arguing that Stephen successfully avoids regressive
sonhood to Bloom. Competent, unexciting criticism.

K8   Feehan, Joseph, ed. DEDALUS ON CRETE: ESSAYS ON THE IMPLI-
     CATIONS OF JOYCE'S *PORTRAIT*. Los Angeles: Saint Thomas More
     Guild, Immaculate Heart College, 1957.
          Four slight lecture papers on aspects of PAYM,
          plus two unconnected essays and the editor's
          brief "Introduction" (pp. 7-10). Includes K22,
          K57, K109, and K124.

K9   Gifford, Don, and Robert J. Seidman. NOTES FOR JOYCE:
     DUBLINERS AND *A PORTRAIT OF THE ARTIST AS A YOUNG MAN*.
     New York: Dutton, 1967.
          See J7.

K10 Halper, Nathan. THE EARLY JAMES JOYCE. New York: Columbia
     Univ. Press, 1973.
          See J8.

K11 Hanson, Christopher. *A PORTRAIT OF THE ARTIST AS A YOUNG
     MAN*. Oxford: Blackwell, 1969.
          Introduction for students, examining with skill
          several fundamental critical problems in the
          interpretation of PAYM. Sections on JJ's "in-
          tentions" and on "significant form," motifs and
          parallels, epiphany, structure, and themes in
          PAYM.

K12 JAMES JOYCE QUARTERLY. 4 (1967), 251-346. "New Perspec-
     tives on the PORTRAIT."
          Contains a prefatory note by the issue's guest
          editor, Richard M. Kain, three commentaries on
          PAYM's biographical backgrounds by George A.
          Little ("James Joyce and Little's Death"), Eoin
          O'Mahony (F116), and Harry J. Pollock ("The Girl
          Joyce did not Marry"), and ten critical essays
          and notes on the novel by Eugene R. August (K28),
          Brian Dibble (K51), Sidney Feshbach (K59), Donald
          J. Foran ("A Mirror Held up to Stephen"), Thomas
          W. Grayson (K72), Marvin Magalaner ("Reflections

on A PORTRAIT OF THE ARTIST"), James Naremore
(K108), Francis X. Newman ("A Source for the
Name 'Dedalus'?"), F. Parvin Sharpless (K133),
and Thomas Zaniello ("The Epiphany and the Ob-
ject-Image Distinction").

K13 Magalaner, Marvin, ed. CRITICAL REVIEWS OF *A PORTRAIT OF
THE ARTIST AS A YOUNG MAN*. New York: Selected Academic
Readings, 1965.
Five previously published essays on PAYM, with
Magalaner's brief "Introduction" (pp. i-iii).
Includes K24, K86, and extracts from G52, G58,
and G72.

K14 Morris, William E., and Clifford A. Nault, eds. PORTRAITS
OF AN ARTIST: A CASEBOOK ON JAMES JOYCE'S *A PORTRAIT OF THE
ARTIST AS A YOUNG MAN*. New York: Odyssey, 1962.
Excellent collection of thirty-six previously
published biographical and critical essays and
extracts, concerning JJ and PAYM, arranged under
several headings: "preliminary considerations,"
"impact," general "readings," "art and autobiography," "esthetic theory," and assorted "considerations." Includes various extracts from JJ's
prose, editorial suggestions for study and writing, a useful checklist of studies, the following essays: H8, H32, H59, H145, K24, K37, K64,
K86, K87, K123, K143, and extracts from B17, B21,
C1, F33, F146, G46, G47, G52, G58, G69, H64,
H121, H219, K141, M50, and P28.

K15 Scholes, Robert, and Richard M. Kain, eds. THE WORKSHOP
OF DAEDALUS: JAMES JOYCE AND THE RAW MATERIALS FOR *A POR-
TRAIT OF THE ARTIST AS A YOUNG MAN*. Evanston, Ill.: Northwestern Univ. Press, 1965.
Compilation of early manuscript materials for and
drafts of PAYM (see B17), biographical backgrounds
for the novel (see F136), and esthetic backgrounds
(e.g., extracts from Aquinas, Shelley, Pater,
Yeats, and other aestheticians and poets--pp. 241-
81).

K16 Schutte, William M., ed. TWENTIETH CENTURY INTERPRETATION
OF *A PORTRAIT OF THE ARTIST AS A YOUNG MAN*. Englewood
Cliffs, N.J.: Prentice-Hall, 1968.
Reprints nine previously published critical es-
says and eight brief "View Points" on PAYM, with

Schutte's biographical and critical "Introduction" (pp. 1-14). Includes K35, K96, K133, and extracts from F33, G47, G52, G76, H32, H195, J56, K34, K108, K141, K143, M22, and M50.

K17 Smith, John Bristow. IMAGERY AND THE MIND OF STEPHEN DEDALUS: A COMPUTER-ASSISTED STUDY OF JOYCE'S *A PORTRAIT OF THE ARTIST AS A YOUNG MAN*. Lewisburg, Pa.: Bucknell Univ. Press, 1980.

Attempts to show that "the dynamic patterns of associations among images on the page reflect the developing structure of Stephen's mind," in PAYM, employing computer assistance to confirm, through numerical data and distributions, what the reasonably sensitive reader already knows. A useful example of computer uses in the humanities, perhaps, but a marginal contribution to JJ studies at best.

K18 Staley, Thomas F. A CRITICAL STUDY GUIDE TO JOYCE'S *A PORTRAIT OF THE ARTIST AS A YOUNG MAN*. Totowa, N.J.: Littlefield, Adams, 1968.

Excellent summary and critique of PAYM, with background information. Far superior to the hack-work cribs usually published in such series.

K19 Staley, Thomas F., and Bernard Benstock, eds. APPROACHES TO JOYCE'S *PORTRAIT*: TEN ESSAYS. Pittsburgh: Univ. of Pittsburgh Press, 1976.

Nine original, commissioned essays, and one reprinted article, on various aspects of PAYM, from a variety of perspectives. Includes K23, K32, K46, K62, K84, K88, K103, K107, K112, and K137.

K20 Sucksmith, Harvey P. JAMES JOYCE: *A PORTRAIT OF THE ARTIST AS A YOUNG MAN*. London: Arnold, 1973.

Superior introduction for students, covering general topics such as theme, structure, characterization, viewpoint, myth and symbol, and style, with conciseness, insight, and sensitivity.

K, ii. General Critical Articles or Chapters on A PORTRAIT
OF THE ARTIST AS A YOUNG MAN.

K21 Adams, Robert M. "The Operatic Novel: Joyce and D'Annun-
     zio." In NEW LOOKS AT ITALIAN OPERA: ESSAYS IN HONOR OF
     DONALD GROUT. Ed. William W. Austin. Ithaca, N.Y.: Cor-
     nell Univ. Press, 1968. Pp. 260-81.
          JJ's nonconsecutive plot and imitative prose
          style indebted to D'Annunzio's programme for
          the "operatic" novel.

K22 Aloyse, Sister M. "The Novelist as Popularizer: Joyce and
     'Psychological' Fiction." In DEDALUS ON CRETE. Ed. Joseph
     Feehan. Pp. 31-43. See K8.
          To the professional psychologist, PAYM clearly
          and properly more art than psychology.

K23 Anderson, Chester G. "Baby Tuckoo: Joyce's 'Features of
     Infancy.'" In APPROACHES TO JOYCE'S *PORTRAIT*. Ed. Thomas
     F. Staley. Pp. 135-69. See K19.
          Infantile sources of Joyce-Stephen's various in-
          tense neuroses revealed in PAYM's opening pages.

K24 -----. "The Sacrificial Butter." ACCENT, 12 (1952), 3-13.
          Symbolic patterns of "the poet as God" and the
          "betrayal-crucifixion" in PAYM, chapter 5. Re-
          printed in K5, K6, K13, and K14.

K25 -----. "The Text of James Joyce's A PORTRAIT OF THE ART-
     IST AS A YOUNG MAN." NEUPHILOLOGISCHE MITTEILUNGEN, 65
     (1964), 160-200.
          Full description of the novel's various pro-
          gressively degenerating texts, from manuscript
          through several early editions. (Note: for
          reasons beyond Anderson's control only some of
          the necessary changes were made in his "textual"
          edition of PAYM, more properly called a "cor-
          rected" edition; see K1).

K26 Andreach, Robert J. "James Joyce." In STUDIES IN STRUC-
     TURE: THE STAGES OF THE SPIRITUAL LIFE OF FOUR MODERN AU-
     THORS. New York: Fordham Univ. Press, 1964. Pp. 40-71.
          Catholic view of PAYM's structure as an inver-
          sion of the five stages of the spiritual life
          (cf. Dante).

K27 Atherton, James S. "Introduction"; "Notes." In JJ's A
     PORTRAIT OF THE ARTIST AS A YOUNG MAN. London: Heinemann,

1964. Pp. ix-xxii; 239-58.
> Biographical backgrounds, general critical com-
> ments on JJ's fictional techniques, and useful
> factual annotations, though less extensive than
> Anderson's (see K1).

K28   August, Eugene R. "Father Arnall's Use of Scripture in
A PORTRAIT." JJQ, 4 (1967), 275-79.
> Irony in Fr. Arnall's choice of texts and in
> his several mistaken comments on them in his
> "hell-fire" sermons. See K12.

K29   Bates, Ronald. "The Correspondence of Birds to Things of
the Intellect." JJQ, 2 (1965), 281-90.
> JJ's bird symbolism a "major element" in PAYM's
> structure.

K30   Beebe, Maurice. "James Joyce: The Return from Exile." In
IVORY TOWERS AND SACRED FOUNTS: THE ARTIST AS HERO IN FIC-
TION FROM GOETHE TO JOYCE. New York: New York Univ. Press,
1964. Pp. 260-95.
> Conflict between art and life in PAYM, and Ste-
> phen's ambivalent dedication to both, intensi-
> fied on the realistic plane and symbolically re-
> solved in U. Excellent comments on JJ's work
> in the *Künstlerroman* tradition. Extract origi-
> nally published in G56 and reprinted in K1.

K31   -----. "The PORTRAIT as Portrait: Joyce and Impression-
ism." In IRISH RENAISSANCE ANNUAL I. Ed. Zack Bowen.
Newark: Univ. of Delaware Press, 1980. Pp. 13-31.
> Relationships between Impressionism in the vis-
> ual arts and the style, theme, form, and aesthe-
> tic theory in PAYM.

K32   Benstock, Bernard. "A Light from Some Other World: Sym-
bolic Structure in A PORTRAIT OF THE ARTIST." In APPROACHES
TO JOYCE'S *PORTRAIT*. Ed. Thomas F. Staley and Benstock.
Pp. 185-211. See K19.
> Surveys major structural symbols in PAYM: eyes,
> heart, color, water, animals.

K33   -----. "The Temptation of St. Stephen: A View of the Villanelle." JJQ, 14 (1976), 31-38.
> Agrees with Rossman (see K128) in seeing the
> villanelle as enfeebled, arguing, in fact, that
> its symbolically masturbatory conclusion is ac-
> complished only through Stephen's actual mas-
> turbation.

K34   Bernhardt-Kabish, Ernest. "Joyce's A PORTRAIT OF THE ART-
      IST AS A YOUNG MAN." EXPLICATOR, 18 (1960), Item No. 24.
         Explicates the line: "Bous Stephanoumenos! Bous
         Stephaneforos" from Stephen's seaside epiphany.
         Extract reprinted in K16.

K35   Booth, Wayne C. "The Problem of Distance in A PORTRAIT
      OF THE ARTIST." In THE RHETORIC OF FICTION. Chicago:
      Univ. of Chicago Press, 1961. Pp. 324-36.
         Ambiguities in presentation of Stephen, in the
         fifth chapter, seen as unintentional and attrib-
         uted to flaws in JJ's narrative technique. Re-
         printed in J3, K1, and K16.

K36   Bowen, Zack. "Stephen's Villanelle: Antecedents, Manifes-
      tations, and Aftermath." MODERN BRITISH LITERATURE, 5
      (1980), 63-67.
         Stephen's villanelle "an amalgam of previous
         images, a rationalization of [his] inferiority,
         and a vision of its own composition." See G63.

K37   Boyd, Elizabeth F. "Joyce's Hell-Fire Sermons." MLN, 75
      (1960), 561-71.
         Describes JJ's primary sources for the hell-fire
         sermons and compares passages. Reprinted in K5
         and K14. Also see K52 and K140.

K38   Brandabur, Edward. "Stephen's Aesthetic in A PORTRAIT OF
      THE ARTIST." In THE CELTIC CROSS: STUDIES IN IRISH CUL-
      TURE AND LITERATURE. Ed. Ray B. Browne, W.J. Roscelli,
      and Richard Loftus. Lafayette, Ind.: Purdue Univ. Studies,
      1964. Pp. 11-21.
         Stephen's aesthetic less important as a guide
         to JJ's views than as a reflection of Stephen's
         psychological development, his escape from re-
         ality. Followed by a brief comment by Maurice
         Beebe (pp. 22-25).

K39   Buckley, Jerome H. "Portrait of James Joyce as a Young
      Aesthete." In SEASON OF YOUTH: THE *BILDUNGSROMAN* FROM
      DICKENS TO GOLDING. Cambridge, Mass.: Harvard Univ. Press
      1974. Pp. 225-47.
         PAYM's modifications upon the *Bildungsroman* con-
         ventions.

K40   Burke, Kenneth. "Fact, Inference, and Proof in the Ana-
      lysis of Literary Symbolism." In TERMS FOR ORDER. Ed.

Stanley E. Hyman. Bloomington: Indiana Univ. Press, 1964.
Pp. 145-72.
  Theoretical discussion of symbol analysis, using
  PAYM as a sample text.

K41   -----. "Three Definitions." KR, 13 (1951), 173-92.
       See J158.

K42   Burrell, Angus. "James Joyce and ULYSSES." In his and
       Dorothy Brewster's MODERN FICTION. New York: Columbia
       Univ. Press, 1934. Pp. 155-217.
         Extended summaries of PAYM (pp. 157-63) and U
         (pp. 163-207), with critical asides and with
         concluding discussion of the moral and critical
         problems of U's "vulgarity."

K43   Carens, James F. "The Motif of Hands in A PORTRAIT OF THE
       ARTIST AS A YOUNG MAN." In IRISH RENAISSANCE ANNUAL II.
       Ed. Zack Bowen. Pp. 139-57. See G14.
         Sexual implications of the novel's hand imagery.

K44   Chapple, J.A.V. DOCUMENTARY AND IMAGINATIVE LITERATURE,
       1880-1920. New York: Barnes and Noble, 1970. Pp. 353-
       64 and passim.
         See J159.

K45   Church, Margaret. "The Adolescent Point of View toward
       Women in Joyce's A PORTRAIT OF THE ARTIST AS A YOUNG MAN."
       In IRISH RENAISSANCE ANNUAL II. Ed. Zack Bowen. Pp. 158-
       65. See G14.
         Stephen's idealization of the female an artist's
         defense against a perceived threat to his iden-
         tity as a creator.

K46   -----. "A PORTRAIT and Giambattista Vico: A Source Study."
       In APPROACHES TO JOYCE'S *PORTRAIT*. Ed. Thomas F. Staley
       and Bernard Benstock. Pp. 77-89. See K19.
         Finds a Viconian pattern operating on "reli-
         gious, psychological, and mythical levels" in
         PAYM.

K47   Connolly, Thomas E. "Kinesis and Stasis: Structural Rhythm
       in Joyce's PORTRAIT OF THE ARTIST." UNIVERSITY REVIEW
       (Dublin), 3 (1966), 21-30.
         Applies Stephen's aesthetic theory to an ana-
         lysis of PAYM's structure. Reprinted, with re-
         visions, in G14.

K48 Dahl, Liisa. "The Influence of Édouard Dujardin's Mono-
logue Intérieur on Joyce [sic] Technique." In ATTI DEL
THIRD INTERNATIONAL JAMES JOYCE SYMPOSIUM. Pp. 134-38.
See G7.
Finds Dujardin's influence, frequently noted in
U, as early as PAYM (chiefly syntactic parallels).

K49 Davis, Edward. "A PORTRAIT OF THE ARTIST AS A YOUNG MAN."
In READINGS IN MODERN FICTION. Cape Town: Simondium,
1964. Pp. 239-57.
Summarizes novel, paraphrases the discussion of
aesthetics in chapter five, and comments on JJ's
diction, characters, and setting.

K50 Delbaere-Garant, Jeanne. "From the Moocow to Navelless
Eve: The Spiral Growth of Stephen Dedalus." RLV, 43
(1977), 131-41.
Spiral structure of PAYM, pursued into the early
episodes of U.

K51 Dibble, Brian. "A Brunonian Reading of Joyce's A PORTRAIT
OF THE ARTIST." JJQ, 4 (1967), 280-85.
Details from the personal life and heretical
thought of Giordano Bruno inform JJ's portrait
of Stephen. See K12.

K52 Doherty, James. "Joyce and HELL OPENED TO CHRISTIANS: The
Edition He Used for His Hell Sermons." MP, 61 (1963), 110-
19.
Identifies exact translation of Pinamonti's
tract (Dublin, 1889), used by JJ for Fr. Arnall's sermons, and compares the two texts.
See K37 and K140.

K53 Drew, Elizabeth A. "James Joyce, 1882-1941: A PORTRAIT
OF THE ARTIST AS A YOUNG MAN." In THE NOVEL: A MODERN
GUIDE TO FIFTEEN ENGLISH MASTERPIECES. New York: Dell,
1963. Pp. 245-61.
Competent introduction to PAYM's principal
themes (growth, art and reality), and its peri-
odic structure.

K54 Egri, Péter. "The Function of Dreams and Visions in A
PORTRAIT and DEATH IN VENICE." JJQ, 5 (1968), 86-102.
Compares JJ's and Mann's explorations of the
artist's psychology.

K55   Ellmann, Richard. "Two Faces of Edward." In EDWARDIANS
       AND LATE VICTORIANS. Ed. Ellmann. New York: Columbia
       Univ. Press, 1960. Pp. 188-210.
           Edwardian qualities of PAYM (e.g., theme of dis-
           passionate revolt, iterative style), among other
           works.

K56   Epstein, Edmund L. "James Joyce and THE WAY OF ALL FLESH."
       JJQ, 7 (1969), 22-29.
           Influence of Samuel Butler's views of paternity
           on JJ's development of the father-son conflict.

K57   Evans, Fallon. "The PORTRAIT as a Literary Work." In
       DEDALUS ON CRETE. Ed. Joseph Feehan. Pp. 13-28. See K8.
           General introductory lecture on PAYM.

K58   Farrell, James T. "Joyce's A PORTRAIT OF THE ARTIST AS A
       YOUNG MAN." In THE LEAGUE OF FRIGHTENED PHILISTINES. New
       York: Vanguard Press, 1945. Pp. 45-59.
           Stresses the realistic social and historical con-
           texts of Stephen's development and the realism of
           JJ's portrait of the artist's mind. Reprinted in
           G30. Also see P11.

K59   Feshbach, Sidney. "A Slow and Dark Birth: A Study of the
       Organization of A PORTRAIT OF THE ARTIST AS A YOUNG MAN."
       JJQ, 4 (1967), 289-300.
           Process of gestation a "precise schematic" organ-
           izing principle in the novel. See K12.

K60   Fortuna, Diane. "The Labyrinth as Controlling Image in
       Joyce's A PORTRAIT OF THE ARTIST AS A YOUNG MAN." BNYPL,
       76 (1972), 120-80.
           Religious purpose (i.e., initiation ritual) and
           topicality (i.e., Evans' excavations in Crete,
           1900-11), of JJ's allusions to the Minoan laby-
           rinth and his labyrinthine symbolism in PAYM.

K61   Gabler, Hans Walter. "The Christmas Dinner Scene, Par-
       nell's Death, and the Genesis of A PORTRAIT OF THE ARTIST
       AS A YOUNG MAN." JJQ, 13 (1975), 27-38.
           Christmas scene retains traces of its textual
           genesis and composition for STEPHEN HERO.

K62   -----. "The Seven Lost Years of A PORTRAIT OF THE ARTIST
       AS A YOUNG MAN." In APPROACHES TO JOYCE'S *PORTRAIT*. Ed.
       Thomas F. Staley and Bernard Benstock. Pp. 25-60. See K19.
           Intensive analysis and critical evaluation of the
           novel's textual evolution (1907-14).

K63   -----. "Towards a Critical Text of James Joyce's POR-
      TRAIT." SB, 27 (1974), 1-53.
          Establishes a "comprehensive textual hypothesis"
          for the preparation of a "critical text" for PAYM.

K64   Garnett, Edward. "Reader's Report." 1916. In THE LET-
      TERS OF JAMES JOYCE. Ed. Richard Ellmann. II, 371-72.
      See C1.
          Rejects PAYM, for Duckworth, as "too discursive,
          formless, unrestrained." Also published in F33.
          Reprinted in G25, J3, K1, and K14.

K65   Geckle, George L. "Stephen Dedalus and W.B. Yeats: The
      Making of the Villanelle." MFS, 15 (1969), 87-96.
          Stephen's ideas of creation derived from Yeats's
          "The Symbolism of Poetry." Argues weakness of
          villanelle. See G65.

K66   Gillam, Doreen M.E. "Stephen Kouros." JJQ, 8 (1971),
      221-32.
          JJ's possible awareness and use of Cretan myth-
          ology, described in Jane Harrison's THEMIS (1912),
          in completing PAYM.

K67   Gillie, Christopher. CHARACTER IN ENGLISH LITERATURE.
      New York: Barnes and Noble, 1965. Pp. 177-87.
          PAYM a dialectical presentation of Stephen's
          evolving, individuated character.

K68   Gordon, Caroline. "Some Readings and Misreadings." SR,
      61 (1953), 384-407.
          PAYM, among several other works, a novel "of a
          soul that is being damned for time and eternity
          caught in the act of foreseeing and foreknowing
          its damnation." Reprinted in K6.

K69   Gordon, William A. "Submission and Autonomy: Identity
      Patterns in Joyce's PORTRAIT." PsyR, 61 (1974-75), 535-55
          Freudian analysis of Stephen's psyche.

K70   Gorman, Herbert. "Introduction." In JJ's A PORTRAIT OF
      THE ARTIST AS A YOUNG MAN. New York: Modern Library,
      1928. Pp. v-xii.
          PAYM a "prelude" to U, particularly in JJ's use
          of stream of consciousness.

K71   Gould, Eric. "The Writer as a New Idiom: Myth and Epiphan

in PORTRAIT OF THE ARTIST." ES, 58 (1977), 501-07.   ✓
Attempted redefinition of the "mythic" quality
of JJ's prose.

K72 Grayson, Thomas W. "James Joyce and Stephen Dedalus: The
Theory of Aesthetics." JJQ, 4 (1967), 310-19.
Implications of JJ's irony for the interpreta-
tion of Stephen's aesthetic theory. See K12.

K73 Halper, Nathan. "The Aesthetics of Joyce: James Joyce and
His Fingernails." In YEATS, JOYCE, AND BECKETT: NEW LIGHT
ON THREE MODERN IRISH WRITERS. Ed. Kathleen McGrory and
John Unterecker. Lewisburg, Pa.: Bucknell Univ. Press,
1976. Pp. 105-09.
JJ's ironic distance from Stephen and his aesthe-
tic (e.g., the doctrine of artistic detachment).
Earlier version published in G7.

K74 Hardy, John Edward. "Joyce's PORTRAIT: The Flight of the
Serpent." In MAN IN THE MODERN NOVEL. Seattle: Univ. of
Washington Press, 1964. Pp. 67-81.
Fine interpretation of PAYM's identity theme,
Oedipal conflict, and multivalent symbolism.

K75 Harvey, Francis. "STEPHEN HERO and A PORTRAIT OF THE ART-
IST AS A YOUNG MAN: The Intervention of Style in a Work of
the Creative Imagination." In A BASH IN THE TUNNEL. Ed.
John Ryan. Pp. 203-07. See F135.
PAYM a *"dead* masterpiece" of stylistic virtuosity, compared to its imaginatively gifted early
version.

K76 Hayman, David. "Daedalian Imagery in A PORTRAIT OF THE
ARTIST AS A YOUNG MAN." In HERIDITAS: SEVEN ESSAYS ON
THE MODERN EXPERIENCE OF THE CLASSICAL. Ed. Frederic Will.
Austin: Univ. of Texas Press, 1964. Pp. 33-54.
Classical myth in PAYM (e.g., labyrinth, monster,
and flight motifs).

K77 -----. "A PORTRAIT OF THE ARTIST AS A YOUNG MAN and L'EDU-
CATION SENTIMENTALE: The Structural Affinities." OL, 19
(1964), 161-75.
Precedents for PAYM's "architectonic structure,"
balance of ironies, and impersonal narration in
Flaubert's *Bildungsroman* (1869).

K78 Helsinger, Howard. "Joyce and Dante." ELH, 35 (1968),
     591-605.
          Dantean elements of PAYM (e.g., Stephen and
          Dante as artist exiles).

K79 Hochman, Baruch. "Joyce's PORTRAIT as Portrait." LITER-
     ARY REVIEW, 22 (1978), 25-55.
          While "radically new" in several respects, PAYM
          indebted to the "central traditions of represen-
          tationalism" (i.e., "novelistic portraiture").

K80 Huneker, James G. "James Joyce." In UNICORNS. New York:
     Scribner's, 1917. Pp. 187-94.
          JJ "indubitably a fresh talent," a naturalist
          in the manner of Chekhov.

K81 Hutchings, William. "Ontogenesis/Phylogenesis: The Pat-
     tern of Historical Development in Chapter IV of A POR-
     TRAIT." JJQ, 15 (1978), 339-46.
          Stephen's development in the fourth chapter
          "recapitulates western intellectual history
          from within a decidedly Catholic point of view."

K82 Jack, Jane H. "Art and A PORTRAIT OF THE ARTIST." EIC,
     5 (1955), 354-64.
          Defends PAYM as a novel of feeling, though
          strenuously designed to pursue the central
          theme of the artist. Reprinted in K6.

K83 Jones, David E. "The Essence of Beauty in James Joyce's
     Aesthetics." JJQ, 10 (1973), 291-311.
          Turns to Aristotle's DE ANIMA and METAPHYSICS
          and Aquinas's COMMENTARY ON *DE ANIMA,* for clar-
          ification of Stephen's theory.

K84 Kain, Richard M. "Epiphanies of Dublin." In APPROACHES
     TO JOYCE'S *PORTRAIT*. Ed. Thomas F. Staley and Bernard
     Benstock. Pp. 91-112. See K19.
          JJ's use of his adolescent "epiphanies" in PAYM
          and the comparatively minor role of the Dublin
          cityscape in the novel.

K85 Karl, Frederick R., and Marvin Magalaner. "James Joyce."
     In A READER'S GUIDE TO GREAT TWENTIETH-CENTURY ENGLISH
     NOVELS. New York: Noonday, 1959. Pp. 205-53.
          Brief survey of JJ's life and summaries, with
          criticism, of PAYM and U.

K86   Kaye, Julian B. "Who is Betty Byrne?" MLN, 71 (1956),
      93-95.
               Suggests JJ's reference is to the mother of J.F.
               Byrne ("Cranly"). Reprinted in K5, K13, and K14.

K87   Kelleher, John V. "The Perceptions of James Joyce." AT-
      LANTIC, 201 (Mar. 1958), 82-90.
               PAYM's organic unity of action, symbolism, form,
               and tone (irony). Reprinted in K14.

K88   Kenner, Hugh. "Joyce's PORTRAIT--A Reconsideration." UNI-
      VERSITY OF WINDSOR REVIEW, 1 (1965), 1-15.
               JJ's view of Stephen neither ironic nor sympa-
               thetic, but moves "as the subject moves." Ken-
               ner's modification of his fully ironic view of
               Stephen (see below). Reprinted, in revised
               form, as "The Cubist Portrait" in K19.

K89   -----. "The PORTRAIT in Perspective." In JAMES JOYCE.
      Ed. Seon Givens. Pp. 132-74. See G30.
               Kenner's enormously influential and controver-
               sial, ironic reading of PAYM. Assimilated into
               G47. Also see Kenner's second thoughts (G48
               and above), as well as his contemporaries' re-
               sponses: K116, K118, K130, and K133.

K90   Kershner, R.B. "Time and Language in Joyce's PORTRAIT OF
      THE ARTIST." ELH, 43 (1976), 604-19.
               Changes in Stephen's senses of space and time and
               in the novel's language reinforce his physical
               and intellectual changes.

K91   Klein, James R. "Lotts, Horse Piss, and Rotted Straw."
      CE, 34 (1973), 952-75.
               Mental instability and the artist's search for
               a "stable" reality (title pun intended?) in the
               "word" (e.g., Stephen). Reprinted, with revi-
               sions, in G43.

K92   Klein, Michael. "Strick's Adaptation of Joyce's PORTRAIT
      OF THE ARTIST: Discourse and Containing Discourse." In
      NARRATIVE STRATEGIES: ORIGINAL ESSAYS IN FILM AND PROSE
      FICTION. Ed. Syndy Conger and Janice R. Welsch. Macomb:
      Western Illinois Univ., 1980. Pp. 37-46.
               Not seen.

K93 Landess, Thomas H. "James Joyce and Aesthetic Gnosticism."
     ModA, 23 (1979), 145-53.
          Parallels Stephen's escape into art with the
          gnostic's search for the "other world of his
          origin."

K94 Lane, Jeremy. "His Master's Voice? The Questioning of
     Authority in Literature." In THE MODERN ENGLISH NOVEL:
     THE READER, THE WRITER, AND THE WORK. Ed. Gabriel Josi-
     povici. New York: Barnes and Noble, 1976. Pp. 113-29.
          The quest to create one's own world, in JJ and
          Kafka (cf. THE TRIAL [1925]).

K95 Lanham, Jon. "The Genre of A PORTRAIT OF THE ARTIST AS
     A YOUNG MAN and 'the rhythm of its structure.'" GENRE,
     10 (1977), 77-102.
          Attempts to clarify novel's ambiguities by de-
          fining PAYM's genre as a hybrid of the related
          modes of apology ("its symbolic organization")
          and confession ("its narrative organization").

K96 Lemon, Lee T. "A PORTRAIT OF THE ARTIST AS A YOUNG MAN:
     Motif as Motivation and Structure." MFS, 12 (1966-67),
     441-52.
          PAYM the first novel to rely principally on mo-
          tifs for structure and meaning. Reprinted in
          K16.

K97 Link, Frederick M. "The Aesthetics of Stephen Dedalus."
     PLL, 2 (1966), 140-49.
          Cautious application of Stephen's theory to JJ's
          novel.

K98 Lord, George deForest. HEROIC MOCKERY: VARIATIONS ON EPIC
     THEMES FROM HOMER TO JOYCE. Newark: Univ. of Delaware
     Press, 1977. Pp. 121-32.
          JJ the "first writer since Virgil and Ovid to
          employ the Minoan myth in its full cycle and
          with its greatest possible range of allusions,"
          in PAYM and "Wandering Rocks" (in U).

K99 Magalaner, Marvin. "James Mangan and Joyce's Dedalus Fam-
     ily." PQ, 31 (1952), 363-71.
          Aspects of Stephen's family life drawn from
          Mangan's.

K100   Manso, Peter. "The Metaphoric Style of Joyce's PORTRAIT."
       MFS, 13 (1967), 221-36.
              Novel's progressive styles "mirror Stephen's
              growth." Analyses of rhythm, structure, and
              style.

K101   Marre, K.E. "Colour Significance in A PORTRAIT OF THE
       ARTIST AS A YOUNG MAN." DUTCH QUARTERLY REVIEW, 7 (1977),
       201-12.
              JJ's symbolic use of primary colors in the
              first chapter (red, white, and green), and
              subsequently the color which results from
              their mixture: grey.

K102   Mason, Michael. "ULYSSES the Sequel to A PORTRAIT? Joyce's
       Plans for the Two Works." ELN, 8 (1971), 296-300.
              Argument against seeing U as a sequel to PAYM,
              convincingly discredited in three replies, by
              Kain, Litz, and Scholes (ELN, 8 [1971], 301-05).

K103   Mitchell, Breon. "A PORTRAIT and the *Bildungsroman* Tra-
       dition." In APPROACHES TO JOYCE'S *PORTRAIT*. Ed. Thomas
       F. Staley and Bernard Benstock. Pp. 61-76. See K19.
              JJ's surprisingly traditional use of *Bildungs-*
              roman conventions (re: structure, style, tech-
              nique, and theme).

K104   Mueller, William R. "James Joyce: Genesis of an Artist."
       In CELEBRATION OF LIFE: STUDIES IN MODERN FICTION. New
       York: Sheed and Ward, 1972. Pp. 9-29.
              Stephen rejects the priestly vocation, though
              he sees the world in theological terms as he
              matures into a "priest" of art.

K105   -----. "The Theme of Vocation: James Joyce's A PORTRAIT
       OF THE ARTIST AS A YOUNG MAN." In THE PROPHETIC VOICE
       IN MODERN FICTION. New York: Association Press, 1959.
       Pp. 17-45.
              Complex relationship between the concept of
              vocation suggested by the novel (identity),
              and that implied by the biblical tradition
              (salvation).

K106   Murry, John Middleton. "The Break-Up of the Novel." YR,
       12 (1922), 288-304.
              The significant and coincidental publication
              of three stream-of-consciousness, sequence

novels in "1913-14" (sic): Proust's SWANN'S
WAY (1912), Dorothy Richardson's POINTED ROOFS
(1915), and JJ's PAYM (1916).

K107   Naremore, James. "Consciousness and Society in A PORTRAIT
OF THE ARTIST." In APPROACHES TO JOYCE'S *PORTRAIT*. Ed.
Thomas F. Staley and Bernard Benstock. Pp. 113-34. See
K19.
Stephen's "ideas, language, and art" affected by
his religion and economic status. JJ as a
social realist.

K108   -----. "Style as Meaning in A PORTRAIT OF THE ARTIST."
JJQ, 4 (1967), 331-42.
PAYM's purposefully "purple" passages reflect
Stephen's still "immature" and "provincial"
character. See K12. Extract reprinted in K16.

✓ K109   Nims, John F. "Dedalus in Crete." In DEDALUS ON CRETE.
Ed. Joseph Feehan. Pp. 77-88. See K8.
Elementary comment on JJ's use of the Daedalus-
Icarus myth.

K110   Noon, William T., S.J. "A PORTRAIT OF THE ARTIST AS A
YOUNG MAN: After Fifty Years." In JAMES JOYCE TODAY. Ed.
Thomas F. Staley. Pp. 54-82. See G75.
Survey of PAYM's critical status and argument
that JJ's "mature point" in PAYM is the futil-
ity of attempting to "replace God through the
creative processes of literature."

K111   -----. "Three Young Men in Rebellion." THOUGHT, 38
(1963), 560-77.
Comparisons among JJ's Dedalus, Butler's Ernest
Pontifex (THE WAY OF ALL FLESH [1903]), and
Salinger's Holden Caulfield (THE CATCHER IN
THE RYE [1951]).

K112   O'Brien, Darcy. "In Ireland after A PORTRAIT." In AP-
PROACHES TO JOYCE'S *PORTRAIT*. Ed. Thomas F. Staley and
Bernard Benstock. Pp. 213-37. See K19.
Effects of PAYM on the works of Seamus Heaney,
Flann O'Brien (i.e., Brian Nolan), Patrick Kav-
anagh, and Conor Cruise O'Brien.

K113   O'Faolain, Sean. "Commentary." In JJ's A PORTRAIT OF
THE ARTIST AS A YOUNG MAN. New York: New American Li-
brary, 1954. Pp. iii-vi, 200-02.
JJ's transformation of reality, and of the

realistic conventions for fiction, creates the
"private world" of his novels.

K114 Pascal, Roy. "The Autobiographical Novel and the Autobiography." EIC, 9 (1959), 134-50.
> Old men write autobiographies (e.g., Wells),
> while young writers transmute and objectify
> their selves through fiction (e.g., C. Bronte,
> Lawrence, JJ).

K115 Pope, Deborah. "The Misprison of Vision: A Comparison
of Stephen's Heaven and Hell in A PORTRAIT OF THE ARTIST
AS A YOUNG MAN." JJQ, 17 (1980), 263-70.
> Ironic parallels between Stephen's visions of
> heaven and hell.

K116 Poss, Stanley H. "A Portrait of the Artist as Beginner."
UKCR, 26 (1960), 189-96.
> Stephen's own self-criticism diminishes the
> irony in his portrait (response to Kenner's
> vigorously ironic reading; see K89 and K118).

K117 -----. "A Portrait of the Artist as Hard-Boiled Messiah."
MLQ, 27 (1966), 68-79.
> Complex responses of the reader to and JJ's
> own ambivalence toward Stephen's "messianic
> impulse."

K118 -----. "Stephen's Words, Joyce's Attitude." RS, 28
(1960), 156-61.
> Early, reasonable response to Kenner's too
> severe view of Dedalus and to the "Stephen-
> hating school of Joyce criticism" generally.
> See K116 above.

K119 Pound, Ezra. "James Joyce: At Last the Novel Appears."
EGOIST, 4, No. 2 (1917), 21-22.
> JJ "produces the nearest thing to Flaubertian
> prose that we have now in English." Reprinted
> in F123, G25 (extract), and K1.

K120 Rader, Ralph W. "Defoe, Richardson, Joyce, and the Concept of Form in the Novel." In AUTOBIOGRAPHY, BIOGRAPHY,
AND THE NOVEL. Ed. William Matthews and Rader. Los Angeles: William Andrews Clark Memorial Library, 1973. Pp.
31-72.
> Formal similarities among MOLL FLANDERS, PAM-
> ELA, PAYM, and U, with special emphasis on the
> authors' approximation of "felt life."

K121   Ranald, Margaret Loftus. "Stephen Dedalus' Vocation and
       the Irony of Religious Ritual." JJQ, 2 (1965), 97-102.
          JJ achieves aesthetic distance in his presen-
          tation of Stephen by associating his actions,
          language, and thought with religious ritual.

K122   Reddick, Bryan. "The Importance of Tone in the Structural
       Rhythm of Joyce's PORTRAIT." JJQ, 6 (1969), 201-18.
          Novel's changes in tone reflect Stephen's de-
          velopment, affect the reader's response to
          Stephen, and suggest a more positive inter-
          pretation of PAYM's ending.

K123   Redford, Grant H. "The Role of Structure in Joyce's POR-
       TRAIT." MFS, 4 (1958), 21-30.
          PAYM's structural pattern (search-rebellion)
          parallels Stephen's theories of the creative
          act. See G64. Reprinted in K5, K6, and K14.

K124   Reilly, James P. *"Non Ego--Non Serviam:* The Problem of
       Artistic Freedom." In DEDALUS ON CRETE. Ed. Joseph Fee-
       han. Pp. 45-52. See K8.
          JJ's (and Stephen's) aestheticism a search for
          freedom and "Transcendence" after the rejection
          of the church and faith.

K125   Riquelme, John Paul. "Pretexts for Reading and for Writ-
       ing: Title, Epigraph, and Journal in A PORTRAIT OF THE
       ARTIST AS A YOUNG MAN." JJQ, 18 (1981), 301-21.
          A "paratextual" analysis of the implications,
          for reader's response, of PAYM's heterogeneous
          textual departures.

K126   Robinson, K.E. "The Stream of Consciousness Technique
       and the Structure of Joyce's PORTRAIT." JJQ, 9 (1971),
       63-84.
          Finds the stylistic and structural elements
          of the stream-of-consciousness technique more
          pervasive in PAYM than generally recognized.

K127   Rossman, Charles. "Stephen Dedalus and the Spiritual-
       Heroic Refrigerating Appartus: Art and Life in Joyce's
       PORTRAIT." In FORMS OF MODERN BRITISH FICTION. Ed. Alan
       W. Friedman. Austin: Univ. of Texas Press, 1975. Pp.
       101-31.
          Stephen's neoplatonic discussion of aesthetics
          related to his "painful, perhaps doomed, effort
          to define and liberate [his] self," his "at-
          tempt at spiritual transcendence."

K128 -----. "Stephen Dedalus' Villanelle." JJQ, 12 (1975),
      281-93.
          The "enormous disparity between [Stephen's]
          intention and fulfillment" revealed, princi-
          pally in the villanelle. Disputes Scholes'
          non-ironic view of Stephen's poem (see K131).
          Also see K33.

K129 Rubin, Louis D. "A Portrait of a Highly Visible Artist."
      In THE TELLER IN THE TALE. Seattle: Univ. of Washington
      Press, 1967. Pp. 141-77.
          The full meaning of PAYM and U "resides in the
          articulated and dramatized presence of the
          authorial personality telling his narrator's
          story" (cf. Proust).

K130 Scholes, Robert. "Stephen Dedalus: *Eiron* and *Alazon*."
      TSLL, 3 (1961), 8-15.
          JJ's presentation of Stephen modulates between
          irony and sympathy, developing traits of both
          pretension *(alazon)* and self-deprecation *(eiron)*
          in his character. In part, a response to Ken-
          ner (K89).

K131 -----. "Stephen Dedalus: Poet or Esthete?" PMLA, 79
      (1964), 484-89.
          Villanelle marks Stephen's maturation into
          artist. Reprinted in K1. Also see K128.

K132 Schorer, Mark. "Technique as Discovery." HudR, 1 (1948),
      67-87.
          JJ succeeds where Lawrence failed (in SONS AND
          LOVERS), allowing his style and "technique to
          discover the full meaning of his subject." Re-
          printed in Schorer's THE WORLD WE IMAGINE (New
          York: Farrar, Straus and Giroux, 1968).

K133 Sharpless, F. Parvin. "Irony in Joyce's PORTRAIT: The
      Stasis of Pity." JJQ, 4 (1967), 320-30.
          JJ's mixed irony and sympathy promote emotional
          stasis toward Stephen. In part, a response to
          Kenner (K89). Also see K12. Reprinted in K16.

K134 Spielberg, Peter. "James Joyce's Errata for American
      Editions of A PORTRAIT OF THE ARTIST." In JOYCE'S *POR-
      TRAIT*. Ed. Thomas E. Connolly. Pp. 318-28. See K6.
          JJ's 1917 errata list for PAYM, assimilated by
          Anderson's corrected edition (1964).

K135   Sprinchorn, Evert. "Joyce: A PORTRAIT OF THE ARTIST AS
        A YOUNG MAN: A Portrait of the Artist as Achilles." In
        APPROACHES TO THE TWENTIETH CENTURY NOVEL. Ed. John
        Unterecker. New York: Crowell, 1965. Pp. 9-50.
            "Key" to the symbols and JJ's symbolic tech-
            nique in PAYM.

K136   Squire, John C. "Mr. James Joyce." In BOOKS IN GENERAL.
        New York: Knopf, 1919. Pp. 245-50.
            JJ a "genuine realist" who lacks form: "It is
            doubtful if he will make a novelist." Extract
            reprinted in G25.

K137   Staley, Thomas F. "Strings in the Labyrinth: Sixty Years
        with Joyce's PORTRAIT." In APPROACHES TO JOYCE'S *PORTRAIT*.
        Ed. Staley and Bernard Benstock. Pp. 3-24. See K19.
            Briefly surveys critical and textual history
            of PAYM.

K138   Steinberg, Erwin R. "The Bird-Girl in A PORTRAIT as Syn-
        thesis: The Sacred Assimilated to the Profane." JJQ, 17
        (1980), 149-63.
            Analysis of the culminating symbol patterns
            in the concluding paragraphs of chapter IV.

K139   Tarbox, Raymond C. "Auditory Experience in Joyce's POR-
        TRAIT." AI, 27 (1970), 301-28.
            Thematic and symbolic significance of Stephen's
            sensitivity to sound.

K140   Thrane, James R. "Joyce's Sermon on Hell: Its Sources
        and Its Background." MP, 57 (1960), 172-98.
            Compares JJ's text with his chief source, Pina-
            monti's HELL OPENED TO CHRISTIANS (1688). Re-
            printed in G57. Also see K37 and K52.

K141   Van Ghent, Dorothy. "On A PORTRAIT OF THE ARTIST AS A
        YOUNG MAN." In THE ENGLISH NOVEL: FORM AND FUNCTION.
        New York: Rinehart, 1953. Pp. 263-76, 463-73.
            Role of language as labyrinth and "creator of
            reality" for the maturing Stephen. Includes
            "Questions for Study." Reprinted in K6. Ex-
            tracts reprinted in K14 and K16.

K142   Van Laan, Thomas F. "The Meditative Structure of Joyce's
        PORTRAIT." JJQ, 1, No. 3 (1964), 3-13.
            Traces the structural pattern of the medita-
            tion, derived from Ignatius Loyola's SPIRITUAL

EXERCISES, both within and among the chapters
of PAYM.

K143 Waith, Eugene M. "The Calling of Stephen Dedalus." CE,
18 (1957), 256-61.
Daedalus and Thoth symbols of the semi-divine,
creative vocation of the artist. Reprinted in
K6, K14, and K16 (extract).

K144 Walsh, Ruth M. "That Pervasive Mass--In DUBLINERS and
A PORTRAIT OF THE ARTIST AS A YOUNG MAN." JJQ, 8 (1971),
205-20.
See J54.

K145 Wasson, Richard. "Stephen Dedalus and the Imagery of
Sight: A Psychological Approach." L&P, 15 (1965), 195-
209.
Stephen's preoccupation with vision "characteristic for people with voyeuristic predi-
lections."

K146 Wells, H.G. "James Joyce." NEW REPUBLIC, 10 (1917),
158-60.
Highly favorable review of PAYM, despite some
distaste for JJ's "cloacal obsession." Reprinted in G25 and K1.

K147 Wilds, Nancy G. "Style and Auctorial Presence in A POR-
TRAIT OF THE ARTIST AS A YOUNG MAN." STYLE, 7 (1973),
39-55.
Story's constantly shifting styles, perspectives, and relations among reader, writer, and
character (creating an "almost cubist effect"),
call attention throughout to JJ's authorial
presence.

K148 Woodbery, Potter. "The Irrelevance of Stephen Dedalus:
Some Reflections on Joyce and the Student Activist Movement." SLitI, 3, No. 2 (1970), 69-78.
Students no longer able to identify with the
aesthete. See G78.

K149 Woodward, A.G. "Technique and Feeling in James Joyce's
A PORTRAIT OF THE ARTIST AS A YOUNG MAN." ESA, 4 (1961),
39-53.
JJ's turn toward increasing technical virtuosity in his work a mask, a "distracting" tactic
for avoiding his intense personal involvement.

L. STUDIES OF *EXILES* (1918)

The following section is subdivided into two parts: i. Books
and Essay Collections on EXILES; and ii. General Critical Articles or Chapters on EXILES.

For facsimiles of JJ's surviving notes, manuscripts, and galley
proofs for EXILES, see vol. 11 of THE JAMES JOYCE ARCHIVE (B10).
For a concordance to EXILES, see Bauerle (D2).

For biographical backgrounds to EXILES, see, in section F above,
Ellmann (F33).

For additional critical commentaries and information on EXILES,
see the following books, in section G above: Benstock (G10),
Benstock and Benstock (G11), Bowen (G13), Brivic (G16), Cixous
(G21), Goldberg (G31), Golding (G32), Gorman (G36), Grose (G37),
Hodgart (G40), Hodgart and Worthington (G41), Kenner (G47, G48),
Levin (G52), Litz (G53), Magalaner and Kain (G58), Moseley (G67),
O'Brien (G70), Tindall (G80), Tysdahl (G82); and the following
studies, entered in other sections of this bibliography: Loss
(H132), Brandabur (J4), Reynolds (M52), Von Phul (N215), and
Sorensen (P5).

For foreign-language studies of EXILES, see section W.

L, i. Books and Essay Collections on EXILES

L1 MacNicholas, John. JAMES JOYCE'S *EXILES*: A TEXTUAL COM-
PANION. New York: Garland, 1979.
    Detailed historical essay on the "personal and
    artistic backgrounds" of JJ's play, including a
    clear and convincing account of its genesis and
    composition, together with the textual apparatus
    for a definitive edition of EXILES. Though Mac-
    Nicholas in unable to publish the edited text as
    such (because of copyright restrictions), he

wisely provides the information and mechanics
for any user of the widely available Viking-
Penguin (1951) paperback to establish the critical text. Conscientious and thorough textual
study.

L, ii. General Critical Articles or Chapters on EXILES

L2 Adams, Robert M. "Light on Joyce's EXILES? A New MS, a
Curious Analogue, and Some Speculations." SB, 17 (1964),
83-105.
Describes the Cornell manuscript of EXILES,
transcribes several passages deleted from the
published version, and speculates on their rel-
evance to the problems of interpretating the
play.

L3 -----. "The Manuscript of James Joyce's Play." YULG, 39
(1964), 30-41.
Variants between published versions of EXILES
and the Yale manuscript (later version than the
Cornell manuscript; see above).

L4 Aitken, D.J.F. "Dramatic Archetypes in Joyce's EXILES."
MFS, 4 (1958), 42-52.
JJ's use of archetypal dramatic personalities.
See G64.

L5 Bandler, Bernard. "Joyce's EXILES." HOUND AND HORN, 6
(1933), 266-85.
Play a most clear statement of the modern theme
of exile. Extract reprinted in G25.

L6 Benstock, Bernard. "EXILES: 'Paradox Lust' and 'Lost Pal-
adays.'" ELH, 36 (1969), 739-56.
Garden of Eden allegory in the play.

L7 -----. "EXILES, Ibsen, and the Play's Function in the Joyce
Canon." BSUF, 11, No. 2 (1970), 26-37.
Examines analogies to Ibsen's plays and parallels
to other works by JJ (particularly the "incon-
clusive" ending).

L8 Brown, Carole, and A.M. Leo Knuth. "James Joyce's EXILES:

The Ordeal of Richard Rowan." JJQ, 17 (1979), 7-20.
Useful reassessment of the play's strengths
and its place in the canon of JJ's works.

L9   Clark, Earl John. "James Joyce's EXILES." JJQ, 6 (1968),
69-78.
Stresses importance of seeing JJ's artistic
and personal needs for exile as major influences on his ideas in EXILES.

L10   Colum, Padraic. "Introduction." In JJ's EXILES. New
York: Viking, 1951. Pp. 7-11.
Play "a series of confessions" and "its end an
act of contrition" motivated by JJ's Catholic
conscience.

L11   Dombrowski, Theo Q. "Joyce's EXILES: The Problem of Love."
JJQ, 15 (1978), 118-27.
Play foreshadows U in its "complexity of feel-
ing" toward love and familial roles.

L12   "EXILES: A Discussion of James Joyce's Plays [sic]." LIT-
TLE REVIEW, 5, No. 9 (1919), 20-27; No. 10 (1919), 44, 49.
Five generally disappointed comments on the
play. Extracts reprinted in G25.

L13   Farrell, James T. "EXILES and Ibsen." In JAMES JOYCE.
Ed. Seon Givens. Pp. 95-131. See G30.
JJ's indebtedness to and identification with
Ibsen.

L14   Fergusson, Francis. "EXILES and Ibsen's Work." HOUND AND
HORN, 5 (1932), 345-53.
Play the logical culmination of Ibsen's tech-
niques and themes, a modern "intellectual dra-
ma," "to end all drama." Extract reprinted in
G25.

L15   -----. "A Reading of EXILES." In JJ's EXILES. Norfolk,
Conn.: New Directions, 1945. Pp. v-xviii.
Influence of Ibsen and JJ's farewell to the
"artist as hero" in the play. Reprinted in
Fergusson's THE HUMAN IMAGE IN DRAMATIC LIT-
ERATURE (1957).

L16   Harmon, Maurice. "Richard Rowan, His Own Scapegoat." JJQ,
3 (1965), 34-40.
Rowan's interior "more timid, doubting self"

progressively unmasked in EXILES (cf. Stephen
Dedalus).

L17 Kestner, Joseph A. "Joyce, Wagner, and Bizet: EXILES,
TANNHÄUSER, and CARMEN." MODERN BRITISH LITERATURE, 5
(1980), 53-62.
     Wagnerian influence on JJ's play and its sig-
     nificant associations with Wagner's and Bizet's
     operas. See G63.

L18 MacCarthy, Desmond. "James Joyce's EXILES." 1918.   In
HUMANITIES. New York: Oxford, 1954. Pp. 88-93.
     Review of JJ's "remarkable" though confusing
     play. Extract reprinted in G25.

L19 Macleod, Vivienne Koch. "The Influence of Ibsen on Joyce."
PMLA, 60 (1945), 879-98; 62 (1947), 573-80.
     Biographical and thematic parallels, chiefly
     in EXILES and STEPHEN HERO.

L20 MacNicholas, John. "Joyce contra Wagner." COMPARATIVE
DRAMA, 9 (1975), 29-43.
     Elements of TÄNNHAUSER and TRISTAN AND ISOLDE
     in EXILES.

L21 -----. "Joyce's EXILES: The Argument for Doubt." JJQ, 11
(1973), 33-40.
     Valuable analysis of EXILES' dramatic strengths
     and "subtle but powerful conclusion," which at-
     taches "dignity to the spiritual suffering aris-
     ing from an entrenched skepticism."

L22 -----. "The Stage History of EXILES." JJQ, 19 (1981),
9-26.
     Surveys reviews of stage productions and argues
     EXILES' viability as a play.

L23 Maher, R.A. "James Joyce's EXILES: The Comedy of Discon-
tinuity." JJQ, 9 (1972), 461-74.
     Pursues implications of JJ's suggestion that
     EXILES is "a comedy in three acts."

L24 Pound, Ezra. "Mr. James Joyce and the Modern Stage."
DRAMA, 6, No. 2 (1916), 122-32.
     EXILES a "dangerous and unstageable" problem
     play. Reprinted in F123 and G25 (extract).

L25   Simon, Elliott M. "James Joyce's EXILES and the Tradition
      of the Edwardian Problem-Play." MD, 20 (1977), 21-35.
          Play dramatically "unfinished," its intellec-
          tual problem unsolved, and its characters de-
          humanized abstractions.

L26   Weber, Roland von. "On and About Joyce's EXILES." In A
      JAMES JOYCE YEARBOOK. Ed. Maria Jolas. Pp. 47-67. See
      G45.
          Describes JJ's "long observation, training and
          study of the dramatic form," stressing the in-
          fluence of D'Annunzio, Hauptmann, and Ibsen.

M. STUDIES OF *ULYSSES* (1922)

The following section is subdivided into three parts: i. Books
and Essay Collections on U; ii. General Critical Articles, or
Chapters on U; and iii. Studies of Individual Episodes, or Chapters of U (identified by JJ's original Homeric titles, as is
the standard practice of JJ's critics):

1. "Telemachus"   10. "Wandering Rocks"
2. "Nestor"   11. "Sirens"
3. "Proteus"   12. "Cyclops"
4. "Calypso"   13. "Nausicaa"
5. "Lotus-Eaters"   14. "Oxen of the Sun"
6. "Hades"   15. "Circe"
7. "Aeolus"   16. "Eumaeus"
8. "Lestrygonians"   17. "Ithaca"
9. "Scylla and Charybdis"   18. "Penelope"

For facsimiles of JJ's surviving notes, manuscript drafts (exclusive of the Rosenbach manuscript, see below), placards, typescripts, and page proofs for U, see vols. 12-27 of THE JAMES
JOYCE ARCHIVE (B10). For transcriptions of the notesheets and
early drafts in the Buffalo and British Museum libraries, see
B15 and B16 respectively. For a facsimile of the Rosenbach
manuscript, see B22. And for a concordance to U, see Hanley
(D6).

For a bibliographical survey of the early editions of U, see
Roberts (E23). For biographical and topographical backgrounds
to U, and for memoirs and reminiscences of JJ during the writ-
ing and publication of U, see, among the works entered in sec-
tion F above: Anderson (F3), Beach (F6), Benco (F8), Borach
(F9), Budgen (F11--also see M8 below), Carens (F16), Cody (F18),
Daly (F25), Delaney (F27), Ellmann (F33, F35), Furbank (F45),
Gogarty (F49, F50, F51, F53), Graham (F56), Hoffmeister (F63),
Huddleston (F66), Hutchins (F67), JAMES JOYCE QUARTERLY (F70,
F72), Kerr (F88), Lidderdale and Nicholson (F92), F.S.L. Lyons
(F94), J.B. Lyons (F95), O'Connor (F114), Parandowski (F118),
Pearl (F120), Pinker (F121), Potts (F122), Pound (F123), Power
(F124), Quinn (F127), Reid (F129), Stephens (F143), Sullivan
(F146), Suter (F147), Svevo (F148), Wagner (F155), and Weaver
(F157).

For additional critical commentaries and information on U, see
the following books, in section G above: Adams (G1, G2), Arnold
(G6), Benstock (G10), Benstock and Benstock (G11), Bolt (G12),
Bowen (G13), Boyle (G15), Brivic (G16), Burgess (G17), Chatter-
jee (G20), Cixous (G21), Cope (G22), Duff (G27), Eruvbetine
(G28), Gillet (G29), Goldberg (G31), Golding (G32), Goldman
(G33, G34), Gorman (G36), Grose (G37), Gross (G38), Hodgart
(G40), Hodgart and Worthington (G41), JAMES JOYCE QUARTERLY
(G42), Jones (G46), Kenner (G47, G48), Knuth (G49), Kronegger
(G51), Levin (G52), Litz (G53), MacCabe (G54), Magalaner and
Kain (G58), Majault (G59), Morse (G66), Moseley (G67), Murillo
(G68), Noon (G69), O'Brien (G70), Peake (G71), Ryf (G72), Smidt
(G74), Stewart (G76), Strong (G77), Tindall (G79, G80), Tysdahl
(G82), Waldron (G83); the following critical articles, in sec-
tion H above: Allott (H3), Anderson (H5), Aronson (H7), Beach
(H10), Bickerton (H19), Cope (H39), Dahl (H42), Dahlberg and
Read (H43), Daiches (H45), DiGaetani (H47), Friedman (H64),
Frierson (H65), Garrett (H70), Glasheen (H76), Glicksburg (H77),
Hendry (H86), Highet (H89), Hoffman (H91, H92, H93), Kaye (H106),
Kenner (H109, H110), Kestner (H112), Korg (H120), Kumar (H121),
Lawrence (H122), Lewis (H126), Loss (H132), Lyons (H136), Mc-
Luhan (H139, H141), Markovic (H144), Melchiori (H147), Mercier
(H148), More (H153), Morse (H155), Muir (H157), Russell (H183),
Savage (H184), Semmler (H192), Seward (H195), Spears (H200),
Stanford (H206), Starkie (H207), Steinberg (H208), Tindall
(H219), Ussher (H220), Von Phul (H224), Watson (H228), West
(H232), White (H233), Wilson (H237); and the following studies,
entered in other sections of this bibliography: Epstein (K7),
Hayman (N23), McCarthy (N31), Connolly (N87), Morse (N171),
Sage (N192), Von Phul (N215), Aubert (P1), Jackson (P4), and
Sorensen (P5). For additional commentary and information on
the individual episodes of U, see the headnotes for section M,
iii below and for each of the episodes within section M, iii.

For foreign-language studies of U, see section X.

M, i. Books and Essay Collections on ULYSSES

See M278, the twenty-six foreign-language titles (X1 through
X26), and the appendix. Also see the following books on in-
dividual episodes: on "Circe": Barkentin (M421), Boldereff
(M422), and Link (X100).

M1 Adams, Robert M. SURFACE AND SYMBOL: THE CONSISTENCY OF
    JAMES JOYCE'S *ULYSSES*. New York: Oxford Univ. Press, 1962.
        Painstaking analysis of JJ's use of fact and
        realistic detail, to determine the extent to
        which U's realistic data are fundamental to its
        submerged symbolic patterns ("piling, scaffold-
        ing, or adornment"). Adams' skeptical response
        to JJ's pedantry and his demonstration of U's
        dead ends and errors have been controversial,
        yet his book contains a wealth of information
        valuable for reading U. Well-written, though
        disconcertingly arrogant.

M2 Almeida, Hermione de. BYRON AND JOYCE THROUGH HOMER: *DON
    JUAN* AND *ULYSSES*. New York: Columbia Univ. Press, 1981.
        Well-written investigation of the informative
        parallels between the two remarkably dissimilar
        authors' correspondingly contrasting masterworks.
        Arguing that Byron and JJ share a basic "ambiv-
        alence" toward Homer in their assimilation and
        adaptation of the epic literary tradition and
        the Homeric "cultural heritage," Almeida demon-
        strates their use of the ODYSSEY as "their first
        pattern" for DON JUAN and U, their variant mod-
        ifications of the epic hero, their unconventional
        attacks on contemporary social ideals (departing
        from the Homeric confirmation of ideals), and
        their exploitation and parody of "all the major
        literary styles" descending from Homer. Ulti-
        mately, DON JUAN and U are comparable as mirrors
        of "the entire Western tradition."

M3 Barrow, Craig Wallace. MONTAGE IN JAMES JOYCE'S *ULYSSES*.
    Madrid and Potomac, Md.: Studia Humanitatis, 1980.
        Summarizes the idea and use of the cinematic
        montage device in fiction and fiction criticism,
        distinguishes the variety of montage techniques,
        and examines JJ's use of montage in U, episode
        by episode.

M4 Benjamin, Judy-Lynn, ed. THE CELTIC BULL: ESSAYS ON JAMES
    JOYCE'S *ULYSSES*. Tulsa, Okla.: Univ. of Tulsa Press, 1966.
        Collects twelve papers from an undergraduate
        honors seminar on U, at Hunter College. Inter-
        esting and occasionally impressive. Essays not
        separately entered and annotated in this guide.

M5   Blamires, Harry. THE BLOOMSDAY BOOK: A GUIDE THROUGH
     JOYCE'S *ULYSSES*. London: Methuen, 1966.
          By far the best reader's guide to U. Blamires'
          explications of each of U's eighteen episodes
          manage both to clarify obscurities for the be-
          ginning reader and to enrich the understanding
          of the experienced Joycean through their run-
          ning commentaries on the developing themes and
          motifs of the novel.

M6   Bonheim, Helmut. JOYCE'S BENEFICTIONS. Berkeley and Los
     Angeles: Univ. of California Press, 1964.
          Study of U and FW, correlating JJ's rebellions
          against social, political, and familial author-
          ity with his iconoclastic assaults on traditional
          literary forms and styles. After an opening dis-
          cussion of JJ's anti-authoritarian temper, Bon-
          heim examines the "heterodoxical" presentation
          of Bloom as failed father and the futile con-
          flicts of self and society in U, and explores
          the degeneration of the father figure, the King
          Mark motif (and other slain or fallen kings),
          the denigrations of church and God, and the "de-
          nunciation of misuses of power" in FW. His final
          chapter interestingly relates JJ's attacks on
          authority to his overriding comic vision.

M7   Bonnerot, Louis, ed. *ULYSSES:* CINQUANTE ANS APRÈS. Paris:
     M. Didier, 1974.
          Twenty-five essays on JJ, principally on U (one
          previously published). Sixteen articles in Eng-
          lish. Includes F109, F141, M78, M89, M119, M163,
          M166, M181, M204, M214, M231, M286, M295, M353,
          M373, M436, X29, X50, and X52.

M8   Budgen, Frank. JAMES JOYCE AND THE MAKING OF *ULYSSES*. Lon-
     don: Grayson, 1934.
          Running commentary on U, prefaced by a memoir
          of meetings and conversations with JJ and in-
          formed throughout by Budgen's and JJ's discus-
          sions of the novel-in-progress. Provides ex-
          ceptional insights into JJ's conception and
          working methods for U. Includes a final chap-
          ter on FW ("Work in Progress"). Reprinted in
          F13.

M9   Burgess, Anthony. JOYSPRICK: AN INTRODUCTION TO THE LANG-
       UAGE OF JAMES JOYCE. London: Deutsch, 1973.
           Misleadingly subtitled collection of commen-
           taries on various aspects of JJ's uses of lang-
           uage, principally in U. Burgess, a profes-
           sional novelist but an amateur linguist, makes
           several perceptive remarks about the fictional
           effects of JJ's language, but embarasses him-
           self in his needless attacks upon academic
           criticism and on the discipline of linguistics.
           While in no way an orderly or profound study,
           Burgess's book does provide some useful com-
           ment on JJ's use of dialect, his sentence struc-
           ture, and his "musicalization" of style.

M10   Caspel, Paul P.J. van. BLOOMERS ON THE LIFFEY: EISEGETI-
       CAL READINGS OF JAMES JOYCE'S *ULYSSES* PART II. Groningen,
       Neth.: Veenstra Visser, 1980.
           Not seen.

M11   Dimes, Louis T. PLAIN TALK ON *ULYSSES* (JAMES JOYCE) BY
       L'HOMME QUI RIT. London: "Comment" Publication, 1942.
           Slight critical commentary. (Pamphlet--19 pp.)

M12   Dujardin, Édouard. LE MONOLOGUE INTÉRIEURE: SON APPARI-
       TION, SES ORIGINES, SA PLACE DANS L'OEUVRE DE JAMES JOYCE.
       Paris: Messein, 1931.
           Recounts the Lazarus-like resurrection from
           obscurity of his early experiment in the inter-
           ior monologue (LES LAURIERS SONT COUPÉS [1887]),
           following its acknowledgement by JJ as the
           source for his monologue technique in U, de-
           fines the interior-monologue technique, dis-
           cusses its origins (e.g., influence of Wagner),
           and describes its sensational popularity among
           writers of the twenties. Includes references
           to U throughout. [In French.]

M13   Egri, Péter. AVANTGARDISM AND MODERNITY: A COMPARISON OF
       JAMES JOYCE'S *ULYSSES* WITH THOMAS MANN'S *DER ZAUBERBERG*
       AND *LOTTE IN WEIMAR*. Trans. Paul Aston. Tulsa, Okla.:
       Univ. of Tulsa Press, 1972.
           Fruitful comparative study, with a Marxist ori-
           entation. Egri distinguishes between JJ's
           avantgardism, which disrupts "the objective,
           plastic, dynamic, and synthesizing view of the
           world of the realistic tradition," and Mann's

modernism, which reaffirms "the objectivity of
reality" in creating the polyphonic novel, a
form embracing diversity, yet within the realist tradition. See X9.

M14   Ellmann, Richard. THE CONSCIOUSNESS OF JOYCE. New York:
      Oxford Univ. Press, 1977.
      Complement to Ellmann's earlier study of the
      themes and patterns of U (below), tracing JJ's
      assimilation and adaptation of his chief lit-
      erary sources. Individual chapters survey
      JJ's use of Homer and the Homeric tradition
      and his debts to Shakespeare (chiefly HAMLET),
      with notes on other literary sources in pas-
      sing. Ellmann's final chapter shifts atten-
      tion to the relations between JJ's aesthetics
      and politics. Insightful, but neither a major
      nor an original contribution. Includes a list
      of approximately 600 titles in JJ's Trieste
      Library.

M15   -----. ULYSSES ON THE LIFFEY. New York: Oxford Univ.
      Press, 1972.
      Strongly affirmative reading of U. Ellmann ex-
      amines the various structures of U, finding
      that the novel proceeds by dialectical triads
      of episodes, maintains four distinct levels of
      meaning throughout (literal, ethical, aesthe-
      tic, anagogic), and parallels the overall de-
      sign of the COMMEDIA ("Inferno," "Purgatorio,"
      "Paradiso"). Fine insights throughout, though
      several basic points have been anticipated by
      others. Extract reprinted in G19.

M16   Field, Saul, and Morton P. Levitt. BLOOMSDAY: AN INTER-
      PRETATION OF JAMES JOYCE'S ULYSSES. Greenwich, Conn.:
      New York Graphic Society, 1972.
      Twenty-five "compotina" prints by Field, on
      various subjects in U, with accompanying crit-
      ical commentary by Levitt (assimilating his
      earlier article on "The Family of Bloom"; see
      M209).

M17   Fischer-Seidel, Therese, ed. JAMES JOYCES ULYSSES:
      NEUERE DEUTSCHE AUFSÄTZE. Frankfurt a.M.: Suhrkamp, 1977.
      Important collection of eleven recent German
      textual and critical commentaries. Includes

the editor's introduction (pp. 11-25), a bibliography (pp. 347-75), extracts from or revisions of B16, M146, M285, M303, and the following essays and extracts of works listed in
part 3, below: Q2 (extract), X15 (extract),
X40, X44, X78, X82, and X100 (extract). [All
items in German.]

M18   French, Marilyn. THE BOOK AS WORLD: JAMES JOYCE'S *ULYSSES*.
      Cambridge, Mass.: Harvard Univ. Press, 1976.
            Study of the dialectical interplay among JJ's
            shifting styles, tones, and points of view,
            and of the reader's shifting sympathies through
            the "journey" of U. After his "initial style"
            in U's first six episodes firmly establishes
            the reader's sympathy with humanity (e.g.,
            Bloom and Stephen), JJ tests and sustains this
            sympathy through increasing the distance of
            his point of view ("city," "world," "universe"),
            the opacity of his style, and the hostility of
            his tone, only to return to affirmation in U's
            coda, or "ricorso," the "Penelope" episode. A
            fine interpretation, though occasionally marred
            by repetitive and turgid writing. See Law-
            rence's similar, but non-affirmative study (M37).
            Also see Lobsien (M38a).

M19   Garvin, John. JAMES JOYCE'S DISUNITED KINGDOM AND THE
      IRISH DIMENSION. Dublin: Gill and Macmillan, 1976.
            Study of U and FW, contending that their basic
            themes, chief characters, topography, and his-
            torical, literary, and musical motifs are "near-
            ly all of Irish, and generally of Dublin, ori-
            gin." Garvin, himself a Dubliner, tracks down
            numerous factual details behind the works and
            mixes them freely with local gossip, anecdotes,
            fragments of JJ's biography, and personal spec-
            ulation, arriving at some useful insights and
            several curious conclusions (e.g., Simon Dedalus
            is the narrator of "Cyclops," JJ is Blazes Boy-
            lan). Overstated thesis, unsystematic illustra-
            tion, and unconvincing interpretation. Extract
            originally published in F71.

M20   Gifford, Don, with Robert J. Seidman. NOTES FOR JOYCE:
      AN ANNOTATION OF JAMES JOYCE'S *ULYSSES*. New York: Dutton,
      1974.
            Excellent reader's companion, providing page-

by-page factual annotations and translations,
and identifying allusions (with context) and
personalities in U. Includes maps for each
episode and an appendix listing the rhetorical
figures used by JJ in the "Aeolus" episode.
Despite errors, more generally useful than
Thornton's ALLUSIONS IN *ULYSSES* (M64).

M21 Gilbert, Stuart. JAMES JOYCE'S *ULYSSES:* A STUDY. 1930.
2nd ed. New York: Knopf, 1952.
Now classic introduction to U's major themes
and techniques, and explications of the individual episodes. Since Gilbert's study was
written in consultation with a JJ who was himself considerably removed from the writing of
U, its emphasis falls on the esoteric elements of
U which prefigure JJ's later interests seen in
FW. Further, Gilbert's explications are dis-
tended by summaries of the novel unnecessary
for a readership which may now easily obtain
the book. Still useful, but Blamires' THE
BLOOMSDAY BOOK is the better reader's guide
(see M5).

M22 Goldberg, S.L. THE CLASSICAL TEMPER: A STUDY OF JAMES
JOYCE'S *ULYSSES*. London: Chatto and Windus, 1961.
Perceptive analysis of the fundamental attitudes underlying JJ's creation of U. Goldberg
defines JJ's "classical temper," which replaced
his morally irresponsible, adolescent, romantic
temper ("militant aestheticism"--STEPHEN HERO,
PAYM), as both a moral and an artistic ideal:
a dramatic and humanistic objectivity which,
beginning with the "local and concrete," finds
a "spiritual completeness and impersonal order"
beyond. This emphasis on objectivity, however,
leads Goldberg into an unfortunate rejection
of U's later chapters as departures from the
ideal. Fine analyses of the aesthetic of PAYM
and U, and of irony, history, symbolism, realism, structure, and values in U. Extracts reprinted in G19 and K16. Also see M376.

M23 Gose, Elliott B., Jr. THE TRANSFORMATION PROCESS IN JOYCE
ULYSSES. Toronto: Univ. of Toronto Press, 1980.
Essentially an overwrought study of the cyclic
patterns and symbols in U. After a lengthy

digression on Bergson, Gose argues that the two
great, complementary influences on JJ's U were
Bruno and Freud, that JJ's Brunian vision of
"nature as the divine in a process of transformation" determines the various cycles of transformation in U (e.g., life-death, creation-de-
struction, digestion, sexuality), and that his
Freudian sense of "the protean and circean
twists of the mind" informs the psychological
transformation of U's characters. JJ's synthesis of Bruno and Freud contributes to his unique
amalgamation of the spiritual and scientific,
sublime and earthy, comic and grotesque in U.
Several intriguing observations, but unneces-
sarily dense and often plodding.

M24 Gottfried, Roy K. THE ART OF JOYCE'S SYNTAX IN *ULYSSES*.
Athens: Univ. of Georgia Press, 1980.
Systematic analyses of JJ's sentence structures
in U, leading to several generally valuable conclusions. JJ uses the traditional rules of syntax, Gottfried argues, in order to transgress
them, creating a "dialectical tension between
syntactic order and expressive form." The mechanics of syntax reinforce the systematic patterns of action and symbolism that JJ employs
to order U; however, his unique use of fragmented constructions, which nevertheless imply
a potential higher order ("as Entelechy"), en-
ables JJ to transgress the patterns of U's
world (e.g., space and time). JJ's transcen-
dence of syntax emphasizes his ultimate, controlling role as "artist-god in the text."
Several brilliant insights, and delightfully
well-written.

M25 Groden, Michael. *ULYSSES* IN PROGRESS. Princeton, N.J.:
Princeton Univ. Press, 1977.
Fine discussion of U's writing history. Groden
argues against the prevailing "revolutionary"
view of U's composition, showing, through close
analyses of the surviving draft materials, U's
"evolutionary" development through three distinct, though related phases of creation: Interior monologue ("Telemachus" and "Scylla and
Charybdis"); the experimentations with parodies
and "imposed styles" ("Wandering Rocks" through

"Oxen of the Sun"); and the turn toward FW in
the last episodes as the composition of U becomes its own subject ("Circe" through "Penelope"). Since traces of all three phases of
composition are clear in the finished work, U
is justly considered a "palimpsest" for JJ's
"development from 1914 to 1922." Several excellent observations. Extract originally published in M34.

M26 Hart, Clive. JAMES JOYCE'S *ULYSSES*. Sidney: Sidney Univ.
Press, 1968.
Good introductory survey of JJ's works prior
to U, study guide to the individual episodes
of U (brief explications with critical comment), and summary critique of U's styles,
techniques, and critical reception. Fine overview for the student, unified by Hart's thesis
that JJ writes "from a thoroughly moralist
point of view," consistently vindicating man
and "man's doings."

M27 Hart, Clive, and A.M. Leo Knuth. A TOPOGRAPHICAL GUIDE TO
JAMES JOYCE'S *ULYSSES*. 2 vols. Colchester, Engl.: WAKE
NEWSLITTER Press, 1975.
Describes JJ's techniques for incorporating
the features of the Dublin cityscape into U
and provides itineraries for the characters'
movements through the eighteen episodes of U.
Includes a list of Dublin addresses and place
names and, in a separate folder, eighteen maps
and three diagrams illustrating the itineraries.

M28 Hart, Clive, and David Hayman, eds. JAMES JOYCE'S *ULYSSES*.
CRITICAL ESSAYS. Berkeley and Los Angeles: Univ. of Cali-
fornia Press, 1974.
"Carefully modulated reassessment of Joyce's
accomplishment" by eighteen distinguished
Joyceans, one original essay per episode. Sev-
eral excellent contributions. Includes M345,
M348, M356, M360, M361, M362, M365, M369, M376,
M386, M393, M401, M412, M414, M428, M438, M446,
and M451.

M29 Hayman, David. *ULYSSES*: THE MECHANICS OF MEANING. Englewood Cliffs, N.J.: Prentice-Hall, 1970.
Introductory discussion of U's "action, charac-

ters, and setting, the thematic uses of analogy,
and the application of paradox, and then the
techniques, the structure, and the styles as
functional aspects of the book's meaning." Several good remarks on JJ's relation to European
literary traditions and on his narrator-"ar-
ranger" persona. A second, revised and enlarged
edition has been announced for 1982 publication
by the Univ. of Wisconsin Press.

M30 Henke, Suzette A. JOYCE'S MORACULOUS SINDBOOK: A STUDY
OF *ULYSSES*. Columbus: Ohio State Univ. Press, 1978.
Original application of the existential and
phenomenological critical methods of the "Geneva
school" (Georges Poulet and J. Hillis Miller),
Husserl, Heidegger, and Sartre, to arrive at
some very unoriginal conclusions about U: "Stephen moves from an enclosed world of determinism
to the existential liberation of artistic consciousness" and Bloom "creates hope out of de-
spair," transforming a "potentially tragic sit-
uation into a comedy of personal triumph," by
demonstrating "charity, sympathy, and the wisdom
of self-control."

M31 Hornik, Marcel P. STUDIES IN JAMES JOYCE: LEOPOLD BLOOM-
CANDAULES. Boar's Hill, Engl.: Lincombe Lodge Research
Library, 1959.
Bloom's unwitting offer of Molly to Stephen
originates in the classical story of Candaules
(Herodotus, HISTORIES) and was probably known
to JJ through its most recent variant, Gide's
play ROI CANDAULE (1900). (Pamphlet--19 pp.)

M32 Huxley, Aldous, Stuart Gilbert, and J. Schwartz. JOYCE
THE ARTIFICER: TWO [sic] STUDIES OF JOYCE'S METHOD. London: Privately Printed, 1952.
Three brief comments on JJ's incremental composition in U and FW. (Pamphlet--19 pp.)

M33 JAMES JOYCE QUARTERLY. 10 (1972), 5-199. "ULYSSES issue."
See M59.

M34 JAMES JOYCE QUARTERLY. 12 (1974-75), 6-168. "Textual
Studies Issue."
Includes M25 (extract), M381, and M407.

M35 Kain, Richard M. FABULOUS VOYAGER: JAMES JOYCE'S *ULYSSES*.
     Chicago: Univ. of Chicago Press, 1947.
         Good introductory study devoted to a variety
         of loosely integrated subjects: U's verbal
         motifs, isolation theme, setting, style, and
         technique, its social, political, and ethical
         criticism, and its ultimately "cosmic" level
         of meaning. Kain also provides several still
         useful factual appendixes on the characters,
         locations, and motifs of U.

M36 Kenner, Hugh. *ULYSSES*. London: Allen and Unwin, 1980.
         Insightful and provocative commentary on U,
         intended to supplant the introductions by Bud-
         gen, Gilbert, Hart, Hayman, et al., yet ad-
         dressed to a reader more than casually ac-
         quainted both with U and with the basic crit-
         ical views of U. Kenner opens with several
         general essays on U (e.g., its relations to
         JJ's other works, its chief characters, and
         its indirections of exposition and language--
         the "aesthetic of delay"), yet, by his study's
         midpoint, he shifts to a succession of commen-
         taries on the increasingly complex individual
         episodes ("Sirens" and after). Still, a clev-
         er, fresh, and welcome addition to the criti-
         cal discussion of U.

M37 Lawrence, Karen. THE ODYSSEY OF STYLE IN *ULYSSES*. Prince-
     ton, N.J.: Princeton Univ. Press, 1981.
         Study of JJ's arbitrary "rhetorical masks,"
         chiefly in "Aeolus" and the "Wandering Rocks"
         through "Penelope," contending that the novel's
         attack on the "authority of style" parallels
         its overall resistance to authoritative inter-
         pretation. Departing from recent critical
         trends which generally argue that meaning and
         coherence are found in the spatial unities of
         U's form, Lawrence finds U's progressively com-
         plex stylistic transformations repeatedly frus-
         trating the reader's expectations of traditional
         narrative sequence, formal coherence, or reve-
         lation of a "single truth" (differing in this
         last regard from French's similar study; see
         M18). In its "general movement...from writing
         to rhetorical exhibition" U becomes an "encyc-
         lopedia" of narrational experiments, a novel

concerned with its own composition as a subject, and, in its diffuse detail and subver-
sion of meaning, an ultimately realistic reflection of the "plurasignificance" of life
itself. Includes a preliminary discussion of
D, and two previously published articles (see
M366 and M445). Also see M38a.

M38   Litz, A. Walton. THE ART OF JAMES JOYCE: METHOD AND DE-
       SIGN IN *ULYSSES* AND *FINNEGANS WAKE*. 1961. Rev. ed. Lon-
       don: Oxford Univ. Press, 1964.
           Excellent and lucid analysis of JJ's method
       for composing his last two novels, based on
       close study of the surviving manuscript ma-
       terials. Litz traces JJ's changing concep-
       tion of his art, through the later revisions
       of U, showing JJ's fundamental movement from
       "exclusion" (e.g., the paring-down of STEPHEN
       HERO into PAYM), to a "process of inclusion"
       involving continual revision, both augmenting
       his material and increasing the density and
       complexity of his medium. This process of
       accretion and elaboration, together with the
       increasing imposition of patterns and designs,
       leads directly to the compositional methods
       of FW ("continual embroidery upon a fixed pat-
       tern"). Litz concludes with a healthily skep-
       tical view of JJ's "pyrrhic triumph" in FW.
       Extracts originally published in G56 and G64.

M38a   Lobsien, Eckard. DER ALLTAG DES *ULYSSES:* DIE VERMITTLUNG
       VON ÄSTHETISCHER UND LEBENSWELTLICHER ERFAHRUNG. Stutt-
       gart: J.B. Metzler, 1978.
           The third important, recent study (also see
       French [M18] and Lawrence [M37]), which seeks
       a departure both from the "classical" inter-
       pretations of U's meaning (i.e., in terms of
       conventional concerns with character and plot;
       e.g., Goldberg [M22]), and from the more recent
       formalist interpretations (i.e., U's meaning
       found in its spatial form; e.g. Ellmann [M15]).
       Lobsein sees the intriguing narrational exper-
       iments of U's later episodes as JJ's means for
       drawing the reader's attention to the arbitrar-
       iness and subjectivity of perception itself.
       While the first half of U may be approached as
       a traditional novel, only in its later stages is
       the reader made aware that the patterns of mean-
       ing found in daily experience *(Alltag)* by its

characters (or in the novel by its commentators), are extrinsic and imposed. U, thus, is
concerned with the subjective perception and
ordering of purportedly objective, everyday re-
alities, not, as is the conventional novel, with
the matter as perceived or ordered. Includes a
lengthy opening discussion of trends in U criticism. [In German.]

M39 Loehrich, Rolf. THE SECRET OF *ULYSSES*: AN ANALYSIS OF
JAMES JOYCE'S *ULYSSES*. McHenry, Ill.: The Compass Press,
1953.
Unsatisfactory and eccentric view of U as an
affirmative "account of how man gains revelation," equally abusing Christianity, Existentialism, and Freudianism in the process.

M40 Luna, Norman. *ULYSSES* AND *AL FILO DEL AGUA*: A TEXTUAL
COMPARATIVE STUDY. Lincoln: Univ. of Nebraska-Lincoln,
Inst. for International Studies, 1976.
Traces the extensive influence of U on Agustin
Yáñez's "labyrinths of language, mythology, arche-
type, and motif" in AL FILO DEL AGUA (1947).
(Monograph--53 pp.)

M41 Macaré, Helen H. A *ULYSSES* PHRASEBOOK. Portola Valley,
Calif.: Woodside Priory, 1981.
Glosses, by page and line, approximately 3,500
difficult or foreign words and phrases in U.

M42 Maddox, James H. JOYCE'S *ULYSSES* AND THE ASSAULT UPON
CHARACTER. New Brunswick, N.J.: Rutgers Univ. Press,
1978.
Sound and insightful discussion of JJ's inno-
vative characterization in U as the correlative
to his experiments with fictional conventions.
U demonstrates the "art of surround and peri-
phery," evoking through massive detail yet
"never naming the center." Similarly, the
soul of a character, for JJ, is at once "know-
able from a thousand perspectives and eternally
mysterious, noumenous." Maddox traces JJ's
establishment of multiple perspectives on the
characters of Stephen, Bloom, and Molly, and
his subsequent "assaults" on the conventions
of realistic characterization, throughout "map-
ping" the shape of their souls as previous
critics have mapped the action of the novel.

M43   Mason, Michael. JAMES JOYCE: *ULYSSES*. London: Arnold,
      1972.
            Elementary introduction to JJ's technical "con-
            ception" of U and to the moral values both ques-
            tioned and inherent in U, together with brief,
            superficial notes on the individual episodes.

M44   Mitchell, Breon. JAMES JOYCE AND THE GERMAN NOVEL, 1922-
      1933. Athens: Ohio Univ. Press, 1976.
            Study of the early German translations of U,
            their contemporary reception, and their impact
            on the narrative techniques of selected German
            authors. Mitchell examines U's direct but su-
            perficial influence on Hans Henny Jahnn's PER-
            RUDJA (1929), its less direct and more complex
            relationship to Alfred Döblin's BERLIN ALEXAN-
            DERPLATZ (1929), and its indirect yet profound
            impact on Hermann Broch's trilogy DIE SCHLAF-
            WANDLER (1931-32). Competent, though limited
            and, at times, plodding.

M45   MOSAIC. 6, No. 1 (1972), 3-245. "ULYSSES and THE WASTE
      LAND Fifty Years After: A Critical Retrospective."
            Nine essays on JJ and U, a collection of illu-
            strations for U by Julien Alberts with an ap-
            preciative critique by R.G. Collins, and eight
            articles on Eliot and THE WASTE LAND. Guest
            editors: Collins and Kenneth McRobbie. Includes
            H176, M70, M187, M205, M226, M299, M319, M368,
            and M397.

M46   Mozley, Charles. CONCERNING *ULYSSES* AND THE BODLEY HEAD.
      Barnet, Engl.: Stellar Press, 1961.
            Comments on U, in celebration of the twenty-
            fifth anniversary of the Bodley Head publica-
            tion of U. (Pamphlet--15 pp.)

M47   Nabokov, Vladimir. LECTURES ON *ULYSSES:* A FACSIMILE OF
      THE MANUSCRIPT. Columbia, S.C.: Bruccoli Clark, 1980.
            Facsimile of Nabokov's mostly handwritten notes
            for his university lectures on U (133 pp.), with
            a brief "Foreword" by A. Walton Litz (n. pag.
            [i-iii]). Nabokov presents a solid, commonsense
            reading of U as essentially a realistic novel
            which develops three related themes: "the hope-
            less past," "the ridiculous and tragic present,"
            and "the pathetic future." First published in
            M244.

M48   Parr, Mary. JAMES JOYCE: THE POETRY OF CONSCIENCE: A STUDY
      OF *ULYSSES*. Milwaukee, Wis.: Inland Press, 1961.
      U presented as JJ's fulfillment of Stephen's
      vow to create the "uncreated conscience" of
      his race. Parr sees the representative modern
      conscience, however, embodied in the figure of
      Charlie Chaplin upon whom, she argues, both
      Leopold Bloom and U (as an organic form), are
      modeled. Correspondingly Parr traces cinematic
      techniques in U. Bizarre, but amusing.

M49   Powys, John Cowper. JAMES JOYCE'S *ULYSSES:* AN APPRECIA-
      TION. London: Village Press, 1975.
      Reprint of Powys's admiring early review (1923).
      (Pamphlet--21 pp.)

M50   Prescott, Joseph. EXPLORING JAMES JOYCE. Carbondale:
      Southern Illinois Univ. Press, 1964.
      Collects seven previously published essays,
      several of them distinguished. Prescott ex-
      amines JJ's increasing play with language
      through his works and comments valuably on
      the relationships between STEPHEN HERO and
      PAYM, but the chief contributions of his col-
      lection are his five discussions of U's Hom-
      eric backgrounds, local allusions, character-
      ization of Stephen and Molly, and stylistic
      realism. Extracts originally published in
      G56 and G57, and reprinted in K5, K6, K14,
      and K16.

M51   Raleigh, John Henry. THE CHRONICLE OF LEOPOLD AND MOLLY
      BLOOM: *ULYSSES* AS NARRATIVE. Berkeley and Los Angeles:
      Univ. of California Press, 1977.
      Interesting and useful reference work, docu-
      menting the "immense and detailed naturalistic
      base" upon which U is constructed. Raleigh
      coalesces the random and various references to
      the Blooms' pasts, their presents, and intima-
      tions of their futures, arranging them into a
      meticulous year-by-year chronicle (essentially
      1865-1904). Finds a naturalistic "Defoe-esque"
      order in U, but not to the exclusion Blakean
      symbolic interpretations.

M52   Reynolds, Mary T. JOYCE AND DANTE: THE SHAPING IMAGINA-
      TION. Princeton, N.J.: Princeton Univ. Press, 1981.
      An intriguing argument for considering Dante,

as well as Homer and Shakespeare, as a decisive
influence on JJ's developing art, most fully
illustrated in his U. Reynolds describes JJ's
reading and maturing understanding of Dante,
traces his Dantean explorations of father figures, of parental themes, and, particularly,
of the theme of love in U (e.g., "Sirens" episode), and compares JJ's and Dante's views of
the poetic imagination and myth-making. Her
concluding chapters draw less impressive con-
nections between Dante and JJ's other works
(PAYM paralleled with LA VITA NUOVA; FW very
briefly treated). Also includes an extended
list of JJ's allusions to Dante (pp. 223-329).

M53 Sandulescu, Constantin-George. THE JOYCEAN MONOLOGUE: A
STUDY OF CHARACTER AND MONOLOGUE IN JOYCE'S *ULYSSES* AGAINST
THE BACKGROUND OF LITERARY TRADITION. Colchester, Engl.:
WAKE NEWSLITTER Press, 1979.
    Not seen.

M54 Schoonbroodt, Jean. POINT OF VIEW AND EXPRESSIVE FORM IN
JAMES JOYCE'S *ULYSSES*. Liege, Belg.: Universitas Catholica
Lovaniensis, 1967.
    Extended commentary on the "Scylla and Charyb-
dis" episode, discussion of the varieties of
interior monologue in U, essays on the liturgical elements in JJ's style and characterization,
and, among several appendixes, an essay on "The
Liturgy in the PORTRAIT." Chaotically organized
and poorly written dissertation.

M55 Schutte, William M. JOYCE AND SHAKESPEARE: A STUDY IN THE
MEANING OF *ULYSSES*. New Haven, Conn.: Yale Univ. Press,
1957.
    Most detailed and still the most authoritative
discussion of the Shakespeare theme in U and
an influential, negative interpretation of U's
meaning. Schutte describes the HAMLET parallels
of the opening episodes and, in the major portion of his study, examines the backgrounds to
and course of Stephen's Shakespeare theory (in-
valid as criticism; brilliant as revelation of
Stephen's character deficiencies and of JJ's
intentions for U). Schutte's analysis of the
dual role of the artist in Stephen's discourse
(as creator and destroyer), his chapter on

Bloom's Shakespearian traits, and his observations on JJ's contrast of Elizabethan order
with modern chaos are especially recommended.
Includes appendixes on the sources for Stephen's
theory and on the Shakespeare allusions in U
(and in STEPHEN HERO and PAYM as well).

M56 Seidel, Michael. EPIC GEOGRAPHY: JAMES JOYCE'S *ULYSSES*.
Princeton, N.J.: Princeton Univ. Press, 1976.
Investigation of JJ's adaptations of epic traditions, myth and symbolism, and narrative
structures, as well as his assimilation of the
commentaries and practices of Blake, Defoe,
Vico, Homer, and the Homeric critics. A major
portion of Seidel's study, expanding Gilbert's
discussion of JJ's debt to Victor Bérard's LES
PHÉNICIENS ET L'ODYSSÉE (1902-03; see M21),
shows how JJ modeled the movement of his characters upon Ulysses' migrations in the ODYSSEY.
Includes twenty-four maps.

M57 Shechner, Mark. JOYCE IN NIGHTTOWN: A PSYCHOANALYTIC IN-
QUIRY INTO *ULYSSES*. Berkeley and Los Angeles: Univ. of
California Press, 1974.
Essays on JJ's psyche as revealed in U. Con-
sidering Stephen's analysis of HAMLET a model
of psychoanalytic criticism, Shechner turns
the tables on JJ, examining the Freudian implications of Stephen's alienation and hostility,
of the psychopathia sexualis of the "Circe" episode, of the virgin and temptress females in
U, and of Stephen's (i.e., JJ's) relationship
with his mother. Unfortunately jargon-laden.
Extract originally published in M59.

M58 Smith, Paul Jordan. A KEY TO THE *ULYSSES* OF JAMES JOYCE.
Chicago: Covici, 1927.
Interesting and sympathetic brief overview of
U, tracing the Homeric correspondences and
praising JJ's capture of the universal "cry of
tortured conscience."

M59 Staley, Thomas F., ed. *ULYSSES: FIFTY YEARS*. Bloomington
Indiana Univ. Press, 1974.
Twelve essays on various aspects of U, viewed
"from the perspective of fifty years," together
with a modest group of photographs of JJ's

"dwellings." Originally published as a special
issue of JJQ (10 [1972], 5-199). Includes M57
(extract), M72, M77, M88, M185, M195, M203, M210,
M215, M276, M285, and M370.

M60 Staley, Thomas F., and Bernard Benstock, eds. APPROACHES
TO *ULYSSES:* TEN ESSAYS. Pittsburgh: Univ. of Pittsburgh
Press, 1970.
> Ten commissioned essays, examining the most di-
> verse and variegated of novels from a corre-
> sponding variety of perspectives. Includes M90,
> M164, M183, M248, M279, M288, M298, M316, M328,
> and extracts from G10 and below.

M61 Steinberg, Erwin R. THE STREAM OF CONSCIOUSNESS AND BE-
YOND IN *ULYSSES*. Pittsburgh: Univ. of Pittsburgh Press,
1973.
> Intensive analysis of JJ's use of the stream-
> of-consciousness technique. Steinberg invest-
> igates the clouded relationship between the
> psychological stream of consciousness and its
> literary approximations, evaluating JJ's suc-
> cess in presenting psychologically convincing
> portraits of U's three major characters (close
> stylistic analysis of "Proteus," "Lestrygonians,"
> and "Penelope"). Steinberg concludes with an
> account of JJ's movement away from stream of
> consciousness toward the "polyphonic technique"
> of FW. Extracts originally published in G65,
> G73, and above. Also see M279.

M62 Sultan, Stanley. THE ARGUMENT OF *ULYSSES*. Columbus: Ohio
State Univ. Press, 1964.
> Forceful and lengthy explication of "what hap-
> pens" in U. Sultan reads U as a conventional
> novel which presents its characters and their
> situations through relatively conventional and
> essentially static means ("Telemachus" through
> "Scylla and Charybdis"); then, after an inter-
> lude ("Wandering Rocks"), U develops its mate-
> rials toward a climax ("Circe") and a resolu-
> tion ("Eumaeus" through "Penelope"), with cor-
> responding expansiveness and increasingly in-
> novative narrative techniques. Sultan sees
> U's resolution as strongly affirmative, as Ste-
> phen finds his father-Messiah and the Blooms
> reunite. Good detailed readings and several
> influential insights.

M63   -----. *ULYSSES, THE WASTE LAND,* AND MODERNISM: A JUBILEE
      STUDY. Port Washington, N.Y.: Kennikat, 1977.
            Comparative study of the most famous of modern-
            ist novels and poems, principally focused on
            those "qualities" and interpretive problems in
            THE WASTE LAND which "reflect a rich set of
            similarities between it" and U, and how those
            similarities illuminate "Modernism as a whole."
            Several good observations.

M64   Thornton, Weldon. ALLUSIONS IN *ULYSSES:* AN ANNOTATED LIST.
      Chapel Hill: Univ. of North Carolina Press, 1968.
            Excellent annotations for virtually all JJ's
            allusions to works of "literature, philosophy,
            theology, history," to "the fine arts," and to
            "popular and folk music" in U. Largely dupli-
            cated by and more limited in scope than Gifford's
            and Seidman's NOTES FOR JOYCE (see M20), though
            often providing more complete and more accurate
            information. See M379, M383, and M437.

M65   Vresswijk, Harry. NOTES ON JOYCE'S *ULYSSES,* PART I (CHAP-
      TERS 1-3): (A VERY FIRST DRAFT). Amsterdam: Van Gennep,
      1971.
            Not seen.

M, ii.   General Critical Articles or Chapters on ULYSSES

M66   Albert, L. "ULYSSES, Cannibals and Freemasons." AD, 2
      (1951), 40-52.
            Masonic rituals and references in U.

M67   Aldington, Richard. "Mr. James Joyce's ULYSSES." 1921.
      In LITERARY STUDIES AND REVIEWS. New York: Dial Press,
      1924. Pp. 192-207.
            The "deplorable" influence of U, the "grave
            stone...of Naturalisme." (Note, however, that
            T.S. Eliot evidently wrote his famous defense
            of U at Aldington's suggestion; see M132). Ex-
            tract reprinted in G25.

M68   Allen, Walter. THE ENGLISH NOVEL: A SHORT CRITICAL HIST-
      ORY. New York: Dutton, 1954. Pp. 423-31.
            Brief overview of U, emphasizing its comedy
            and variety.

M69 Barrett, William. "Myth or the Museum?" In TIME OF NEED:
     FORMS OF IMAGINATION IN THE TWENTIETH CENTURY. New York:
     Harper and Row, 1972. Pp. 312-50.
          Argues JJ's essential traditionalism as realist
          (U) and mythmaker (FW).

M70 Beausang, Michael. "Seeds for Planting of Bloom." MOSAIC,
     6, No. 1 (1972), 11-22.
          Vegetation-hero and divine king archetypes in
          U. See M45.

M71 Beebe, Maurice. "James Joyce: The Return from Exile." In
     IVORY TOWERS AND SACRED FOUNTS: THE ARTIST AS HERO IN FIC-
     TION FROM GOETHE TO JOYCE. New York: New York Univ. Press,
     1964. Pp. 260-95.
          See K30.

M72 -----. "ULYSSES and the Age of Modernism." In *ULYSSES:*
     FIFTY YEARS. Ed. Thomas F. Staley. Pp. 172-88. See M59.
          JJ's characteristically "modernist" traits:
          formalism, ironic detachment, use of myth, and
          "reflexivism" (inward-turning).

M73 Begnal, Michael H. "The Mystery Man of ULYSSES." JML, 2
     (1972), 565-68.
          Suggests the "man in the macintosh" is the
          Irish poet Mangan.

M74 Bennett, Arnold. "James Joyce's ULYSSES." 1922. In THE
     AUTHOR'S CRAFT, AND OTHER CRITICAL WRITINGS. Ed. Samuel
     Hynes. Lincoln: Univ. of Nebraska Press, 1968. Pp. 211-
     17.
          Extravagant praise and extravagant blame; de-
          spite brilliance, JJ "has made novel-reading
          into a fair imitation of penal servitude." Ex-
          tract reprinted in G25.

M75 Bennett, John Z. "Unposted Letter: Joyce's Leopold Bloom."
     BuR, 14, No. 1 (1966), 1-13.
          Study of Bloom's character and of the possibil-
          ities suggested, if not realized, for its fur-
          ther development.

M76 Benstock, Bernard. "L. Bloom as Dreamer in FINNEGANS
     WAKE." PMLA, 82 (1967), 91-97.
          Elements of Bloom's character and conscious-
          ness assimilated into the dreamer in FW.

M77   -----. "ULYSSES Without Dublin." In *ULYSSES:* FIFTY YEARS.
       Ed. Thomas F. Staley. Pp. 90-117. See M59.
       Fine commentary on and summary of the major
       contemporary reviews of U.

M78   -----. "What Stephen Says: Joyce's Second Portrait of the
       Artist." In *ULYSSES:* CINQUANTE ANS APRÈS. Ed. Louis Bon-
       nerot. Pp. 137-52. See M7.
       Stephen's potential artistry not to be found
       in what he says or writes in U, but in the
       creative imagination revealed in his thoughts.

M79   Benstock, Shari. "The Double Image of Modernism: Matisse's
       Etchings for ULYSSES." ConL, 21 (1980), 450-79.
       Though not based on a knowledge of JJ's text,
       Matisse's 1935 illustrations, in their method,
       "rather cleverly complemented that of" U. In-
       cludes ten illustrations.

M80   -----. "The Evasion Principle: A Search for Survivors in
       ULYSSES." MFS, 24 (1978), 159-79.
       Bloom's "self-protective" mask and tactics of
       "evasion" enable him to attain equanimity in a
       novel, too, masked and evasive.

M81   -----. "ULYSSES as Ghoststory." JJQ, 12 (1975), 396-413.
       Ghosts in the novel and ghostly qualities in
       its characters.

M82   -----. "Who Killed Cock Robin? The Sources of Free Indi-
       rect Style in ULYSSES." STYLE, 14 (1980), 259-73.
       JJ's deliberate manipulation of conventional
       narration effectively kills the idea of the
       narrator and provides a *locus classicus* for
       the free indirect style as a narrative tech-
       nique.

M83   Benstock, Shari, et al. "Narrative in ULYSSES." In JOYCE
       & PARIS. Ed. Jacques Aubert and Maria Jolas. II, 33-58.
       See G8.
       Two-day panel discussion of JJ's narrative
       techniques in U, studied in four sample pas-
       sages.

M84   Berger, Alfred Paul. "James Joyce, Adman." JJQ, 3 (1965),
       25-33.
       JJ's fascination with advertising and over 100
       references to ads in U.

M85 Blackmur, R.P. "The Jew in Search of a Son: Joyce's
     ULYSSES." 1948. In ELEVEN ESSAYS IN THE EUROPEAN NOVEL.
     New York: Harcourt, 1964. Pp. 27-47.
          U expresses in its difficult and fragmented
          technique and its theme of fragmentation (the
          "gaps" between individuals and generations),
          the breakdowns in modern culture.

M86 Blodgett, Harriet. "Joyce's Time Mind in ULYSSES: A New
     Emphasis." JJQ, 5 (1967), 22-29.
          JJ's concern for clock time equal to his con-
          cern for historical and durational time in U.

M87 Bowen, Zack. "Libretto for Bloomusalem in Song: The Music
     of Joyce's ULYSSES." In NEW LIGHT ON JOYCE. Ed. Fritz
     Senn. Pp. 149-66. See G73.
          JJ's use of musical references, motifs, and
          techniques.

M88 Boyle, Robert, S.J. "Miracle in Black Ink: A Glance at
     Joyce's Use of His Eucharistic Image." In *ULYSSES:* FIFTY
     YEARS. Ed. Thomas F. Staley. Pp. 47-60. See M59.
          JJ's use of the Eucharistic image in U rein-
          forces Ellmann's affirmative reading (see M15).

M89 -----. "Mystery in ULYSSES." In *ULYSSES:* CINQUANTE ANS
     APRÈS. Ed. Louis Bonnerot. Pp. 243-61. See M7.
          Importance of the mystery that can be "appre-
          hended only, never comprehended," learned by
          JJ in his study of theology, necessarily in-
          corporated into his own created world.

M90 -----. "The Priesthoods of Stephen and Buck." In AP-
     PROACHES TO *ULYSSES.* Ed. Thomas F. Staley and Bernard
     Benstock. Pp. 29-60. See M60.
          Buck as a false, "usurping priest" and Stephen
          as a Jesuitical priest of art. The arguments
          of this and the above two essays are partly as-
          similated and extended in Boyle's JAMES JOYCE'S
          PAULINE VISION (see G15).

M91 -----. "ULYSSES as Frustrated Sonata Form." JJQ, 2 (1965),
     247-54.
          Amplifies musical analogues of Pound's obser-
          vation of a three-part, sonata structure in U
          (see M255).

M92   Briand, Paul L., Jr. "The Catholic Mass in James Joyce's
      ULYSSES." JJQ, 5 (1968), 312-22.
            Finds U's construction paralleling the three-
            part structure of the Mass. See supplemental
            note, by Patrick A. McCarthy, JJQ, 7 (1970),
            132-37. Also see M331.

M93   Broch, Hermann. "Joyce and the Present Age." 1936. Trans.
      Eugene Jolas and Maria Jolas. In À JAMES JOYCE YEARBOOK.
      Ed. Maria Jolas. Pp. 68-108. See G45.
            In U, JJ anticipates many of the most recent
            technical experiments (e.g., musical atonality)
            and themes (e.g., relativity) of contemporary
            art. See X5.

M94   Brooke, Jocelyn. "Proust and Joyce: The Case for the Pro-
      secution." ADAM INTERNATIONAL REVIEW, Nos. 297-98 (1961),
      pp. 5-66.
            Extended comparative discussion of themes and
            techniques in U and in Proust's A LA RECHERCHE
            DU TEMPS PERDU (1912-27), with several "swipes"
            at the uncritical adulators of both authors.

M95   Brooks, Cleanth. "Joyce's ULYSSES: Symbolic Poem, Biog-
      raphy, or Novel?" In IMAGINED WORLDS: ESSAYS ON SOME ENG-
      LISH NOVELS AND NOVELISTS IN HONOUR OF JOHN BUTT. Ed.
      Maynard Mack and Ian Gregor. London: Methuen, 1968. Pp.
      419-39.
            Defends U as a novel, finding coherence in JJ's
            use of symbolic paradigms for structure (e.g.,
            the dog-god pattern).

M96   Bryer, Jackson R. "Joyce, ULYSSES, and the LITTLE REVIEW."
      SAQ, 66 (1967), 148-64.
            Examines U's incomplete serial publication
            (1918-20) and the rarely discussed first cen-
            sorship trial (1921).

M97   Burgum, Edwin B. "ULYSSES and the Impasse of Individual-
      ism." In THE NOVEL AND THE WORLD'S DILEMMA. New York:
      Oxford Univ. Press, 1947. Pp. 95-108.
            U a cynical chronicle of frustration, a product
            of the post-war decadence.

M98   Burrell, Angus. "James Joyce and ULYSSES." In his and
      Dorothy Brewster's MODERN FICTION. New York: Columbia
      Univ. Press, 1934. Pp. 155-217.
            See K42.

M99   Campbell, Joseph. "Contransmagnificandjewbangtantiality."
      SLitI, 3, No. 2 (1970), 3-18.
           In U, JJ translates the Christian imagery of
           the Incarnation into Oriental terms, finding
           mankind consubstantial with the transcendent
           divinity through individual transubstantiation.
           Explicates title word from "Proteus." See G78.

M100 Caserio, Robert L. PLOT, STORY, AND THE NOVEL. Princeton,
      N.J.: Princeton Univ. Press, 1979. Pp. 237-48.
           U's varieties of technique demonstrate the
           "artificial and provisional nature of all nar-
           rative order, especially the order that is the
           family plot."

M101 Cazamian, Louis. "L'Oeuvre de James Joyce." REVUE ANGLO-
      AMERICAINE, 2, No. 2 (1924), 97-113.
           U an intriguing, though fatiguing 'laboratory
           experiment.' Extract translated and reprinted
           in G25.

M102 Chesterton, G.K. "On Phases of Eccentricity." In ALL I
      SURVEY: A BOOK OF ESSAYS. London: Methuen, 1933. Pp. 62-
      68.
           Serious modern play with language and style
           (JJ and Stein), "consists of doing as a nov-
           elty what a Victorian did long ago as a joke."
           Extract reprinted in G25.

M103 Cohen, Keith. FILM AND FICTION: THE DYNAMICS OF EXCHANGE.
      New Haven, Conn.: Yale Univ. Press, 1979.
           Theoretical comparisons of cinematic and nar-
           rative techniques (e.g., time, point of view,
           and montage in U).

M104 Cohn, Dorrit. TRANSPARENT MINDS: NARRATIVE MODES FOR PRE-
      SENTING CONSCIOUSNESS IN FICTION. Princeton, N.J.: Prince-
      ton Univ. Press, 1978. Pp. 82-88, 91-98, 217-34, and pas-
      sim.
           Considerable discussion of U to illustrate
           varieties of narrative techniques (e.g., quoted
           monologue, narrated monologue [cf. *erlebte
           rede*], autonomous monologue [e.g., "Penelope"]).

M105 Coleman, Elliott. "A Note on Joyce and Jung." JJQ, 1,
      No. 1 (1963), 11-16.
           JJ's influence on Jung, through U, chiefly his

helping Jung "to see that the fragmentation
of the world...was a part of the creative
process." See M180.

M106 Collins, Joseph. "Ireland's Latest Literary Antinomian:
      James Joyce." In THE DOCTOR LOOKS AT LITERATURE. London:
      Allen and Unwin, 1923. Pp. 35-60.
      Grudging admiration for JJ's creation of "a
      world, and a chaotic one in which no decent
      person wants to live." Extract reprinted in
      G25.

M107 Colum, Mary. "The Confessions of James Joyce." FREEMAN,
      5 (1922), 450-52.
      Despite its technical originality, U a con-
      ventional representative of the Rousseau-
      Strindberg type of confessional literature.
      (Review--admired by JJ.) Extract reprinted
      in G25.

M108 Cope, Jackson I. "The Rhythmic Gesture: Image and Aesthe-
      tic in Joyce's ULYSSES." ELH, 29 (1962), 67-89.
      Attributes both the "form" and the "cause" of
      U to JJ's developing conception of aesthetic
      rhythm (1902 and after).

M109 Croessmann, H.K. "Joyce, Gorman, and the Schema of ULYSSES:
      An Exchange of Letters--Paul L. Léon, Herbert Gorman, Ben-
      nett Cerf." In A JAMES JOYCE MISCELLANY, SECOND SERIES.
      Ed. Marvin Magalaner. Pp. 9-14. See G56.
      Letters documenting a controversy among Gor-
      man, Léon, and Cerf over the proposed publi-
      cation of the U schema.

M110 Cronin, Anthony. "The Advent of Bloom." In A QUESTION
      OF MODERNITY. London: Secker and Warburg, 1966. Pp. 58-96.
      JJ's expansion of the realistic novel to pre-
      sent a full approximation of the "texture" of
      life: "Conversation, anecdote, thought, des-
      ultory impression, image and happening are
      freed at last from their long subordination
      to plot." Extract reprinted in G19.

M111 Crosman, Robert. "Who Was M'Intosh?" JJQ, 6 (1968), 128-
      36.
      Identifies M'Intosh as Bloom's *Döppelganger*.

M112   Curtius, Ernst Robert.   "Technique and Thematic Develop-
       ment of James Joyce."   Trans. Eugene Jolas.   TRANSITION,
       Nos. 16-17 (1929), pp. 310-25.
              JJ's accomplished yet "sterile" employment of
              stream of consciousness.   Extract reprinted
              in G25.   Also see X6.

M113   Daiches, David.   "The Importance of ULYSSES."   In NEW
       LITERARY VALUES: STUDIES IN MODERN LITERATURE.   Edinburgh:
       Oliver and Boyd, 1936.   Pp. 69-82.
              U significant for its new technique of char-
              acterization, escape from "dimensional limi-
              tations" of time, and "new and dangerous treat-
              ment of language."

M114   Dalton, Jack P.   "The Text of ULYSSES."   In NEW LIGHT ON
       JOYCE.   Ed. Fritz Senn.   Pp. 99-119.   See G73.
              Describes the corrupt state of the 1961 Random
              House "corrected" edition.

M115   Damon, S. Foster.   "The Odyssey in Dublin; with a Post-
       script, 1947."   1929.   In JAMES JOYCE.   Ed. Seon Givens.
       Pp. 203-42.   See G30.
              Discerning early study of U's sources and its
              symbolic, spiritual, and psychological levels
              of meaning (cf. Homer, Dante, and Shakespeare),
              which also stresses the simplicity of the
              novel's story.   Reprinted in G25.

M116   Daniel-Rops, Henry.   "Une Technique Nouvelle: Le Monologue
       Intérieur."   LE CORRESPONDENT, No. 1664 (1932), pp. 281-
       305.
              The history and dynamics of the interior mono-
              logue technique, with special reference to
              Dujardin and JJ.   Extract translated and re-
              printed in G25.

M117   Day, Robert Adams.   "Joyce's Gnomons, Lenehan, and the
       Persistence of an Image."   NOVEL, 14 (1980), 5-19.
              See J99.

M118   -----.   "Joyce's Waste Land and Eliot's Unknown God."
       In LITERARY MONOGRAPHS.   Vol. 4.   Ed. Eric Rothstein.
       Madison: Univ. of Wisconsin Press, 1971.   Pp. 139-210,
       218-26.
              Detailed demonstration of Eliot's compression
              and transformation in THE WASTE LAND of the

themes, the symbolism and, especially, the
structure of the "expansive" U.

M119 Deane, Seamus. "ULYSSES: The Exhaustion of Literature
and the Literature of Exhaustion." In *ULYSSES*: CINQUANTE
ANS APRÈS. Ed. Louis Bonnerot. Pp. 263-74. See M7.
    JJ's recognition that "traditional literature
    is exhausted and that future literature must
    make of this exhaustion either a theme, or an
    organizing principle, or a point of departure."

M120 Delbaere-Garant, Jeanne. "From the Moocow to Navelless
Eve: The Spiral Growth of Stephen Dedalus." RLV, 43
(1977), 131-41.
    See K50.

M121 DiBernard, Barbara. "Parallax as Parallel, Paradigm, and
Paradox in ULYSSES." EIRE, 10, No. 1 (1975), 69-84.
    Astronomical use of the term "parallax," as
    defined by Robert Ball (referred to by Bloom),
    an important structural element in U.

M122 Doody, Terrence A. "DON QUIXOTE, ULYSSES, and the Idea
of Realism." NOVEL, 12 (1979), 197-214.
    Parallel conceptions of realism underlying
    the two works.

M123 Drew, Elizabeth A. "The Difficulties of Joyce's ULYSSES."
CEA CRITIC, 14, No. 2 (1952), 1, 6.
    U less important for its stylistic and tech-
    nical originality than for its "fundamental
    deep conservatism" and "profound moral state-
    ments." See G18.

M124 Duncan, Joseph E. "The Modality of the Audible in Joyce's
ULYSSES." PMLA, 72 (1957), 286-95.
    JJ's treatment of sound reviewed in light of
    Aristotle's "idea of perception and modality."

M125 Dundes, Alan. "Study of Folklore in Literature and Culture: Identification and Interpretation." JOURNAL OF
AMERICAN FOLKLORE, 78 (1965), 136-42.
    Notes JJ's use of folklore elements and ex-
    amines Stephen's "fox and grandmother" riddle.

M126 Eddins, Dwight. "ULYSSES: The Search for the Logos."
ELH, 47 (1980), 804-19.
    Stephen's and Bloom's successful "struggle to

find a logos comprehensive and flexible enough
to deal with the chaotic multiplicity of experience."

M127   Edel, Leon. "Introduction." In Édouard Dujardin's WE'LL
       TO THE WOODS NO MORE. Trans. Stuart Gilbert. New York:
       New Directions, 1957. Pp. vii-xxvii.
             Stresses influence of Dujardin's interior mon-
          ologue on JJ's techniques in U.

M128   -----. "The Mind's Eye View." In THE MODERN PSYCHOLOGI-
       CAL NOVEL. 1955. Rev. ed. New York: Grosset and Dunlap,
       1964. Pp. 75-93.
             Distinct qualities of the three streams of
          consciousness in U, "the fountain-head of the
          modern psychological novel." (Numerous addi-
          tional comments on JJ, passim.)

M129   Edgar, Pelham. "Psycho-Analysis and James Joyce." In
       THE ART OF THE NOVEL: FROM 1700 TO THE PRESENT TIME. New
       York: Macmillan, 1933. Pp. 301-19.
             Admires JJ's presentation of the waking un-
          conscious mind in U.

M130   Edwards, Calvin R. "The Hamlet Motif in Joyce's ULYSSES."
       WR, 15 (1950), 5-13.
             Finds the archetypes for several of U's char-
          acters and situations in HAMLET.

M131   Eggers, Tilly. "Darling Milly Bloom." JJQ, 12 (1975),
       386-95.
             Function and significance of Milly's charac-
          ter.

M132   Eliot, T.S. "ULYSSES, Order, and Myth." DIAL, 75 (1923),
       480-83.
             Frequently quoted (and reprinted) praise of
          JJ's innovative mythical structure: "the myth-
          ical method [is] a step toward making the mod-
          ern world possible for art." Reprinted in G25
          (extract) and G30. Also see M67.

M133   Empson, William. "The Theme of ULYSSES." KR, 18 (1956),
       26-52.
             Straight-forward biographical reading. Ste-
          phen is JJ, and U commemorates the turning
          point in his career which led him to write D.
          Reprinted with revisions in G57.

M134   Esslinger, Pat M., and Duane R. Carr. "Hugh (Blazes)
       Boylan: The Last O'Neill." EIRE, 10, No. 2 (1975), 32-
       43.
              Irish historical backgrounds amplify the sig-
              nificance of the contest between Boylan and
              Bloom ("the new Irishman").

M135   Evans, William A. "Wordagglutinations in Joyce's ULYSSES."
       SLitI, 3, No. 2 (1970), 27-36.
              Statistical analysis of JJ's experimental
              "weldings of two or more single words to pro-
              duce units with special meanings." See G78.

M136   Fehr, Bernhard. "James Joyces ULYSSES." ENGLISCHE
       STUDIEN, 60 (1925), 180-205.
              Correlates JJ's "spatialization" of time and
              memory with contemporary relativist philosophy
              (e.g., Bergson and Russell). Extract trans-
              lated (ineptly) from the original German and
              reprinted in G25.

M137   Fiedler, Leslie. "Bloom on Joyce; or, Jokey for Jacob."
       In NEW LIGHT ON JOYCE. Ed. Fritz Senn. Pp. 195-208.
       See G73.
              Personal response to U, in praise of Bloom.

M138   Fischer, Emeric. "Le Monologue Intérieur dans l'ULYSSE
       de James Joyce." LA REVUE FRANÇAISE, 28 (1933), 445-53.
              Notes the logical and grammatical structure
              and coherence in JJ's use of the interior mon-
              ologue. Extract translated and reprinted in
              G25.

M139   Fitzpatrick, William P. "Joyce's Shakespeare: Reflections
       in Circe's Mirror." MODERN BRITISH LITERATURE, 2 (1977),
       64-74.
              Shakespeare becomes a "complex symbol" in U,
              representing both the struggle of the modern
              artist to create and a synthesizing force
              drawing together the portraits of Stephen and
              Bloom.

M140   -----. "The Myth of Creation: Joyce, Jung, and ULYSSES."
       JJQ, 11 (1974), 123-44.
              Jungian analysis of mother fixation and rite
              of initiation themes in "Oxen of the Sun,"
              "Circe," and "Penelope."

M141   Fogel, Daniel Mark. "Symbol and Context in ULYSSES:
       Joyce's 'Bowl of Bitter Waters' and Passover." ELH,
       46 (1979), 710-21.
           JJ's use of the "chief symbolic elements of
           the Passover ritual" in U.

M142   Ford, Ford Madox. "ULYSSES and the Handling of Indecen-
       cies." ENGLISH REVIEW, 35 (1922), 538-48.
           Ford's ambivalent response to JJ. Extract
           reprinted in G25.

M143   Ford, Jane. "Why is Milly in Mullingar?" JJQ, 14 (1977),
       436-49.
           Suggests sublimated incest in Bloom's "preoc-
           cupation with his daughter." See G43.

M144   Forster, E.M. ASPECTS OF THE NOVEL. New York: Harcourt,
       1927. Pp. 177-80.
           Regards U as a "fantasy."

M145   Frank, Joseph. "Spatial Form in Modern Literature." 1945.
       In THE WIDENING GYRE: CRISIS AND MASTERY IN MODERN LITER-
       ATURE. New Brunswick, N.J.: Rutgers Univ. Press, 1963.
       Pp. 3-62.
           JJ's appropriation and amplification of Flau-
           bert's technique of spatial counterpoint
           (chiefly pp. 14-19).

M146   Gabler, Hans Walter. "Werkentstehung und Textsituationen
       des ULYSSES." In JAMES JOYCES *ULYSSES:* NEUERE DEUTSCHE
       AUFSÄTZE. Ed. Therese Fischer-Seidel. Pp. 58-79. See
       M17.
           Important commentary on the novel's composi-
           tion and textual history, by the editor of
           the forthcoming critical edition. [In German.]
           See M159 and M191.

M147   Gaskell, Philip. "Joyce, ULYSSES, 1922." In FROM WRITER
       TO READER: STUDIES IN EDITORIAL METHOD. New York: Oxford
       Univ. Press, 1978. Pp. 213-44.
           Brief history of U's complex textual evolu-
           tion, suggesting various approaches to pre-
           paring and presenting a critical edition.

M148   Geckle, George L. "Stephen Dedalus as Lapwing: A Symbolic
       Center of ULYSSES." JJQ, 6 (1968), 104-14.
           Lapwing imagery corroborates picture of Ste-
           phen as a "faithless" failure in U.

M149   Gibbon, Monk. "The Unraised Hat." In A BASH IN THE TUN-
       NEL. Ed. John Ryan. Pp. 209-12. See F135.
           Pompous outrage at JJ's baseness; JJ no di-
           vinity, despite his worshippers.

M150   Giedion-Welcker, Carola. "Zum ULYSSES von James Joyce."
       NEUE SCHWEIZER RUNDSCHAU, 21 (1928), 18-32.
           Extended appreciation and critique of U's
           topics, themes, techniques, and episodes.
           Extract translated (ineptly) and reprinted
           in G25.

M151   Gindin, James. "James Joyce." In HARVEST OF A QUIET EYE:
       THE NOVEL OF COMPASSION. Bloomington: Indiana Univ. Press,
       1971. Pp. 222-36.
           JJ a "social novelist," in scope and in themes,
           creating an intricate balance between criticism
           and compassion for humanity.

M152   Glasheen, Adaline. "Another Face for Proteus." JAMES
       JOYCE REVIEW, 1, No. 2 (1957), 3-8.
           Stephen an Orestes figure.

M153   Glikin, Gloria H. "Variations on a Method." JJQ, 2 (1964),
       42-49.
           JJ's possible influence on Dorothy Richard-
           son's stream-of-consciousness novel sequence,
           PILGRIMAGE (1915-38).

M154   Goldknopf, David. "Realism in the Novel." In THE LIFE
       OF THE NOVEL. Chicago: Univ. of Chicago Press, 1972.
       Pp. 177-98.
           U, WOMEN IN LOVE (1920), and the higher real-
           ism of modern fiction.

M155   Gordon, John. "Notes in Response to Michael Seidel's
       'ULYSSES' Black Panther Vampire.'" JJQ, 15 (1978), 229-
       35.
           Extends Seidel's discussion of Bloom's asso-
           ciation with the "Black Panther Vampire" fig-
           ure (see M282).

M156   Grabo, Carl. THE TECHNIQUE OF THE NOVEL. New York:
       Scribner's, 1928. Pp. 281-86.
           U a "hoax" upon critics.

M157   Greenway, John. "A Guide through James Joyce's ULYSSES."
       CE, 17 (1955), 67-78.
              Superficial, episode-by episode summaries.

M158   Groden, Michael. "Criticism in New Composition: ULYSSES
       and THE SOUND AND THE FURY." TCL, 21 (1975), 265-77.
              Faulkner's successful incorporation of JJ's
              "techniques into his own artistic sensibil-
              ity."

M159   -----. "Editing Joyce's ULYSSES: An International Ef-
       fort." SCHOLARLY PUBLISHING, 12 (1980), 37-54.
              Describes the procedures followed for the
              forthcoming textual edition of U. See M146
              and M191.

M160   Hall, Vernon. "Joyce's Use of DaPonte and Mozart's DON
       GIOVANNI." PMLA, 66 (1951), 78-84.
              Examines JJ's allusions to Mozart's opera
              (libretto by DaPonte), and their appropriate-
              ness.

M161   Hardy, Barbara. "Form as End and Means in ULYSSES." OL,
       19 (1964), 194-200.
              The essential appropriateness of U's "highly
              schematic," yet neither abstract nor reduc-
              tive form.

M162   Harris, Wendell V. "Molly's 'Yes': The Transvaluation
       of Sex in Modern Fiction." TSLL, 10 (1968), 107-18.
              Sex as an affirmation of life (U, among other
              works).

M163   Hart, Clive. "The Sexual Perversions of Leopold Bloom."
       In *ULYSSES: CINQUANTE ANS APRÈS.* Ed. Louis Bonnerot. Pp.
       131-36. See M7.
              U "contains no active moral paradigm" and
              Bloom's "so-called" sexual perversions "do
              not really matter" in interpreting the novel.

M164   Hayman, David. "The Empirical Molly." In APPROACHES TO
       ULYSSES. Ed. Thomas F. Staley and Bernard Benstock. Pp.
       103-35. See M60.
              Attempts a composite portrait of Molly (based
              on what is said and *not said* about her in U),
              and speculates on the motives and causes for
              her infidelity.

M165   -----. "Forms of Folly in Joyce: A Study of Clowning in
        ULYSSES." ELH, 34 (1967), 260-83.
            Techniques and significance of broad comedy
            and farce in U. Also see N122.

M166   -----. "Language of/as Gesture in Joyce." In *ULYSSES:*
        CINQUANTE ANS APRÈS. Ed. Louis Bonnerot. Pp. 209-21.
        See M7.
            Language that gestures (i.e., both oral lang-
            uage, with gestures, and intonation) and phy-
            sical gestures as language in JJ (chiefly U).

M167   Heine, Arthur. "Shakespeare in James Joyce." SHAKESPEARE
        ASSOCIATION BULLETIN, 24 (1949), 56-70.
            Lists 257 "quotations, adaptations, and echoes
            from Shakespeare" in U. See M237.

M168   Henderson, Philip. "Stephen Daedalus [sic] versus Bloom."
        In THE NOVEL TODAY: STUDIES IN CONTEMPORARY ATTITUDES.
        London: Lane, 1936. Pp. 81-87.
            Misreading, seeing JJ (i.e., Stephen) at war
            with Bloom's sensibility: "That Joyce is Ste-
            phen Daedalus there can be little doubt."

M169   Henig, Suzanne. "ULYSSES in Bloomsbury." JJQ, 10 (1973),
        203-08.
            The Woolfs frustrated willingness to publish
            U, despite some doubts of its merit.

M170   Henke, Suzette A. "Joyce's Bloom: Beyond Sexual Posses-
        siveness." AI, 32 (1975), 329-34.
            Both Bloom (through masturbation) and Molly
            (through adultery) transcend erotic love, to-
            gether attaining ideal love *("agape")*.

M171   Herring, Phillip F. "The Bedsteadfastness of Molly Bloom."
        MFS, 15 (1969), 49-61.
            Molly neither an affirmative nor a negative
            character; rather, like the other characters,
            she is "human, at once sympathetic, repulsive
            and amusing." See G65.

M172   -----. "Experimentation with a Landscape: Pornotopography
        in ULYSSES--The Phallocy of Imitative Form." MFS, 20
        (1974), 371-78.
            Facetious commentary on JJ's traditional use
            of "topography [;] for lewd and indecent pur-
            poses" however.

M173   -----. "Toward an Historical Molly Bloom." ELH, 45
       (1978), 501-21.
              Examines U's factual details to "test the
              verisimilitude of Molly."

M174   Hoffmann, Frederick J. "The Authority of the Common-
       place: Joyce's Bloomsday." KR, 22 (1960), 316-23.
              Bloom, unlike Emma Bovary, presented sympa-
              thetically as a "hero of the commonplace" as
              JJ "makes a virtue of a multitude of human
              defects" (cf. Flaubert).

M175   Hollington, Michael. "Svevo, Joyce, and Modernist Time."
       In MODERNISM, 1890-1930. Ed. Malcolm Bradbury and James
       McFarlane. Harmondsworth, Engl.: Penguin, 1976. Pp.
       430-42.
              "Non-events" in JJ (U) and Svevo (CONFESSIONS
              OF ZENO [1923]) related to their characterist-
              ically modern sense of irony (frustration of
              "temporal expectations").

M176   Howarth, Herbert. "THE WASTE LAND and Joyce." In NOTES
       ON SOME FIGURES BEHIND T.S. ELIOT. Boston: Houghton Mif-
       flin, 1964. Pp. 242-46.
              JJ's and Eliot's "reciprocal creative borrow-
              ing" (U, THE WASTE LAND [1922], FW).

M177   Humphrey, Robert. "Joyce's Daedal Network." In STREAM
       OF CONSCIOUSNESS IN THE MODERN NOVEL. Berkeley and Los
       Angeles: Univ. of California Press, 1954. Pp. 87-99.
              JJ's ingenious designs and patterns in U nec-
              essary to counteract the formlessness inherent
              in the stream-of-consciousness technique.

M178   Hyman, Louis. "Some Aspects of the Jewish Background of
       ULYSSES." In THE JEWS OF IRELAND: FROM THE EARLIEST TIMES
       TO THE YEAR 1910. Shannon: Irish Univ. Press, 1972. Pp.
       167-92.
              Identifies Jews referred to in U and discusses
              JJ's handling of Jewish subjects.

M179   Iser, Wolfgang. "Patterns of Communication in Joyce's
       ULYSSES." In THE IMPLIED READER: PATTERNS OF COMMUNICA-
       TION IN PROSE FICTION FROM BUNYAN TO BECKETT. Baltimore:
       Johns Hopkins Univ. Press, 1974. Pp. 196-233.
              JJ's use of myth, archetype, and experimental
              style presents the reader with the task of de-
              ciphering meaning in U. See X51.

M180 Jung, Carl G. "ULYSSES: A Monologue." 1932. In THE
      SPIRIT IN MAN, ART, AND LITERATURE. Trans. R.F.C. Hull.
      Princeton, N.J.: Princeton Univ. Press, 1966. Pp. 109-
      34.
            The psychologist's exasperated, uncomprehend-
            ing, and very "subjective" response to U as
            an example of literary schizophrenia. Extract
            reprinted in G25. Also see M105 and X54.

M181 Kain, Richard M. "The Cosmic View in ULYSSES." In
      ULYSSES: CINQUANTE ANS APRÈS. Ed. Louis Bonnerot. Pp.
      275-86. See M7.
            Explores JJ's indications that one important
            perspective on the events and personages of
            U is cosmic; they are to be "seen from the in-
            finite distances of space and time."

M182 -----. "Homeric Geography, Strabo to Bérard." In ATTI
      DEL THIRD INTERNATIONAL JAMES JOYCE SYMPOSIUM. Pp. 184-
      92. See G7.
            JJ's familiarity with Homeric geography and
            archaeology.

M183 -----. "Motif as Meaning: The Case of Leopold Bloom."
      In APPROACHES TO *ULYSSES*. Ed. Thomas F. Staley and Ber-
      nard Benstock. Pp. 61-101. See M60.
            JJ's creation of pattern out of fragments and
            details awesome, but imperfect. Includes a
            reconstructed biographical chronology for
            Bloom.

M184 -----. "The Position of ULYSSES Today." In JAMES JOYCE
      TODAY. Ed. Thomas F. Staley. Pp. 83-95. See G75.
            Surveys the contemporary critical positions
            on the main areas of study of U (e.g., the
            text, exegesis, thematics, interpretation,
            and symbolism).

M185 -----. "The Significance of Stephen's Meeting Bloom: A
      Survey of Interpretations." In *ULYSSES:* FIFTY YEARS. Ed.
      Thomas F. Staley. Pp. 147-60. See M59.
            Summarizes ten distinct approaches to the in-
            terpretation of U's anticlimactic climax.

M186 -----. "Treasures and Trifles in ULYSSES." In LITTERS
      FROM ALOFT. Ed. Ronald Bates and Harry J. Pollock. Pp.
      1-14. See G9.
            A serendipitous excursion around and about
            JJ's U. Entertaining afterdinner speech.

M187   -----. "ULYSSES as a Classic: Some Anniversary Reconsid-
       erations." MOSAIC, 6, No. 1 (1972), 57-62.
              General comments on the enduring reputation
              of U as one of "the last universal great books
              in English." See M45.

M188   Kaplan, Harold J. "Stoom: The Universal Comedy of James
       Joyce." In THE PASSIVE VOICE: AN APPROACH TO MODERN FIC-
       TION. Athens: Ohio Univ. Press, 1966. Pp. 43-91.
              JJ's solipsistic and cosmic view of a universe
              which is comic, since "his creatures, being
              human, continue to act 'lovingly.'"

M189   Karl, Frederick R., and Marvin Magalaner. "James Joyce."
       In A READER'S GUIDE TO GREAT TWENTIETH-CENTURY ENGLISH
       NOVELS. New York: Noonday, 1959. Pp. 205-53.
              See K85.

M190   Kaye, Julian B. "A Portrait of the Artist as Blephen-
       Stoom." In A JAMES JOYCE MISCELLANY, SECOND SERIES. Ed.
       Marvin Magalaner. Pp. 79-91. See G56.
              Bloom and Stephen *both* fictional projections
              of JJ himself.

M191   Kenner, Hugh. "The Computerized ULYSSES: Establishing
       the Text Joyce Intended." HARPER'S, 260 (Apr. 1980),
       89-95.
              Describes the principles and methodology of
              Hans Walter Gabler's forthcoming textual edi-
              tion of U. See M146 and M159.

M192   -----. "Faulkner and Joyce." In FAULKNER, MODERNISM,
       AND FILM: FAULKNER AND YOKNAPATAWPHA, 1978. Ed. Evans
       Harrington and Ann J. Abadie. Jackson: Univ. Press of
       Mississippi, 1979. Pp. 20-33.
              Correspondences between U and THE SOUND AND
              THE FURY (1929).

M193   -----. "Homer's Sticks and Stones." JJQ, 6 (1969), 285-
       98.
              JJ's principal view of Homer as "an observer
              and ingenious transposer of actualities," al-
              ready developed by Samuel Butler under the
              influence of Schliemann's archaeological dis-
              coveries, not the only view of Homer suggested
              by U. Assimilated into H110.

M194 -----. "James Joyce: Comedian of the Inventory." In
THE STOIC COMEDIANS: FLAUBERT, JOYCE, AND BECKETT. Boston: Beacon Press, 1963. Pp. 30-66.
    Part of U's comedy lies in JJ's exhaustive
comic inventories (curbed some by concern for
verisimilitude, but unchecked in FW).

M195 -----. "Molly's Masterstroke." In ULYSSES: FIFTY YEARS.
Ed. Thomas F. Staley. Pp. 19-28. See M59.
    Facetious speculation on Molly's possible fi-
delity to Bloom.

M196 -----. "The Rhetoric of Silence." JJQ, 14 (1977), 382-
94.
    JJ's tendency to tell his reader's things,
indirectly, by deliberately not telling them
things.

M197 Kettle, Arnold. "James Joyce: ULYSSES." In AN INTRODUC-
TION TO THE ENGLISH NOVEL. Vol. 2. HENRY JAMES TO THE
PRESENT. London: Hutchinson, 1951. Pp. 135-51.
    JJ's failure to produce a complex epic por-
trait of man "in his full and staggering complexity," in part compensated by the comedy
and compassion of U.

M198 Killham, John. "'Ineluctable Modality' in Joyce's ULYSSES."
UTQ, 34 (1965), 269-89.
    Illuminates Stephen's "wonderfully ambiguous"
Aristotelianism through U.

M199 Kimball, Jean. "Freud, Leonardo, and Joyce: The Dimensions of a Childhood Memory." JJQ, 17 (1980), 165-82.
    Features of Leonardo DaVinci, analyzed by
Freud in a 1910 essay owned by JJ, assimilated into JJ's portraits of Stephen and
Bloom (principally in U).

M200 -----. "James Joyce and Otto Rank: The Incest Motif in
ULYSSES." JJQ, 13 (1976), 366-82.
    Traces JJ's debts to contemporary psychoana-
lytic theories besides those of Freud and
Jung. See G43.

M201 Kimpel, Ben D. "The Voices of ULYSSES." STYLE, 9 (1975),
283-319.
    Comments on JJ's multiple narrative techniques.

M202 Klug, Michael A. "The Comic Structure of Joyce's ULYSSES."
      EIRE, 11, No. 1 (1976), 63-84.
          Links "between the structure and resolution"
          of U and "those of conventional comedy."

M203 Knuth, A.M. Leo. "Joyce's Verbal Acupuncture." In *ULYSSES:*
      FIFTY YEARS. Ed. Thomas F. Staley. Pp. 61-71. See M59.
          Traces some intriguing clusters of puzzles
          and signals (e.g., "S.O.S.") in U, with a
          defense of such critical "detection."

M204 -----. "The Ring and the Cross in Joyce's ULYSSES." In
      ULYSSES: CINQUANTE ANS APRÈS. Ed. Louis Bonnerot. Pp.
      181-88. See M7.
          Structural and symbolic significance of the
          figure of the "ring encircling the cross" in
          U.

M205 Kopper, Edward A. "ULYSSES and James Joyce's Use of Com-
      edy." MOSAIC, 6, No. 1 (1972), 45-55.
          Kinds, qualities, and purposes of comedy in
          U. See M45.

M206 Larbaud, Valery. "The ULYSSES of James Joyce." CRITERION,
      1 (1922), 94-103.
          Early appreciation of U, by a distinguished
          critic and friend of JJ, originally published
          in the most prestigious contemporary French
          literary journal (see X58). Extract reprinted
          in G25. Also see M242.

M207 Leslie, Shane. "ULYSSES." QR, 238 (1922), 219-34.
          U "gruesome" in its realism, "unquotable,"
          "unreviewable," "unreadable," and by this
          reviewer, evidently unread. Representative
          early critical response to U. Extract re-
          printed in G25.

M208 Levine, Jennifer Schiffer. "Originality and Repetition
      in FINNEGANS WAKE and ULYSSES." PMLA, 94 (1979), 106-20.
          JJ's deconstruction of language through his
          experimental styles in FW and his use of
          cliché in U.

M209 Levitt, Morton P. "The Family of Bloom." In NEW LIGHT
      ON JOYCE. Ed. Fritz Senn. Pp. 141-48. See G73.
          Bloom's archetypal Jewishness. Assimilated
          into M16.

M210 -----. "A Hero for Our Time: Leopold Bloom and the Myth
of ULYSSES." In *ULYSSES:* FIFTY YEARS. Ed. Thomas F.
Staley. Pp. 132-46. See M59.
    Continued functioning of archetypes in U,
    "itself a new myth" rather than a mere com-
    pilation of mythic "formulas."

M211 -----. "Two Odysseys-Kazantzakis and Joyce." In ATTI
DEL THIRD INTERNATIONAL JAMES JOYCE SYMPOSIUM. Pp. 172-
77. See G7.
    JJ and Kazantzakis both "borrow more from the
    post-Homeric tradition than from Homer him-
    self."

M212 Littmann, Mark E., and Charles A. Schweighauser. "Astro-
nomical Allusions, Their Meaning and Purpose in ULYSSES."
JJQ, 2 (1965), 238-46.
    Stresses importance of JJ's astronomical ref-
    erences for U's theme and structure.

M213 Litz, A. Walton. "The Genre of ULYSSES." In ATTI DEL
THIRD INTERNATIONAL JAMES JOYCE SYMPOSIUM. Pp. 149-57.
See G7.
    U, "at its deepest reaches, denies the valid-
    ity of genres and seeks to be wholly itself."
    Surveys attempts to define U's "genre." Re-
    printed in THE THEORY OF THE NOVEL, ed. John
    Halperin (New York: Oxford Univ. Press, 1974).

M214 -----. "The Last Adventures of ULYSSES." PULC, 28 (1967),
63-75.
    Amplifies and documents the role of Sylvia
    Beach in publishing U (too modestly described
    by Beach herself; see F6). Reprinted in M7.

M215 -----. "Pound and Eliot on ULYSSES: The Critical Tradition." In *ULYSSES:* FIFTY YEARS. Ed. Thomas F. Staley.
Pp. 5-18. See M59.
    Traces Pound's and Eliot's various responses
    to U and U's impact on their own creative
    work.

M216 Lorch, Thomas M. "The Relationship Between ULYSSES and
THE WASTE LAND." TSLL, 6 (1964), 123-33.
    Similarities of theme and technique in the
    two works.

M217 Lyons, John O. "The Man in the Macintosh." In A JAMES
      JOYCE MISCELLANY, SECOND SERIES. Ed. Marvin Magalaner.
      Pp. 133-38. See G56.
      Identifies M'Intosh as James Duffy of "A Pain-
      ful Case" (D). See M263.

M218 McAleer, Edward C. "The Ignorance of Mr. Bloom." In
      STUDIES IN HONOR OF JOHN C. HODGES AND ALWIN THALER. Ed.
      Richard B. Davis and John L. Livesay. Knoxville: Univ.
      of Tennessee Press, 1961. Pp. 121-29.
      Summarizes Bloom's modest intellectual make
      up, concluding he may be "saved," for he
      knows not his ignorance.

M219 McBride, Margaret. "At Four She Said." JJQ, 17 (1979),
      21-39; 18 (1981), 417-31.
      Bloom's preoccupation with time and suppres-
      sion of his time consciousness.

M220 -----. "Watchwords in ULYSSES: The Stylistics of Sup-
      pression." JEGP, 77 (1978), 356-66.
      Time references in U tied to Bloom's sexual
      anxieties.

M221 MacCarthy, Desmond. "Joyce's ULYSSES." In CRITICISM.
      London: Putnam, 1932. Pp. 296-311.
      JJ's skepticism, "morose delectation in dirt,"
      derisive, unrobust wit, and exploration of
      "blind psychological alleys."

M222 McLean, Andrew M. "Joyce's ULYSSES and Döblin's ALEXAN-
      DERPLATZ BERLIN." CL, 25 (1973), 97-113.
      Technical and structural influences of U on
      Döblin's novel (1929).

M223 McMillan, Dougald. "Influences of Gerhart Hauptmann in
      Joyce's ULYSSES." JJQ, 4 (1967), 107-19.
      Attributes a "number of important themes,
      character types, and techniques" in U to JJ's
      reading of Hauptmann.

M224 McNelly, Willis E. "Liturgical Deviations in ULYSSES."
      JJQ, 2 (1965), 291-98.
      Surveys JJ's several, clearly unintentional
      inaccuracies in his references to Catholic
      liturgy.

M225   Magalaner, Marvin. "The Anti-Semitic Limerick Incidents
       and Joyce's 'Bloomsday.'" PMLA, 68 (1953), 1219-23.
       The first stirring of antisemitism in Ireland
       "became big news" in Dublin's newspapers and
       magazines during the summer of 1904.

M226   -----. "The Humanization of Stephen Dedalus." MOSAIC,
       6, No. 1 (1972), 63-67.
       Finds JJ's creation of Stephen in U "three-
       dimensional and full-blooded" despite the
       frequent critical contention that JJ "deper-
       sonalized" his character. See M45.

M227   Mason, Ellsworth. "James Joyce: Moralist." TCL, 1 (1956),
       196-206.
       At the core of his work is found JJ's "simple,
       conservative, essentially Christian" affirma-
       tion of man's spiritual value.

M228   Mason, Michael. "ULYSSES the Sequel to A PORTRAIT? Joyce's
       Plans for the Two Works." ELN, 8 (1971), 296-300.
       See K102.

M229   -----. "Why is Leopold Bloom a Cuckold?" ELH, 44 (1977),
       171-88.
       Attempts to reconcile Bloom's "cuckoldhood"
       with his heroism.

M230   Mayhew, George. "Joyce on Shakespeare." SOUTHWESTERN
       JOURNAL, 5 (1950), 109-26.
       Reviews Stephen's Shakespeare theory and its
       implications for JJ's themes in U.

M231   Mays, J.C.C. "Some Comments on the Dublin of ULYSSES."
       In *ULYSSES:* CINQUANTE ANS APRÈS. Ed. Louis Bonnerot.
       Pp. 83-98. See M7.
       The partiality and incompleteness of the Dub-
       lin presented in U.

M232   Melnick, Daniel C. "Dissonant ULYSSES--A Study of How
       To Read Joyce." TCL, 26 (1980), 45-63.
       U approached in light of Nietzsche's defini-
       tion and analysis of the "dissonant sensibil-
       ity."

M233   Miller, Henry. "The Universe of Death." PHOENIX, 1,
       No. 1 (1938), 33-64.
       JJ and Proust living-dead writers (in contrast

to the dead, yet still vital D.H. Lawrence),
and U a tomb for the disintegrating remains
of the modern imagination.

M234 Miller-Budnitskaya, R. "James Joyce's ULYSSES." Trans.
N.J. Nelson. DIALECTICS, No. 5 (1938), pp. 6-26.
Representative Marxist view of U as an anar-
chical "self-negation" of contemporary Western civilization, "permeated with political,
religious, national and racial hatred." Extract reprinted in G25. Also see X64.

M235 Moholy-Nagy, Laszlo. VISION IN MOTION. Chicago: Theobald, 1947. Pp. 341-51.
Parallels among U, FW, and experiments with
space-time relationships in the visual arts
(particularly cubism).

M236 Monnier, Adrienne. "Joyce's ULYSSES and the French Public." 1940. Trans. Sylvia Beach. KR, 8 (1946), 430-44.
The "first French reader" and publisher of
the French translation summarizes her responses to U and those of a few compatriots.
Extract reprinted in G25. Also see X68.

M237 Morse, B.J. "Mr. Joyce and Shakespeare." ENGLISCHE
STUDIEN, 65 (1930), 367-81.
Early discussion of JJ's systematic allusions
to Shakespeare and incorporation of Shakespearian motifs in U. Includes a preliminary list
of JJ's direct quotations from Shakespeare,
superseded by Heine (see M167).

M238 Morse, J. Mitchell. "Karl Gutzkow and the Modern Novel."
JGE, 15 (1963), 175-89.
JJ "discovered and made viable" Gutzkow's
theory of a "simultaneous" novel (chiefly in
U and FW). Also published in JJQ, 2 (1964),
13-17.

M239 -----. "Molly Bloom Revisited." In A JAMES JOYCE MIS-
CELLANY, SECOND SERIES. Ed. Marvin Magalaner. Pp. 139-
49. See G56.
Profoundly negative view of Molly as perverse,
repulsive, and corrupt, the "very center of
paralysis" in U.

M240 Moss, Roger. "Difficult Language: The Justification of
      Joyce's Syntax in ULYSSES." In THE MODERN ENGLISH NOVEL:
      THE READER, THE WRITER AND THE WORK. Ed. Gabriel Josi-
      povici. New York: Barnes and Noble, 1976. Pp. 130-48.
      JJ's "difficult" language in U justified as a
      reinforcement of his central themes: the dif-
      ficulties of perception, expression, and ac-
      tion.

M241 Muir, Edwin. THE STRUCTURE OF THE NOVEL. London: Hogarth,
      1928. Pp. 126-33.
      JJ's Homeric plan for U "purely contingent and
      theoretical, not the animating principle of
      the whole."

M242 Murry, John Middleton. "Mr. Joyce's ULYSSES." NATION
      AND ATHENAEUM, 31 (1922), 124-25.
      Finds U an extremely "individualist" work,
      disputing Larbaud's praise for the novel as
      a major contribution to the European literary
      tradition (see M206). Extract reprinted in
      G25.

M243 Myers, Walter L. THE LATER REALISM: A STUDY OF CHARAC-
      TERIZATION IN THE BRITISH NOVEL. Chicago: Univ. of Chi-
      cago Press, 1927. Pp. 70-73 and passim.
      JJ's "deliriously dadaistic" presentation of
      the incongruities of fictional character.

M244 Nabokov, Vladimír. "James Joyce: ULYSSES." In his LEC-
      TURES ON LITERATURE. Ed. Fredson Bowers. New York: Har-
      court, 1980. Pp. 285-370.
      Nabokov's university lectures on U, edited
      from his papers (see M47). Includes several
      illustrations and diagrams from Nabokov's
      lecture notes and reading copy of U.

M245 Niemayer, Carl. "A ULYSSES Calendar." JJQ, 13 (1976),
      163-93.
      Chronological notes on dates, or datable events
      concerning the Blooms (1816-Sept. 1904).

M246 Noon, William T., S.J. "Is ULYSSES Immoral or All-Moral?
      In JAMES JOYCE: HIS PLACE IN WORLD LITERATURE. Ed. Wolo-
      dymyr T. Zyla. Pp. 103-14. See G85.
      Questions the validity of the question of U's
      morality.

M247   Oates, Joyce Carol. "Jocoserious Joyce." CRITICAL IN-
       QUIRY, 2 (1976), 677-88.
              Comic qualities of U, "the greatest single
              work of art in our tradition."

M248   O'Brien, Darcy. "Some Determinants of Molly Bloom." In
       APPROACHES TO *ULYSSES*. Ed. Thomas F. Staley and Bernard
       Benstock. Pp. 137-55. See M60.
              Molly reflects JJ's own sexual ambivalence,
              his characteristically Irish mixture of fear
              and contempt for women.

M249   Pearce, Richard. "Experimentation with the Grotesque:
       Comic Collisions in the Grotesque World of ULYSSES." MFS,
       20 (1974), 378-84.
              Literal and symbolic collisions in U (cf.
              Sergei Eisenstein's montage technique).

M250   Perlmutter, Ruth. "Joyce and Cinema." BOUNDARY 2, 6 (1978),
       481-502.
              Cinematic qualities of the novel.

M251   Pimentel, Luz Aurora. "An Examination of One Aspect in
       the Art of Proust and Joyce." CLS, 17 (1980), 447-57.
              "External reality" as "the starting point
              towards the perception and recreation of
              psychological realities" in U and A LA RECHER-
              CHE DU TEMPS PERDU (1912-27).

M252   Pinsker, Sanford. "ULYSSES and the Post-Modern Temper."
       MQ, 15 (1974), 406-16.
              Defends U against the attacks of "post-modern"
              critics (e.g., Leslie Fiedler).

M253   -----. "ULYSSES as Ghost-Story." In RENAISSANCE AND
       MODERN. Ed. Murray J. Levith. Syracuse: Syracuse Univ.
       Press, 1976. Pp. 119-32.
              The "spectral horrors" of Stephen's interior
              life.

M254   Poss, Stanley. "ULYSSES and the Comedy of the Immobil-
       ized Act." ELH, 24 (1957), 65-83.
              Persuasive argument against affirmative read-
              ings of U: "there is no transcendental sig-
              nificance in the meeting of Stephen and Bloom."

M255   Pound, Ezra. "James Joyce et Pécuchet." 1922. Trans.
       Fred Bornhauser. SHENANDOAH, 3, No. 3 (1952), 9-20.
            Influential discussion of JJ's Flaubertian
            realism, his satiric intention, his achieve-
            ment of ·form, and his variations upon the
            father and son theme in U. Expansion of es-
            say below. Reprinted in F123 [in French]
            and G25 (extract). Also see G47, M91, and
            X73.

M256   -----. "Paris Letter: ULYSSES." DIAL, 72 (1922), 623-29.
            JJ's work praised as superior to Proust's or
            James's and as the perfection of the stylistic
            and formal innovations of Flaubert. Reprinted
            in F123. Also see above.

M257   Prescott, Joseph. "Notes on Joyce's ULYSSES." MLQ, 13
       (1952), 149-62.
            Sixty-two annotations for U, beginning the
            process of annotation carried out more comp-
            rehensively and systematically by Gifford
            and Seidman (M20) and Thornton (M64).

M258   Rader, Ralph W. "Defoe, Richardson, Joyce, and the Con-
       cept of Form in the Novel." In AUTOBIOGRAPHY, BIOGRAPHY,
       AND THE NOVEL. Ed. William Matthews and Rader. Los Ang-
       eles: William Andrews Clark Memorial Library, 1973. Pp.
       31-72.
            See K120.

M259   -----. "Exodus and Return: Joyce's ULYSSES and the Fic-
       tion of the Actual." UTQ, 48 (1978), 149-71.
            JJ's novel revolutionary not in shaping life
            "to our feelings," but in shaping "our feel-
            ings to life as it is." JJ's aesthetic in
            light of the reader's response.

M260   Radford, F.L. "King, Pope, and Hero-Martyr: ULYSSES and
       the Nightmare of Irish History." JJQ, 15 (1978), 275-323.
            Excellent discussion and clarification of the
            related roles of Edward VII, Leo XIII, and
            Robert Emmet, in the immediate historical
            memory of Dublin in 1904.

M261   Raleigh, John Henry. "Bloom as a Modern Epic Hero."
       CRITICAL INQUIRY, 3 (1977), 583-98.
            Bloom's epic heroism "largely internal and

known only, in most part, to himself, and to
the reader." Surveys Bloom's archetypal dimensions.

M262 -----. "Victorian Morals and the Modern Novel." PR, 25
(1958), 241-64.
U's amorality culminates one important pattern
of anti-Victorian reaction (cf. James, Conrad,
Woolf).

M263 -----. "Who Was M'Intosh?" JAMES JOYCE REVIEW, 3 (1959),
59-62.
Speculates that Mr. Duffy, of "A Painful Case,"
is the man in the mackintosh. See M217.

M264 Richardson, Malcolm, II. "Joycean Irony and Mozart's DON
GIOVANNI." CLS, 17 (1980), 93-101.
Bloom vicariously plays the roles of both Leo-
porello and Don Giovanni.

M265 Ridgeway, Ann. "Two Authors in Search of a Reader." JJQ,
1, No. 4 (1964), 41-51.
Parallels between U and Sterne's TRISTRAM SHANDY
(1759-67).

M266 Roberts, John H. "James Joyce: From Religion to Art."
NEW HUMANIST, 7 (May-June 1934), 7-13.
U, the sequel to PAYM, is a "concrete expres-
sion of the aesthetic theory of tragedy stated
in the earlier work." Extract reprinted in
G25.

M267 Roberts, R.F. "Bibliographical Notes on James Joyce's
ULYSSES." COLOPHON, n.s. 1 (1936), 565-79.
See E23.

M268 Robinson, Fred Miller. "Joyce: ULYSSES." In THE COMEDY
OF LANGUAGE: STUDIES IN MODERN COMIC LITERATURE. Amherst:
Univ. of Massachusetts Press, 1980. Pp. 25-50.
JJ's comic conceptions and techniques in U,
with special emphasis on "Ithaca" and "Pene-
lope."

M269 Rogers, Howard Emerson. "Irish Myth and the Plot of
ULYSSES." ELH, 15 (1948), 306-27.
Clarifies JJ's extensive use of Irish mythology to pattern and to systematize U (cf.
the Homeric parallels).

M270   Rubin, Louis D. "A Portrait of a Highly Visible Artist."
        In THE TELLER IN THE TALE. Seattle: Univ. of Washington
        Press, 1967. Pp. 141-77.
                See K129.

M271   Russell, H.K. "The Incarnation in ULYSSES." MFS, 4 (1958),
        53-61.
                Theological reading (Bloom as Christ). See
                G64.

M272   Russell, Stanley C. "A Baedeker to Bloom." JJQ, 3 (1966),
        226-35.
                Examines the "manifold personality" of Bloom.

M273   Ryan, John. "*Rosevean:* ULYSSES' Silent Ship." DUBLIN
        MAGAZINE, 10, No. 2 (1973), 42-52.
                History of "*the* ship" of U (with illustra-
                tions). See G26.

M274   Rychner, Max. "Wirklichkeit im Roman--Zum ULYSSES von
        James Joyce." In IN MEMORIAM JAMES JOYCE. Ed. Carola
        Giedion-Welcker. Pp. 32-36. See F47.
                JJ's creation of patterns of significance
                within U's dense texture of realistic detail.
                Extract translated (ineptly) and reprinted
                in G25. Also see X77.

M275   Schiffer, Paul S. "'Homing, upstream': Fictional Closure
        and the End of ULYSSES." JJQ, 16 (1979), 283-98.
                The true conclusion of U to be found in its
                achievement of "equanimity" through style
                (especially the underlying lyricism) in its
                last three episodes.

M276   Scholes, Robert. "ULYSSES: A Structuralist Perspective."
        In ULYSSES: FIFTY YEARS. Ed. Thomas F. Staley. Pp. 161-
        71. See M59.
                Introduction to the structuralist interpreta-
                tion of U.

M277   Schotz, Myra Glazer. "Parallax in ULYSSES." DR, 59
        (1979), 487-99.
                JJ's use of the parallax idea for motif, theme,
                structure, and narrative technique.

M278   Schutte, William M. "An Index of Recurrent Elements in
        ULYSSES." JJQ, 13 (1975), through JJQ, 17 (1979).
                Episode-by-episode listing of recurring "ele-

ments" in U (e.g., figures, themes, motifs,
tag lines). Announced for book publication by
Southern Illinois Univ. Press (Feb. 1982).

M279 Schutte, William M., and Erwin R. Steinberg. "The Fic-
tional Technique of ULYSSES." In APPROACHES TO *ULYSSES*.
Ed. Thomas F. Staley and Bernard Benstock. Pp. 157-78.
See M60.
    Surveys the various permutations of conscious-
    ness and the rhythmic devices used by JJ to
    create a "fluid succession of presents." Par-
    tially assimilated into M61.

M280 Scofield, Martin. "'Methinks I see my father': Joyce's
ULYSSES." In THE GHOSTS OF *HAMLET*: THE PLAY AND MOD-
ERN WRITERS. Cambridge: Cambridge Univ. Press, 1980.
Pp. 59-72.
    Reviews JJ's use of HAMLET for theme and motif
    in U.

M281 Seidel, Michael. "ULYSSES." In HOMER TO BRECHT: THE
EUROPEAN EPIC AND DRAMATIC TRADITION. Ed. Seidel and
Edward Mendelson. New Haven, Conn.: Yale Univ. Press,
1977. Pp. 123-39.
    JJ, while assimilating various archetypal pat-
    terns from epic literature, makes important
    modifications in traditional epic structure
    (i.e., U cyclic rather than linear).

M282 -----. "ULYSSES' Black Panther Vampire." JJQ, 13 (1976),
415-27.
    The interrelated panther and vampire images
    (both flesh-seeking ghost figures), in their
    specific association with Bloom, act as por-
    tents of Bloom's potentially malign influence
    on Stephen. Also see M155.

M283 Seldes, Gilbert. "ULYSSES." NATION, 115 (1922), 211-12.
    Perceptive early review (admired by JJ), not-
    ing U's Nietzschean "tragic gaiety" and defend-
    ing its Dantean "local and private" elements.
    Extract reprinted in G25.

M284 Senn, Fritz. "Bloom among the Orators: The Why and the
Wherefore and All the Codology." In IRISH RENAISSANCE
ANNUAL I. Ed. Zack Bowen. Newark: Univ. of Delaware
Press, 1980. Pp. 168-90.
    Skill in speech, an epic characteristic, super-

abundant in Dublin but denied to Bloom as part
of his isolation (cf. Moses and Parnell as in-
articulate speakers).

M285   -----. "Book of Many Turns." In *ULYSSES:* FIFTY YEARS.
Ed. Thomas F. Staley. Pp. 29-46. See M59.
   Protean elusiveness of U--JJ's METAMORPHOSES--
   for the critic. Reprinted with revisions, in
   German, in M17.

M286   -----. "The Rhythm of ULYSSES." In *ULYSSES:* CINQUANTE
ANS APRÈS. Ed. Louis Bonnerot. Pp. 33-43. See M7.
   Manifold interconnections among U's episodes,
   in the midst of their radical stylistic differences, create the novel's "rhythm."

M287   -----. "'Scareotypes': On Some Trenchant Renditions in
ULYSSES." MODERN BRITISH LITERATURE, 5 (1980), 22-28.
   A "few prolegomenous glances" at "the nature
   and use of cliché" in U. See G63.

M288   -----. "ULYSSES in Translation." In APPROACHES TO
ULYSSES. Ed. Thomas F. Staley and Bernard Benstock.
Pp. 249-86. See M60.
   Special problems and new perspectives afforded
   by the translation of U. Earlier version pub-
   lished as "Seven against ULYSSES," in G42.

M289   Shapiro, Stephen A. "Leopold Bloom and Gulley Jimson:
The Economics of Survival." TCL, 10 (1964), 3-11.
   Bloom and Jimson as modern comic heroes (cf.
   Joyce Cary's THE HORSE'S MOUTH [1944]).

M290   Shloss, Carol. "Choice Newseryreels: James Joyce and
the IRISH TIMES." JJQ, 15 (1978), 325-38.
   The newspaper as subject in, source for, and,
   through stylistic variety, analogue to U.

M291   Slade, Carole. "The Dantean Journey through Dublin."
MODERN LANGUAGE STUDIES, 6, No. 1 (1976), 12-21.
   Parallels to the DIVINE COMEDY and allusions
   to Dante in U.

M292   Smith, Don N. "Musical Form and Principles in the Scheme
of ULYSSES." TCL, 18 (1972), 79-92.
   Forced application of sonata form to U.

M293   Smyer, Richard I. "Orwell and Joyce." In PRIMAL DREAM
       AND PRIMAL CRIME: ORWELL'S DEVELOPMENT AS A PSYCHOLOGICAL
       NOVELIST. Columbia: Univ. of Missouri Press, 1979. Pp.
       41-58.
           Superficial influences of U on Orwell's A
           CLERGYMAN'S DAUGHTER (1935).

M294   Solomon, Albert J. "A Moore in ULYSSES." JJQ, 10 (1973),
       215-27.
           JJ's references to George Moore and allusions
           to his works.

M295   Solomon, Margaret C. "Character as Linguistic Mode: A
       New Look at Streams-of-Consciousness in ULYSSES." In
       ULYSSES: CINQUANTE ANS APRÈS. Ed. Louis Bonnerot. Pp.
       111-30. See M7.
           Reexamination of JJ's characterization from
           the perspective of structuralist linguistics.

M296   Spencer, John. "A Note on the 'Steady Monologuy of the
       Interiors.'" REL, 6, No. 2 (1965), 32-41.
           JJ's use of "different linguistic forms" and
           "features" to distinguish modes of narration,
           in turn to elicit varied responses from the
           reader.

M297   Spilka, Mark. "Leopold Bloom as Jewish Pickwick: A Neo-
       Dickensian Perspective." NOVEL, 13 (1979), 121-46.
           JJ's and Dickens's comparable reflections of
           and reactions to bourgeois society and their
           similarly humane and magnanimous characteriza-
           tion.

M298   Staley, Thomas F. "Stephen Dedalus and the Temper of
       the Modern Hero." In APPROACHES TO ULYSSES. Ed. Staley
       and Bernard Benstock. Pp. 3-28. See M60.
           The sensitive yet weak Stephen, confronting
           the modern world, "reflects in all his pain
           and anguish, and even nastiness, the temper
           of the modern hero."

M299   -----. "ULYSSES: Fifty Years in the Joycean Conundrum."
       MOSAIC, 6, No. 1 (1972), 69-76.
           Surveys the foreign reception of U. See M45.

M300   -----. "ULYSSES and World Literature." In JAMES JOYCE:
       HIS PLACE IN WORLD LITERATURE. Ed. Wolodymyr T. Zyla.
       Pp. 39-52. See G85.
           Traces the major criticism of U and notes the

novel's direct influences on recent world literature.

M301 Stanford, William B. "The Mysticism That Pleased Him:
A Note on the Primary Source of Joyce's ULYSSES." ENVOY,
5 (May 1951), 62-69.
JJ's first recognition of the allegorical pos-
sibilities of the Ulysses theme in his youth-
ful reading of Charles Lamb's ADVENTURES OF
ULYSSES (1808). See F36. Reprinted in F111
and F135. Also see below.

M302 -----. THE ULYSSES THEME: A STUDY IN THE ADAPTABILITY
OF A TRADITIONAL HERO. 1954. 2nd ed. Oxford: Black-
well, 1963. Pp. 211-22 and passim.
JJ's synthesis of the various traditional aspects of the Ulysses character. See above.

M303 Stanzel, Franz K. "ULYSSES." In NARRATIVE SITUATIONS
IN THE NOVEL. Trans. J.P. Pusack. Bloomington: Indiana
Univ. Press, 1971. Pp. 121-44.
The multiplicity of narrative techniques in
U unified by the monologist of the novel, the
prevailing authorial consciousness. Extract
reprinted, in original German, in M17. Also
see X83.

M304 Stavrou, C.N. "Gulliver's Voyage to the Land of Dubliners." SAQ, 59 (1960), 490-99.
Parallels between U and GULLIVER'S TRAVELS
(1726).

M305 -----. "The Love Songs of J. Swift, Bernard Shaw, and
J.A.A. Joyce." MQ, 6 (1965), 135-62.
Parallels and contrasts in the three Irish-
men's view of woman (e.g., Molly).

M306 Stein, Sol. "The Aesthetics of James Joyce's ULYSSES."
UKCR, 18 (1952), 241-54.
Subjective summary of "the predominant qual-
ities of feeling evoked" by U.

M307 Stern, Frederick C. "The Other Parnell." EIRE, 7, No. 3
(1972), 3-12.
Backgrounds to JJ's use of Charles Stewart
Parnell's older brother, John Howard Parnell,
as a minor figure in U.

M308 Sternfeld, Frederick W. "Poetry and Music--Joyce's
      ULYSSES." In SOUND AND POETRY: ENGLISH INSTITUTE ESSAYS
      1956. Ed. Northrop Frye. New York: Columbia Univ. Press,
      1957. Pp. 16-54.
            Various aspects of JJ's use of music in U
            (e.g., rhythms, "modes of expression," struc-
            ture).

M309 Stonier, George Walter. "Gog Magog." In GOG MAGOG, AND
      OTHER CRITICAL ESSAYS. London: Dent, 1933. Pp. 1-42.
            JJ's concern for form and style, rather than
            meaning, symptomatic of the modern writer's
            isolation (chiefly U). Extract reprinted in
            G25.

M310 Storey, Robert. "The Argument of ULYSSES, Reconsidered."
      MLQ, 40 (1979), 175-95.
            JJ's compulsive remaking of himself into an
            "unindividuated creature of self-abnegation,"
            traced through U in the growing ascendancy of
            Noman-Bloom.

M311 Taylor, Anne Robinson. "Modern Primitives: Molly Bloom
      and James Joyce, with a Note on D.H. Lawrence." In MALE
      NOVELISTS AND THEIR FEMALE VOICES: LITERARY MASQUERADES.
      Troy, N.Y.: Whitston, 1981. Pp. 189-228.
            Woman, in both JJ and Lawrence, seen ambivalently
            as a symbol of the primitive consciousness and
            as a source of the archetypal qualities of "un-
            consciousness, irrationality, undifferentiated
            acceptance, mother love, and sex."

M312 Thomas, Brook. "The Artistic Touch of the Hidden Hand."
      JJQ, 15 (1977), 36-42.
            The hidden hand of JJ himself detected in
            small details within both the counterfeit
            world of U and the counterfeit image of him-
            self, Stephen.

M313 -----. "Formal Re-creation: Re-reading and Re-joycing
      the Re-rightings of ULYSSES." GENRE, 13 (1980), 337-54.
            Uniqueness of the U reading experience partly
            attributable to JJ's compositional technique,
            itself the result of his repeated reading of
            what he had already written. (Useful view of
            recent reader-response criticism of U.) Also
            see G44.

M314   -----. "Reading, Writing, and Joyce's Dublin." MODERN
       BRITISH LITERATURE, 5 (1980), 73-79.
           The "solitary act" of writing the "possible
           alternative" to the "communal act" of speech,
           "other than silence," both for the Dubliners
           in U and for JJ. See G63.

M315   Thompson, Lawrance R. A COMIC PRINCIPLE IN STERNE--MERE-
       DITH--JOYCE. Oslo: Univ. of Oslo British Institute, 1954.
           The profound seriousness of the authors' sim-
           ilar use of comic, mock-heroic, and satirical
           conventions (cf. A SENTIMENTAL JOURNEY [1768]
           and THE ORDEAL OF RICHARD FEVEREL [1859]).

M316   Thornton, Weldon. "The Allusive Method in ULYSSES." In
       APPROACHES TO *ULYSSES*. Ed. Thomas F. Staley and Bernard
       Benstock. Pp. 235-48. See M60.
           Integral relationship between JJ's allusive
           technique, which constantly draws analogies,
           and his central theme: "the need for an ade-
           quate synthesis of all the dichotomies of mod-
           ern experience" (cf. Eliot).

M317   Tillyard, E.M.W. "Joyce: ULYSSES." In THE EPIC STRAIN
       IN THE ENGLISH NOVEL. London: Chatto and Windus, 1963.
       Pp. 187-96.
           U has the size, variety, and ambitious con-
           ception of the classical epic, but lacks the
           genre's formal unity and "positive faith."

M318   Timpe, Eugene F. "ULYSSES and the Archetypal Feminine."
       In PERSPECTIVES IN LITERARY CRITICISM. Ed. Joseph Strel-
       ka. University Park: Pennsylvania State Univ. Press,
       1968. Pp. 199-213.
           JJ's use of the "Great Mother archetypal pat-
           tern," in light of Neumann's discussion of the
           archetype in THE GREAT MOTHER (1955).

M319   Tindall, William York. "Mosaic Bloom." MOSAIC, 6, No. 1
       (1972), 3-9.
           Moses analogues in U. See M45.

M320   Tolomeo, Diane. "Leopold Bloom and the Law of Falling
       Bodies: Joyce's Use of the Fall in ULYSSES." ENGLISH
       STUDIES IN CANADA, 5 (1979), 301-10.
           Man's physical and spiritual, literal and sym-
           bolic falls part of U's "artistic structure."

M321   Tomasi, Barbara R.   "The Fraternal Theme in Joyce's
       ULYSSES." AI, 30 (1973), 177-91.
              Freudian "patriarchal/fraternal dichotomy...
              basic in" U.

M322   Torrance, Robert M.   "Ulysses and Hermes in Modern Times:
       Leopold Bloom and Felix Krull." In THE COMIC HERO. Cam-
       bridge, Mass.: Harvard Univ. Press, 1978. Pp. 240-73.
              JJ's and Mann's comic transformations of epic
              heroes, in U and FELIX KRULL (1922; rev. ed.
              1954).

M323   Toynbee, Philip.   "A Study of James Joyce's ULYSSES."
       In JAMES JOYCE. Ed. Seon Givens. Pp. 243-84. See G30.
              Generally admiring and perceptive essay (an-
              ticipates Robert Adams' skeptical view of
              JJ's "superfluous" obscurities; see M1).

M324   Troy, William.   "Stephen Dedalus and James Joyce." NATION,
       138 (1934), 187-88.
              Important early and emphatic distinction be-
              tween JJ and his character Stephen. Reprinted
              in Troy's SELECTED ESSAYS, ed. Stanley E. Hy-
              man (New Brunswick, N.J.: Rutgers Univ. Press,
              1967).

M325   Vickery, John B.   "James Joyce: ULYSSES and the Anthro-
       pological Reality"; "James Joyce: ULYSSES and the Artist
       as Dying God"; "James Joyce: ULYSSES and the Human Scape-
       goat." In THE LITERARY IMPACT OF *THE GOLDEN BOUGH*.
       Princeton, N.J.: Princeton Univ. Press, 1973. Pp. 346-
       57; 358-80; 381-407.
              Archetypal patterns, myth, and ritual in U
              generally, and specialized studies of the
              dying god and scapegoat archetypes. Also
              see H222.

M326   Vogel, Jane.   "The Consubstantial Family of Stephen Ded-
       alus." JJQ, 2 (1965), 109-32.
              U a "draft" of JJ's optimistic vision of the
              family "refounded on the idea of consubstan-
              tial (generic) as opposed to accidental (ge-
              netic) relatedness," despite separations of
              race, age, space, and time.

M327   Von Abele, Rudolph.   "ULYSSES: The Myth of Myth." PMLA,
       69 (1954), 358-64.
              Questions the prevalent mythopoeic interpre-

tations of U, suggesting JJ's critics are attempting to confer "democratic respectability"
on an esoteric, coterie novel.

M328 Waidner, H. Frew. "ULYSSES by Way of CULTURE AND ANARCHY."
In APPROACHES TO *ULYSSES*. Ed. Thomas F. Staley and Bernard Benstock. Pp. 179-97. See M60.
For JJ in U, Arnold's Hebrew-Hellenic dichot-
omy less influential than his distinction between the "man of culture" and the "Philistine,"
in CULTURE AND ANARCHY (1869).

M329 Waldock, Arthur J.A. "James Joyce." In JAMES, JOYCE,
AND OTHERS. London: Williams and Norgate, 1937. Pp.
30-52.
General appreciation of JJ's workmanship,
humor, language, and technical "virtuosity."

M330 Walkley, R. Barrie. "The Bloom of Motherhood: Couvade
as a Structural Device in ULYSSES." JJQ, 18 (1979), 55-
67.
Primitive customs of fatherhood knowingly alluded to by JJ in Bloom's maternal-paternal
nature.

M331 Walsh, Ruth. "In the Name of the Father and of the Son...
Joyce's Use of the Mass in ULYSSES." JJQ, 6 (1969), 321-
47.
While allusions to the Mass serve many purposes in U, they are neither "indigenous to
Bloom's background" nor integral to U's structure (contra Briand, see M92). Also see J54.

M332 Ward, Alfred C. THE NINETEEN-TWENTIES: LITERATURE AND
IDEAS IN THE POST-WAR DECADE. London: Methuen, 1930.
Pp. 55-59.
JJ as a modernist experimenter, in the con-
text of the literary movements of the twenties.

M333 Warner, William B. "The Play of Fictions and Succession
of Styles in ULYSSES." JJQ, 15 (1977), 18-35.
JJ's play with styles paralleled with Bloom's
life, itself "a kind of play with fictions."

M334 Weinstein, Arnold L. VISION AND RESPONSE IN MODERN FIC-
TION. Ithaca, N.Y.: Cornell Univ. Press, 1974. Pp. 167-
90.
JJ communicates knowledge through form and

relationships rather than through character
and plot. Epistemological reading.

M335   West, Alick. "James Joyce: ULYSSES." 1937.   In CRISIS
AND CRITICISM, AND SELECTED LITERARY ESSAYS. London:
Lawrence and Wishart, 1975. Pp. 143-80.
Socialist reading, finding in JJ's shift of
allegiance from Stephen to Bloom "a new vision of society growing out of a new social
basis" (cf. Marx).

M336   White, John. "ULYSSES: The Metaphysical Foundations and
Grand Design." MFS, 15 (1969), 27-34.
JJ's "universal nature" as creator, artist,
and god expressed in his grand design, artic-
ulating "the life of the human mind and heart."
See G65.

M337   White, Patrick. "The Key in ULYSSES." JJQ, 9 (1971),
10-25.
U's key-motif fully examined.

M338   -----. "Vico's Institution of Burial in ULYSSES." BSUF,
14, No. 4 (1973), 59-68.
Vico's influence on JJ's attitudes toward
burial in U.

M339   Williams, Raymond. THE ENGLISH NOVEL FROM DICKENS TO
LAWRENCE. London: Chatto and Windus, 1970. Pp. 164-68.
U, less opaque than FW, a most satisfactory
expression of modern fragmentation.

M340   Worthen, William B. "Eliot's ULYSSES." TCL, 27 (1981),
166-77.
Notes the extensive debts to JJ's novel present in the earlier drafts of Eliot's poems.

M341   Worthington, Mabel P. "Irish Folk Songs in Joyce's
ULYSSES." PMLA, 71 (1956), 321-29.
Provides texts and annotations for JJ's ref-
erences to forty-three Irish songs.

M342   Wykes, David. "The ODYSSEY of ULYSSES." TSLL, 10 (1968),
301-16.
Attempts to distinguish the incidental and
trivial from the fundamental and significant
parallels to Homer in U.

M343   Zhantieva, D.G. "Joyce's ULYSSES." 1967. Trans. Anne
       White. In PRESERVE AND CREATE: ESSAYS IN MARXIST LITER-
       ARY CRITICISM. Ed. Gaylord C. LeRoy and Ursula Beitz.
       New York: Humanities, 1973. Pp. 138-72.
                JJ's "sharp perception of the evil reigning"
                in bourgeois society drives him to the char-
                acteristic pessimism of Western intellectuals.
                See X89.

M344   Zimmerman, Michael. "Leopold Paula Bloom: The New Womanly
       Man." L&P, 29 (1979), 176-84.
                "Bloom's simultaneous physical and psycholog-
                ical satisfaction in being filled full...con-
                stitutes his fundamental femaleness."

M, iii. Studies of Individual Episodes

See headnote to section M above. Several of the general studies
of JJ, entered in section G above, contain episode-by-episode
commentaries on U. See Adams (G2), Arnold (G6), Bowen (G13),
Burgess (G17), Duff (G27), Golding (G32), Gorman (G36), Grose
(G37), Hodgart (G40), Hodgart and Worthington (G41), Jones (G46),
Kenner (G47*), Moseley (G67), O'Brien (G70*), Peake (G71*), and
Tindall (G80). Several of the books and essay collections on
U, entered in section M, i above, likewise devote a substantial
portion of their contents to episode-by-episode discussions of
the novel. See Barrow (M3), Blamires (M5*), Budgen (M8*), Ell-
mann (M15*), French (M18*), Garvin (M19), Gifford and Seidman
(M20*), Gilbert (M21*), Hart (M26), Hart and Knuth (M27), Hart
and Hayman (M28), Henke (M30), Kain (M35), Kenner (M36*), Macaré
(M41), Maddox (M42), Mason (M43), Nabokov (M47), Seidel (M56),
Smith (M58), Sultan (M62*), and Thornton (M64*). Among the articles entered in section M, ii above, also see Greenway (M157),
Karl and Magalaner (M189), and Schutte (M278*). (* The starred
items are especially recommended for any intensive study of a
particular episode of the novel.)

"Telemachus"

For other important commentaries and information on this episode, see, in addition to the titles listed in the headnote to
section M, iii above, the following studies: Gogarty (F51),
JAMES JOYCE QUARTERLY (G42), Porter (H172), Groden (M25), Litz

(M38), Schutte (M55), Steinberg (M61), Vresswijk (M65), Blackmur (M85), Boyle (M90), Fogel (M141), Rogers (M269), Toynbee
(M323), and Boldereff (M422).

M345   Benstock, Bernard. "'Telemachus.'" In JAMES JOYCE'S
       ULYSSES. Ed. Clive Hart and David Hayman. Pp. 1–16.
       See M28.
              Episode explication, stressing the major
              themes and symbol patterns introduced.

M346   Klein, A.M. "The Black Panther (A Study in Technique)."
       ACCENT, 10 (1950), 139–55.
              Extravagant interpretation of the liturgical
              and Biblical symbols in the episode.

M347   Levenston, E.A. "Narrative Technique in ULYSSES: A Styl-
       istic Comparison of 'Telemachus' and 'Eumaeus.'" LANG-
       UAGE AND STYLE, 5 (1972), 260–75.
              Close linguistic analysis and comparison of
              JJ's styles in the two episodes.

"Nestor"

For other important commentaries and information on this episode, see, in addition to the titles listed in the headnote to
section M, iii above, the following studies: Ellmann (F33),
Adams (M1), Loehrich (M39), Vresswijk (M65), Blackmur (M85),
and Prescott (M257). Also see X92.

M348   Epstein, Edmund L. "'Nestor.'" In JAMES JOYCE'S *ULYSSES*.
       Ed. Clive Hart and David Hayman. Pp. 17–28. See M28.
              Fallacies of history and "the proper way to
              regard the stream of human history," chief
              concerns of the episode.

M349   Klein, A.M. "'A Shout in the Street': An Analysis of the
       Second Chapter of Joyce's ULYSSES." NEW DIRECTIONS, No:
       13 (1951), pp. 327–45.
              Tabulates thirty-six (!) Viconian cycles in
              the episode.

M350   Stern, Frederick C. "Pyrrhus, Fenians, and Bloom." JJQ,
       5 (1968), 211–28.
              Clarifies the Irish political backgrounds to
              "Nestor" and "Cyclops."

"Proteus"

For other important commentaries and information on this epi-
sode, see, in addition to the titles listed in the headnote to
section M, iii above, the following studies: Cross (G24), Daich
(H45), Scott (H188), Magalaner (J11), Gose (M23), Litz (M38),
Schutte (M55), Steinberg (M61), Vresswijk (M65), Blackmur (M85)
Campbell (M99), Delbaere-Garant (M120), Duncan (M124), Humphrey
(M177), Killham (M198), Prescott (M257), Rogers (M269), Bolder-
eff (M422), and Aubert (P1).

M351   Day, Robert Adams. "How Stephen Wrote his Vampire Poem."
       JJQ, 17 (1980), 183-97.
              Reviews source of and discusses JJ's inten-
              tions for Stephen's "poem-to-be (a good one)."

M352   -----. "Joyce, Stoom, King Mark: 'Glorious Name of Iris
       Goose.'" JJQ, 12 (1975), 211-50.
              Intensive analysis of a sentence of the epi-
              sode, finding a network of associations to
              JJ's other works.

M353   Egri, Péter. "Towards Poetry in Prose in the 'Proteus'
       Episode of James Joyce's ULYSSES." In *ULYSSES: CINQUANT*
       ANS APRÈS. Ed. Louis Bonnerot. Pp. 153-60. See M7.
              Episode's "highly polyphonic text and texture"
              approaches the condition of poetry.

M354   Hayman, David. "Stephen on the Rocks." JJQ, 15 (1977),
       5-17.
              Suggests Stephen masturbates at the conclusion
              of the episode.

M355   Herr, Cheryl T. "Theosophy, Guilt, and 'That Word Known
       to All Men' in Joyce's ULYSSES." JJQ, 18 (1980), 45-54.
              Problem of language and reality in the episode
              related to Boehme's monism and Blavatsky's oc-
              cultism.

M356   Morse, J. Mitchell. "'Proteus.'" In JAMES JOYCE'S *ULYSSE*
       Ed. Clive Hart and David Hayman. Pp. 29-49. See M28.
              Fine analysis of thought in the episode, stress-
              ing Stephen's need and failure to "grasp the
              beast" of concrete reality in order to become
              an artist.

M357 Vitoux, Pierre. "Aristotle, Berkeley, and Newman [sic,
      Newton] in 'Proteus' and FINNEGANS WAKE." JJQ, 18 (1981),
      161-75.
           The triadic relationship of Berkeleyan ideal-
           ism, Aristotelian materialism and Newtonian
           empiricism in "Proteus" and FW.

M358 Voelker, Joseph C. "'Proteus' and the VATICINIA of Marsh's
      Library: Joyce's Subjunctive Selves." EIRE, 14, No. 4
      (1979), 133-41.
           Backgrounds to JJ's interest in mysticism and
           rejection of the mystic prophet he might have
           been: "Swift-Joachim [Abbas]-Elisha-Stephen."

M359 Von Phul, Ruth. "The Boast of Heraldry in the 'Proteus'
      Episode of ULYSSES." JML, 1 (1971), 399-405.
           Allusions to heraldry in episode amplify JJ's
           characterization of Stephen.

"Calypso"

For other important commentaries and information on this episode, see, in addition to the titles listed in the headnote to
section M, iii above, the following studies: Knuth (G49), Caspel (M10), McBride (M219), Prescott (M257), and Boldereff
(M422). Also see X28 and X66.

M360 Glasheen, Adaline. "'Calypso.'" In JAMES JOYCE'S ULYSSES.
      Ed. Clive Hart and David Hayman. Pp. 51-70. See M28.
           While they could be a sexually viable pair,
           Bloom and Molly remain alienated because of
           the disorders of Bloom's will (here deline-
           ated).

"Lotus-Eaters"

For other important commentaries and information on this episode, see, in addition to the titles listed in the headnote to
section M, iii above, the following studies: Caspel (M10), Litz
(M38), Prescott (M257), and Boldereff (M422). Also see X66 and
X93.

M361   Herring, Phillip F.   "'Lotuseaters.'"   In JAMES JOYCE'S
       ULYSSES.   Ed. Clive Hart and David Hayman.   Pp. 71-89.
       See M28.
              Episode "forecasts" JJ's "creative techniques
              in later sections," his "major motifs," and
              his use of the Homeric analogy.

"Hades"

For other important commentaries and information on this epi-
sode, see, in addition to the titles listed in the headnote to
section M, iii above, the following studies: Adams (M1), Caspel
(M10), Goldberg (M22), Begnal (M73), Crosman (M111), Lyons
(M217), Prescott (M257), Raleigh (M263), Toynbee (M323), White
(M338), and Wykes (M342).   Also see X66.

M362   Adams, Robert M.   "'Hades.'"   In JAMES JOYCE'S *ULYSSES*.
       Ed. Clive Hart and David Hayman.   Pp. 91-114.   See M28.
              The "genesis," "classical parallel," themes,
              techniques, and verifiable details of the
              episode.

"Aeolus"

For other important commentaries and information on this epi-
sode, see, in addition to the titles listed in the headnote to
section M, iii above, the following studies: Ellmann (F33),
Goldman (G34), MacCabe (G54), Adams (M1), Caspel (M10), Groden
(M25), Litz (M38), Loehrich (M39), Reynolds (M52), Blackmur
(M85), Day (M117), Prescott (M257), Senn (M287), and Boldereff
(M422).

M363   Briskin, Irene Orgel.   "Some New Light on 'The Parable
       of the Plums.'"   JJQ, 3 (1966), 236-51.
              Explicates the biblical and mythological al-
              lusions in Stephen's parable, an "essential
              and integral part" of U's themes and struc-
              ture.

M364   Halperen, Max.   "The Uninvited Guest in James Joyce's
       'Aeolus.'"   In A FAIR DAY IN THE AFFECTIONS: LITERARY

ESSAYS IN HONOR OF ROBERT B. WHITE, JR. Ed. Jack M. Durant and M. Thomas Hester. Raleigh, N.C.: Winston, 1980.
Pp. 187-96.
> Episode's headlines betray JJ's emerging at-
> tempt to "evade" or distort a world he is "un-
> able to face."

M365   Hodgart, Matthew J.C. "'Aeolus.'" In JAMES JOYCE'S
ULYSSES. Ed. Clive Hart and David Hayman. Pp. 115-30.
See M28.
> Explication, with special attention to JJ's
> rhetorical devices.

M366   Lawrence, Karen R. "'Aeolus': Interruption and Inventory."
JJQ, 17 (1980), 389-405.
> Through its headlines, this episode invites
> the reader's initial, "radical questioning of
> the authority of its writing." Assimilated
> into M37.

M367   Tompkins, Phillip. "James Joyce and the Enthymeme: The
Seventh Episode of ULYSSES." JJQ, 5 (1968), 199-205.
> The overall plan of U, the "extended enthymeme
> by example (or incomplete analogy)," embodied
> within the "Aeolus" episode.

"Lestrygonians"

For other important commentaries and information on this episode, see, in addition to the titles listed in the headnote to
section M, iii above, the following studies: Daiches (H45),
Adams (M1), Caspel (M10), Goldberg (M22), Groden (M25), Steinberg (M61), Prescott (M257), and Boldereff (M422).

M368   Anderson, Chester G. "Leopold Bloom as Dr. Sigmund Freud."
MOSAIC, 6, No. 1 (1972), 23-43.
> JJ's conscious and systematic allusions to
> three works by Freud throughout the episode.
> See M45.

M369   Friedman, Melvin J. "'Lestrygonians.'" In JAMES JOYCE'S
ULYSSES. Ed. Clive Hart and David Hayman. Pp. 131-46.
See M28.
> JJ's narrational devices, with comparisons to
> the LITTLE REVIEW version of the episode (1919).

M370   Schutte, William M. "Leopold Bloom: A Touch of the Art-
       ist." In *ULYSSES: FIFTY YEARS*. Ed. Thomas F. Staley.
       Pp. 118-31. See M59.
            Importance of episode for establishing the
            "essential elements" of Bloom's character
            (here surveyed).

M371   Swanson, Roy A. "Edible Wandering Rocks: The Pun as Al-
       legory in Joyce's 'Lestrygonians.'" GENRE, 5 (1972),
       385-403.
            JJ's sustained play with the word "rock" in
            the episode.

"Scylla and Charybdis"

For other important commentaries and information on this epi-
sode, see, in addition to the titles listed in the headnote to
section M, iii above, the following studies: Kain (F84), Chat-
terjee (G20), MacCabe (G54), Magalaner and Kain (G58), Noon
(G69), Scott (H188), Adams (M1), Caspel (M10), Goldberg (M22),
Groden (M25), Schoonbroodt (M54), Schutte (M55), Shechner
(M57), Beebe (M71), Berger (M84), Edwards (M130), Fitzpatrick
(M139), Heine (M167), Mayhew (M230), Morse (M237), Prescott
(M257), Rogers (M269), Russell (M271), Scofield (M280), Stern-
feld (M308), and Boldereff (M422). Also see X70.

M372   Duncan, Edward. "Unsubstantial Father: A Study of the
       HAMLET Symbolism in Joyce's ULYSSES." UTQ, 19 (1950),
       126-40.
            Explication of Stephen's Shakespeare theory.

M373   Feshbach, Sidney. "A New Passion: The Ninth Chapter of
       ULYSSES." In *ULYSSES: CINQUANTE ANS APRÈS*. Ed. Louis
       Bonnerot. Pp. 169-79. See M7.
            Examines the levels of the episode's narra-
            tion and its complexity of structure, with
            analogy to Cubist principles of design.

M374   Jenkins, Ralph. "Theosophy in 'Scylla and Charybdis.'"
       MFS, 15 (1969), 35-48.
            Stephen's sexual and spiritual perversion,
            as theosophist. See G65.

M375 Kain, Richard M. "James Joyce's Shakespeare Chronology."
      MR, 5 (1964), 342-55.
            Introduction to and commentary on JJ's notes
            on Shakespeare (reprinted pp. 349-55), used
            for composing episode.

M376 Kellogg, Robert. "'Scylla and Charybdis.'" In JAMES
      JOYCE'S ULYSSES. Ed. Clive Hart and David Hayman. Pp.
      147-79. See M28.
            Discussion of the episode's dialogue tech-
            nique, "romantic" temper (countering Gold-
            berg's discussion of JJ's "classical temper"
            [M22]), literary theory, symbolic polarities,
            and affirmation of conjugal love.

M377 Kershner, R.B. "Artist, Critic, and Performer: Wilde
      and Joyce on Shakespeare." TSLL, 20 (1978), 216-29.
            Influence of Wilde's PORTRAIT OF MR. W.H.
            (1889; 1921), on Stephen's theory.

M378 Lennam, Trevor. "The Happy Hunting Ground: Shakespearian
      Dramatis Personae in the 'Scylla and Charybdis' Episode
      of James Joyce's ULYSSES." UTQ, 29 (1960), 386-97.
            Characters in "Scylla and Charybdis" based
            on Shakespearian prototypes, from HAMLET.
            Reprinted in G57.

M379 Marcus, Phillip L. "Notes on Irish Elements in 'Scylla
      and Charybdis.'" JJQ, 10 (1973), 312-20.
            Supplements the annotations of Thornton (M64)
            and Schutte (M383).

M380 Peery, William. "The Hamlet of Stephen Dedalus." TEXAS
      STUDIES IN ENGLISH, 31 (1952), 109-19.
            Argues for a greater recognition of HAMLET's
            influence on JJ's style ("enrichment"), themes
            ("paternity theme"), and character portrayal
            (Stephen as Hamlet) in U.

M381 Quillian, William H. "Shakespeare in Trieste: Joyce's
      1912 HAMLET Lectures." JJQ, 12 (1974), 7-63.
            Reproduces, with commentary, JJ's notes for
            his lectures (1912-13). Useful background
            for Stephen's HAMLET discussion in the epi-
            sode. See M34.

M382   Radford, F.L. "'Christfox in Leather Trews': The Quaker
       in the Library in ULYSSES." ELH, 39 (1972), 441-58.
          Explains JJ's allusions to George Fox, founder
          of the Society of Friends, in the ninth epi-
          sode.

M383   Schutte, William M. "Allusions in 'Scylla and Charybdis':
       A Supplement to Weldon Thornton's List." JJQ, 7 (1970),
       315-25.
          Useful annotations.

M384   Sharpe, Garold. "The Philosophy of James Joyce." MFS,
       9 (1963), 120-26.
          Asserts that Stephen's HAMLET theory "is the
          most comprehensive statement of James Joyce's
          metaphysical beliefs."

"Wandering Rocks"

For other important commentaries and information on this epi-
sode, see, in addition to the titles listed in the headnote to
section M, iii above, the following studies: Knuth (G49), Adams
(M1), Caspel (M10), Groden (M25), Lawrence (M37), Reynolds
(M52), Humphrey (M177), Kettle (M197), Prescott (M257), Stern
(M307), and Boldereff (M422). Also see X94.

M385   Cronin, Edward J. "Of Mirrors and Maps and Houses with
       Gardens: Joyce's 'Wandering Rocks,' Chapter X, ULYSSES."
       NDQ, 48, No. 1 (1980), 40-52.
          Corrects Hart's discussion of JJ's "inten-
          tional errors" in episode (see below), and
          describes JJ's detailed, mirror-pattern for
          the episode's design.

M386   Hart, Clive. "'Wandering Rocks.'" In JAMES JOYCE'S
       ULYSSES. Ed. Hart and David Hayman. Pp. 181-216. See
       M28.
          Commentary on JJ's ambivalent relationship
          with the city, analysis of the episode's in-
          terpolations, and elaborate time chart of
          its action. See above.

M387   Lane, Mervin. "A Synecdochic Reading of 'Wandering
       Rocks' in ULYSSES." WHR, 28 (1974), 125-40.
          Reads episode as a synecdochic microcosm
          of U.

M388 Lord, George deForest. HEROIC MOCKERY: VARIATION ON EPIC
      THEMES FROM HOMER TO JOYCE. Newark: Univ. of Delaware
      Press, 1977. Pp. 121-32.
            See K98.

M389 Melchiori, Giorgio. "The 'Wandering Rocks,' or the Re-
      jection of Stephen Dedalus." E&S, 28 (1975), 58-75.
            Episode "the moment and the place" in JJ's
            work where his rejection of Stephen "becomes
            absolutely clear," where he is "abolished as
            a representative of the human condition."

M390 Raspa, Richard. "The 'Wandering Rocks' of ULYSSES." LHY,
      16, No. 1 (1975), 131-52.
            Episode thematically ordered by the counter-
            point between moral values and surface manners.

M391 Wenke, John. "Charity: The Measure of Morality in 'Wan-
      dering Rocks.'" EIRE, 15, No. 1 (1980), 100-13.
            Episode demonstrates both the "moral dispo-
            sitions" of U's major and minor characters
            and the central importance of charity in JJ's
            "nontranscendental" ethics.

"Sirens"

For other important commentaries and information on this episode, see, in addition to the titles listed in the headnote to
section M, iii above, the following studies: Ellmann (F33),
Goldman (G34), Levin (G52), MacCabe (G54), Strong (G77), Friedman (H64), Caspel (M10), Gottfried (M24), Groden (M25), Kain
(M35), Lawrence (M37), Litz (M38), Reynolds (M52), Sternfeld
(M308), and Worthington (M341). Also see X95.

M392 Cole, David W. "Fugal Structure in the 'Sirens' Episode
      of ULYSSES." MFS, 19 (1973), 221-26.
            JJ's fugal development of his themes (e.g.,
            prelude, subject, countersubject).

M393 Cope, Jackson I. "'Sirens.'" In JAMES JOYCE'S ULYSSES.
      Ed. Clive Hart and David Hayman. Pp. 217-42. See M28.
            "Sirens" U's stylistic and thematic "turning
            point."

M394   French, Marilyn. "The Voices of the Sirens in Joyce's
       ULYSSES." JNT, 8 (1978), 1-10.
       JJ's manipulation of narrative voice in the
       episode.

M395   Honton, Margaret. "Thou Lost One: All Songs on that Theme
       in 'Sirens.'" JJQ, 17 (1979), 41-48.
       Explores the triadic structure of the episode
       (fuga per canonem).

M396   Levin, Lawrence L. "The 'Sirens' Episode as Music: Joyce's
       Experiment in Prose Polyphony." JJQ, 3 (1965), 12-24.
       Examines the musical qualities of JJ's style
       and argues that the structure of the episode
       is based on the canon form, not the fugue, nor
       the *fuga per canonem.*

M397   Noon, William T., S.J. "'Songs the Syrens Sang.'" MOSAIC,
       6, No. 1 (1972), 77-83.
       JJ's exercise in musical form, with passing
       comparisons to Eliot. See M45.

M398   Solomon, Margaret C. "Striking the Lost Chord: The Motif
       of 'Waiting' in the 'Sirens' Episode of ULYSSES." In
       YEATS, JOYCE, AND BECKETT: NEW LIGHT ON THREE MODERN IRISH
       WRITERS. Ed. Kathleen McGrory and John Unterecker. Lewis-
       burg, Pa.: Bucknell Univ. Press, 1976. Pp. 92-104.
       JJ's play upon "all possible variations" of
       the episode's "waiting" motif (e.g., hesita-
       tion, serving, weight, and so on).

M399   Whaley, Helen. "The Role of the Blind Piano Tuner in
       Joyce's ULYSSES." MFS, 16 (1971), 531-35.
       The "croppy" boy's symbolic, technical, and
       thematic associations in U.

"Cyclops"

For other important commentaries and information on this episode, see, in addition to the titles listed in the headnote to
section M, iii above, the following studies: Ellmann (F33),
MacCabe (G54), Adams (M1), Caspel (M10), Goldberg (M22), Gose
(M23), Groden (M25), Lawrence (M37), Litz (M38), Schoonbroodt
(M54), Prescott (M257), Russell (M271), and Senn (M284). Also
see B15, B16, and X96.

M400 Biro, Diana. "Leopold in Noman's Land: The 5:00 Chapter of ULYSSES." THOTH, 11, No. 2 (1971), 9-21.
JJ's use of three distinct perspectives (hostile-narrator; objective-dialogue; comic-interpolations), to refine his basically sympathetic portrait of Bloom.

M401 Hayman, David. "'Cyclops.'" In JAMES JOYCE'S ULYSSES. Ed. Clive Hart and Hayman. Pp. 243-75. See M28.
Commentary on JJ's complex "juggling" of themes and styles in his "mixed media" chapter, noting its narrator's retrospective point of view. See M405.

M402 Mantell, Deborah Byrd. "Leopold Bloom: Joyce's Loveless Irishman, or Everlasting Caricature of the Serious World?" In IRISH RENAISSANCE ANNUAL II. Ed. Zack Bowen. Pp. 115-38. See G14.
JJ's view of Irish political history and its relationship to his portrait of Bloom in the episode.

M403 Pringle, Mary Beth. "Funfersum: Dialogue as Metafictional Technique in the 'Cyclops' Episode of ULYSSES." JJQ, 18 (1981), 397-416.
JJ's deliberate blurring of distinctions between his "I-narrator" and his parodies emphasizes the unreality of both narrative voices.

M404 Rankin, H.D. "Joyce's Satyr-Play: The 'Cyclops' Episode in ULYSSES." AGORA, 2, No. 2 (1973), 3-12.
JJ's use of themes characteristic of Greek satyric drama (cf. Euripides' THERSITES).

M405 Schneidau, Herbert. "One Eye and Two Levels: On Joyce's 'Cyclops.'" JJQ, 16 (1979), 95-104.
Speculations on the reader's response to the displaced narration of the chapter (noted by Hayman; see M401), suggesting the narrator is, in effect, JJ himself. Followed by a "Response," by David Hayman, pp. 105-10. See G44.

M406 Schoenberg, E.I. "The Identity of the 'Cyclops' Narrator in James Joyce's ULYSSES." JML, 5 (1976), 534-39.
Implausible suggestion that Simon Dedalus is the anonymous narrator. Also see M19.

M407   Schwartzman, Myron. "The V.A.8 Copybook: An Early Draft
       of the 'Cyclops' Chapter of ULYSSES with Notes on Its
       Development." JJQ, 12 (1974), 64-122.
            Transcription of the copybook, with commentary
            on JJ's working methods. See M34.

M408   Staples, Hugh B. "'Composition of Place': The Setting
       of 'Cyclops.'" JJQ, 13 (1976), 393-99.
            JJ's later revisions of episode exploit the
            "historical and political overtones" of con-
            temporary Dublin details.

M409   Stern, Frederick C. "Pyrrhus, Fenians, and Bloom." JJQ,
       5 (1968), 211-28.
            See M350.

"Nausicaa"

For other important commentaries and information on this episode, see, in addition to the titles listed in the headnote to
section M, iii above, the following studies: Ellmann (F33),
Cross (G24), Knuth (G49), Deakin (H46), Magalaner (H143), Caspel (M10), Groden (M25), Lawrence (M37), Litz (M38), Schoonbroodt (M54), Shechner (M57), Henke (M170), Humphrey (M177),
McBride (M220), Prescott (M257), and Boldereff (M422). Also
see B16, X97, and X98.

M410   Brick, Allan. "The Madman in His Cell: Joyce, Beckett,
       Nabokov, and Stereotypes." MR, 1 (1959), 41-55.
            Gerty MacDowell illustrates JJ's perceptive
            analysis of the "imprisonment of the contem-
            porary mind by mass culture" (cf. Beckett
            and Nabokov).

M411   Issacs, Neil D. "The Autoerotic Metaphor in Joyce, Sterne,
       Lawrence, Stevens, and Whitman." L&P, 15 (1965), 92-106.
            JJ's rhythmic, onanistic style.

M412   Senn, Fritz. "'Nausicaa.'" In JAMES JOYCE'S ULYSSES.
       Ed. Clive Hart and David Hayman. Pp. 277-311. See M28.
            Miscellany of often excellent notes and ob-
            servations on the episode's themes, tech-
            niques, and larger relationships to the novel.

"Oxen of the Sun"

For other important commentaries and information on this episode, see, in addition to the titles listed in the headnote to
section M, iii above, the following studies: Ellmann (F33),
Chatterjee (G20), Adams (M1), Caspel (M10), Gose (M23), Gottfried (M24), Groden (M25), Lawrence (M37), Litz (M38), Schoonbroodt (M54), Fitzpatrick (M140), and Boldereff (M422). Also
see B16.

M413   Allison, June W. "A Literary Coincidence? Joyce and
        Plato." JJQ, 16 (1979), 267-82.
                Parallels between Plato's SYMPOSIUM and the
                episode.

M414   Atherton, James S. "'The Oxen of the Sun.'" In JAMES
        JOYCE'S *ULYSSES*. Ed. Clive Hart and David Hayman. Pp.
        313-39. See M28.
                JJ's sources for and adaptations of his prose
                models in his "exercise in imitative form."

M415   Bauerle, Ruth. "A Sober Drunken Speech: Stephen's Par-
        odies in 'The Oxen of the Sun.'" JJQ, 5 (1967), 40-46.
                Stephen's conscious parodies of the Last Sup-
                per and the Mass in the episode.

M416   Cohn, Alan M. "Joyce's Notes on the End of 'Oxen of the
        Sun.'" JJQ, 4 (1967), 194-201.
                Reprints JJ's notes, supplied to his German
                translator Georg Goyert (in 1927). See G42.

M417   Gordon, John. "The Multiple Journeys of 'Oxen of the
        Sun.'" ELH, 46 (1979), 158-72.
                JJ's organic development of linguistic, lit-
                erary, historical, political, Biblical, cos-
                mic, and biographical patterns through the
                episode. See G35.

M418   Iser, Wolfgang. "Doing Things in Style: An Interpreta-
        tion of 'The Oxen of the Sun' in James Joyce's ULYSSES."
        In THE IMPLIED READER: PATTERNS OF COMMUNICATION IN PROSE
        FICTION FROM BUNYAN TO BECKETT. Baltimore: Johns Hopkins
        Univ. Press, 1974. Pp. 179-95.
                JJ's style in the episode, a microcosm of the
                entire novel, imposes "form on an essentially
                formless reality." See X99.

M419   Klein, A.M.   "'The Oxen of the Sun.'"   HERE AND NOW, 1
        (1949), 28-48.
                Intensive symbolic analysis of the foetal
                development of the episode.

M420   Weiss, Daniel.   "The End of the 'Oxen of the Sun': An
        Analysis of the Boosing Scene in James Joyce's ULYSSES."
        ANALYST, No. 9 (1955), pp. 1-16.
                Attempted gloss and explication of the cha-
                otic final pages of the episode.   Also see
                various addenda submitted by several critics:
                ANALYST, No. 10 (1956), pp. 10-18.

"Circe"

For other important commentaries and information on this epi-
sode, see, in addition to the titles listed in the headnote to
section M, iii above, the following studies: Ellmann (F33),
Cross, (G24), Levin (G52), MacCabe (G54), Tysdahl (G82), Hoff-
man (H91), Kaye (H106), Epstein (K7), Adams (M1), Caspel (M10),
Goldberg (M22), Gose (M23), Gottfried (M24), Groden (M25), Kain
(M35), Lawrence (M37), Litz (M38), Loehrich (M39), Parr (M48),
Reynolds (M52), Schoonbroodt (M54), Schutte (M55), Shechner
(M57), Fitzpatrick (M139, M140), Hart (M163), Hayman (M165),
Kain (M185), Poss (M254), Prescott (M257), Rogers (M269), Rus-
sell (M271), and Sternfeld (M308).   Also see B15, B16, X100,
X101, and X102.

M421   Barkentin, Marjorie.   JAMES JOYCE'S *ULYSSES* IN NIGHTTOWN.
        New York: Modern Library, 1958.
                Interesting dramatic adaptation of the "Circe"
                episode, plus some other vestiges of the novel,
                performed on Broadway in 1958 and revived in
                1974.

M422   Boldereff, Frances M.   A BLAKEAN TRANSLATION OF JOYCE'S
        "CIRCE".   Woodward, Pa.: Classic Non-Fiction Library,
        1965.
                Bizarre close reading of the "Circe" episode,
                prefaced by general commentary on the rest of
                U, discovering throughout JJ's "appropriation"
                and application of Blake's language, symbolism,
                and themes.   Methodologically unsound and of-
                ten eccentric.

M423 Bowen, Zack, et al. "'Circe': Why, What and How?" In
JOYCE & PARIS. Ed. Jacques Aubert and Maria Jolas. II,
11-26. See G8.
Five brief papers on various aspects of the
episode.

M424 Goldman, Arnold. "Stephen's Parleyvoo: ULYSSES, pp. 672-
674." JJQ, 8 (1971), 157-62.
Focuses on Stephen's perilous position of
near-prostitute at his "lowest point" in U.

M425 Harkness, Marguerite. "'Circe': The Mousetrap of ULYSSES."
JJQ, 12 (1975), 259-72.
The mousetrap, play-within-a-play in HAMLET,
and "Circe" function similarly in preparing
"the way for change."

M426 Henke, Suzette A. "James Joyce and Joris-Karl Huysmans:
What Was Leopold Bloom Doing with that Circus-Lady?" MOD-
ERN BRITISH LITERATURE, 5 (1980), 68-72.
"Bloom's kinky behavior" inspired by "Huysmans'
rage for the dramatic enactment of erotic fan-
tasy" in À REBOURS (1884). See G63.

M427 Jarrell, Mackie L. "Joyce's Use of Swift's POLITE CON-
VERSATION in the 'Circe' Episode of ULYSSES." PMLA, 72
(1957), 545-54.
JJ's "parodic use of the proverb" in the episode directly indebted to Swift (traces numerous "borrowings" and parallels).

M428 Kenner, Hugh. "'Circe.'" In JAMES JOYCE'S *ULYSSES*. Ed.
Clive Hart and David Hayman. Pp. 341-62. See M28.
Symbolic, technical, and thematic significance
of role-playing in U's dramatic episode, with
analyses of Bloom's fantasies and Stephen's
delusions.

M429 Leithauser, Gladys Garner, and Paul Sporn. "Hypsospadia:
Linguistic Guidepost to the Themes of the 'Circe' Episode
of ULYSSES." JML, 4 (1974), 109-14.
JJ's modification of the medical neologism
"*hypo*spadia," altering the Greek prefix to
"*hypso*," gives a positive meaning to the term
(i.e., androgynous evolution rather than de-
volution).

M430   May, Keith M. OUT OF THE MAELSTROM: PSYCHOLOGY AND THE
        NOVEL IN THE TWENTIETH CENTURY. London: Elek, 1977. Pp.
        28-33.
            JJ's use of Freud's triadic "scheme" to de-
            scribe the mind's action (unconscious-precon-
            scious-conscious).

M431   Paley, Morton D. "Blake in Nighttown." In A JAMES JOYCE
        MISCELLANY, THIRD SERIES. Ed. Marvin Magalaner. Pp. 175-
        87. See G57.
            Compares JJ's and Blake's ideas and esoteric
            symbolism.

M432   Schneider, Ulrich. "Freemasonic Signs and Passwords in
        the 'Circe' Episode." JJQ, 5 (1968), 303-11.
            Clarifies Masonic themes and ritual elements
            in the episode.

M433   Silverstein, Norman. "Bruno's Particles of Reminiscence."
        JJQ, 2 (1965), 271-80.
            Close analysis of the meaning implicit in a
            line of JJ's text, and clarification of his
            allusion to Bruno's ARS MEMORIAE.

M434   -----. "Evolution of the Nighttown Setting." In THE
        CELTIC MASTER. Ed. Maurice Harmon. Pp. 27-36. See G39.
            Stages of composition for and evolution of
            the expressionistic setting in "Circe."

M435   -----. "Magic on the Notesheets of the 'Circe' Episode."
        JJQ, 1, No. 4 (1964)", 19-26.
            Examines JJ's notes on magic for the episode.
            (See addenda and corrigenda, JJQ, 2 [1965],
            217-26.)

M436   -----. "Stephen Dedalus as Harlequin." In *ULYSSES*: CIN-
        QUANTE ANS APRÈS. Ed. Louis Bonnerot. Pp. 197-202. See
        M7.
            Episode's implied parallel to Milton's COMUS,
            with Stephen as Harlequin.

"Eumaeus"

For other important commentaries and information on this episode, see, in addition to the titles listed in the headnote to
section M, iii above, the following studies: Kenner (G48), Gose

(M23), Groden (M25), Lawrence (M37), Litz (M38), Reynolds (M52), Schoonbroodt (M54), Prescott (M257), and Schiffer (M275). Also see B16.

M437 Bass, Richard K. "Additional Allusions in 'Eumaeus.'" JJQ, 10 (1973), 321-29.
      Useful supplement to Thornton's listing (see M64).

M438 Bruns, Gerald L. "'Eumaeus.'" In JAMES JOYCE'S ULYSSES. Ed. Clive Hart and David Hayman. Pp. 363-83. See M28.
      Spirit of romance (the "poetic") collapses and is displaced by the "spirit of ordinary life" ("realistic poetry") in episode.

M439 Levenston, E.A. "Narrative Technique in ULYSSES: A Stylistic Comparison of 'Telemachus' and 'Eumaeus.'" LANGUAGE AND STYLE, 5 (1972), 260-75.
      See M347.

M440 McLain, Evelyn N. "'Alle Schiffe Brücken': Joyce's ULYSSES Resolved." SOUTH CENTRAL BULLETIN, 30 (1970), 209-11.
      Elements of Viconian and Thomistic thought in the episode.

M441 Raleigh, John Henry. "On the Way Home to Ithaca: The Functions of the 'Eumaeus' Section in ULYSSES." In IRISH RENAISSANCE ANNUAL II. Ed. Zack Bowen. Pp. 13-114. See G14.
      Detailed discussion of the historical and political backgrounds of the episode and forceful defense of JJ's "wonderfully energetic and creative" prose style.

M442 Thomas, Brook. "The Counterfeit Style of 'Eumaeus.'" JJQ, 14 (1976), 15-24.
      Episode's style represents, with humor, Bloom's idea of "fine writing."

"Ithaca"

For other important commentaries and information on this episode, see, in addition to the titles listed in the headnote to section M, iii above, the following studies: Cross (G24), Goldman (G34), Levin (G52), Kaye (H106), Adams (M1), Goldberg (M22),

Gose (M23), Gottfried (M24), Groden (M25), Litz (M38), Reynolds
(M52), Schoonbroodt (M54), Kain (M181), Littmann and Schweig-
hauser (M212), Prescott (M257), Robinson (M268), Russell (M271),
Schiffer (M275), and Boldereff (M422). Also see B16.

M443   Benstock, Bernard. "Dateline 'Ithaca': The News from
       Eccles Street." MODERN BRITISH LITERATURE, 5 (1980),
       29-42.
              Review of episode and of its treatment by
              various critics, with a tentative classifi-
              cation of the major "sources" of the infor-
              mation presented. See G63.

M444   Fleishman, Avrom. "Science in 'Ithaca': An Examination
       of the Physical Sciences in ULYSSES." 1967. In FICTION
       AND THE WAYS OF KNOWING. Austin: Univ. of Texas Press,
       1978. Pp. 136-48.
              JJ's original use of science in literature
              (chiefly classical mechanics and astronomy)
              paralleled to Einstein's original extrapola-
              tions upon Newtonian physics.

M445   Lawrence, Karen R. "Style and Narrative in the 'Ithaca'
       Chapter of Joyce's ULYSSES." ELH, 47 (1980), 559-74.
              JJ's anti-literary style and abondonment of
              narrative, in the episode, paradoxically il-
              lustrate both the limitations of style and
              form in fiction and JJ's skill in their ma-
              nipulation. Assimilated into M37.

M446   Litz, A. Walton. "'Ithaca.'" In JAMES JOYCE'S ULYSSES.
       Ed. Clive Hart and David Hayman. Pp. 385-405. See M28.
              Commentary on JJ's obsessive realism and sym-
              bolism, and survey of the "problems" of the
              episode.

M447   Madtes, Richard E. "Joyce and the Building of 'Ithaca.'"
       ELH, 31 (1964), 443-59.
              Close study of JJ's "accretive" development
              of the episode through its successive stages
              of composition.

M448   Marre, K.E. "Experimentation with a Symbol from Mythol-
       ogy: The Courses of the Comets in the 'Ithaca' Chapter
       of ULYSSES." MFS, 20 (1974), 385-90.
              Stephen as "comet" in the episode (cf. Aris-
              totelian cosmology).

M449 Watson, Edward A. "Stoom-Bloom: Scientific Objectivity
versus Romantic Subjectivity in the 'Ithaca' Episode of
Joyce's ULYSSES." UNIVERSITY OF WINDSOR REVIEW, 2, No.
1 (1966), 11-25.
Through "omission of any element of subjectivity or human emotion" in the language of the
episode, JJ effectively reinforces our sense
of Bloom's "basic humanity."

M450 Weinstein, Norman. "The 'Ithaca' Chapter of ULYSSES:
Notes on Science, Number and Poetic Structure." SOUTHERN
REVIEW (Adelaide, Australia), 12 (1979), 3-22.
The poetic elements and effects of JJ's most
prosaic episode.

"Penelope"

For other important commentaries and information on this epi-
sode, see, in addition to the titles listed in the headnote to
section M, iii above, the following studies: Ellmann (F33),
Semmler (H192), Goldberg (M22), Groden (M25), Lawrence (M37),
Litz (M38), Schoonbroodt (M54), Shechner (M57), Steinberg (M61),
Blackmur (M85), Cohn (M104), Edel (M128), Fitzpatrick (M140),
Harris (M162), Hayman (M164), Herring (M171, M173), Humphrey
(M177), Kenner (M195), Morse (M239), O'Brien (M248), Prescott
(M257), Robinson (M268), Schiffer (M275), Taylor (M311), and
Timpe (M318). Also see B16 and X103.

M451 Boyle, Robert, S.J. "'Penelope.'" In JAMES JOYCE'S ULYSSES.
Ed. Clive Hart and David Hayman. Pp. 407-33. See M28.
Affirmative reading of the unfathomably mysterious Molly's and the novel's affirmations
of life.

M452 Card, James Van Dyck. "'Contradicting': The Word for
Joyce's 'Penelope.'" JJQ, 11 (1973), 17-26.
Contradiction the episode's "guiding princi-
ple."

M453 ------. "A Gibraltar Sourcebook for 'Penelope.'" JJQ, 8
(1971), 163-75.
Study of JJ's use of a source (GIBRALTAR, by
Henry M. Field [1889]), offers insight into
his methods of composition.

M454   Tolomeo, Diane. "The Final Octagon of ULYSSES." JJQ,
       10 (1973), 439-54.
           Episode's octagonal structure and Viconian
           patterning.

M455   Voelker, Joşeph C. "Molly Bloom and the Rhetorical Tra-
       dition." CLS, 16 (1979), 146-64.
           Rhetorical parallels among Chaucer's "Wife
           of Bath," Erasmus's Stultitia (in ENCOMIUM
           MORIAE, in THE PRAISE OF FOLLY), and JJ's
           Molly Bloom.

M456   -----. "'Nature it is': The Influence of Giordano Bruno
       on James Joyce's Molly Bloom." JJQ, 14 (1976), 39-48.
           JJ's concept of women related to Bruno's idea
           of Nature.

N. STUDIES OF *FINNEGANS WAKE* (1939)

The following section is subdivided into two parts: i. Books
and Essay Collections on FW; and ii. General Critical Articles,
or Chapters on FW.

The WAKE NEWSLITTER [sic] is a unique, "title-centered" periodical devoted principally to brief notes on and explications
of FW (see N45, below).

For facsimiles of JJ's extensive notebooks for FW, see vols.
28-43 of THE JAMES JOYCE ARCHIVE (B10). Vols. 44-63 of the
ARCHIVE contain facsimiles of the numerous surviving drafts,
fair copies, typescripts, proofs, galleys, errata pages, and
TRANSITION pages of FW, arranged according to the chapter di-
visions of the published work. For additional transcriptions
of the FW manuscripts and notebooks, see B1, B7, B12, and B19.

For a concordance to FW, see Hart (D7). For glossaries and
lexicons of the foreign-language words and word-elements in
FW, see Tysdahl (G82), Bonheim (N11), Christiani (N15), O'Hehir
(N39, N40), and WAKE NEWSLITTER (N45).

For a bibliographical survey of the part-publication of FW as
"Work in Progress" (1924-38), see Spoerri (E27). For biograph-
ical backgrounds to FW and for memoirs and reminiscences of JJ
during the years of its writing and publication, see Budgen
(F11), Crosby (F23), Ellmann (F33), Finneran (F39), Gluck (F48),
Hoffmeister (F63), Hutchins (F68), JAMES JOYCE QUARTERLY (F69),
E. Jolas (F73), M. Jolas (F74), Lidderdale and Nicholson (F92),
Lyons (F95), McGrory (F99), McMillan (F100), Mercanton (F105),
Paul (F119), Potts (F122), Pound (F123), Power (F124), Stephens
(F143), Sullivan (F146), Wagner (F155), and Weaver (F157).

For additional critical commentaries and information on FW, see
the following books, in section G above: Adams (G1, G2), Arnold
(G6), Boyle (G15), Brivic (G16), Burgess (G17), Chatterjee (G20),
Cixous (G21), Cope (G22), CRANE BAG (G23), Duff (G27), Hart (in
G27a), Gillet (G29), Goldberg (G31), Golding (G32), Goldman
(G33, G34), Grose (G37), Gross (G38), Hodgart (G40), Hodgart

and Worthington (G41), JAMES JOYCE QUARTERLY (G42), Jones (G46), Kenner (G47), Knuth (G49), Levin (G52), Litz (G53), MacCabe (G54), Magalaner and Kain (G58), Majault (G59), Manganiello (G60), Martin (G61), Morse (G66), Moseley (G67), Murillo (G68), Noon (G69), O'Brien (G70), Peake (G71), Ryf (G72), Smidt (G74), Stewart (G76), Strong (G77), Tindall (G79, G80), TRANSITION (G81), Tysdahl (G82), Waldron (G83); the following critical articles, in section H above: Benstock (H18), Colum (H36), Daiches (H45), Forster (H61), Friedman (H64), Garrett (H70), Goodheart (H79), Hendry (H86), Hoffman (H93), Kenner (H109, H110), Klawitter (H118), Litz (H128), McLuhan (H139), Markovic (H144), Mercier (H148), Morse (H155), Poirier (H171), Russell (H183), Semmler (H192), Ussher (H220), Weidlé (H230), Weir (H231), White (H233), Wilson (H237); and the following studies, entered in other sections of this bibliography: Epstein (K7), Budgen (M8), Burgess (M9), Reynolds (M52), Steinberg (M61), Kenner (M194), Aubert (P1), and Jackson (P4).

For foreign-language studies of FW, see section Y.

N, i. Books and Essay Collections on FINNEGANS WAKE

Also see Y1 through Y9.

N1 THE ANALYST. Nos. 10, 12, 15-17, 19-24 (1956-65).
        Eleven issues devoted wholly or in part to an-
        notations and explications of FW. Of particu-
        lar value are Adaline Glasheen's analyses of
        the "thunderwords" in FW (No. 23 [1964], 1-29),
        John V. Kelleher's notes on FW (No. 12 [1957],
        9-15; No. 15 [1958], 9-13), and Fritz Senn's
        discussion of Zurich allusions in FW (No. 19
        [1960], 1-23). Items not entered separately
        or annotated in this guide.

N2 Atherton, James S. THE BOOKS AT THE WAKE: A STUDY OF LIT-
        ERARY ALLUSIONS IN JAMES JOYCE'S *FINNEGANS WAKE*. New York:
        Viking, 1960.
        Learned, well-written study of the occurrence
        and significance of literary allusions in FW
        which provides, in fact, an important general
        interpretation of the novel, despite the spe-
        cialized approach suggested by its subject.
        Atherton divides JJ's principal literary sources

into three main categories: the "structural
books" that determined the "eclectic logic" of
FW's construction (e.g., works by Vico, Bruno,
Lévy-Bruhl), the major works of the European
and Celtic literary traditions, from medieval
manuscripts through Ibsen, and the principal
"Sacred Books" of mankind (e.g., the BIBLE,
BOOK OF THE DEAD, EDDAS, KORAN), that, together synthesized in and "superimposed" upon
FW, transform the work into a universal history. Includes an "Alphabetical List of Literary Allusions." Addenda published in JJQ, 2
(1965), 142-49. See N26. Also see N69 and
N165.

N3   Beckett, Samuel, et al. OUR EXAGMINATION ROUND HIS FACT-
IFICATION FOR INCAMINATION OF "WORK IN PROGRESS." Paris:
Shakespeare and Co., 1929.
Important collection of analyses, appreciations,
and explications, by 'twelve disciples,' published in part to correct the popular miscon-
ception that FW was inexplicable, surrealist,
or automatic writing. Several times reissued
and still valuable. Includes two letters in
protest and the following: N53, N68, N74, N107,
N141, N156, N157, N159, N179, N191, N192, and
N222.

N4   Begnal, Michael H., and Fritz Senn, eds. A CONCEPTUAL
GUIDE TO *FINNEGANS WAKE*. University Park: Pennsylvania
State Univ. Press, 1974.
Thirteen commentaries on the chapters of FW,
variously divided among as many critics, ambig-
uously intended to present a unified view of
FW, "as *novel,*" through diversity. Fine guide
for the experienced reader, though several essays are too narrow to provide a general overview. Includes N47, N56, N58, N67, N73, N95,
N99, N133, N149, N161, N176, N199, and N203.

N5   Begnal, Michael H., and Grace Eckley. NARRATOR AND CHAR-
ACTER IN *FINNEGANS WAKE*. Lewisburg, Pa.: Bucknell Univ.
Press, 1975.
Unusual combined publication of two unrelated
monographs. Begnal's "The Dreamers at the Wake:
A View of Narration and Point of View" approaches
FW as an experimental yet traditional novel, ar-

guing that JJ uses multiple points of view to
create a narrative of "several people...dream-
ing together." The body of his essay explores
each of these voices (e.g., HCE, ALP, Shem,
Shaun, the omniscient narrator). Eckley's
"Queer Mrs. Quickenough and Odd Miss Doddpeb-
ble: The Tree and the Stone in FINNEGANS WAKE"
discusses the epic and mythic dimensions and
the symbol and character polarities of JJ's
dialogue of the washerwomen, the "Anna Livia
Plurabelle" section of FW. Extracts of Begnal's monograph originally published in G9,
and of Eckley's in N27.

N6 Benstock, Bernard. JOYCE-AGAIN'S WAKE: AN ANALYSIS OF *FIN-
NEGANS WAKE*. Seattle: Univ. of Washington Press, 1965.
Valuable study of various aspects of FW, neither intended as nor providing a coherent interpretation of the book. Rather, Benstock
surveys the major confusions about FW, among
its readers as well as its critics ("What We
Still Don't Know About FINNEGANS WAKE"), discusses JJ's political and religious beliefs as
reflected in FW, examines the comic and poetic
dimensions of FW, attempts to define the genre
of FW (cf. Fielding's concept of the comic epic
in prose), and argues, through a study of the
autobiographical elements of FW, the "humanity"
of JJ's last novel. Includes an appendix pre-
senting a model analysis of the several levels
of meaning in "The Tale of Jarl von Hoother and
the Prankquean" (FW, pp. 21-23). See N98.

N7 Best, Nigel. DAWN: A STUDY OF THE PRESENT AGE AND *FINNEGANS
WAKE* THROUGH A CLOSE LOOK AT FW PAGE 594: ONE PAGE SUFFI-
CIENT FOR OUR TIME. 1979. 2nd ed. New Plymouth, N.Z.:
Dawn, 1979.
Not seen.

N8 Boldereff, Frances M. HERMES TO HIS SON THOTH: BEING
JOYCE'S USE OF GIORDANO BRUNO IN *FINNEGANS WAKE*. Law-
renceville, N.J.: Classic Non-fiction Library, 1968.
Unsatisfactory exercise in association. Boldereff views FW as a product of the Hermetic
tradition, through Bruno, and examines its "direct references" to Bruno. Her final chapter
also freely associates JJ with the Russian revolutionary Alexander Herzen, his countryman

Yeats, and the American novelists Melville and
Hawthorne. Enthusiastic, effusive, and poorly-
written. Also see below.

N9   -----. READING *FINNEGANS WAKE*. New York: Barnes and
Noble, 1959.
        Two-part study of FW, the first section argu-
    ing that the novel should be read as "the
    greatest poem about [a] country that has ever
    been written of any land, including Greece"
    and the second section providing extensive
    glosses for its references to Irish history,
    literature, language, and geography. Bolder-
    eff makes a number of intriguing connections
    between JJ's method and the techniques of
    early Irish literature and several interest-
    ing observations on Irish history in FW, but
    uncritical enthusiasm as frequently leads her
    to extravagant claims and eccentric distor-
    tions. Boldereff's two studies of FW (also
    see above) are, despite some slight merits,
    examples of the worst abuses of cultist crit-
    icism.

N10   Bonheim, Helmut. JOYCE'S BENEFICTIONS. Berkeley and Los
Angeles: Univ. of California Press, 1964.
        See M6.

N11   -----, comp. A LEXICON OF THE GERMAN IN *FINNEGANS WAKE*.
Berkeley and Los Angeles: Univ. of California Press, 1967.
        Lists, with translations and line location, ap-
    proximately 5,000 words wholly or partly óf Ger-
    man origin. Scrupulously done.

N12   Brown, Norman O. CLOSING TIME. New York: Random House,
1973.
        Ostentatiously "experimental" juxtaposition
    of passages from Vico's NEW SCIENCE and FW,
    plus a few other works, creating a "dialogue"
    between JJ and Vico, with sparse commentary
    by Brown. Brown does demonstrate ingenuity
    in his technique, however, developing a num-
    ber of interesting correlations between the
    authors' views of history, "origins," and
    language.

N13   Cage, John. WRITING THROUGH *FINNEGANS WAKE*. Tulsa, Okla.:
Univ. of Tulsa Press, 1978.
        The composer's tracing of JJ's name through

the text of FW, in the form of "mesotics"
(similar to acrostics and defined in Cage's
brief "Introduction"). An exercise in composition, making no claim that JJ intended
thus to bury his name throughout FW. Extract
originally published in N24.

N14   Campbell, Joseph, and Henry Morton Robinson. A SKELETON
      KEY TO *FINNEGANS WAKE*. New York: Harcourt, 1944.
      Influential early attempt to find pattern and
      meaning within the "complex and amazing nar-
      rative" of FW, offering several tentative in-
      terpretations which have too often been taken
      for gospel. After a preliminary synopsis of
      FW and a sample close reading of its opening
      four pages, Campbell and Robinson provide a
      section-by-section explication of the text.
      Their commentary is replete with insights, as
      well as curious blunders and dubious emphases
      (e.g., their overstatement of FW's mythic di-
      mension). All in all, this remains a valuable
      introduction to FW, if used with caution. See N223.

N15   Christiani, Dounia Bunis. SCANDINAVIAN ELEMENTS OF *FIN-
      NEGANS WAKE*. Evanston, Ill.: Northwestern Univ. Press,
      1965.
      Eight chapters surveying JJ's assimilation of
      Scandinavian culture, history, and literature
      (e.g., HCE as "Ostman" and "Odin," the influ-
      ences of Ibsen, Kierkegaard, and Strindberg),
      and an extensive glossary of Scandinavian
      words used in or suggested by JJ's word-com-
      pounds in FW (with page and line references
      and annotations). Extract originally pub-
      lished in N26.

N16   Dalton, Jack P., and Clive Hart, eds. TWELVE AND A TILLY:
      ESSAYS ON THE OCCASION OF THE 25TH ANNIVERSARY OF *FINNEGANS
      WAKE*. Evanston, Ill.: Northwestern Univ. Press, 1965
      [1966].
      Twelve original essays on FW, of varying in-
      terest and quality, with a poem on JJ by Pad-
      raic Colum. Includes N48, N76, N90, N111,
      N113, N128, N136, N144, N155, N166, N175, and
      N197.

N17   DiBernard, Barbara.   ALCHEMY AND *FINNEGANS WAKE*.   Albany:
      State Univ. of New York Press, 1980.
           Traces sources in Hermetic and occult literature
           for several themes and image patterns cohering
           within FW. DiBernard sees JJ using alchemy as
           a "central" metaphor "for change and the artis-
           tic process" and as a "source or analogue" for
           many of FW's major themes (examined in succes-
           sive chapters): "incest, colors, forgery, death
           and rebirth, the dream form, the use of excre-
           ment, the Golden Age, number symbolism, the
           macrocosm-microcosm theory, and the reconcilia-
           tion of opposites." Well-written, but greatly
           exaggerates JJ's knowledge of alchemy. Extract
           originally published in N29.

N18   Drachler, Jacob.   ID-GRIDS AND EGO-GRAPHS: A CONFABULATION
      WITH *FINNEGANS WAKE*.   Brooklyn, N.Y.: Gridgraffiti Press,
      1978.
           Forty-four drawings, inspired by passages in
           FW.

N19   Garvin, John.   JAMES JOYCE'S DISUNITED KINGDOM AND THE
      IRISH DIMENSION.   Dublin: Gill and Macmillan, 1976.
           See M19.

N20   Glasheen, Adaline.   A THIRD CENSUS OF *FINNEGANS WAKE*: AN
      INDEX OF THE CHARACTERS AND THEIR ROLES.   Berkeley and Los
      Angeles: Univ. of California Press, 1977.
           Third revised and expanded edition of Glasheen's
           indispensable guide to the characters in FW
           (first published in 1956; second edition, 1963).
           Glasheen presents an extended "Synopsis" of FW
           (also in its third revised form), a chart list-
           ing schematically the transforming identities
           of major figures ("Who is Who When Everybody is
           Somebody Else"), and an alphabetical index of
           the characters in FW (with identification, oc-
           casional interpretive remarks, and page and
           line references for their mention). Extremely
           useful. See N165.

N21   Hart, Clive.   STRUCTURE AND MOTIF IN *FINNEGANS WAKE*. Evan-
      ston, Ill.: Northwestern Univ. Press, 1962.
           The single most important general study of FW,
           offering a perceptive view of the novel's funda-
           mental structural principles and defining, with

impressive illustration, the nature and extent
of JJ's use of *leitmotif.* After an opening
survey of FW's general characteristics, Hart
devotes four chapters to the clarification of
its structure ("Cyclic Form," "Dream-Structure"--
stressing the dream-within-a-dream elements--
"The Circle," and "The Cross"), and three chapters to JJ's use of motifs, as distinguished
from themes and symbols ("Correspondences,"
"Leitmotif," and "Two Major Motifs" [i.e.,
"Quinet" and "The Letter"]). Among the appendixes is an extensive listing of approximately 700 motifs, exclusive of literary and
song allusions. Extract reprinted in G19.

N22   Hart, Clive, and Fritz Senn, eds. A *WAKE* DIGEST. Sydney:
      Sydney Univ. Press, 1968.
      Useful gathering of twenty-four mostly brief
      essays on FW, by ten critics, divided into
      three categories: "Source Studies and General
      Explication," "Linguistic Studies," and "Notes."
      All but four essays previously published in the
      WAKE NEWSLITTER (see N45). For the two most
      substantial contributions, see N117 and N196.

N23   Hayman, David. JOYCE ET MALLARMÉ. 2 vols. Paris: Les
      Lettres Modernes, 1956.
      Singles out Stéphane Mallarmé as the most impor-
      tant influence, among the French symbolists, on
      JJ's developing conception of his art, drawing
      specific correlations between Mallarmé's so-
      called "stylistique de la suggestion" and JJ's
      "classical temperament" and theory of the art-
      ist's impersonality. Hayman describes the
      comparatively superficial suggestivity of U
      (association of ideas, motifs, symbols, struc-
      tural devices) and the "suggestive intégrale"
      of structure, language, and symbolism in FW.
      Includes extensive comparisons of UN COUP DE
      DÉS (1897) and FW and essays on "éléments Mal-
      larméens" in FW (e.g., paraphrases, allusions,
      evocations, etc.). [In French.]

N24   Hayman, David, and Elliott Anderson, eds. IN THE WAKE OF
      THE *WAKE.* Madison: Univ. of Wisconsin Press, 1978.
      Miscellany, containing four articles on FW and
      its influence, an anthology of eleven works by

as many authors, written in the tradition of FW
(including Samuel Beckett, John Cage [see N13],
Augusto de Campos, Hélène Cixous, William Gass,
Maurice Roche, and Philippe Sollers), and two
interviews (with Roche and Sollers). Only the
four articles are directly pertinent to the
study of FW. Reprinted from original publication in N43. Includes N81, N100, N129, and N198.

N25 Huxley, Aldous, Stuart Gilbert, and J. Schwartz. JOYCE
     THE ARTIFICER: TWO [sic] STUDIES OF JOYCE'S METHOD. Lon-
     don: Privately Printed, 1952.
          See M32.

N26 JAMES JOYCE QUARTERLY. 2 (1965), 142-216.
          Heterogeneous collection of eight articles on
          FW, by James S. Atherton (extract from N2), Ron-
          ald Bates (N52), Bernard Benstock (N60, N61),
          Dounia Bunis Christiani (extract from N15), Da-
          vid Hayman (N127), Brendan O'Hehir (extract
          from N39), and Hugh B. Staples ("Joyce and Crypt-
          ology: Some Speculations"). Guest editor: David
          Hayman.

N27 JAMES JOYCE QUARTERLY. 9 (1971), 174-269. "FINNEGANS
     WAKE Issue."
          Contains eight articles on FW, by Arthur T.
          Broes (N69), James W. Cerney ("Joyce's Mental
          Map"), W.V. Costanzo ("The French Version of
          FINNEGANS WAKE"), Grace Eckley (extract from
          N5), A.M. Leo Knuth ("The FINNEGANS WAKE Trans-
          lation Panel at Trieste"--synopsis published
          in G7), Ronald J. Koch ("Giordano Bruno and
          FINNEGANS WAKE"), Kevin M. McCarthy ("Turkish
          References in FINNEGANS WAKE"), and Timothy
          Ranson ("The P-p-p-p-power of the Words, Words,
          Words").

N28 JAMES JOYCE QUARTERLY. 11 (1974), 307-405. "FINNEGANS
     WAKE Issue."
          Collects a previously published parody of FW,
          by Sean Kelly (from NATIONAL LAMPOON), a sample
          page of an Italian translation of FW by Luigi
          Schenoni, and seven essays on FW, by William F.
          Dohmen (N92), David Hayman (N122), A.M. Leo
          Knuth (N148), Eric McLuhan (N162), Margot C.
          Norris (extract from N38), Manfred Pütz ("The
          Identity of the Reader in FINNEGANS WAKE"), and
          Ruth Von Phul (N214).

N29   JAMES JOYCE QUARTERLY.   14 (1977), 237-325.   "FINNEGANS
      WAKE Issue."
            Seven essays representative of recent scholar-
            ship on FW, prefaced by a brief introductory
            review of the state of FW studies, by the is-
            sue's guest editor, Bernard Benstock.   Includes
            articles by J.C. Baird and Coilin Owens ("Shem
            as Crucified Word"), Morris Beja (N29), Marion
            W. Cumpiano (N89), Barbara DiBernard (extract
            from N17), James D. Wallace (N217), Franklin
            Walton (N218), and Lorraine Weir ("The Choreog-
            raphy of Gesture: Marcel Jousse and FINNEGANS
            WAKE").

N30   Litz, A. Walton.   THE ART OF JAMES JOYCE: METHOD AND DE-
      SIGN IN *ULYSSES* AND *FINNEGANS WAKE*.   1961.   Rev. ed.   Lon-
      don: Oxford Univ. Press, 1964.
            See M38.

N31   McCarthy, Patrick A.   THE RIDDLES OF *FINNEGANS WAKE*.   Ruth-
      erford, N.J.: Fairleigh Dickinson Univ. Press, 1980.
            Finding JJ's model for FW the riddle itself,
            which forces the reader "to think, to question,
            to doubt, and to work out the thread of corre-
            spondences that form the basis of...human life,"
            McCarthy briefly describes and categorizes the
            riddle in traditional literature and folklore,
            surveys the riddles of U, and explicates the
            major riddles of FW: the three riddles in the
            "quiz" section, Shem's riddle, the Prankquean's
            riddle, and the "heliotrope" riddle.   Modest in
            scope, but insightful and entertaining.

N32   McHugh, Roland.   THE *FINNEGANS WAKE* EXPERIENCE.   Berkeley
      and Los Angeles: Univ. of California Press, 1981.
            An absorbing chronicle of McHugh's "learning
            to read" FW, pursued in conjunction with his
            studies of entomology, from 1964 to present.
            McHugh is not so presumptuous as to assert
            that his approach to the understanding of FW
            should be the model for all readers first un-
            dertaking the work, yet his account does sug-
            gest some basic strategies for its reading.
            After presenting an overview of FW's demands,
            by explicating four sample passages from FW's
            four chapters, McHugh recalls his initial read-
            ing of FW, his deliberate avoidance of "other

people's opinions" until he felt confident of
his basic grasp of the novel, his subsequent
study of the various commentaries and reference
works (the most worthwhile elements of which
he has condensed and included with his own readings in his ANNOTATIONS FOR *FINNEGANS WAKE;* see
N34), his participation in various symposia and
study groups (which he generally found disap-
pointing), and his researches into the manuscripts, notebooks, and Irish backgrounds of FW.
An intriguing and, at times, amusing story of one
man's obsession with an equally obsessive author's most challenging work.

N33 -----. THE SIGLA OF *FINNEGANS WAKE*. Austin: Univ. of
Texas Press, 1976.
Introduction to FW attempting to displace the
concentration of most such introductions on
the narrative of FW, such as it may be, by
tracing the occurrence and transmutations of
several key figures and concepts through the
text. The importance of these "certain characters or conceptual patterns" for JJ is evident in his use of sigla, or various geometri-
cal signs, to distinguish them in his manuscripts and letters (e.g., ⋔ = Earwicker; Δ =
Anna Livia). McHugh convincingly demonstrates
the intricate design of FW, the ascendency and
submersion of fourteen distinct concepts in
the novel, yet begs the questions of JJ's overall purpose and meaning.

N34 -----, ed. ANNOTATIONS FOR *FINNEGANS WAKE*. Baltimore:
Johns Hopkins Univ. Press, 1980.
Awesome compilation of glosses and notes, re-
produced on pages roughly twice the size of,
but corresponding to, the Viking text of FW
and placed on the page in the same general
area as the terms annotated are found in the
text. McHugh supplies "the cream of all available exegesis [of FW] in as condensed and accessible a form as possible," drawing extensively from previously published word lists,
allusion lists, censuses, and concordances,
and from the marginal annotations in texts of
several distinguished FW scholars. Immensely
useful, though the brevity demanded by the
typographical format is often disconcerting.

N35   Manning, Mary. PASSAGES FROM *FINNEGANS WAKE* BY JAMES
      JOYCE: A FREE ADAPTATION FOR THE THEATER. Cambridge,
      Mass.: Harvard Univ. Press, 1957.
           Dramatic rendering of FW, providing the novel's
           "general flavor without the aid of any keys."

N36   Mink, Louis O., ed. A *FINNEGANS WAKE* GAZETTEER. Bloom-
      ington: Indiana Univ. Press, 1978.
           Two-part concordance of JJ's nearly 8,000 al-
           lusions to real and imaginary geographical
           locations and to historical events in FW. The
           first part identifies, line-by-line, all such
           allusions. The second part is an alphabetical
           annotation for the allusions (with page and
           line locations). Includes several introduc-
           tory essays on JJ's topographical and histor-
           ical references. Useful.

N37   Motz, Reighard. TIME AS JOYCE TELLS IT. Mifflinburg,
      Pa.: Mulford Colebrook, [1977].
           Enthusiastic and confused praise for JJ's treat-
           ment of time in FW, and extensive annotations
           for time references throughout the novel.

N38   Norris, Margot C. THE DECENTERED UNIVERSE OF *FINNEGANS
      WAKE:* A STRUCTURALIST ANALYSIS. Baltimore: Johns Hopkins
      Univ. Press, 1977.
           Excellent application of structuralist theories
           of criticism, language, myth, and psychology
           to FW, a work, originating in the same "intel-
           lectual currents of early twentieth century
           Europe" that led to the structuralist movement.
           Norris discounts the conservative, novelistic
           approaches current in FW studies, in her open-
           ing chapter, and proceeds to examine FW's rela-
           tivist ("decentered") narrative, its interre-
           lated themes and characters, its dreamer's re-
           lationship to his necessarily unidentifiable
           self, its language, and its philosophical im-
           plications, with impressive reference to the
           theories of Derrida, Heidegger, Lacan, and
           Levi-Strauss, among others. Persuasive argu-
           ment for a nonrealistic reading of FW. Extract
           originally published in N28.

N39   O'Hehir, Brendan, comp. A GAELIC LEXICON FOR *FINNEGANS
      WAKE* AND GLOSSARY FOR JOYCE'S OTHER WORKS. Berkeley and

Los Angeles: Univ. of California Press, 1967.
Page and line references, phonetic pronunci-
ations, and translations for all Gaelic words
used or echoed by JJ in FW. Includes a similar glossary for JJ's other works (pp. 333-53)
and numerous supplementary notes. Extract
originally published in N26.

N40 O'Hehir, Brendan, and John M. Dillon, comps. A CLASSICAL
LEXICON FOR *FINNEGANS WAKE; A GLOSSARY OF THE GREEK AND
LATIN IN THE MAJOR WORKS OF JOYCE. Berkeley and Los Ang-
eles: Univ. of California Press, 1977.
Identifies and translates classical words in
FW (pp. 1-514) and in JJ's other works (pp.
516-90), with several supplementary appendixes
and brief notes.

N41 Solomon, Margaret C. ETERNAL GEOMATER: THE SEXUAL UNIVERSE
OF *FINNEGANS WAKE*. Carbondale: Southern Illinois Univ.
Press, 1969.
Analyses of FW's sexual themes, from the role
of ALP to the implications of various forms
of sexual activity, of its closely related ex-
cremental symbolism (e.g., "T," "P," tea, and
various numbers), and of its underlying sexual
structure. Important treatment of an undeni-
ably major facet of JJ's work. Extract originally published in G39.

N42 Tindall, William York. A READER'S GUIDE TO *FINNEGANS WAKE*.
New York: Farrar, Straus and Giroux, 1969.
Section-by-section explication of FW, the re-
sult of "almost thirty years" of committee discussion and private study. Commentaries are
paired with miscellaneous notes and observations ("dumps") within each section.

N43 TRI-QUARTERLY. No. 38 (1977), pp. 3-209. "In the Wake
of the WAKE."
See N24.

N44 Troy, Mark L. MUMMERIES OF RESURRECTION: THE CYCLE OF
OSIRIS IN *FINNEGANS WAKE*. Stockholm: Almqvist and Wik-
sell, 1976.
Examination of JJ's use of ancient Egyptian
materials in FW. Troy correlates several of
JJ's stylistic techniques to the Egyptian

scribe's manipulations of language, stresses
JJ's assimilation of Egyptian theology, notes
his appropriation of Egyptian symbols, emblems,
and deities, and traces his extensive variations upon the Osiris myths. Methodical and
uninspired.

N45   WAKE NEWSLITTER. Nos. 1-18 (1962-63); n.s. 1, No. 1
(1964--).
Newsletter devoted to brief studies and explications of FW. Also includes several listings
of JJ's uses of various minor languages in FW.
Published bi-monthly. Contains items far too
numerous for individual entry in this guide.
Several articles reprinted in N22. Also, see
the ten-year index issue (Vol. 8, 1971).

N, ii.   General Critical Articles or Chapters on FINNEGANS WAKE

N46   Atherton, James S. "FINNEGANS WAKE: 'The Gist of the
Pantomime.'" ACCENT, 15 (1955), 14-26.
FW's pantomime elements, in several senses of
the word.

N47   -----. "Shaun A/Book III, Chapter i." In A CONCEPTUAL
GUIDE TO *FINNEGANS WAKE*. Ed. Michael H. Begnal and Fritz
Senn. Pp. 149-72. See N4.
Explicates the fourteen questions put to Shaun
in the chapter.

N48   -----. "Sport and Games in FINNEGANS WAKE." In TWELVE
AND A TILLY. Ed. Jack P. Dalton and Clive Hart. Pp. 52-
64. See N16.
Glosses JJ's use of horse-racing and cricket
argot.

N49   -----. "To Give Down the Banks and Hark from the Tomb!"
JJQ, 4 (1967), 75-83.
JJ's incorporation of references to HUCKLEBERRY
FINN (1884), into FW.

N50   Aubert, Jacques. "Notes on the French Element in FINNEGANS
WAKE." JJQ, 5 (1968), 110-24.
Annotates JJ's use of the French language and
"allusions to French civilization" in FW.

N51   Barrett, William. "Myth or the Museum?" In TIME OF NEED:
      FORMS OF IMAGINATION IN THE TWENTIETH CENTURY. New York:
      Harper and Row, 1972. Pp. 312-50.
            See M69.

N52   Bates, Ronald. "The Feast Is a Flyday." JJQ, 2 (1965),
      174-87.
            Argues the "core date" for FW is Easter (3
            Apr.), 1904. See N26.

N53   Beckett, Samuel. "Dante... Bruno. Vico.. Joyce." In OUR
      EXAGMINATION. By Beckett, et al. Pp. 3-22. See N3.
            Bruno's and Vico's thought in FW and parallels
            between FW and the DIVINE COMEDY. Reprinted
            in F135.

N54   Begnal, Michael H. "FINNEGANS WAKE and the Nature of Nar-
      rative." MODERN BRITISH LITERATURE, 5 (1980), 43-52.
            FW's many-layered plot. See G63.

N55   -----. "James Joyce and the Mythologizing of History." In
      DIRECTIONS IN LITERARY CRITICISM: CONTEMPORARY APPROACHES
      TO LITERATURE. Ed. Stanley Weintraub and Philip Young.
      University Park: Pennsylvania State Univ. Press, 1973. Pp.
      211-19.
            JJ's belief that the significance of the past
            can be grasped only on the level of myth: Myth
            orders, history atomizes.

N56   -----. "Love that Dares to Speak its Name/Book II, Chap-
      ter iv." In A CONCEPTUAL GUIDE TO *FINNEGANS WAKE*. Ed.
      Begnal and Fritz Senn. Pp. 139-48. See N4.
            Commentary on the Tristan and Isolde legend
            and the transformations of Mamalujo (e.g.,
            Matthew-Mark-Luke-John) in the chapter.

N57   Beja, Morris. "Dividual Chaoses: Case Histories of Mul-
      tiple Personality and FINNEGANS WAKE." JJQ, 14 (1977),
      241-50.
            Documents JJ's interest in and use of several
            case histories of "dissociation of personality"
            in FW. See N29. Also see N110.

N58   Benstock, Bernard. "Concerning Lost Historeve/Book I,
      Chapter v." In A CONCEPTUAL GUIDE TO *FINNEGANS WAKE*. Ed.
      Michael H. Begnal and Fritz Senn. Pp. 33-55. See N4.
            Explication of "the most cohesive and least

digressive chapter" of FW, with special emphasis on the "all-important letter" featured in
the chapter.

N59 -----. "Every Telling Has a Taling: A Reading of the Nar-
rative of FINNEGANS WAKE." MFS, 15 (1969), 3-25.
Attempt to trace the "fine vein" of FW's story.
See G65.

N60 -----. "A FINNEGANS WAKE Address Book." JJQ, 2 (1965),
195-203.
Lists the addresses of FW's "characters." See
N26.

N61 -----. "The Gastronome's FINNEGANS WAKE." JJQ, 2 (1965),
188-94.
Lists JJ's food references. See N26.

N62 -----. "L. Boom as Dreamer in FINNEGANS WAKE." PMLA, 82
(1967), 91-97.
See M76.

N63 Bierman, Robert. "'White and Pink Elephants': FINNEGANS
WAKE and the Tradition of 'Unintelligibility.'" MFS, 4
(1958), 62-70.
Argues the traditional heritage and ultimate
intelligibility of FW. See G64.

N64 Bishop, John Peale. "FINNEGANS WAKE." 1940. In THE COL-
LECTED ESSAYS OF JOHN PEALE BISHOP. Ed. Edmund Wilson.
New York: Scribner's, 1948. Pp. 146-65.
Appreciative review of the themes, technique,
and structure of FW, JJ's final "break with
the Flaubertian tradition." Extract reprinted
in G25.

N65 Bogan, Louise. "FINNEGANS WAKE." 1939. 1944. In SELECTED
CRITICISM: PROSE, POETRY. New York: Noonday, 1955. Pp.
142-53.
Admiring review of JJ's "enormous and baffling
book" (extract reprinted in G25), and comment
on its reflection of JJ's complex personality.

N66 Boyle, Robert, S.J. "FINNEGANS WAKE, Page 185: An Explication." JJQ, 4 (1966), 3-16.
Finds, in the passage examined, JJ's defense
for his ambition "to turn vulgarity and sca-
tology to his artistic purpose."

N67 -----. "Portrait of the Artist as Balzacian Wilde Ass/Book
I, Chapters vii-viii." In A CONCEPTUAL GUIDE TO *FINNEGANS
WAKE*. Ed. Michael H. Begnal and Fritz Senn. Pp. 71-82.
See N4.
> JJ's continuing preoccupation with portraits
> of the artist.

N68 Brion, Marcel. "The Idea of Time in the Work of James
Joyce." Trans. Robert Sage. In OUR EXAGMINATION. By
Samuel Beckett, et al. Pp. 25-33. See N3.
> Time, seen as "the dissociation of moments,"
> the "primary element at the base" of JJ's work
> (chiefly FW).

N69 Broes, Arthur T. "More Books at the WAKE." JJQ, 9 (1971),
189-217.
> Extensive supplement to Atherton (N2). See N27.

N70 -----. "Shakespeare in FINNEGANS WAKE." HAB, 25 (1974),
304-17.
> Play-by-play list of Shakespeare allusions.

N71 -----. "Swift the Man in FINNEGANS WAKE." ELH, 43 (1976),
120-40.
> Swift, a "central, if not the chief historical
> figure" in FW, as his life provides both a
> "primary source for the characteristics" of
> Earwicker and an illustration of FW's basic
> "esthetic and philosophical tenets."

N72 -----. "Swift's Works in FINNEGANS WAKE." ENGLISH STUDIES
IN CANADA, 5 (1979), 167-86.
> Extended discussion of JJ's allusions to and
> quotations from Swift's works in FW.

N73 Buckalew, Ronald E. "Night Lessons on Language/Book II,
Chapter ii." In A CONCEPTUAL GUIDE TO *FINNEGANS WAKE*. Ed.
Michael H. Begnal and Fritz Senn. Pp. 93-115. See N4.
> Linguist's study of JJ's language backgrounds,
> training, and explorations in the "night les-
> sons" chapter.

N74 Budgen, Frank. "James Joyce's 'Work in Progress' and Old
Norse Poetry." In OUR EXAGMINATION. By Samuel Beckett,
et al. Pp. 37-46. See N3.
> Early discussion of Scandinavian elements in
> JJ's work, chiefly FW. Possibly written with
> JJ's supervision.

N75   -----. "Joyce's Chapters of Going Forth by Day." HORIZON,
       4 (1941), 172-91.
              FW as a "resurrection myth." Reprinted in F13,
              G25 (extract), and G30.

N76   -----. "Resurrection." In TWELVE AND A TILLY. Ed. Jack
       P. Dalton and Clive Hart. Pp. 11-15. See N16.
              Resurrection myth as the main strand through
              the labyrinth of FW.

N77   Burgess, Anthony. "What It's All About." In A SHORTER
       FINNEGANS WAKE. Ed. Burgess. Pp. xi-xxviii. See B20.
              General summary of and commentary on FW. See
              H63.

N78   Burgum, Edwin B. "The Paradox of Skepticism in FINNEGANS
       WAKE." In THE NOVEL AND THE WORLD'S DILEMMA. New York:
       Oxford Univ. Press, 1947. Pp. 109-19.
              The cynicism which forms the philosophic core
              of the novel and JJ's self-destructive aesthe-
              tic must finally "disgust us."

N79   Busi, Frederick. "Joycean Echoes in WAITING FOR GODOT."
       RS, 43 (1975), 71-87.
              Immediate and general influences of FW on Beck-
              ett's play (1952).

N79a   Butler, Christopher. AFTER THE *WAKE*: AN ESSAY ON THE CON-
       TEMPORARY AVANT-GARDE. New York: Oxford Univ. Press, 1981.
       Passim.
              Occasional references to FW as an influence
              on or example of post-modernist techniques in
              art, literature, and music.

N80   Campbell, Joseph. "Finnegan the Wake." CHIMERA, 4, No.
       3 (1946), 39-63.
              FW from the perspective of Egyptian mythology.
              Reprinted in G30.

N81   Campos, Haroldo de. "Sanscreed Latinized: The WAKE in
       Brazil and Hispanic America." In IN THE WAKE OF THE *WAKE*.
       Ed. David Hayman and Elliott Anderson. Pp. 54-62. See
       N24.
              Impression of FW in Brazil, particularly on
              the "Concrete Poetry" movement.

N82 Carlson, Marvin. "Henrik Ibsen and FINNEGANS WAKE." CL,
     12 (1960), 133-41.
           Elements of Ibsen in FW. (For a fuller dis-
           cussion, see Tysdahl [G82]).

N83 Chase, Richard V. "FINNEGANS WAKE: An Anthropological
     Study." AMERICAN SCHOLAR, 13 (1944), 418-26.
           Responds to several typical objections to FW,
           defending it as a brilliant and fundamentally
           "orthodox" book.

N84 Christiani, Dounia Bunis. "The Polyglot Poetry of FIN-
     NEGANS WAKE." In JAMES JOYCE: HIS PLACE IN WORLD LITER-
     ATURE. Ed. Wolodymyr T. Zyla. Pp. 23-38. See G85.
           Survey of FW's chief characteristics, with an-
           swers for the hypothetical reader's questions.

N85 Coleman, Elliott. "Heliotropical Noughttime: Light and
     Color in FINNEGANS WAKE." TQ, 4, No. 4 (1961), 162-77.
           JJ's purposeful use of the color spectrum and
           light and darkness in FW.

N86 Colum, Padraic. "Preface." In JJ's ANNA LIVIA PLURABELLE.
     New York: Crosby Gaige, 1928. Pp. vii-xix.
           General comments on the flow and language of
           the Anna Livia section. Assimilated into F19.
           Extract reprinted in G25.

N87 Connolly, Cyril. "The Position of Joyce." 1929. In THE
     CONDEMNED PLAYGROUND: ESSAYS: 1927-1944. New York: Mac-
     millan, 1946. Pp. 1-15.
           JJ's "new work respect-worthy and readable.
           There is nothing insane in its conception nor
           bogus in its execution." Extract reprinted
           in G25.

N88 Connolly, Thomas E. "Introduction." In SCRIBBLEDEHOBBLE.
     Ed. Connolly. Pp. vii-xxii. See B19.
           Describes the contents, composition, and or-
           ganization of JJ's "Ur-Workbook" for FW.

N89 Cumpiano, Marion W. "The Salmon and Its Leaps in FINNEGANS
     WAKE." JJQ, 14 (1977), 255-73.
           JJ's multivalent use of salmon imagery and al-
           lusions. See N29.

N90   Dalton, Jack P. "Advertisement for the Restoration." In
      TWELVE AND A TILLY. Ed. Dalton and Clive Hart. Pp. 119-
      37. See N16.
            Plea for a careful textual edition of FW.

N91   Dobrée, Bonamy. MODERN PROSE STYLE. 1935. 2nd ed. Ox-
      ford: Clarendon Press, 1964. Pp. 245-51.
            JJ's "poetic," yet destructive style.

N92   Dohmen, William F. "'Chilly Spaces': Wyndham Lewis as
      Ondt." JJQ, 11 (1974), 368-86.
            JJ's "light-hearted interpretation" of the
            Lewis-Joyce controversy in FW. See N28.

N93   Dolmatch, Theodore B. "Notes and Queries Concerning the
      Revisions of FINNEGANS WAKE." MLQ, 16 (1955), 142-48.
            Comments on six different texts of the "Anna
            Livia Plurabelle" section.

N94   Eagleton, Terry. EXILES AND EMIGRÉS: STUDIES IN MODERN
      LITERATURE. New York: Schocken, 1970. Pp. 171-74.
            JJ's use of myth in light of structuralist
            anthropology (cf. Eliot and Levi-Strauss).

N95   Eckley, Grace. "Looking Forward to a Brightening Day/Book
      IV, Chapter i." In A CONCEPTUAL GUIDE TO *FINNEGANS WAKE*.
      Ed. Michael H. Begnal and Fritz Senn. Pp. 211-36. See N4.
            Summarizes the four dramatic episodes: baptism,
            debate, letter, and monologue, of the final
            chapter, or "ricorso" of FW.

N96   -----. "Shem Is a Sham But Shaun Is a Ham, or Samuraising
      the Twins in FINNEGANS WAKE." MFS, 20 (1974), 469-81.
            Argues against the common contention that Shem
            and Shaun are projections of one identity, merg-
            ing at various points in FW.

N97   Edel, Leon. "James Joyce and His New Work." UTQ, 9 (1939),
      68-81.
            Review essay, stressing JJ's appeal to the ear:
            FW is "as near to music as prose can come." Ex-
            tract reprinted in G25.

N98   Epstein, Edmund L. "Interpreting FINNEGANS WAKE: A Half-
      Way House." JJQ, 3 (1966), 252-71.
            Hails the appearance of Benstock's study of FW
            (see N6) as the beginning of a new era in JJ
            criticism, when FW shall be approached as any
            other novel.

N99   -----. "The Turning Point/Book I, Chapter vi." In A
       CONCEPTUAL GUIDE TO *FINNEGANS WAKE*. Ed. Michael H. Beg-
       nal and Fritz Senn. Pp. 56-70. See N4.
            Explication of the "Questions" chapter and
            consideration of the chapter's place in the
            novel as a whole.

N100   Finney, Michael. "Eugene Jolas, TRANSITION, and the Rev-
       olution of the Word." In IN THE WAKE OF THE *WAKE*. Ed.
       David Hayman and Elliott Anderson. Pp. 39-53. See N24.
            Distinguishes between Jolas's program for
            "reconstructing language" and JJ's practice
            in FW. See N141 and N143.

N101   Fleming, William S. "Formulaic Rhythms in FINNEGANS WAKE."
       STYLE, 6 (1972), 19-37.
            JJ's repeated use of formula rhythms for
            structure and meaning.

N102   Frye, Northrop. "Quest and Cycle in FINNEGANS WAKE." In
       FABLES OF IDENTITY. New York: Harcourt, 1963. Pp. 256-
       64.
            JJ's relationship to the epic tradition, via
            the "mythological poets of the Romantic period"
            (cf. Blake's myth of Albion).

N103   Gandleman, Claude. "FINNEGANS WAKE and the Anthropomor-
       phic Landscape." JML, 7 (1979), 39-50.
            Specific relationships between JJ's style in
            FW and sixteenth-century Mannerist art (e.g.,
            anthropomorphic and anamorphic landscape).

N104   -----. "Joyce, Pre-Raphaelism, Art Nouveau: Pictorial
       Influences on FINNEGANS WAKE." OL, 30 (1975), 277-85.
            Influence of the "artistic currents" of JJ's
            youth on theme and style in FW.

N105   Garzilli, Enrico. "Myth, Dream, and Self: FINNEGANS WAKE--
       James Joyce." In CIRCLES WITHOUT CENTER: PATHS TO THE
       DISCOVERY AND CREATION OF SELF IN MODERN LITERATURE. Cam-
       bridge, Mass.: Harvard Univ. Press, 1972. Pp. 65-74.
            Dreaming in FW related to modern man's "hid-
            den search for self."

N106   Giedion-Welcker, Carola. "'Work in Progress': A Linguis-
       tic Experiment by James Joyce." Trans. Eugene Jolas.
       TRANSITION, Nos. 19-20 (1930), pp. 174-83.
            Perceptive early commentary on the relation

of JJ's "word alchemy" to experiments of modernist painters. Reprinted in F47 and G25
(extract). Also see Y17.

N107   Gilbert, Stuart. "Prolegomena to 'Work in Progress.'"
In OUR EXAGMINATION. By Samuel Beckett, et al. Pp. 49-
75. See N3.
Attempts to describe what FW is "all about"
and why JJ makes "it so difficult," with sample explication of a passage.

N108   -----. "Sketch of a Scenario of 'Anna Livia Plurabelle.'"
In A JAMES JOYCE YEARBOOK. Ed. Maria Jolas. Pp. 10-19.
See G45.
Sketch for dramatic (or cinematic) staging of
the opening passages of the Anna Livia episode,
prepared in 1935 with JJ's assistance.

N109   Gillet, Louis. "Joyce's Testament: FINNEGANS WAKE." Trans.
D.D. Paige. QR, 1 (1944), 87-99.
Extravagant appreciation of FW, as contrast
and complement to U, a "multivalent" book
"touching all the problems of life...all the
human and divine questions."

N110   Glasheen, Adaline. "FINNEGANS WAKE and the Girls from
Boston, Mass." HudR, 7 (1954), 89-96.
JJ's use of the theory of multiple personal-
ity in developing his technique of multiple
characterization (re: Morton Prince, THE DIS-
SOCIATION OF A PERSONALITY [1905]). Also see
N57.

N111   Gleckner, Robert F. "Byron in FINNEGANS WAKE." In TWELVE
AND A TILLY. Ed. Jack P. Dalton and Clive Hart. Pp. 40-
51. See N16.
Several significant patterns of allusion to
Byron in FW.

N112   -----. "Joyce and Blake: Notes Toward Defining a Literary
Relationship." In A JAMES JOYCE MISCELLANY, THIRD SERIES.
Ed. Marvin Magalaner. Pp. 188-225. See G57.
JJ "absorbed, modified, reshaped and fused
[Blake] into the fabric of his own vision,"
particularly in FW.

N113 Halper, Nathan. "The Date of Earwicker's Dream." In
      TWELVE AND A TILLY. Ed. Jack P. Dalton and Clive Hart.
      Pp. 72-90. See N16.
           Several speculations on the timing of FW
           (placing the dream on 18-19 Mar. 1922).

N114 -----. "James Joyce and Rebecca West." PR, 16 (1949),
      761-63.
           Speculates on JJ's allusions to West in FW.

N115 -----. "James Joyce and the Russian General." PR, 18
      (1951), 424-31.
           Explicates the mentions of Buckley shooting
           a Russian general.

N116 Harrington, John P. "Swift through Le Fanu and Joyce."
      MOSAIC, 12, No. 3 (1979), 49-58.
           Correspondences among Swift's POLITE CONVER-
           SATION (1738), Le Fanu's THE HOUSE BY THE
           CHURCHYARD (1863), and FW.

N117 Hart, Clive. "The Elephant in the Belly: Exegesis of
      FINNEGANS WAKE." In A *WAKE* DIGEST. Ed. Hart and Fritz
      Senn. Pp. 3-12. See N22.
           Proposes a "limited number of working hypo-
           theses and axioms" for FW explication, in re-
           action to the "twin extremes" of too eccentric
           exegesis and too great insistence on "the pri-
           macy of Joyce's initial and particular inten-
           tions."

N118 -----. "FINNEGANS WAKE in Perspective." In JAMES JOYCE
      TODAY. Ed. Thomas F. Staley. Pp. 135-65. See G75.
           Excellent survey of FW's critical history and
           practical suggestions for reading the novel.

N119 -----. "Notes on the Text of FINNEGANS WAKE." JEGP, 59
      (1960), 229-39.
           Clarifies, amplifies, and supplements Higgin-
           son's notes on the omitted passages in FW
           (e.g., six omissions intended by JJ, eight
           more discovered by Hart). See N131.

N120 Hassan, Ihab. "Joyce-Beckett: A Scenario in Eight Scenes
      and a Voice"; "(   ): FINNEGANS WAKE and the Post-modern
      Imagination." In PARACRITICISMS: SEVEN SPECULATIONS OF
      THE TIMES. Urbana: Univ. of Illinois Press, 1975. Pp.
      63-73; 77-94.
           Comparison of JJ and Beckett and deliberately

untitled dialogue with himself on several aspects of FW. First essay originally published
in G73.

N121 Hayman, David. "Dramatic Motion in FINNEGANS WAKE." TEXAS
STUDIES IN ENGLISH, 37 (1958), 155-76.
Analysis of "Butt and Taff" episode shows JJ's
achievement of dramatic movement, despite the
apparent timeless, spaceless, stasis of FW.

N122 -----. "Farcical Themes and Forms in FINNEGANS WAKE."
JJQ, 11 (1974), 323-42.
Sequel to Hayman's discussion of comedy and
its forms in U (see M165). Also see N28.

N123 -----. "From FINNEGANS WAKE: A Sentence in Progress."
PMLA, 73 (1958), 136-54.
Studies through the complete manuscripts the
purpose and process of JJ's fourteen-year,
thirteen-stage evolution of a single sentence
of FW. A model for close textual analysis of
the novel.

N124 -----. "Introduction." In A FIRST-DRAFT VERSION OF *FIN-
NEGANS WAKE*. Ed. Hayman. Pp. 3-43. See B7.
Excellent history of FW's composition and re-
vision, and discussion of JJ's intentions.

N125 -----. "Nodality and the Infra-Structure of FINNEGANS
WAKE." 1976. JJQ, 16 (1979), 135-49.
Affirms value of seeing FW's structure as
nodal, rather than linear, circular, or non-
existent. Reprinted, in translation, from Y8.
Also see G44.

N126 -----. "Notes for the Staging of FINNEGANS WAKE." In A
JAMES JOYCE MISCELLANY, THIRD SERIES. Ed. Marvin Magalaner. Pp. 278-93. See G57.
Suggests that dramatic adaptors concentrate on
one section of the book (e.g., the pub scene
in section II).

N127 -----. "Pound at the Wake or the Uses of a Contemporary.'
JJQ, 2 (1965), 204-16.
JJ's use of Pound, his name, his conversation,
his writings, and his "pet literary concerns"
in FW. See N26.

N128   -----. "'Scribbledehobbles' and How They Grew: A Turning
        Point in the Development of a Chapter." In TWELVE AND A
        TILLY. Ed. Jack P. Dalton and Clive Hart. Pp. 107-18.
        See N16.
                Discusses one of the few passages discarded
                from FW.

N129   -----. "Some Writers in the Wake of the WAKE." In IN THE
        WAKE OF THE *WAKE*. Ed. Hayman and Elliott Anderson. Pp.
        3-38. See N24.
                Extended survey of writers, chiefly outside
                English and American literature, working in
                the experimental tradition of FW.

N130   -----. "Tristan and Isolde in FINNEGANS WAKE: A Study of
        the Sources and Evolution of a Theme." CLS, 1 (1964), 93-
        112.
                Influence of the Tristan and Isolde legend on
                JJ and his integration of the theme into FW.

N131   Higginson, Fred H. "Notes on the Text of FINNEGANS WAKE."
        JEGP, 55 (1956), 451-56.
                Lists twenty-nine passages omitted from FW's
                final text by typesetter's error. See N119.

N132   -----. "The Text of FINNEGANS WAKE." In NEW LIGHT ON
        JOYCE. Ed. Fritz Senn. Pp. 120-30. See G73.
                Argues the need for a "developmental variorum"
                text of FW.

N133   Hodgart, Matthew J.C. "Music and the Mime of Mick, Nick,
        and the Maggies/Book II, Chapter i." In A CONCEPTUAL GUIDE
        TO *FINNEGANS WAKE*. Ed. Michael H. Begnal and Fritz Senn.
        Pp. 83-92. See N4.
                Glosses JJ's allusions to demonology, chil-
                dren's games, and opera (the "microstructure"
                of the chapter).

N134   -----. "Shakespeare and FINNEGANS WAKE." CAMBRIDGE JOUR-
        NAL, 6 (1953), 735-52.
                Identifies numerous allusions to Shakespeare
                and his plays in FW, suggesting their rela-
                tion to the "themes and character-types of
                the novel."

N135   -----. "'Work in Progress.'" CAMBRIDGE JOURNAL, 6 (1952),
        23-39.
                Defends FW from charges of perverse obscur-

antism, demonstrating the accessibility of
several of its major thematic patterns and
the "firm base in psychological realism" of
its mythological structure.

N136   Hoffman, Frederick J.   "'The Seim Anew': Flux and Family
in FINNEGANS WAKE."   In TWELVE AND A TILLY.   Ed. Jack P.
Dalton and Clive Hart.   Pp. 16-25.   See N16.
FW's tensions between order and chaos, family
and flux, and its unique suggested solutions
for the "problems of father-family and creator-
creature relationship."

N137   Howarth, Herbert.   "THE WASTE LAND and Joyce."   In NOTES
ON SOME FIGURES BEHIND T.S. ELIOT.   Boston: Houghton Mif-
flin, 1964.   Pp. 242-46.
See M176.

N138   Jarrell, Mackie L.   "Swiftiana in FINNEGANS WAKE."   ELH,
26 (1959), 271-94.
JJ's allusions to Swift "more extensive and
more central to the novel than one might sup-
pose."

N139   Johnston, Denis.   "Clarify Begins At: The Non-Information
of FINNEGANS WAKE."   MR, 5 (1964), 357-64.
JJ's teasing refusal to provide the consis-
tent factual data found in his earlier works.

N140   Jolas, Eugene.   "Homage to the Myth Maker."   TRANSITION,
No. 27 (1938), pp. 169-75.
Valedictory comment on "Work in Progress,"
eighteen parts of which had appeared in Jolas'
TRANSITION, and remarks on its forthcoming
book publication.   Reprinted in F100 and G25
(extract).

N141   -----.   "The Revolution of Language and James Joyce."   In
OUR EXAGMINATION.   By Samuel Beckett, et al.   Pp. 79-92.
See N3.
Hails JJ as the exemplar of the modern writer's
disintegration of the word and "subsequent reconstruction on other planes."   Also see N100
and N143.

N142   Jolas, Eugene, Elliot Paul, and Robert Sage.   "First Aid
to the Enemy."   TRANSITION, No. 9 (1927), pp. 161-76.
Emphatic counterattack on the "simian" xeno-

phobe Wyndham Lewis's diatribes against the
literary avant garde (especially JJ and Stein).
Extract reprinted in G25.

N143 Jolas, Eugene, et al. "The Revolution of the Word (A Symposium)." MODERN QUARTERLY, 5 (1929), 273-92.
Six writers, including Stuart Gilbert, Herbert
Gorman, and Robert Sage, as well as Jolas,
call for the revolutionary "reconstruction"
and revivification of the word in literature
and hail JJ's "Work in Progress" as a vindica-
tion of their manifesto. Also see N100, N141,
N152, and N193.

N144 Kain, Richard M. "'Nothing Odd Will Do Long': Some Thoughts
on FINNEGANS WAKE Twenty-Five Years Later." In TWELVE AND
A TILLY. Ed. Jack P. Dalton and Clive Hart. Pp. 91-98.
See N16.
FW, though "ineradicably flawed," will contin-
ue to fascinate as the "Everest of literature,
a constant challenge to the courageous and the
foolhardy."

N145 Kelleher, John V. "Identifying the Irish Printed Sources
for FINNEGANS WAKE." IRISH UNIVERSITY REVIEW, 1 (1971),
161-77.
Comments on a generous number of Irish histories and reference works exploited by JJ in FW.

N146 Kenner, Hugh. "Approaches to the Artist as a Young Language Teacher." In ¡VIVA VIVAS! ESSAYS IN HONOR OF ELISEO
VIVAS. Ed. Henry Regnery. Indianapolis, Ind.: Liberty,
1976. Pp. 333-53.
JJ's independent discovery of DeSaussure's
principle of language as non-referential,
traced to his Berlitz teaching career, culminates in the abstract language of FW. Par-
tially assimilated into G48.

N147 Kiralis, Karl. "Joyce and Blake: A Basic Source for FIN-
NEGANS WAKE." MFS, 4 (1958-59), 329-34.
Blake's JERUSALEM (1820) suggested as a prim-
ary source.

N148 Knuth, A.M. Leo. "FINNEGANS WAKE: A Product of the Twen-
ties." JJQ, 11 (1974), 310-22.
Contemporary references in and influences on
FW. See N28.

N149 Kopper, Edward A. "'but where he is eaten': Earwicker's
      Tavern Feast/Book II, Chapter iii." In A CONCEPTUAL GUIDE
      TO *FINNEGANS WAKE*. Ed. Michael H. Begnal and Fritz Senn.
      Pp. 116-38. See N4.
            Commentary on the tavern feast chapter, con-
            centrating on JJ's references both to nine-
            teenth-century Irish politics and to the Bat-
            tle of Balaclava.

N150 Korg, Jacob. "The Language of FINNEGANS WAKE." In LANG-
      UAGE IN MODERN LITERATURE: INNOVATION AND EXPERIMENT. New
      York: Barnes and Noble, 1979. Pp. 201-25.
            In its multiplicity and ambiguity FW "dis-
            closes a universe of language" which is "in-
            finite." Expanded discussion of JJ's verbal
            experimentation (see H120).

N151 Langdon, M. "Some Reflections of Physics in FINNEGANS
      WAKE." JJQ, 17 (1980), 359-77.
            Relates "certain structural patterns" of FW
            to "some basic conceptions of particle and
            relativistic physics."

N152 Leavis, Frank R. "Joyce and 'The Revolution of the Word.'"
      SCRUTINY, 2 (1933), 193-201.
            The "spuriousness" and the pervasive "mechan-
            ical manipulation" of FW. Considers JJ's ex-
            periments with language destructive and nihil-
            istic. See N143.

N153 Leeming, H. "'Lepoglas' izhe 'susheiavat': James Joyce's
      Slavonic Optophones." SEER, 55 (1977), 289-309.
            Explains and categorizes JJ's slavonic allu-
            sions.

N154 Levine, Jennifer Schiffer. "Originality and Repetition
      in FINNEGANS WAKE and ULYSSES." PMLA, 94 (1979), 106-20.
      See M208.

N155 Litz, A. Walton. "Uses of the FINNEGANS WAKE Manuscripts.
      In TWELVE AND A TILLY. Ed. Jack P. Dalton and Clive Hart
      Pp. 99-106. See N16.
            Manuscripts valuable for establishing a crit-
            ical text or illustrating the continuity of
            JJ's technical development, between U and FW's
            publication, but "not indispensable" for in-
            terpretation of FW ("an independent creation").

N156 Llona, Victor. "I Dont [sic] Know What to Call it but
      its [sic] Mighty Unlike Prose." In OUR EXAGMINATION. By
      Samuel Beckett, et al. Pp. 95-102. See N3.
          Miscellaneous notes on the language and style
          of JJ's philological "divertissement."

N157 McAlmon, Robert. "Mr. Joyce Directs an Irish Word Ballet."
      In OUR EXAGMINATION. By Samuel Beckett, et al. Pp. 105-
      16. See N3.
          Finds in JJ's prose the evocative power of
          music and the "gesticulative quality" of the
          dance.

N158 McCarthy, Patrick A. "'Our Wee Free State': FINNEGANS
      WAKE and Irish Independence." MODERN BRITISH LITERATURE,
      2 (1977), 75-80.
          JJ's ambivalence toward the recently estab-
          lished Irish Free State and basic view of the
          state and art as irreconcilable.

N159 McGreevy, Thomas. "The Catholic Element in 'Work in Prog-
      ress.'" In OUR EXAGMINATION. By Samuel Beckett, et al.
      Pp. 119-27. See N3.
          JJ's fundamental Catholicism (not to be con-
          fused with piety) in his "purgatorial" FW.
          Reprinted in F135.

N160 McHugh, Roland. "A European FINNEGANS WAKE Study Group."
      In ATTI DEL THIRD INTERNATIONAL JAMES JOYCE SYMPOSIUM. Pp.
      311-19. See G7.
          Calls for and reports the results of communal
          reading of FW. See N32.

N161 -----. "Recipis for the Price of the Coffin/Book I, Chap-
      ters ii-iv." In A CONCEPTUAL GUIDE TO *FINNEGANS WAKE*. Ed.
      Michael H. Begnal and Fritz Senn. Pp. 18-32. See N4.
          Helpful explication and paraphrase of the pro-
          gression of scenes in the early chapters of FW.

N162 McLuhan, Eric. "The Rhetorical Structure of FINNEGANS
      WAKE." JJQ, 11 (1974), 394-404.
          The thunderwords as a structural principle in
          FW. See N28.

N163 McMichael, Charles T., and Ted R. Spivey. "Chaos--hur-
      ray!--is come again': Heroism in James Joyce and Conrad
      Aiken." SLitI, 3, No. 2 (1970), 65-68.
          Notes on superficial similarities between FW

and Aiken's THE COMING FORTH BY DAY OF OSIRIS
JONES (1931). See G78.

N164 Magalaner, ·Marvin. "The Myth of Man: Joyce's FINNEGANS
WAKE." UKCR, 16 (1950), 265-77.
    JJ's fusion of "numerous conceptions of myth
    into a greater whole, his own myth of man" in
    FW.

N165 Mercier, Vivian. "In the Wake of the Fianna: Some Addi-
tions and Corrections to Glasheen and a Footnote or Two
to Atherton." In A JAMES JOYCE MISCELLANY, THIRD SERIES.
Ed. Marvin Magalaner. Pp. 226-38. See G57.
    Supplements Atherton (N2) and Glasheen (N20).

N166 -----. "James Joyce and the Macaronic Tradition." In
TWELVE AND A TILLY. Ed. Jack P. Dalton and Clive Hart.
Pp. 26-35. See N16.
    Relates JJ's polyglot vocabulary to traditional,
    often academic games with language.

N167 Mink, Louis O. "Reading FINNEGANS WAKE." SHR, 9 (1975),
1-16.
    Several analogies between reading FW and "the
    scientific inquiry into nature."

N168 Moholy-Nagy, Laszlo. VISION IN MOTION. Chicago: Theobald,
1947. Pp. 341-51.
    See M235.

N169 Montgomery, Niall. "Joyeux Quicum Ulysee...Swissairis
Dubellay Gadelice." ENVOY, 5 (May 1951), 31-43.
    Stresses the wit and sheer fun in JJ's word-
    play. See F36. Reprinted in F111 and F135.

N170 -----. "The PERVIGILIUM PHOENICIS." NEW MEXICO QUARTER-
LY, 23 (1953), 437-72.
    Mirrors, echoes, word-play, anagrams, and
    Irish Catholicism in FW.

N171 Morse, J. Mitchell. "Burrus, Caseous, and Nicholas of
Cusa." MLN, 75 (1960), 326-34.
    JJ's use of Nicholas of Cusa's ideas, in U
    and FW (chiefly).

N172 -----. "1132." JJQ, 3 (1966), 272-75.
    Historical significance of the year 1132 con-
    tributes to the number's symbolism in FW.

N173 -----. "HCE's Chaste Ecstasy." YR, 56 (1967), 397-405.
      HCE's unnamed offense in Phoenix Park could as
      easily have been religious (e.g., prayer) as
      sexual.

N174 -----. "Karl Gutzkow and the Modern Novel." JGE, 15
      (1963), 175-89.
            See M238.

N175 -----. "On Teaching FINNEGANS WAKE." In TWELVE AND A
      TILLY. Ed. Jack P. Dalton and Clive Hart. Pp. 65-71.
      See N16.
            Teaching the "Prankquean" episode of FW to the
            "uninitiated."

N176 -----. "Where Terms Begin/Book I, Chapter i." In A CON-
      CEPTUAL GUIDE TO *FINNEGANS WAKE*. Ed. Michael H. Begnal
      and Fritz Senn. Pp. 1-17. See N4.
            General discussion of Vico's influence on FW
            as theoretical historian and model personality.

N177 Noon, William T., S.J. "'Roll Away the Reel World': New
      Delvings into the Dream-Stuff of Quarter-Century-Old FIN-
      NEGANS WAKE." AMERICA, 111 (1964), 517-20.
            Shakespeare as the "dreamer" in FW.

N178 O'Faolain, Sean. "Style and the Limitation of Speech."
      CRITERION, 8 (1928), 67-87.
            Affirms the richness of JJ's "ahistoric," but
            not revolutionary language. Extract reprinted
            in G25.

N179 Paul, Elliot. "Mr. Joyce's Treatment of Plot." In OUR
      EXAGMINATION. By Samuel Beckett, et al. Pp. 131-37.
      See N3.
            FW's elastic language and setting, and its
            archetypal plot motifs ordered within a de-
            sign "dictated by the mind" of JJ.

N180 Peery, William. "Shakhisbeard at FINNEGANS WAKE." TEXAS
      STUDIES IN ENGLISH, 30 (1951), 243-57.
            JJ's references to Shakespeare's name and al-
            lusions to the titles and texts of his plays.

N181 Peter, John. "Joyce and the Novel." KR, 18 (1956), 619-
      32.
            Reasonable attack on FW as a retreat "not only
            from the immediacy of human experience but ul-
            timately from human experience itself."

N182 Polhemus, Robert M. "Joyce's FINNEGANS WAKE (1924-39):
      The Comic Gospel of 'Shem.'" In COMIC FAITH: THE GREAT
      TRADITION FROM AUSTEN TO JOYCE. Chicago: Univ. of Chi-
      cago Press, 1980. Pp. 294-337.
            JJ's profanation of the sacred and sanctifica-
            tion of the profane in his comic Bible, firmly
            within the tradition of nineteenth-century
            British comic fiction. (Analysis of the "Shem"
            section, FW, pp. 169-95.)

N183 Powys, John Cowper. "FINNEGAN'S [sic] WAKE." In OBSTI-
      NATE CYMRIC: ESSAYS 1935-1947. Carmarthen, Wales: Druid
      Press, 1947. Pp. 19-36.
            Appreciation. Prefers FW's mythic power and
            "large, ample, mellow, mischievous acceptance
            of all human obliquity" as morally superior
            to the ill-tempered U.

N184 Prescott, Joseph. "Concerning the Genesis of FINNEGANS
      WAKE." PMLA, 69 (1954), 1300-02.
            Correspondence with Harriet Weaver lays to
            rest Jolas' assertion (see F73) that she pro-
            vided the seminal inspiration for FW.

N185 Purdy, Strother B. "Mind Your Genderous: Toward a WAKE
      Grammar." In NEW LIGHT ON JOYCE. Ed. Fritz Senn. Pp.
      46-78. See G73.
            Over-interpretation of FW attributable to the
            failure to study its words, its original "gram-
            mar" in context (i.e., sentence and larger
            structures).

N186 Raleigh, John Henry. "'My Brother's Keeper'--Stanislaus
      Joyce and FINNEGANS WAKE." MLN, 68 (1953), 107-10.
            JJ's "mixture of mockery and affection" in
            his references to his brother in FW.

N187 Ramnoux, Clemence. "The Finn Cycle: The Atmosphere and
      Symbols of a Legend." Trans. Maria Jolas. In A JAMES
      JOYCE YEARBOOK. Ed. Maria Jolas. Pp. 130-58. See G45.
            General, archetypal study of the Finn legend.
            Useful background to FW's mythological sources.

N188 Ransom, John Crowe. "The Aesthetic of FINNEGANS WAKE."
      KR, 1 (1939), 424-28.
            JJ, in his verbal techniques, "suggests some
            extreme exponent of surrealist or 'abstraction-
            ist' painting."

N189   Richardson, Dorothy. "Adventure for Readers." LIFE AND
       LETTERS TODAY, 22 (July 1939), 45-52.
              The "inexhaustible entertainment" of FW. Ex-
              tract reprinted in G25.

N190   Robinson, Henry Morton. "Hardest Crux Ever." In A JAMES
       JOYCE MISCELLANY, SECOND SERIES. Ed. Marvin Magalaner.
       Pp. 195-207. See G56.
              On JJ's use of "HCE" word-play and the theme
              of martyrdom in FW.

N191   Rodker, John. "Joyce & His Dynamic." In OUR EXAGMINATION.
       By Samuel Beckett, et al. Pp. 141-46. See N3.
              JJ's experiment with language, demanding the
              reader's participation in the act of communi-
              cation, creates a unique symbiosis between
              author and audience.

N192   Sage, Robert. "Before ULYSSES--and After." In OUR EX-
       AGMINATION. By Samuel Beckett, et al. Pp. 149-70. See
       N3.
              FW a logical development in the "firm mount-
              ing line" of JJ's career and his works, in
              toto, an "indivisible whole."

N193   Salemson, Harold J. "James Joyce and the New Word." MOD-
       ERN QUARTERLY, 5 (1929), 293-312.
              Praises JJ's revolutionary reconstruction of
              language. See N143.

N194   Schavrien, Judy. "Joyce, Shakespeare, and Pulsebeat Poe-
       try." JJQ, 18 (1981), 147-87.
              Compares rhythmic qualities of style in JJ's
              and Shakespeare's later works.

N195   Schlauch, Margaret. "The Language of James Joyce." SCI-
       ENCE AND SOCIETY, 3 (1939), 482-97.
              Lucid justification of JJ's polyphonic, "in-
              credibly elastic" language in FW. Extract
              reprinted in G25.

N196   Senn, Fritz. "Every Klitty of a Scolderymeid: Sexual-
       Political Analogies." In A *WAKE* DIGEST. Ed. Clive Hart
       and Senn. Pp. 27-38. See N22.
              JJ's insistent correlation of sexual and po-
              litical power in FW.

N197   -----. "Insects Appalling." In TWELVE AND A TILLY. Ed.
       Jack P. Dalton and Clive Hart. Pp. 36-39. See N16.
           Insects in FW represent "animal vitality," re-
           flect the work's "perpetual" metamorphoses,
           and suggest JJ's incest theme.

N198   Sollers, Philippe. "Joyce & Co." Trans. Stephen Heath.
       In IN THE WAKE OF THE *WAKE*. Ed. David Hayman and Elliott
       Anderson. Pp. 107-21. See N24.
           Miscellany of comments on FW (e.g., the po-
           litically revolutionary implications of its
           language; JJ's matricidal tendencies).

N199   Solomon, Margaret C. "The Porters: A Square Performance
       of Three Tiers in the Round/Book III, Chapter iv." In A
       CONCEPTUAL GUIDE TO *FINNEGANS WAKE*. Ed. Michael H. Begnal
       and Fritz Senn. Pp. 201-10. See N4.
           Commentary on the interludes and dramatic-
           cinematic tableaux of the Porter chapter.

N200   Solomon, Margaret C., et al. "Joyce's Corpus as Word-
       Machine." In JOYCE & PARIS. Ed. Jacques Aubert and Maria
       Jolas. II, 79-92. See G8.
           Ill-fated attempt to define, through panel
           discussion, JJ's approach to language in FW.

N201   Spender, Stephen. "Tradition-Bound Literature and Tra-
       ditionless Painting." In THE STRUGGLE OF THE MODERN.
       Berkeley and Los Angeles: Univ. of California Press, 1963.
       Pp. 189-206 and passim.
           JJ's language and "machinery of dream and
           metaphor" in FW compared to techniques in
           modern visual arts.

N202   Splittner, Randolph. "The Sane and Joyful Spirit." JJQ,
       13 (1976), 350-65.
           Attempts a Freudian analysis of JJ's motiva-
           tions in writing FW, finding him achieving,
           through his various techniques, a momentary
           "reconciliation of all [his] lost and sundered
           selves." See G43.

N203   Staples, Hugh B. "Growing Up Absurd in Dublin/Book III,
       Chapters ii-iii." In A CONCEPTUAL GUIDE TO *FINNEGANS
       WAKE*. Ed. Michael H. Begnal and Fritz Senn. Pp. 173-
       200. See N4.
           Commentary on two relatively accessible chap-
           ters, with biographical speculations, "considera-
           tions of thematic patterns," notes, and glosses.

N204   Stevenson, Ronald. "MacDiarmid, Joyce, and Busoni: Towards
       a Music-Aesthetic of Literature." In HUGH MACDIARMID: A
       FESTSCHRIFT. Ed. K.D. Duval and Sydney G. Smith. Edin-
       burgh: Duval, 1962. Pp. 141-54.
              Parallels in the aesthetic and practice of JJ
              in fiction (FW), MacDiarmid in poetry, and
              Busoni in music.

N205   Stuart, Michael. "Joyce after ULYSSES." THIS QUARTER,
       2 (1929), 242-48.
              Praises the humor and verbal inspiration of
              JJ's "'universal' history." Extract reprinted
              in G25.

N206   Sullivan, Kevin. "THE HOUSE BY THE CHURCHYARD: James
       Joyce and Sheridan Le Fanu." In MODERN IRISH LITERATURE:
       ESSAYS IN HONOR OF WILLIAM YORK TINDALL. Ed. Raymond J.
       Porter and James D. Brophy. New York: Iona College Press
       and Twayne, 1972. Pp. 315-34.
              JJ's allusions to Le Fanu's novel (1863) in
              FW.

N207   Swinson, Ward. "Riddle in FINNEGANS WAKE." TCL, 19 (1973),
       165-80.
              JJ's awareness of the "riddle traditions in
              folklore" and his use of riddles in FW (e.g.,
              the riddle contest situation).

N208   Thompson, Francis J. "A Portrait of the Artist Asleep."
       WR, 14 (1950), 245-53.
              Identifies JJ, "alias Stephen Dedalus," as
              the dreamer in FW.

N209   Thuente, Mary Helen. "'Traditional Innovations': Yeats
       and Joyce and Irish Oral Tradition." MOSAIC, 12, No. 3
       (1979), 91-104.
              JJ's use of folk-tale elements and his depic-
              tion of "the process of oral narrative" in FW
              (cf. Yeats).

N210   Troy, William. "Notes on FINNEGANS WAKE." PR, 6 (1939),
       97-110.
              Perceptive, if somewhat miscellaneous early
              review of FW. Reprinted in G25 (extract),
              G30, and in Troy's SELECTED ESSAYS, ed. Stan-
              ley E. Hyman (New Brunswick, N.J.: Rutgers
              Univ. Press, 1967).

N211 Vickery, John B. "FINNEGANS WAKE and Sexual Metamorpho-
      sis." ConL, 13 (1972), 213-42.
          JJ's incorporation of various topics from
          Frazer's discussion of ritual, in THE GOLDEN
          BOUGH [3rd ed., 1907-15], to reinforce his
          theme of sexual metamorphosis.

N212 -----. "James Joyce: FINNEGANS WAKE and the Rituals of
      Mortality." In THE LITERARY IMPACT OF *THE GOLDEN BOUGH*.
      Princeton, N.J.: Princeton Univ. Press, 1973. Pp. 408-
      23.
          JJ's assimilation and exploitation of myth and
          archetype from Frazer's THE GOLDEN BOUGH, like
          FW an "encyclopedic effort to show that man's
          religious expressions throughout history re-
          volve around the ideas of sex, death, immortal-
          ity, and law." Also see H222.

N213 Vitoux, Pierre. "Aristotle, Berkeley, and Newman [sic,
      Newton] in 'Proteus' and FINNEGANS WAKE." JJQ, 18 (1981),
      161-75.
          See M357.

N214 Von Phul, Ruth. "CHAMBER MUSIC at the WAKE." JJQ, 11
      (1974), 355-67.
          Close analysis of the sixth poem in CHAMBER
          MUSIC, based on similar themes found in FW.
          See N28.

N215 -----. "Circling the Square: A Study of Structure." In
      A JAMES JOYCE MISCELLANY, THIRD SERIES. Ed. Marvin Maga-
      laner. Pp. 239-77. See G57.
          PAYM, U, EXILES, and FW a tetralogy, and FW's
          structure "recapitulates the total design."

N216 -----. "Who Sleeps at Finnegans Wake?" JAMES JOYCE RE-
      VIEW, 1, No. 2 (1957), 27-38.
          Identifies the dreamer as Jerry Earwicker,
          i.e., Shem (i.e., JJ himself), and FW's theme
          as the attainment of reconciliation with the
          father.

N217 Wallace, James D. "Noodynaady's Actual Ingrate Tootle."
      JJQ, 14 (1977), 290-99.
          Traces pattern of JJ's allusions to Blake's
          "Nobodaddy." See N29.

N218   Walton, Franklin. "Wilde at the WAKE." JJQ, 14 (1977),
       300-12.
           JJ's references to Oscar Wilde. See N29.

N219   Weir, Lorraine. "Phoenix Park in FINNEGANS WAKE." IRISH
       UNIVERSITY REVIEW, 5 (1975), 230-49.
           Phoenix Park associated with both violence
           and sexuality in FW.

N220   Wilder, Thornton. "Giordano Bruno's Last Meal in FINNEGANS
       WAKE." HudR, 16 (1963), 74-79.
           Discusses JJ's interweaving of the trial, tor-
           ture, and death of Bruno into FW, pp. 404-07.

N221   Williams, William Carlos. "A Note on the Recent Work of
       James Joyce (1927)." In his SELECTED ESSAYS. New York:
       Random House, 1954. Pp. 75-79.
           JJ's style the modern's approach to truth
           through the "breakup of beautiful words."
           Extract reprinted in G25.

N222   -----. "A Point for American Criticism." In OUR EXAGMIN-
       ATION. By Samuel Beckett, et al. Pp. 173-85. See N3.
           Rebecca West's criticism of JJ (see H232),
           symptomatic of British "critical orthodoxy."
           Argues that American critics will be better
           able to cope with FW. Reprinted in Williams's
           SELECTED ESSAYS (New York: Random House, 1954),
           pp. 80-90.

N223   Wilson, Edmund. "The Autobuses and the Earwickers"; "A
       Guide to FINNEGANS WAKE." 1943. 1944. In CLASSICS AND
       COMMERCIALS: A LITERARY CHRONICLE OF THE FORTIES. New
       York: Farrar, Straus and Giroux, 1950. Pp. 81-86; 182-
       89.
           Wilder's debt to FW, in THE SKIN OF OUR TEETH
           (1942), and praise for Campbell's and Robin-
           son's SKELETON KEY (N14), without benefit of
           which Wilson was nevertheless able to write
           his masterful essay on FW (see below).

N224   -----. "The Dream of H.C. Earwicker." 1939. In THE
       WOUND AND THE BOW. New York: Oxford Univ. Press, 1947.
       Pp. 243-71.
           Still an exemplary introduction to FW and
           overview of its "action" and technique. Re-
           printed in G30.

N225   Wilson, Robert Anton. "Joyce and Tao." JAMES JOYCE RE-
       VIEW, 3 (1959), 8-16.
       Taoist affirmation found in FW.

N226   Worthington, Mabel P. "American Folk Songs in Joyce's
       FINNEGANS WAKE." AMERICAN LITERATURE, 28 (1956), 197-210.
       Discusses and lists JJ's references to Amer-
       ican songs.

N227   -----. "The Moon and the Sidhe: Songs of Isabel." In NEW
       LIGHT ON JOYCE. Ed. Fritz Senn. Pp. 167-79. See G73.
       Songs of young girlhood in FW.

N228   -----. "Nursery Rhymes in FINNEGANS WAKE." JOURNAL OF
       AMERICAN FOLKLORE, 70 (1957), 37-48.
       Comments on JJ's allusive techniques and lists
       sixty-eight rhymes referred to in FW.

N229   Zaniello, Thomas A. "The Thirteenth Disciple of James
       Joyce: Abraham Lincoln Gillespie." JML, 7 (1979), 51-61.
       The impact of JJ's verbal techniques on the
       generally unknown American expatriate writer
       Gillespie (1895-1944).

P. STUDIES OF JOYCE'S MISCELLANEOUS WRITINGS

The following section is subdivided into two parts: i. Books
and Essay Collections on the Miscellaneous Writings; and ii.
General Critical Articles, or Chapters on the Miscellaneous
Writings.

JJ's principal miscellaneous writings, discussed in the studies listed in this section, include his critical essays and
reviews, "epiphanies," poems, posthumously-published prose and
fiction fragments (i.e., GIACOMO JOYCE and STEPHEN HERO), and
translations. For discussions of JJ as a letter-writer, see
Anderson (F2), Hampshire (F59), Trilling (F152), and Holthausen
(R16).

For facsimiles of the surviving notes, manuscripts, typescripts,
and proofs for the miscellaneous writings, see vols. 1-3 and
7-8 of THE JAMES JOYCE ARCHIVE (B10). For concordances to the
COLLECTED POEMS, see Doyle (D3), to GIACOMO JOYCE, see LaPorte
(D9), and to STEPHEN HERO, see Anderson (D1).

For a bibliographical checklist of JJ's uncollected poetry, see
Doyle (E10). For biographical backgrounds to the miscellaneous
writings, see, in section F above, Ellmann (F33), Pound (F123),
Richards (F130), and Sullivan (F146).

For additional critical commentaries and information on the
miscellaneous writings, see the following books, in section G
above: Benstock and Benstock (G11), Bowen (G13), CAHIERS VIC-
TORIENS (G17a), Cixous (G21), Goldberg (G31), Golding (G32),
Gorman (G36), Grose (G37), Hodgart (G40), Hodgart and Worthington (G41), JAMES JOYCE QUARTERLY (G42), Kenner (G47), Levin
(G52), Litz (G53), MacCabe (G54), Magalaner and Kain (G58),
Majault (G59), Manganiello (G60), Moseley (G67), Murillo (G68),
Noon (G69), O'Brien (G70), Peake (G71), Ryf (G72), Tindall
(G80), Tysdahl (G82); the following critical articles, in sec-
tion H above: Aronson (H7), Kestner (H112), Pound (H173), Stew-
art (H211), Vickery (H222); and the following study, entered
elsewhere in this bibliography: Prescott (M50).

For foreign-language studies of the miscellaneous writings, see section Z.

Note: Several discussions of JJ's aesthetics, entered in section H above, draw their illustrations from STEPHEN HERO, the fragmentary early version of PAYM. See especially: Baker (H8), Beebe (H11), Beja (H13), Connolly (H38), and Scholes (H186). For other discussions of JJ's aesthetics, not necessarily treating STEPHEN HERO in depth, see the headnote to the PAYM section, K above. Furthermore, many of the biographical backgrounds to and critical discussions of PAYM, listed in the headnote to section K or entered within that section, are equally relevant to the study of STEPHEN HERO.

P, i. Books and Essay Collections on Joyce's Miscellaneous Writings

Also see Z1, Z2, and Z3.

P1 Aubert, Jacques. INTRODUCTION A L'ESTHÉTIQUE DE JAMES JOYCE. Paris: M. Didier, 1973.
     Excellent discussion of JJ's aesthetics, tracing his developing ideas through his undergraduate essays, his essays on the drama (particularly "Drama and Life"), his tentative explorations of Ibsen, Mangan, and the modern audience ("Day of the Rabblement"), and his Paris and Pola notebooks. While principally occupied with less well known documents, Aubert is concerned throughout with the relationship of JJ's theories to his practice, particularly in "les oeuvres cruciales," U and FW (e.g., JJ's views of Aristotle and Stephen's, in the "Proteus" episode of U). [In French.]

P2 Brandabur, Edward. A SCRUPULOUS MEANNESS: A STUDY OF JOYCE'S EARLY WORK. Urbana: Univ. of Illinois Press, 1971.
     See J4.

P3 Hughes, Herbert, ed. THE JOYCE BOOK. London: Sylvan Press, 1933.
     Musical settings of the POMES PENYEACH by thirteen different composers (including Antheil, Bax, Goossens, Roussel, and Sessions), with brief notes on JJ's poetry by Padraic Colum, James Stephens, and Arthur Symons (Symons reprinted in G25).

P4   Jackson, Selwyn. THE POEMS OF JAMES JOYCE AND THE USE OF
     POEMS IN HIS NOVELS. Frankfort: Lang, 1978.
          Analyses of CHAMBER MUSIC and POMES PENYEACH,
          together with essays on JJ's use of poems in
          PAYM, U, and FW. Jackson avoids discussing
          the lyric, or poetic qualities of JJ's experi-
          ments in prose, and concentrates on "isolating
          the specific function" of poems in each work,
          from the "unfinished, ambiguous" villanelle in
          PAYM (a reflection of Stephen's character), to
          the "rich and spectacular ornaments" on the
          prose "fabric" of FW. A useful, modest study.

P5   Sorensen, Dolf. JAMES JOYCE'S AESTHETIC THEORY: ITS DEVEL-
     OPMENT AND APPLICATION. Amsterdam: Rodopi, 1977.
          Monograph study of JJ's evolving ideas of art
          in his essays, notebooks, letters, STEPHEN HERO,
          and EXILES, reexamining the now familiar influ-
          ences of Aquinas, Ibsen, and Vico. Sorensen,
          however, fundamentally fails to distinguish be-
          tween JJ's views and those expressed by his
          characters and, arguing that JJ's aesthetic was
          continuously and consistently applied in his
          fiction, distorts the development of JJ's art.
          Weak and unoriginal.

P, ii. General Critical Articles or Chapters on Joyce's Miscellaneous Writings

P6   Anderson, Chester G. "James Joyce's 'Tilly.'" PMLA, 73
     (1958), 285-98.
          Full analysis of the first lyric in POMES PENY-
          EACH (with a fundamental misreading), and com-
          ment on its relation to JJ's major fiction.

P7   Baker, James R. "Joyce's CHAMBER MUSIC: The Exile of the
     Heart." ArQ, 15 (1959), 349-56.
          Collection's unity and characteristic Joycean
          theme: "the conflict of love and creativity."

P8   Berrone, Louis. JAMES JOYCE IN PADUA. Ed. and trans. Ber-
     rone. Pp. xiii-xxviii, 43-71, 73-101, 105-38. See B11.
          Distended discussion of JJ's attempted matricu-
          lation at Padua, of his examination essays there,
          and of "obscure words and phrases" in the essays.

P9   Bowen, Zack. "Goldenhair: Joyce's Archetypal Female." L&P,
      17 (1967), 219-28.
          Virgin-temptress figure in CHAMBER MUSIC reap-
          pears throughout the works.

P10   Connolly, Thomas E. "STEPHEN HERO Revisited." JAMES JOYCE
      REVIEW, 3 (1959), 40-46.
          JJ's manuscript revisions of STEPHEN HERO show
          his maturing attitudes and art.

P11   Farrell, James T. "Postscript on STEPHEN HERO." In JAMES
      JOYCE. Ed. Seon Givens. Pp. 190-97. See G30.
          Notes differences in style, focus, and perspec-
          tive between PAYM and STEPHEN HERO. (Postscript
          to Farrell's article on PAYM, see K58.)

P12   Feshbach, Sidney. "Writ Our Bit as Intermidgets: Classi-
      cal Rhetoric in the Early Writing of James Joyce." JJQ,
      17 (1980), 379-87.
          JJ's response to the classical rhetoric he was
          taught, illustrated here by his schoolboy es-
          say "Trust Not Appearances," informs his rhetor-
          ical experiments throughout his career.

P13   Fisher, Marvin. "James Joyce's 'Ecce Puer': The Return
      of the Prodding Gaul." UKCR, 25 (1959), 265-71.
          Close analysis of poem and assertion of its
          central place in JJ's work (the "paternity"
          theme).

P14   Groden, Michael. "James Joyce and the Classical, Romantic,
      and Medieval Tempers." MODERN BRITISH LITERATURE, 5 (1980),
      10-21.
          Traces in JJ's critical writings the develop-
          ment and later modifications of "his theory
          of the tempers." See G63.

P15   Harvey, Francis. "STEPHEN HERO and A PORTRAIT OF THE ART-
      IST AS A YOUNG MAN: The Intervention of Style in a Work of
      the Creative Imagination." In A BASH IN THE TUNNEL. Ed.
      John Ryan. Pp. 203-07. See F135.
          See K75.

P16   Howarth, Herbert. "CHAMBER MUSIC and Its Place in the
      Joyce Canon." In JAMES JOYCE TODAY. Ed. Thomas F. Staley.
      Pp. 11-27. See G75.
          Poems a partially successful attempt at "mus-
          ical" verse.

P17 Kain, Richard M. "Two Book Reviews by James Joyce." PMLA,
     67 (1952), 291-94.
         Background information on two early review es-
         says (1902-03), contained in THE CRITICAL WRIT-
         INGS (B4).

P18 Macleod, Vivienne Koch. "The Influence of Ibsen on Joyce."
     PMLA, 60 (1945), 879-98; 62 (1947), 573-80.
         See L19.

P19 Mason, Ellsworth. "Introduction." In THE EARLY JOYCE. Ed.
     Stanislaus Joyce and Mason. Pp. 2-5. See B5.
         Brief consideration of JJ's qualities as a
         critic.

P20 Perkins, Jill. JOYCE AND HAUPTMANN. Ed. Perkins. Pp. 1-
     7, 9-15, 17-27, 29-45, 133-66. See B13.
         Critical and textual discussions of JJ's early
         translation of VOR SONNENAUFGANG (c. 1901),
         arguing the influence of Hauptmann as well as
         Ibsen on his work and including notes for the
         play.

P21 Russel, Myra. "The Elizabethan Connection: The Missing
     Score of James Joyce's CHAMBER MUSIC." JJQ, 18 (1981),
     133-45.
         Argues JJ's poems most profitably read with
         Elizabethan conventions for lyrics and music
         in mind.

P22 Scholes, Robert. "In Search of James Joyce." JJQ, 11
     (1973), 5-16.
         JJ's resistance to Pater's "idealizing" aes-
         thetic in his early criticism, theory, and
         practice (the "epiphanies").

P23 -----. "James Joyce, Irish Poet." JJQ, 2 (1965), 255-70.
         Sees JJ's "allegorical habit of mind" and al-
         lusive methods "in action on a small scale" in
         his poetry, and judges him "one of the greatest"
         Irish poets (cf. Yeats).

P24 Scott, Bonnie Kime. "The Woman in the Black Straw Hat: A
     Transitional Priestess in STEPHEN HERO." JJQ, 16 (1979),
     407-16.
         Implications of Stephen's encounter with a
         mysterious female figure in STEPHEN HERO, in-
         fluenced by JJ's reading of Yeats, Renan, and
         Buddhist theology.

P25   Sen, M.K.   "The 'Poetry' of James Joyce."   In FRESH GROUNDS
      IN ENGLISH LITERATURE.   New Delhi: Chand, 1974.   Pp. 141-60.
          JJ's lyrics have charm, but he may be "remem-
          bered by posterity," as a poet, only for two
          poems: "A Prayer" and "Ecce Puer."

P26   Silverman, Oscar A.   "Introduction."   In JJ's EPIPHANIES.
      Ed. Silverman.   Pp. ix-xvi.   See B6.
          Discusses the importance of the epiphany tech-
          nique in JJ's work.

P27   Sisson, C.H.   ENGLISH POETRY, 1900-1950: AN ASSESSMENT.
      London: Hart-Davis, 1971.   Pp. 68-70.
          JJ's failures as a poet and his affinities
          with the imagists.

P28   Spencer, Theodore.   "Introduction."   In JJ's STEPHEN HERO.
      Ed. Spencer.   Pp. 7-19.   See B21.
          On the state of the surviving manuscript of
          JJ's early version of PAYM and on its relation
          to the published novel.   Extracts reprinted in
          J1 and K14.

P29   Staley, Thomas F.   "The Poet Joyce and the Shadow of Swift."
      In JONATHAN SWIFT: TERCENTENARY ESSAYS.   Ed. Winston Weath-
      ers and Staley.   Tulsa, Okla.: Univ. of Tulsa Press, 1967.
      Pp. 39-52.
          Swiftian qualities of JJ's satiric broadsides
          ("Gas from a Burner" and "The Holy Office").

P30   -----.   "Some Observations on the Early Development of
      Joyce's Art."   In INTROSPECTION: THE ARTIST LOOKS AT HIM-
      SELF.   Ed. Donald E. Hayden.   Tulsa, Okla.: Univ. of Tulsa
      Press, 1971.   Pp. 29-40.
          JJ's views on art (c. 1903), culled from his
          early essays and notebooks.

P31   Stern, Richard G.   "Proust and Joyce Underway: JEAN SANTEUIL
      and STEPHEN HERO."   KR, 18 (1956), 486-96.
          Parallels between the two writers' evolving
          views of their art found in similar posthum-
          ously published fragments (JEAN SANTEUIL pub-
          lished 1952).

P32   Tindall, William York.   "Introduction"; "The Texts of CHAM-
      BER MUSIC"; "Notes to the Poems."   In JJ's CHAMBER MUSIC.
      Ed. Tindall.   New York: Columbia Univ. Press, 1954.   Pp.
      3-98; 99-106; 181-225.
          Full discussion of the poems' composition,

publication, and significance, and controversial scatalogical interpretation of the collection. Includes commentary on the manuscripts
and extensive critical notes on the individual
poems.

P33 Tobin, Patricia. "A Portrait of the Artist as Autobiogra-
pher: Joyce's STEPHEN HERO." GENRE, 6 (1973), 189-203.
     Considers STEPHEN HERO "the far more reliable
     source of autobiographical truth" (cf. PAYM).

P34 Von Phul, Ruth. "CHAMBER MUSIC at the WAKE." JJQ, 11
     (1974), 355-67.
          See N214.

P35 Zabel, Morton Dauwen. "The Lyrics of James Joyce." POETRY,
     36 (1930), 206-13.
          JJ's integration of continental, English, and
          Irish elements to achieve "his own poetic char-
          acter for the first time" in POMES PENYEACH.
          Extract reprinted in G25.

PART 3. MAJOR FOREIGN-LANGUAGE STUDIES

This selective checklist of major foreign-language publications
concerning JJ is subdivided into sections paralleling those of
the preceding secondary bibliography of JJ studies (part 2).
While the entries are only slightly annotated, their placement
within the various topical subdivisions give some indication
of their contents.

A cross-reference number has been provided for each title which
is entered elsewhere in this guide and annotated, from original
publication or from subsequent whole or partial publication in
translation. Occasionally translations of titles have been provided for works appearing in less familiar languages. In rare
cases the language of the publication is noted at the conclusion
of the entry, if it is not evident from either the title or the
place of publication.

Q. BIBLIOGRAPHIES

Also see E11, E18, E29, F72, H6, M299, U1, V2, and V5.

Q1   Cianci, Giovanni. LA FORTUNA DI JOYCE IN ITALIA: SAGGIO E
     BIBLIOGRAFIA (1917-1972). Bari, Italy: Adriatica, 1974.
        Essay-survey and topical checklists.

Q2   Franke, Rosemarie. JAMES JOYCE UND DER DEUTSCHE SPRACHBE-
     REICH: ÜBERSETZUNG, VERBREITUNG UND KRITIK IN DER ZEIT VON
     1919-1967. Berlin: Privately published, 1970.
        Extract reprinted in M17.

Q3   Gheerbrant, Bernard, ed. JAMES JOYCE: SA VIE, SON OEUVRE,
     SON RAYONNEMENT. Paris: La Hune, 1949.
        See E12.

Q4   Moro, Koichi. "An Aspect of Joyce's Method (1): Critical
     Evaluations in Japan; (2): A Historical Survey of Critical
     Evaluation in Japan." JOSAI JINBUN KENKYU (Sakado, Jap.),
     6 (1979), 29-48; 7 (1980), 83-97. [In Japanese.]

Q5   Voswinckel, Barbara, and Erika Joerden. JAMES JOYCE, 1882-
     1941. Hamburg: Hamburger Öffentlichen Bücherhallen, 1965.

R. BIOGRAPHIES, MEMOIRS, REMINISCENCES, INTERVIEWS

R1 Alajouanine, Th. "Valery Larbaud et le monologue intérieur
(d'après ses lettres inédites à Édouard Dujardin)." In
VALERY LARBAUD SOUS DIVERS VISAGES. Paris: Gallimard, 1973.
Pp. 113-36.

R2 Beach, Sylvia. "ULYSSES à Paris." MERCURE DE FRANCE, 309
(1950), 12-29.
Includes a letter to Beach from G.B. Shaw (1921—
in French). See R20.

R3 Benco, Silvio. "Un Illustre Scrittore Inglese a 'Trieste.'"
UMANA, 1, No. 4 (July 1918), 1-3.
See F8.

R4 Borach, Georges. "Gespräche mit James Joyce." DIE NEUE
ZÜRICHER ZEITUNG, 3 May 1931.
See F9.

R5 Burgauer, Arnold. JAMES JOYCE IN ZÜRICH. Zurich: Pro
Helvetia, 1973.

R6 Castris, A. Leone de. "Svevo e Joyce." In ITALO SVEVO.
Pisa: Nistri-Lischi, 1966. Pp. 323-40.

R7 Crise, Stelio. EPIPHANIES & PHADOGRAPHS: JOYCE E TRIESTE.
Milan: All'insegna del pesce d'oro, 1967.
See F22.

R8 Dujardin, Édouard, and Valery Larbaud. "Autour du monologue
intérieur: La correspondance Dujardin-Larbaud." Ed. Frida
S. Weissman. CAHIERS DES AMIS DE VALERY LARBAUD, No. 14
(Mar. 1976), pp. 1-45.

R9 Francini-Bruni, Alessandro. JOYCE INTIMO SPOGLIATO IN
PIAZZA. Trieste: La Editoriale Libraria, 1922.
See F42.

R10   -----. "Ricordi personali su James Joyce." NUOVA ANTO-
        LOGIA, 441 (Sep.-Dec. 1947), 71-79.

R11   Frank, Nino. "L'ombre qui avait perdue son homme." In
        MÉMOIRE BRISÉE. Paris: Calmann-Levy, 1967. Pp. 27-64.
            See F43.

R12   -----. "Souvenirs sur James Joyce." LA TABLE RONDE (Par-
        is), No. 23 (Nov. 1949), pp. 1671-93.
            See F43.

R13   Giedion-Welcker, Carola. "Begegnungen mit James Joyce."
        In her SCHRIFTEN, 1926-1971: STATIONEN ZU EINEM ZEITBILD.
        Ed. Reinhold Hohl. Cologne: M. DuMont Schauberg, 1973.
        Pp. 53-74.
            See F46.

R14   -----, ed. IN MEMORIAM JAMES JOYCE. Zurich: Fretz and
        Wasmuth, 1941.
            See F47.

R15   Hoffmeister, Adolf. "James Joyce"; "Osobnost James Joyce."
        In PODOBY. Praque: Ceskoslovensky Spisovatel, 1961. Pp.
        71-78; 118-26.
            See F63.

R16   Holthusen, Hans Egon. "Die Literatur der verbrannten Erde:
        James Joyce in seinen Briefen." In KREISELKOMPASS: KRITISCHE
        VERSUCHE ZUR LITERATUR DER EPOCHE. Munich and Zurich: R.
        Piper, 1976. Pp. 109-37, 231-32.

R17   Kerr, Alfred. "Joyce en Angleterre." LES NOUVELLES LIT-
        TÉRAIRES (Paris), No. 691 (Jan. 1936), pp. 6-12.
            See F88.

R18   Léon, Paul. "In Memory of Joyce." POÉSIE, No. 5 (1942),
        p. 35. [In French.]
            See F90.

R19   Mercanton, Jacques. LES HEURES DE JAMES JOYCE. 1963.
        Lausanne: Éditions l'Age d'Homme, 1967.
            See F105.

R20   MERCURE DE FRANCE. 309 (1950), 5-58.
            Four memoir-essays, plus several of JJ's poems
            in translation. Includes R2 and X67.

R21   MERCURE DE FRANCE. 349 (1963), 9-170. "Sylvia Beach (1887-
      1962)."
          Forty brief articles, several translated from
          English and most touching on JJ.

R22   Nordio, Mario. "Gli anni Triestini di James Joyce." ATENEO
      VENETO, 6 (1968), 77-86.

R23   Núñez, Estuardo. "James Joyce y Victor Llona." REVISTA
      PERUANA DE CULTURA, No. 7-8 (June 1966), pp. 221-28.

R24   Parandowski, Jan. "Spotkanie z Joyce'em" ["Meeting with
      Joyce"]. 1948. In DZIELA WYBRANE. Warsaw: Czytelnik,
      1959. III, 468-77.
          See F118.

R25   Recklinghausen, Daniel von. JAMES JOYCE: CHRONIK VON LEBEN
      UND WERK. Frankfurt a.M.: Suhrkamp, 1968.

R26   Rocco-Bergera, Niny. "I vincoli Triestini di James Joyce";
      "La gelosia in James Joyce e Italo Svevo." In DUE SAGGI
      SU JAMES JOYCE. Trieste: Edizioni UMANA, 1971. Pp. 7-49;
      53-71.

R27   Senn, Fritz. JAMES JOYCE PUB ZÜRICH. Zurich: Schweizerische
      Bankgesellschaft, 1978.
          Monograph (56 pp.) occasioned by the opening
          of the James Joyce Pub.

R28   Soupault, Philippe. SOUVENIRS DE JAMES JOYCE. 1943. Paris:
      Charlot, 1945.
          See F139.

R29   Stark, Helmuth. "Eine Begegnung aus dem Jahr 1915." AK-
      ZENTE, 8 (Apr. 1961), 155-57.

R30   Straumann, Heinrich. "Letzte Begegnung mit Joyce." DU
      (Zurich), 8, No. 12 (1948), 31-32.
          See F145.

R31   Svevo, Italo. "James Joyce." 1927. IL CONVEGNO, 18 (Jan.
      1938), 135-58.
          See F148.

R32   Tuoni, Dario de. RICORDO DI JOYCE A TRIESTE. Milan: All'in-
      segna del pesce d'oro, 1966.
          See F153.

R33   Vinding, Ole. "James Joyce i Kφbenhavn."   In VEJEN TIL
      DEN HALVE VERDEN. Copenhagen: Gyldendal, 1963. Pp. 198–
      209.
            See F72 and F154.

R34   Zhantieva, D.G. DZHEIMS DZHOIS [JAMES JOYCE]. Moscow:
      Izdatelstvo "Vyshaya Shkola," 1967.

S. BOOK-LENGTH CRITICAL STUDIES AND ESSAY COLLECTIONS

Also see the numerous books, essay collections, monographs, and pamphlets on JJ's individual works (D, PAYM, U, FW) and miscellaneous writings, listed in sections U, V, X, Y, Z below.

S1 Ara, Masato, and Shoichi Saeki, eds. JOISU NYUMON [AN IN-
   TRODUCTION TO JAMES JOYCE]. 1960. Rev. ed. Tokyo: Nanundo,
   1966.
       Twenty-five essays, by various hands.

S2 Aravantinou, Manto. TA HELLENIKA TOU TZAIEMS TZOYS [THE
   HELLENISM OF JAMES JOYCE]. Athens: Hermes, 1977.

S3 L'ARC. 36 (1968), 1-97. "Joyce et le roman contemporain."
       Sixteen brief articles on and two excerpts from
       JJ.

S4 Arnold, Armin. JAMES JOYCE. Berlin: Colloquium Verlag,
   1963.
       See G6.

S5 ATTI DEL THIRD INTERNATIONAL JAMES JOYCE SYMPOSIUM TRIESTE--
   14-18 GIUGNO 1971. Trieste: Universita Degli Studi, 1974.
       See G7.

S6 Aubert, Jacques, and Maria Jolas, eds. JOYCE & PARIS: 1902...
   1920-1940...1975. 2 vols. Paris: Éditions du C.N.R.S.,
   1979.
       See G8.

S7 Blengio-Brito, Rául. INTRODUCCIÓN A JOYCE. Montevideo:
   Ano Internacional del Libro Biblioteca Nacional, 1972.

S8 Borel, Jacques, et al. JOYCE. Buenos Aires: Jorge Alvarez,
   1969.
       Nine articles, several translated from English.

S9 Brasil, Assis. JOYCE: O ROMANCE COMO FORMA. Rio de Janeiro
   Livros do Mundo Inteiro, 1971.

S9a CAHIERS VICTORIENS & ÉDOUARDIENS. No. 14 (1981), pp. 1-121. "Studies in the Early Joyce."
See G17a.

S10 CAMP DE L'ARPA. No. 52 (June 1978), pp. 5-44. [In Spanish] Seven essays, with miscellaneous materials concerning JJ.

S11 CHANGE. No. 11 (May 1972), pp. 9-222. [In French.] Twenty essays, a poem, and an excerpt from JJ in translation.

S12 Cixous, Hélène. L'EXIL DE JAMES JOYCE: OU L'ART DU REMPLACEMENT. Paris: Grasset, 1968.
See G21.

S13 Davies, Aneirin Talfan. YR ALLTUD RHAGARWEINIAD I WEITHIAU JAMES JOYCE. London: Gwasg Foyle, 1944. [In Welsh.]

S14 Debenedetti, Giacomo, ed. INTRODUZIONE A JOYCE. TUTTE LE OPERE DI JAMES JOYCE. Vol. 1. Milan: Mondadori, 1967. Extracts of major JJ criticism, in Italian translation, introducing a five-volume Italian edition of JJ's works.

S15 Duytschaever, Joris. JAMES JOYCE. Brugge, Belg.: Desclée de Brouwer, 1970. [In Flemish.]

S16 Fischer [-Seidel], Therese. BEWUSSTSEINSDARSTELLUNG IM WERK VON JAMES JOYCE VON *DUBLINERS* ZU *ULYSSES*. Frankfurt a.M.: Athenaeum Verlag, 1973.

S17 Gillet, Louis. STÈLE POUR JAMES JOYCE. Marseilles: Éditions du Sagittaire, 1941.
See G29.

S18 Giorgianni, Enio. INCHIESTA SU JAMES JOYCE. Milan: Epiloghi di Perseo, 1934.

S19 Gozzi, Francesco. LA POESIA DI JAMES JOYCE. Bari, Italy: Adriatica, 1974.

S20 Guidi, Augusto. IL PRIMO JOYCE. Rome: Edizioni di Storia e Letteratura, 1954.

S21 Haan, Jacques den. JOYCE: MYTHE VAN ERIN. 1948. 2nd ed. Amsterdam: De Bezige Bij, 1967.

S22   Hayman, David, ed. CONFIGURATION CRITIQUE DE JAMES JOYCE,
      II. Paris: Lettres Modernes, 1965.
      Eleven major criticisms, translated from Eng-
      lish. Sequel to S40.

S23   Ito, Hitoshi. JOYCE. Tokyo: Kenkyusha, 1969.

S24   Ito, Sei, ed. JOISU KENKYŪ [A STUDY OF JOYCE]. 1955. Rev.
      ed. Tokyo: Eihôsha, 1965.
      Nineteen essays.

S25   LEVENDE TALEN. No. 269 (1970), pp. 413-83. "Joyce Nummer."
      Thirteen articles, chiefly in Dutch.

S26   LITERATURA NA ŚWIECIE. No. 5 (May 1973), pp. 3-382. [In
      Polish.]
      Ten essays on JJ. Includes English "summary"
      (p. 382).

S27   Lutter, Tibor. JAMES JOYCE. Budapest: Gondolat, 1959.

S28   MAGAZINE LITTÉRAIRE. No. 161 (1980), pp. 8-45. "Dossier
      James Joyce."
      Ten brief articles.

S29   Majault, Joseph. JAMES JOYCE. Paris: Éditions Universi-
      taires, 1963.
      See G59.

S30   Marengo-Vaglio, Carla. INVITO ALLA LETTURA DI JAMES JOYCE.
      Milan: Mursia, 1977.

S31   Maruya, Saiichi, ed. GENDAI SAKKA RON: JAMES JOYCE [STUD-
      IES OF A MODERN AUTHOR: JAMES JOYCE]. Tokyo: Hayakawa
      Shobo, 1974.

S32   Mayoux, Jean-Jacques. JAMES JOYCE. Paris: Gallimard,
      1965.

S33   Mochizuki, Mitsuko. JAMES JOYCE KENKYU JOSETSU [INTRODUC-
      TION TO JOYCE]. Kyoto: Yamaguchi, 1979.

S33a Multhaup, Uwe. JAMES JOYCE. Darmstadt: Wissenschaftliche
      Buchgesellschaft, 1980.

S34   Oda, Motoi. JOYCE E NO MICHI [AN APPROACH TO JOYCE]. Tokyo
      Kenkyusha, 1979.

S35 Oishi, Shun'ichi. JAMES JOYCE NO BUNGAKU [THE WRITINGS OF JAMES JOYCE]. Kyoto: Apolon Sha, 1978.

S36 Oketani, Hideaki. JEIMUSU JOISU. Tokyo: Kinokuniya Shoten, 1964.

S37 Paci, Francesca Romana. VITA E OPERE DI JAMES JOYCE. Bari, Italy: Laterza, 1968.

S38 Paris, Jean. JAMES JOYCE PAR LUI-MEME. Paris: Éditions du Seuil, 1957.
         Includes numerous photographs and several extracts from JJ's works.

S39 Pinguentini, Gianni. JAMES JOYCE IN ITALIA. Florence: Liberia Commissionaria Sansoni, 1963.

S40 Prescott, Joseph, ed. CONFIGURATION CRITIQUE DE JAMES JOYCE. Paris: Lettres Modernes, 1959.
         Thirteen major essays and a bibliographical checklist (from G64), translated from English. Also see S22.

S41 Rothe, Wolfgang. JAMES JOYCE. Wiesbaden: Limes Verlag, 1957.

S42 Schulte, Edvige. L'EROE ALL'ANTIPODO (PER UN'INTERPRETAZIONE DI JAMES JOYCE). Naples: Liguori, 1973.

S43 SECOLUL 20. No. 2 (1965), pp. 17-156. "James Joyce." [In Rumanian.]
         Four articles on JJ and several translations from his fiction and poetry.

S44 Senn, Fritz. JAMES JOYCE: AUFSÄTZE VON FRITZ SENN. Zurich: Max-Geilinger-Stiftung, 1972.
         Seven previously-published essays.

S45 Taha, Taha Mahmud. MASU AT JIMS JUYIS, HAYATUHU WA-FANNUHU WA-DIRASAT LI-A MALIH [A JAMES JOYCE ENCYCLOPEDIA: HIS LIFE, ART, AND WORKS]. Kuwait: Wakâlat al-Matbu'ât, 1975.

S46 TEL QUEL. No. 83 (1980), pp. 23-102. [In French.]
         Three articles, with miscellaneous materials related to JJ. Includes H96.

S47 UMANA (Trieste). 20 (May-Sep. 1971), 2-68.
         Twenty-two mostly brief articles, many concerning JJ and Svevo.

S48   UTOPIA (Eindhoven, Neth.).   8 (June 1969), 6-28.
      Five essays.

S49   Valverde, José María.   CONOCER JOYCE Y SU OBRA.   Barcelona:
      Dopesa, 1978.

S50   Vargas, Manuel Arturo.   JAMES JOYCE.   Madrid: EPESA, 1972.

T.   GENERAL CRITICAL ARTICLES OR CHAPTERS ON JOYCE

T1   Altschul, Carlos. "Hacia una interpretacion del hombre
     Joyce." SUR, No. 260 (1959), pp. 24-36.

T2   Astre, Georges-Albert. "Joyce et la durée." L'AGE NOUVEAU,
     No. 45 (Jan. 1950), pp. 29-38.

T3   Bihalji-Merin, Oto. "Dzems Dzojs" ["James Joyce"]. In
     GRADITELJI MODERNE MISLI U LITERATURI I UMETNOSTI. Bel-
     grade: Prosveta, 1965. Pp. 75-113.

T4   Bini, Luigi. "James Joyce esule ribelle." LETTURE, 16
     (1961), 163-82.

T5   Bonifacino, Victor. "James Joyce." In ENSAYOS BELIGERANTES:
     BERTRAND RUSSELL--JAMES JOYCE. Montevideo: Alfa, 1960. Pp.
     75-96.

T6   Caspel, Paul P.J. van. "Van Dublin naar Harlingen: Joyce
     en Vestdijk." In TAAL EN LETTERKUNDIG GASTENBOEK VOOR PROF.
     DR. G.A. VAN ES. Ed. G. Kazemier and Caspel. Groningen,
     Neth.: Archief voor de Nederlandse Syntaxis, 1975. Pp.
     117-87.

T7   Cixous, Hélène. "Emsemble Joyce." In PRÉNOMS DE PERSONNE.
     Paris: Éditions du Seuil, 1974. Pp. 231-331.

T8   -----. "Joyce, la ruse de l'écriture." POÉTIQUE, No. 4
     (1970), pp. 419-32.

T9   D'Agostino, Nemi. "Reflessioni su Joyce." In FRIENDSHIP'S
     GARLAND: ESSAYS PRESENTED TO MARIO PRAZ ON HIS SEVENTIETH
     BIRTHDAY. Ed. V. Gabrieli. Rome: Edizioni di Storia e
     Letteratura, 1966. II, 253-67.

T10 Debenedetti, Giacomo. "Svevo e Joyce." In IL ROMANZO DEL
     NOVECENTO. Milan: Garzanti, 1971. Pp. 558-94.

T11 Delattre, Floris. "L'influence de Marcel Proust et James
     Joyce." In LE ROMAN PSYCHOLOGIQUE DE VIRGINIA WOOLF. 1932.
     2nd ed. Paris: J. Vrin, 1967. Pp. 142-71.

T12 Destéfano, José R. BAUDELAIRE Y OTRAS RUTAS DE LA NUEVA
     LITERATURA. Buenos Aires: "El Ateneo," 1945. Pp. 221-40.

T13 Drescher, Horst W. "James Joyce und Virginia Woolf: Ästhe-
     tik, Funktion und Form des Modernen Romans." In ENGLISCHE
     UND AMERIKANISCHE LITERATURTHEORIE: STUDIEN ZU IHRER HIS-
     TORISCHEN ENTWICKLUNG. Ed. Rüdiger Ahrens and Erwin Wolff.
     Heidelberg: Carl Winter, 1979. II, 344-61.

T14 Durzak, Manfred. "Die Ästhetik des polyhistorischen Romans:
     James Joyce." In HERMANN BROCH: DER DICHTER UND SEINE ZEIT.
     Stuttgart: W. Kohlhammer, 1968. Pp. 76-113.

T15 Egri, Péter. "Ibsen, Joyce, Shaw." FILOLÓGIAI KÖZLÖNY,
     13 (1966), 109-33. [In Hungarian.]

T16 Faj, Attila. "La filosofia Vichiana in Joyce." FORUM ITAL-
     ICUM, 2 (1968), 470-82.

T17 Fricker, Robert. "James Joyce." In DER MODERNE ENGLISCHE
     ROMAN. 1958. 2nd ed. Gottingen, Neth.: Vandenhoeck and
     Ruprecht, 1966. Pp. 103-23.

T18 Fuentes, Carlos. CERVANTES, O LA CRÍTICA DE LA LECTURA.
     Mexico City: Editorial Joaquin Mortiz, 1976. Pp. 95-110.

T19 Füger, Wilhelm. "Der Brief als Bau-Element des Erzählens:
     Zum Funktionswandel des Einlagebriefes im neueren Roman,
     dargelegt am Beispiel von Dostojewski, Thomas Mann, Kafka
     und Joyce." DEUTSCHE VIERTELJAHRSSCHRIFT, 51 (1977), 628-
     58.

T20 Gandon, Yves. "Examen de Conscience Littéraire de James
     Joyce, Irlandais." In IMAGÉRIES CRITIQUES. Ed. Edgar Mal-
     fere. Paris: Société Française d'Éditions Littéraires et
     Techniques, 1933. Pp. 181-92.

T21 Garcia-Ponce, Juan. "Musil y Joyce." REVISTA DE BELLAS
     ARTES, 13 (1967), 13-31.
          See H69.

T22 Garcia-Sabell D. "James Joyce i a loita pola communica-
     cion total." In ENSAIOS. Vigo, Spain: Galaxia, 1963. Pp.
     97-190. [In Galician.] "James Joyce y la lucha por la

communicación total." In TRES SINTOMAS DE EUROPA: JAMES JOYCE, VINCENT VAN GOGH, JEAN-PAUL SARTRE. Madrid: Ediciones de la Revista de Occidente, 1968. Pp. 9-101. [In Castilian.]

T23 Gide, André. "Interviews Imaginaires." LE FIGARO, 30-31 May 1942.
See H72.

T24 Gresset, Michel. "A propos de Joyce." NOUVELLE REVUE FRANÇAISE, 28 (1966), 510-14.

T25 Höllerer, Walter. "Die Epiphanie als Held des Romans." AKZENTE, 8 (1961), 125-36, 275-85.

T26 Houdebine, Jean-Louis, and Phillipe Sollers. "La Trinité de Joyce." TEL QUEL, 83 (1980), 36-88.
See H96.

T27 Irinoda, Masaaki. "Hermann Broch no James Joyce taiken shiron" ["A Study of Hermann Broch's Exposure to James Joyce"]. TOKYO SUISAN DAIGAKU RONSHU [REPORTS OF THE TOKYO UNIV. OF FISHERIES], 1 (1966), 59-72; 2 (1967), 45-64; 4 (1969), 105-21.

T28 Jacquot, Jean. "Exégètes et interprèts de James Joyce." EA, 12 (1959), 30-46; 15 (1962), 46-63.

T29 Le Breton, Georges. "La Méthod de James Joyce." MERCURE DE FRANCE, 351 (1964), 123-32.

T30 Markow-Totevy, Georges. "André Gide et James Joyce." MERCURE DE FRANCE, 339 (1960), 272-90.

T31 Mason, Eudo C. "James Joyce." In ENGLISCHE DICHTER DER MODERNE: IHR LEBEN UND WERK. Ed. Rudolf Sühnel and Dieter Riesner. Berlin: Schmidt, 1971. Pp. 285-98.

T32 Mayoux, Jean-Jacques. "L'Hérésie de James Joyce." EM, 2 (1951), 199-225.

T33 Melchiori, Giorgio. "James Joyce." In I CONTEMPORANEI: LETTERATURA INGLESE. Ed. Vito Amoruso and Francesco Binni. Rome: Luciano Lucarini, 1977. I, 347-74.

T34 -----. "James, Joyce, e D'Annunzio." In D'ANNUNZIO E IL SIMBOLISMO EUROPEO. Ed. Emilio Mariano. Milan: Il Saggiatore, 1976. Pp. 299-311.

T35   Mercanton, Jacques. "James Joyce." In POÈTES DE L'UNIVERS.
      Paris: Éditions Albert Skira, 1947. Pp. 13-90.

T36   Mirsky, Dmitri P. "Dzheims Dzhois" ["James Joyce"]. AL-
      MANAKH: GOD 16 (Moscow), No. 1 (1933), pp. 428-50.
      See H150.

T37   Monod, Sylvère. "James Joyce." HISTOIRE DE LA LITTÉRATURE
      ANGLAISE DE VICTORIA À ELISABETH II. Paris: Armand Colin,
      1970. Pp. 305-12.

T38   Moravia, Alberto. "Omaggio a Joyce." PROSPETTIVE, 4, Nos.
      11-12 (1940), 12-13.

T39   Nojima, Hidekatsu. EGUZAILU NO BUNGAKU: JOISU, ERIOTTO,
      RORENSU NO BA'AI [THE LITERATURE OF EXILE: THE CASE OF
      JOYCE, ELIOT, LAWRENCE]. Tokyo: Nanundo, 1963.

T40   Praz, Mario. "James Joyce." In JAMES JOYCE, THOMAS STEARNS
      ELIOT: DUE MAESTRI DEI MODERNI. Turin: Edizioni Rai Radio-
      televisione Italiana, 1967. Pp. 3-82.
      See H176.

T41   Reichert, Karl. "Reise ans Ende der Möglichen: James
      Joyce." In ROMANANFÄNGE: VERSUCH ZU EINER POETIK DES RO-
      MANS. Ed. Norbert Miller. Berlin: Literarisches Collo-
      quium, 1965. Pp. 317-43.

T42   Revol, E.L. "Elementos de Joyce." In LA TRADICIÓN IMAG-
      INARIA DE JOYCE A BORGES. Cordoba, Argentina: TEUCO, 1971.
      Pp. 10-29.

T43   Schramke, Jürgen. "Die Zeit." In ZUR THEORIE DES MODERNEN
      ROMANS. Munich: C.H. Beck, 1974. Pp. 99-138.

T44   Straumann, Heinrich. "Das Zeitproblem im englischen und
      amerikanischen Roman: Sterne, Joyce, Faulkner, und Wilder."
      In DAS ZEITPROBLEM IM 20. JAHRHUNDERT. Ed. R.W. Meyer.
      Bern: Francke, 1964. Pp. 140-60.

T45   Taranienko, Zbigniew. "Czas i przestrzen J'a" ["Time and
      Space in Joyce"]. STUDIA FILOZOFICZNE (Warsaw), 61 (1969)
      97-118.

T46   Tessier, Thérèse. "Thomas Moore et James Joyce." CAHIERS
      DU CENTRE D'ÉTUDES IRLANDAISES, No. 3 (1978), pp. 23-29.

T47 Trilling, Jacques. "James Joyce, ou l'écriture matricide."
     ÉTUDES FREUDIENNES, No. 7-8 (Apr. 1973), pp. 7-70.

T48 Urnov, D. "Portret Dz. Dzojsa--pisatelja i 'proroka.'"
     ZNAMIA (Moscow), 35 (1965), 315-34. German translation:
     "James Joyce: Schriftsteller und 'Prophet.'" KUNST UND
     LITERATUR, 13 (1965), 1029-55.

T49 Viebrock, Helmut. "James Joyce: Mensch und Werk." AKZENTE,
     8 (1961), 137-45.

T50 Wais, Kurt. "Shakespeare und die neueren Erzähler: Von
     Bonaventura und Manzoni bis Laforgue und Joyce." In SHAKE-
     SPEARE, SEINE WELT--UNSERE WELT. Ed. Gerhard Müller-Schwefe.
     Tubingen: Max Niemeyer, 1964. Pp. 96-133.

T51 Wicht, Wolfgang. VIRGINIA WOOLF, JAMES JOYCE, UND T.S.
     ELIOT: KUNSTKONZEPTIONEN UND KÜNSTLERGESTALTEN. Berlin:
     Akademie-Verlag, 1981. Pp. 103-71.

T52 Wolff-Windegg, Philipp. "Auf der Suche nach dem Symbol:
     James Joyce und W.B. Yeats." SYMBOLON, 5 (1966), 39-52.

T53 Ziolkowski, Theodore. "James Joyce's Epiphanie und die
     Überwindung der empirischen Welt in der Modernen deutschen
     Prose." DEUTSCHE VIERTELJAHRSSCHRIFT FÜR LITERATURWISSEN-
     SCHAFT UND GEISTESGESCHICHTE, 35 (1961), 594-616.

U. STUDIES OF *DUBLINERS* (1914)

U, i. Books and Essay Collections on DUBLINERS

Also see U6 below.

U1 Reichert, Klaus, Fritz Senn, and Dieter E. Zimmer eds.
     MATERIALIEN ZU JAMES JOYCES *DUBLINERS*. Frankfurt a.M.:
     Suhrkamp, 1969.
        Collects, in German translation, early reviews,
        background materials, and several essays on D,
        in a companion volume for Zimmer's German trans-
        lation of D (1969). Includes an extensive bib-
        liography of international criticism of D.

U, ii. General Critical Articles or Chapters on DUBLINERS

U2 Corti, Claudia. "La sinfonia rella paralisi di Dublino."
     STUDI INGLESI (Rome), 2 (1975), 257-74.

U3 Halter, Peter. "Die Epiphanien in James Joyces DUBLINERS."
     In KATHERINE MANSFIELD UND DIE KURZGESCHICHTE. Zurich:
     Francke, 1972. Pp. 56-73.

U, iii. Studies of Individual Stories

"The Sisters"

U4 Kruse, Horst. "Joyce: 'The Sisters.'" In DIE ENGLISCHE
     KURZGESCHICHTE. Ed. Karl Heinz Goller and Gerhard Hoffmann
     Dusseldorf: August Bagel, 1973. Pp. 147-61, 368-72.

"Clay"

U5 Bernhart, Walter. "'Human Nature's Intricacies' and 'Rig-
    orous Truth': Joyces 'Clay,' Becketts 'Dante and the Lob-
    ster' und die Individuation." ARBEITEN AUS ANGLISTIK UND
    AMERIKANISTIK, 1 (1976), 25-64; 2 (1977), 63-98.

U6 Ceserani, Remo. ARGILLA: INTERPRETAZIONE DI UN RACCONTO
    DI JAMES JOYCE. Naples: Guida, 1975.
        Translation of "Clay," with a commentary.

"Grace"

U7 Gozzi, Francesco. "Dante nell'inferno di Joyce." EM, 23
    (1972), 195-229.

V. STUDIES OF *A PORTRAIT OF THE ARTIST AS A YOUNG MAN* (1916)

V, i. Books and Essay Collections on A PORTRAIT OF THE ARTIST
AS A YOUNG MAN

V1   Cianci, Giovanni. L'ALTERITÀ DELL'ARTISTA: *A PORTRAIT OF
     THE ARTIST AS A YOUNG MAN* DI JAMES JOYCE. Palermo: S.F.
     Flaccovio, 1972.

V2   Füger, Wilhelm, ed. JAMES JOYCES *PORTRAIT:* DAS *JUGENDBILD-
     NIS* IM LICHTE NEUERER DEUTSCHEN FORSCHUNG. Munich: Wilhelm
     Goldmann Verlag, 1972.
          Eight bibliographical, critical, and textual
          articles on PAYM. Includes an extended inter-
          national bibliography of criticism on PAYM.

V3   Mietzner, Hartmut. IMMANENZ UND TRANSZENDENZ IN JOYCES
     A PORTRAIT OF THE ARTIST AS A YOUNG MAN UND *ULYSSES*. Frank-
     furt a.M.: Peter Lang, 1978.

V4   Multhaup, Uwe. DAS KÜNSTLERISCHE BEWUSSTSEIN UND SEINE
     GESTALTUNG IN JAMES JOYCES *PORTRAIT* UND *ULYSSES*. Frankfurt
     a.M.: Peter Lang, 1973.

V5   Reichert, Klaus, and Fritz Senn, eds. MATERIALIEN ZU JAMES
     JOYCES *EIN PORTRÄT DES KÜNSTLERS ALS JUNGER MANN*. Frankfurt
     a.M.: Suhrkamp, 1975.
          Selected background materials, letters, reviews,
          and eight critical articles. All items trans-
          lated into German. Includes notes for the text
          and an extensive bibliography of international
          criticism of PAYM.

V, ii. General Critical Articles or Chapters on A PORTRAIT
OF THE ARTIST AS A YOUNG MAN

V6   Chardin, Philippe. "Sortie du dédale et temps retrouvé:
      Les dénouements de A LA RECHERCHE DU TEMPS PERDU de Proust
      et de A PORTRAIT OF THE ARTIST AS A YOUNG MAN de Joyce."
      In ÉTUDES PROUSTIENNES. Paris: Gallimard, 1979. III, 95-
      120.

V7   Erzgräber, Willi. "James Joyce: A PORTRAIT OF THE ARTIST
      AS A YOUNG MAN." In DER MODERNE ENGLISCHE ROMAN: INTER-
      PRETATIONEN. Ed. Horst Oppel. Berlin: Erich Schmidt, 1965.
      Pp. 78-114.

V8   Füger, Wilhelm. "Joyces PORTRAIT und Nietzsche." ARCADIA,
      7 (1972), 231-59.

V9   -----. "Türsymbolik in Joyces PORTRAIT." GERMANISCHE-
      ROMANISCHE MONATSSCHRIFT, n.s. 22 (1972), 39-57.

V10   Gerard, Albert. "Le Dédale de James Joyce." REVUE NOU-
      VELLE, 27 (1958), 493-501.

V11   Gozzi, Francesco. "Archetipi biblici nel PORTRAIT di
      Joyce." STUDI INGLESI (Rome), 2 (1975), 233-55.

V12   Kahn, Ludwig W. "James Joyce: Der Künstler als Luzifer
      und als Heiland." LITERATUR UND GLAUBENSKRISE. Stuttgart:
      W. Kohlhammer Verlag, 1964. Pp. 109-13.

V13   Koljevic, Svetozar. "Roman o recima: Ogled o Dzojsovom
      portretu umetnika u mladosti" ["A Novel about Words: An
      Essay on Joyce's A PORTRAIT OF THE ARTIST AS A YOUNG MAN"].
      KNJIZEVNOST (Belgrade), 22 (1967), 1-16.

V14   Löffler, Renate. "James Joyce: A PORTRAIT OF THE ARTIST
      AS A YOUNG MAN." In LITERARÄSTHETISCHES MODELL UND WER-
      TUNG: EIN VERSUCH MIT TEXTBEISPIELEN. Bern: Herbert Lang;
      Frankfurt a.M.: Peter Lang, 1975. Pp. 70-99; 165-74.

V15   Ludwig, Hans-Werner. "Stephen Dedalus als Sprachkünstler:
      James Joyces Künstlerbildnis zwischen Ästhetizismus und
      Moderne." ANGLIA, 94 (1976), 98-120.

V16   Vidan, Ivo. "Ravnodusnost tvorac" ["The Indifferent Art-
      ist"]. IZRAZ (Sarajevo), 8 (1960), 515-23.

V17 Zaccaria, Paola. "Segno e ideologia in A PORTRAIT OF THE
     ARTIST AS A YOUNG MAN." ANGLISTICA (Naples), 22, No. 2
     (1979), 155–89.

W. STUDIES OF *EXILES*

W1 Genieva, E. IU. "Dzhois i Ibsen." VESTNIK MOSKOVSKOGO
    UNIVERSITETA, No. 10, 3 (May–June 1971), pp. 32–41.

W2 Jacquot, Jean. "Réflexions sur les EXILES de Joyce." EA,
    9 (1956), 337–43.

W3 Reichert, Klaus. "Der nicht aufhebarre Zweiful: ...Über
    den Stellenwert der VERBANNTEN im Gesamtwerk von Joyce."
    THEATER HEUTE, 14 (Aug. 1973), 32. [Reichert's 1968 trans-
    lation of EXILES follows, pp. 33–52].

X. STUDIES OF *ULYSSES* (1922)

X, i. Books and Essay Collections on ULYSSES

Also see X100, below.

X1   Baake, Josef. DAS RIESENSCHERZBUCH *ULYSSES*. Bonn: Peter
      Hanstein, 1937.

X2   -----. SINN UND ZWECK DER REPRODUKTIONSTECHNIK IN *ULYSSES*
      VON JAMES JOYCE. Bonn: Hagen, 1937.
      Includes portions of study above.

X3   Bajarlfa, Juan Jacobo. LITERATURA DE VANGUARDIA--DEL
      ULISES DE JOYCE Y LAS ESCUELAS POETICAS. Buenos Aires:
      Collección Universal, 1946.

X3a   Bangsgaard, Poul Holm. MACINTOSH OG MOLLY: EN ANALYSE AF
      TO PERSONER I JAMES JOYCES *ULYSSES* OG EN KRITISK GENNEMGANG
      AF DELE AF JOYCE LITTERATUREN. Copenhagen: James Joyce
      Society of Copenhagen, 1977.

X4   Bonnerot, Louis, ed. *ULYSSES:* CINQUANTE ANS APRÈS. Paris:
      M. Didier, 1974.
        See M7.

X5   Broch, Hermann. JAMES JOYCE UND DIE GEGENWART. Vienna:
      Reichner, 1936.
        See M93.

X6   Curtius, Ernst Robert. JAMES JOYCE UND SEIN *ULYSSES*.
      Zurich: Neue Schweizer Rundschau, 1929.
        See M112.

X7   DeAngelis, Giulio. GUIDA ALLA LETTURA DELL'*ULISSE* DI J.
      JOYCE. 1961. Rev. ed. Milan: Lerici, 1964.

X8   Dujardin, Édouard. LE MONOLOGUE INTÉRIEURE: SON APPARI-
     TION, SES ORIGINES, SA PLACE DANS L'OEUVRE DE JAMES JOYCE.
     Paris: Messien, 1931.
          See M12.

X9   Egri, Péter. JAMES JOYCE ES THOMAS MANN. Budapest: Aka-
     démiai, 1967.
          See M13.

X10 Esch, Arno. JAMES JOYCE UND SEIN *ULYSSES*. Cologne and
     Opladen: Westdeutsche Verglag, 1970.

X11 Fischer-Seidel, Therese, ed. JAMES JOYCES *ULYSSES*: NEUERE
     DEUTSCHE AUFSÄTZE. Frankfurt a.M.: Suhrkamp, 1977.
          See M17.

X12 Flora, Francesco. POESIA E IMPOESIA NELL'*ULISSE* DI JOYCE.
     Milan: Nuova academia, 1962.

X13 Goll, Ivan, et al. DER HOMER UNSERER ZEIT: DEUTSCHLAND
     IN ERWARTUNG DES *ULYSSES* VON JAMES JOYCE: LETZTE GELEGEN-
     HEIT ZUR SUBSKRIPTION. Zurich: Rhein Verlag, 1927.
          Four essays.

X14 Hentze, Rudolfe. DIE PROTEISCHE WANDLUNG IM *ULYSSES* VON
     JAMES JOYCE UND IHRE SPIEGELUNG IM STIL. Marburg: Elwert,
     1933.

X15 Kreutzer, Eberhard. SPRACH UND SPIEL IM *ULYSSES* VON JAMES
     JOYCE. Bonn: H. Bouvier, 1969.
          Extract reprinted in M17.

X16 Lagercrantz, Olof. ATT FINNAS TIL: EN STUDIE I JAMES
     JOYCES ROMAN *ODYSSEUS*. Stockholm: Wahlström and Wistraud;
     Helsingfors: Söderström, 1970.

X17 Lobsien, Eckard. DER ALLTAG DES *ULYSSES*: DIE VERMITTLUNG
     VON ÄSTHETISCHER UND LEBENSWELTLICHER ERFAHRUNG. Stutt-
     gart: J.B. Metzler, 1978.
          See M38a.

X18 Mietzner, Hartmut. IMMANENZ UND TRANSZENDENZ IN JOYCES
     A PORTRAIT OF THE ARTIST AS A YOUNG MAN UND *ULYSSES*. Frank-
     furt a.M.: Peter Lang, 1978.

X19 Multhaup, Uwe. DAS KÜNSTLERISCHE BEWUSSTSEIN UND SEINE
     GESTALTUND IN JAMES JOYCES *PORTRAIT* UND *ULYSSES*. Frankfurt
     a.M.: Peter Lang, 1973.

X20   Naganowski, Egon. TELEMACH W LABIRYNCIE ŚWIATA: O TWÓR-
        CZOŚCI JAMESA JOYCE'A. 1962. 3rd ed. Warsaw: Czytelnik,
        1971.

X21   Riekenberg, Wolfgang-Hans. JAMES JOYCES *ULYSSES:* VERSUCH
        EINER KULTURSOZIOLOGISCHEN DEUTUNG. Frankfurt a.M.: Haag
        und Herchen Verlag, 1980.

X22   Schmuhl, Norbert. ERFAHRUNGEN DES AUFBRUCHS: AUF PERSPEC-
        TIVITÄT UND APERSPECTIVITÄT IN JAMES JOYCES *ULYSSES*. Frank-
        furt a.M.: Peter Lang; Bern: Herbert Lang, 1976.

X23   Schneider, Ulrich. DIE FUNKTION DER ZITATE IM *ULYSSES*
        VON JAMES JOYCE. Bonn: H. Bouvier, 1970.

X23a   Schöneich, Christoph. EPOS UND ROMAN: JAMES JOYCES *ULYS-
        SES:* BEITRAG ZU EINER HISTORISIERTEN GATTUNGSPOETIK. Hei-
        delberg: Carl Winter Universitätsverlag, 1981.

X24   SECOLUL 20. No. 200 (1977), pp. 50-92. "Permanenta
        Joyce." [In Rumanian.]
            Four essays on U.

X25   Vandenbergh, John. AANTEKENINGEN BIJ JAMES JOYCE'S *ULYS-
        SES*. 1969. 4th ed. Amsterdam: De Bezige Bij, 1977.

X26   Vidan, Ivo. ROMANI STRUJE SVIJESTI: JAMES JOYCE *ULIKS,*
        WILLIAM FAULKNER *BUKA I BEJES* [STREAM OF CONSCIOUSNESS
        NOVELS: JAMES JOYCE'S *ULYSSES*, WILLIAM FAULKNER'S *THE
        SOUND AND THE FURY*]. Zagreb: Skolska Knjiga, 1971.

X, ii.   General Critical Articles or Chapters on ULYSSES

X27   Aquin, Hubert. "Considérations sur la forme romanesque
        d'ULYSSE de James Joyce." In L'OEUVRE LITTÉRAIRE ET SES
        SIGNIFICATIONS. Ed. Renée Legris and Pierre Pagé. Mon-
        treal: Presses de l'Univ. du Quebec, 1970. Pp. 53-66.

X28   Bier, Jean-Paul. "James Joyce et Karl Bleibtreu: Sens
        et fonction d'une allusion littéraire dans ULYSSES."
        REVUE DE LITTÉRATURE COMPARÉE, 40 (1970), 215-23.

X29   Bonnerot, Louis. "James Joyce et David Jones: Contacts
        et Confrontation." In *ULYSSES:* CINQUANTE ANS APRÈS. Ed.
        Bonnerot. Pp. 223-42. See X4.
            See M7.

X30 Cambon, Glauco. "La traduzione italiana d'ULISSE." VELTRO,
     6 (1962), 579-96.

X31 Camerino, Aldo. "L'ULISSE." OSSERVATORE POLITICO LETTER-
     ARIO, 6 (Dec. 1960), 68-77.

X32 -----. "L'ULISSE di Joyce dopo un quarto di secolo,"
     1943; "Le traduzioni da Joyce," 1955; "'Arriva ULISSE,'"
     1960; "Una chiave per ULISSE," 1964. In SCRITTORI DI
     LINGUA INGLESE. Milan and Naples: Riccardo Ricciardi,
     1968. Pp. 234-38, 239-41, 242-45, 246-47.

X33 Cazamian, Louis. "L'Oeuvre de James Joyce." REVUE ANGLO-
     AMERICAINE, 2, No. 2 (1924), 97-113.
         See M101.

X34 D'Agostino, Nemi. "ULISSE o la ricerca della condizione
     umana." BELFAGOR, 16 (Jan. 1961), 96-102.

X35 Daniel-Rops, Henry. "Une Technique Nouvelle: le monologue
     Intérieure." LE CORRESPONDENT, No. 1664 (1932), pp. 281-
     305.
         See M116.

X36 Decker, Heinz. "Der innere Monolog: Zur analyse des ULYS-
     SES." AKZENTE, 8 (Apr. 1961), 99-125.

X37 Döblin, Alfred. "ULYSSES von Joyce." DAS DEUTSCHE BUCH
     (Leipzig), 8 (1928), 84-85.

X38 Durzak, Manfred. "Hermann Broch und James Joyce." DEUTSCHE
     VIERTELJAHRSSCHRIFT FÜR LITERATURWISSENSCHAFT UND GEISTES-
     GESCHICHTE, 40 (1966), 391-433.

X39 Duytschaever, Joris. "Joyce--Dos Passos--Döblin: Einfluss
     oder Analogie?" In MATERIALIEN ZU ALFRED DÖBLINS *BERLIN
     ALEXANDERPLATZ*. Ed. Matthias Prangel. Frankfurt a.M.:
     Suhrkamp, 1975. Pp. 136-49.

X40 Esch, Arno. "James Joyce und Homer: Zur Frage der ODYSSEE-
     Korrespondenzen in ULYSSES." In LEBENDE ANTIKE: SYMPOSIUM
     FÜR RUDOLF SÜHNEL. Ed. Horst Meller and Hans-Joachim Zim-
     merman. Berlin: E. Schmidt, 1967. Pp. 423-32.
         Reprinted, with revision, in M17.

X41 Fehr, Bernhard. "James Joyces ULYSSES." ENGLISCHE STUDIEN,
     60 (1925), 180-205.
         See M136.

X42   Fiol, J.M., and J.C. Santoyo. "Joyce, ULYSSES, y España."
      PAPELES DE SON ARMADANS (Mallorca), 66 (1972), 121-40.

X43   Fischer, Eméric. "Le Monologue intérieur dans l'ULYSSE
      de James Joyce." LA REVUE FRANÇAISE, 28 (1933), 445-53.
      See M138.

X44   Fischer-Seidel, Therese. "Charakter als Mimesis und Rhet-
      orik Bewusstseindarstellung in Joyces ULYSSES." In JAMES
      JOYCES *ULYSSES:* NEUERE DEUTSCHE AUFSÄTZE. Ed. Fischer-
      Seidel. Pp. 309-43. See X11.
      See M17.

X45   Füger, Wilhelm. "Lapwing: Nachträge zu einer vieldisku-
      tierten ULYSSES-Stelle." ANGLIA, 94 (1976), 121-39.

X46   Gabler, Hans Walter. "Werkenstehung und Textsituationen
      des ULYSSES." In JAMES JOYCES *ULYSSES:* NEUERE DEUTSCHE
      AUFSÄTZE. Ed. Therese Fischer-Seidel. Pp. 58-79. See
      X11.
      See M146.

X47   Giedion-Welcker, Carola. "Zum ULYSSES von James Joyce."
      NEUE SCHWEIZER RUNDSCHAU, 21 (1928), 18-32.
      See M150.

X48   Gilbert, Stuart. "ULYSSES, par James Joyce." NOUVELLE
      REVUE FRANÇAISE, 32 (1929), 567-79.

X49   Gonzalez, Manuel Pedro. "El ULISES cuarenta anos depues."
      CUADERNOS AMERICANOS, 22 (1963), 210-27.

X50   Guiguet, Jean. "Virginia Woolf et James Joyce: Un prob-
      lème de dates et de tempéraments." In *ULYSSES:* CINQUANTE
      ANS APRÈS. Ed. Louis Bonnerot. Pp. 23-31. See X4.
      See M7.

X51   Iser, Wolfgang. "Der Archetyp als Leerform: Erzählschablo-
      nen und Kommunikation in Joyces ULYSSES." In DER IMPLIZITE
      LESER: KOMMUNIKATIONS-FORMEN DES ROMANS VON BUNYAN BIS
      BECKETT. Munich: Fink, 1972. I, 300-58.
      See M179. Assimilates X99.

X52   Jacquet, Claude. "Les plans de Joyce pour ULYSSE." In
      ULYSSES: CINQUANTE ANS APRÈS. Ed. Louis Bonnerot. Pp.
      45-82. See X4.
      See M7.

X53 Jeremic, Ljubisa. "Unutrasnji monolog kod Tolstoja i Dzojsa." DELO, 12 (1966), 1242-60, 1390-1406.

X54 Jung, Carl G. "ULYSSES: Ein Monolog." EUROPAISCHE REVUE, 8 (1932), 547-66.
See M180.

X55 Kaiser, Gerhard R. "Joyce, ULYSSES." In PROUST, MUSIL, JOYCE: AUM VERHÄLTNIS VON LITERATUR UND GESELLSCHAFT AM PARADIGMA DES ZITATS. Frankfurt a.M.: Athenaeum, 1972. Pp. 145-225.

X56 Koljevic, Svetozar. "Igra svesti i postojanja u Dzojsovom ULISU" ["The Interplay of Consciousness and Existence in Joyce's ULYSSES"]. IZRAZ (Serajevo), 10 (1966), 429-43.

X57 Larbaud, Valery. "A propos de James Joyce et de ULYSSES." NOUVELLE REVUE FRANÇAISE, 24 (1925), 1-17.

X58 -----. "James Joyce." NOUVELLE REVUE FRANÇAISE, 18 (1922), 385-409.
See M206.

X59 Lewicki, Zbignew. CZAS W PROZIE STRUMIENIA SWIADOMOSCI: ANALIZA *ULISSESSA* JA J'A ORAZ *WSCIEKLOSCI I WRZASKU* I *KIEDY UMIERAM* WILLIAMA FAULKNERA [TIME IN PROSE FICTION: ANALYSES OF *ULYSSES* BY JAMES JOYCE, AND *THE SOUND AND THE FURY* AND *AS I LAY DYING* BY WILLIAM FAULKNER]. Warsaw: Panstwowe Wydawnictwo Naukowe, 1975.

X60 Lundkvist, Artur. IKARUS' FLYKT. Stockholm: Albert Bonniers, 1939. Pp. 73-112 and passim.

X61 Macias, Raul. "ULISES: mito y realidad." UNION (Havana), 2 (Jan.-Apr. 1963), 101-10.

X62 Mercanton, Jacques. "James Joyce." EUROPE, 46 (1938), 433-71. [In French.]

X63 Mikhalskaya, N.P. "ULISS Dzheimsa Dzhoisa." UCHENYE ZAPISKI, MOSKOVSKII GOSUDARSTVENNYI PEDAGOGICHESKII IN-STITUT IMENI LENINA, 304 (1968), 3-33.

X64 Miller-Budnitskaya, R. "ULISS Dzheimsa Dzhoisa." 1934. INTERNATIONAL LITERATURE, No. 4 (1935), pp. 106-16.
See M234.

X65   Mirković, Radoslava. "Tehnika toka svesti u Dzojsovom
      ULISU." DELO (Belgrade), 17 (1971), 1102-20.

X66   Mochizuki, Mitsuko. "[The Meanings of Episodes 4, 5, 6
      in Joyce's ULYSSES.]" DOSHISHA WOMAN'S COLLEGE OF LIBERAL
      ARTS, ANNUAL REPORTS OF STUDIES (Kyoto), 21 (1970), 338-
      65. [In Japanese.]

X67   Monnier, Adrienne. "La Traduction d'ULYSSE." MERCURE DE
      FRANCE, 309 (May 1950), 30-37.
            See R20.

X68   -----. "L'ULYSSE de Joyce et le Public français." LA
      GAZETTE DES AMIS DES LIVRES (Paris), 3, No. 10 (1940),
      50-64.
            See M236.

X69   Moretti, Franco. "Il lungo addio: ULYSSES e la fine del
      capitalismo liberale." STUDI INGLESI (Rome), 3-4 (1976-
      77), 313-45.

X70   Paris, Jean. "Hamlet et ses frères." CAHIERS RENAUD-BAR-
      RAULT, 57 (Nov. 1966), 63-89.

X71   Pimentel, Osmar. "James Joyce (cá entre nós)." In A
      LÂMPADA E O PASSADO: ESTUDIOS DE LITERATURA E PSICOLOGIA.
      São Paulo: Conselho Estadual de Cultura, Commisão de Lit-
      eratura, 1968. Pp. 63-78.

X72   Plebe, Armando. "L'ULISSE di Joyce e l'estetica dell'arte
      al quadrato." GIORNALE CRITICO DELLA FILOSOFIA ITALIANA,
      41 (1962), 219-37.

X73   Pound, Ezra. "James Joyce et Pécuchet." MERCURE DE FRANCE
      156 (1922), 307-20.
            See M255.

X74   Raimond, Michel. "Le monologue intérieur." In LA CRISE
      DU ROMAN: DES LENDEMAINS DU NATURALISME AUX ANNÉES VINGT.
      Paris: Jose Corti, 1966. Pp. 257-98.

X75   Rauter, Hebert. "ULYSSES." In DER ENGLISCHE ROMAN VON
      MITTELALTER ZUR MODERNE. Ed. Franz K. Stanzel. Dussel-
      dorf: August Bagel, 1969. II, 317-55.

X76   Rosenberg, Kurt. "James Joyce: Ein Wanderer ins Reich
      des Unbewussten." GEIST UND ZEIT, No. 4 (1959), pp. 114-
      27.

X77   Rychner, Max. "Wirklichkeit im Roman--Zum ULYSSES von
        James Joyce." DIE TAT, 18-19 Jan. 1941.
            See M274. Reprinted in F47.

X78   Schneider, Ulrich. "Alttestamentarische Anspielungen im
        ULYSSES." In JAMES JOYCES *ULYSSES:* NEUERE DEUTSCHE AUF-
        SÄTZE. Ed. Therese Fischer-Seidel. Pp. 189-212. See X11.
            See M17.

X79   Servotte, Herman. "ULYSSES: De triomf van de kunst." In
        DE VERTELLER IN DE ENGELSE ROMAN: EEN STUDIE OVER ROMAN-
        TECNIEK. Hasselt, Belg.: Uitgeverij Heideland, 1965. Pp.
        113-64.

X80   Simon, Irène. FORMES DU ROMAN ANGLAIS DE DICKENS À JOYCE.
        Liege, Belg.: Faculté de Philosophie et Lettres, 1949. Pp.
        388-437.

X81   Sozonova, I. "Chelovek i khod istorii (I.e., nabliudenii
        nad TIKHIM DONOM)" ["Man and the Course of History (I.e.,
        Observations on AND QUIET FLOWS THE DON)"]. VOPROSY LIT-
        ERATURY, 6 (Jan. 1962), 179-92.

X82   Stanzel, Franz K. "Die Personalisierung des Erzählaktes
        im ULYSSES." In JAMES JOYCES *ULYSSES:* NEUERE DEUTSCHE
        AUFSÄTZE. Ed. Therese Fischer-Seidel. Pp. 284-308. See
        X11.
            See M17.

X83   -----. DIE TYPISCHEN ERZÄHLSITUATIONEN IM ROMAN. Vienna:
        W. Braumuller, 1955. Pp. 122-44.
            See M303.

X84   Sühnel, Rudolf. "Die literarischen Voraussetzungen von
        Joyces ULYSSES." GERMANISCH-ROMANISCHE MONATSSCHRIFT, 12
        (1962), 202-11.

X85   Todorov, Tzvetan. "Le récit primitif." TEL QUEL, No. 30
        (1967), pp. 47-55.

X86   Varela-Jacome, Benito. "James Joyce y el impacto del
        ULISES." RENOVACION DE LA NOVELA EN EL SIGLO XX. Barce-
        lona: Ediciones Destino, 1967. Pp. 144-71.

X87   Vestdijk, Simon. "Hoofdstukken over ULYSSES." 1934. In
        LIER EN LANCET. Rotterdam: Nijgh & Van Ditmar, 1960. Pp.
        90-125.

X88 Wetzel, Heinz. "Spuren des ULYSSES in THE WASTE LAND."
     In BANALE VITALITÄT UND LÄHMENDES ERKENNEN: DREI VERGLEI-
     CHENDE STUDIEN ZU T.S. ELIOTS *THE WASTE LAND*. Bern and
     Frankfurt a.M.: Herbert Lang, 1974. Pp. 39-60, 66-69.

X89 Zhantieva, D.G. "Dzheims Dzhois." In ANGLISKII ROMAN
     XX VEKA. Moscow: Izdatelstvo "Nauka," 1967. Pp. 14-67.
          See M343.

X90 Zolla, Elemire. "Joyce o l'apoteosi del fantasticare."
     In STORIA DEL FANTASTICARE. Milan: Bompiani, 1964. Pp.
     177-91.

X91 Zweig, Stefan. "Anmerkung zum ULYSSES." NEUE RUNDSCHAU,
     39 (1928), 476-79.

X, iii. Studies of Individual Episodes

"Nestor"

X92 Kiasaschwili, Niko. "Die 'Nestor'-Episode als Paradigma
     des ULYSSES." Trans. Ingeburg Hucke. In ERZÄHLTE WELT:
     STUDIEN ZUR EPIK DES 20. JAHRHUNDERTS. Ed. Helmut Brandt
     and Nodar Kakabadse. Berlin and Weimar: Aufbau, 1978. Pp.
     320-36.

"Lotus Eaters"

X93 Topia, André. "Contrepoints joyciens." POÉTIQUE, No. 27
     (1976), pp. 351-71.
          See X96.

"Wandering Rocks"

X94 Guidacci, Margherita. "Sul capitolo X dell'ULISSE." HU-
     MANITAS, 17 (Feb. 1962), 130-37.

"Sirens"

X95   Koegler, Horst. "James Joyce oder die Literarische Meta-
morphose der Musik." SCHWEIZERISCHE MUSIKZEITUNG UND
SANGERBLATT, 93 (1953), 257-60.

"Cyclops"

X96   Topia, André. "Contrepoints joyciens." POÉTIQUE, No. 27
(1976), pp. 351-71.
        See X93.

"Nausicaa"

X97   Hohoff, Curt. "Die schwarze Summa des James Joyce." HOCH-
LAND, 51 (1958-59), 534-44.

X98   Köhler, Erich. "Nausikaa, Danae, und Gerty McDowell: Zur
Literaturgeschichte des Feuerwerkes." In LEBENDE ANTIKE:
SYMPOSIUM FÜR RUDOLF SÜHNEL. Ed. Horst Meller and Hans-
Joachim Zimmerman. Berlin: E. Schmidt, 1967. Pp. 451-72.

"Oxen of the Sun"

X99   Iser, Wolfgang. "Hisorische Stilformen in Joyces ULYSSES:
Zur Interpretation des Kapitels 'The Oxen of the Sun.'"
In LEBENDE ANTIKE: SYMPOSIUM FÜR RUDOLF SÜHNEL. Ed. Horst
Meller and Hans-Joachim Zimmerman. Berlin: E. Schmidt,
1967. Pp. 433-50.
        See M418. Incorporated into X51.

"Circe"

X100   Link, Viktor. BAU UND FUNKTION DER "CIRCE"-EPISODE IM
ULYSSES VON JAMES JOYCE. Bonn: Rheinische Friedrich-

Wilhelms-Univ., 1970.
    Extract reprinted in M17.

X101   Paris, Jean. "Joyce au bordel." CAHIERS DE LA COMPAGNIE
        MADELEINE·RENAUD--JEAN-LOUIS BARRAULT, No. 37 (Feb. 1962),
        pp. 32-36.

X102   Wirpsza, Witold. "Matnia i siec." DIALOG (Warsaw), 9
        (Dec. 1964), 104-12.

"Penelope"

X103   Potvin, Claudine. "Lecture de 'Pénélope': La Notion de
        désir chez Joyce." MOSAIC, 12, No. 3 (1979), 59-67.

Y.   STUDIES OF *FINNEGANS WAKE* (1939)

Y, i. Books and Essay Collections on FINNEGANS WAKE

Y1   Bouchet, André du. JAMES JOYCE: *FINNEGANS WAKE*. Paris:
Gallimard, 1962.

Y2   Campos, Augusto de, and Haroldo de Campos, eds. PANAROMA
DO *FINNEGANS WAKE*. 1962. 2nd ed. São Paulo: Editora Per-
spectiva, 1971.
Six essays, with related materials on FW.

Y3   Eco, Umberto. LE POETICHE DI JOYCE: DALLA *SUMMA* AL *FINNE-
GANS WAKE*. 1962. 2nd ed. Milan: Bompiani, 1966.

Y4   Hayman, David. JOYCE ET MALLARMÉ. 2 vols. Paris: Les
Lettres Modernes, 1956.
See N23.

Y5   Jacquet, Claude. JOYCE ET REBELAIS: ASPECTS DE LA CRÉATION
VERBALE DANS *FINNEGANS WAKE*. Paris: M. Didier, 1972.

Y6   Meneghelli, Pietro. LA LETTERA DI JOYCE. Rome: Lestoille
Editrice, 1978.

Y7   Obradovic, Adeheid B. DIE BEHANDLUNG DER RÄUMLICHHEIT IM
SPATEREN WERK DES JAMES JOYCE. Marburg: Marburg Universi-
tät, 1934.

Y8   POÉTIQUE. 26 (1976), 131-251. "FINNEGANS WAKE." Ed. Hélène
Cixous.
Collects eight original essays on FW. Includes
N125.

Y9   Settanni, Ettore. JAMES JOYCE E LA PRIMA VERSIONE ITALIANA
DEL *FINNEGANS WAKE*. Venice: Cavallino, 1955.

Y, ii.   General Critical Articles or Chapters on FINNEGANS WAKE

Y10   Aubert, Jacques. "FINNEGANS WAKE: Pour en finir avec les traductions?" JJQ, 4 (1967), 217-22.
          See G42.

Y11   Borges, Jorge Luis. "Joyce y los Neologismos." SUR, No. 62 (1939), pp. 59-61.

Y12   Campos, Augusto de. "Um lance de 'des' do GRANDE SERTÃO." REVISTA DO LIVRE, 4 (Dec. 1959), 9-28.

Y13   Cesare, Lorenzo. "La metafora joyciana: Un'analisi della favola 'The Ondt and the Gracehoper.'" STRUMENTI CRITICI, 12 (1978), 332-52.

Y14   Eco, Umberto. "Le moyen âge de James Joyce." Trans. Louis Bonalumi. TEL QUEL, No. 11 (1962), 39-52; No. 12 (1963), 83-92.

Y15   -----. "Semantica della metafora." In LE FORME DEL CON- TENUTO. Milan: Bompiani, 1971. Pp. 93-125.

Y16   Giedion-Welcker, Carola. "Die Funktion der Sprache in der Heutigen Dichtung." TRANSITION, No. 22 (1933), pp. 90-100.

Y17   -----. "Ein Sprachliches Experiment von James Joyce." NEUE SCHWEIZER RUNDSCHAU, 22 (1929), 660-71.
          See N106.

Y18   Gillet, Louis. "A propos de FINNEGANS WAKE." BABEL, 1 (1940), 101-13.
          See N109.

Y19   Gysen, René. "Links en rechts." KOMMA, 2 (1966), 57-63.

Y20   Henrici, Waldtraud Barbara. "Anspielungen auf Ibsens Dramen in FINNEGANS WAKE." OL, 23 (1968), 127-60.

Y21   Hildesheimer, Wolfgang. "Übersetzung und Interpretation einer Passage aus FINNEGANS WAKE von James Joyce." In INTERPRETATIONEN. Frankfurt a.M.: Suhrkamp, 1969. Pp. 7-29.

Y22   Jacquet, Claude. "Fonctions du language dans FINNEGANS WAKE: Néologismes et glossolalies." In AUTOUR DE L'IDÉE DE NATURE, HISTOIRE DES IDÉES ET CIVILISATION, PÉDAGOGIE, ET DIVERS. Paris: M. Didier, 1978. Pp. 253-66.

Y23 Jolas, Eugene. "Elucidation du Monomythe de James Joyce."
     CRITIQUE, 4 (1948), 579-95.

Y24 MacCarvill, Eileen. "Les Années de Formation de James
     Joyce à Dublin." ARCHIVES DES LETTRES MODERNES, No. 12
     (1958), 1-31.

Y25 Mason, Eudo C. "Joyces FINNEGANS WAKE." In EXZENTRISCHE
     BAHNEN: STUDIEN ZUM DICHTERBEWUSSTSEIN DER NEUZEIT. Got-
     tingen, Neth.: Vandenhoeck and Ruprecht, 1963. Pp. 284-92.

Y26 Mercanton, Jacques. "FINNEGANS WAKE (notes pour une 'In-
     troduction à la méthode de Joyce')." NOUVELLE REVUE FRAN-
     ÇAISE, 27 (1939), 858-64.

Y27 Naganowski, Egon. "La nuit au bord du fleuve de la vie;
     essai d'interpretation de FINNEGANS WAKE." LETTRES NOU-
     VELLES, 11 (Feb.-Mar. 1964), 80-94.

Y28 Paris, Jean. "Finnegans, wake!" UNIVERS PARALLÈLES II:
     LE POINT AVEUGLE: POÉSIE, ROMAN. Paris: Éditions de Seuil,
     1975. Pp. 223-35.

Y29 Pelorson, Georges. "FINNEGANS WAKE de James Joyce, ou
     les Livres de l'homme." REVUE DE PARIS, 1 (Sep. 1939),
     227-35.

Y30 Petitjean, Armand M. "El Tratamiento del Lenguaje en
     Joyce." SUR, No. 78 (1941), pp. 42-59.

Y31 Rabaté, Jean-Michel. "La 'missa parodia' de FINNEGANS
     WAKE." POÉTIQUE, No. 17 (1974), pp. 75-95.

Y32 Rump, Gerhard Charles. "FINNEGANS WAKE, oder: Das Uni-
     versum des James Joyce." In SPRACHNETZE: STUDIEN ZUR LIT-
     ERARISCHEN SPRACHVERWENDUNG. Ed. Rump. Hildesheim: Georg
     Olms, 1976. Pp. 141-219.

Y33 Schmidt, Arno. DER TRITON MIT DEM SONNENSCHIRM: GROSS-
     BRITANNISCHE GEMÜTSERGETZUNGEN. Karlsruhe: Stahlberg,
     1969. Pp. 194-328.

Y34 Tello, Jaime. "Un experimento joyceano." REVISTA NACIONAL
     DE CULTURA, 29 (Sep.-Dec. 1961), 61-79.

Y35 Verdin, Simonne. "Tradlire Joyce: Journal d'une lecture."
     COURRIER DU CENTRE INTL. D'ÉTUDES POÉTIQUES, No. 132-34
     (1979), pp. 1-39.

Y36 Werckmeister, O.K.   "Das Book of Kells in FINNEGANS WAKE."
     NEUE RUNDSCHAU, 77 (1966), 44-63.

Z.   STUDIES OF JOYCE'S MISCELLANEOUS WRITINGS

Z, i. Books and Essay Collections on Joyce's Miscellaneous
Writings

Z1   Aubert, Jacques. INTRODUCTION A L'ESTHÉTIQUE DE JAMES
     JOYCE. Paris: M. Didier, 1973.
          See P1.

Z2   Corsini, Gianfranco, and Giorgio Melchiori, eds. JOYCE AS
     AN ITALIAN WRITER: REGARDING SCRITTI ITALIANI DI JAMES JOYCE.
     Milan: Mondadori, 1979.
          See B14.

Z3   Putzeys-Alvares, Guillermo. LOS JUICIOS LITERARIOS EN JAMES
     JOYCE. Mexico City: UNAM, Inst. de Investigaciones Filo-
     sóficas, 1974.

Z, ii. General Critical Articles or Chapters on Joyce's Miscellaneous Writings

Z4   Forster, Jean-Paul. "Joyce, STEPHEN HERO, et Stephen Ded-
     alus." ÉTUDES DE LETTRES, 9 (1966), 149-64.

Z5   Puccini, Dario. "Neruda traduttore di Joyce." In STUDI
     DI LETTERATURA SPAGNOLA. Rome: Facoltà di Magistero e
     Facoltà di Lettere dell'Univ. di Roma, 1965. Pp. 234-41.
          Neruda's translations of JJ's poetry.

Z6   Risset, Jacqueline. "Joyce traduit par Joyce." TEL QUEL,
     55 (1973), 47-58.

APPENDIX: STUDY GUIDES

With the exception of the last item, the titles listed here are
mostly plot summaries, with interspersed, elementary commentary,
and offer little of interest or value even to the beginning
reader of JJ's works. They are entered in this volume to make
the record of monograph- and book-length publications on JJ more
nearly complete.

Brown, Richard K. JOYCE'S *A PORTRAIT OF THE ARTIST AS A YOUNG
MAN*. New York: Barrister, 1966.

Ellis, Charles R., et al. *A PORTRAIT:* A CRITICAL COMMENTARY.
New York: R.D.M., 1963.

Handley, Graham. BRODIE'S NOTES ON JAMES JOYCE'S *A PORTRAIT
OF THE ARTIST AS A YOUNG MAN*. London: Pan Books, 1977.

Hopper, J.L. A COMPREHENSIVE OUTLINE OF JOYCE'S *PORTRAIT OF
THE ARTIST*. East Longmeadow, Mass.: Harvard Outline Co., 1965.

Lilly, Katherine A. *A PORTRAIT OF THE ARTIST AS A YOUNG MAN*
BY JAMES JOYCE: NOTES. Lincoln, Neb.: Cliff's Notes, 1964.

Morton, Richard. *ULYSSES*. Lincoln, Neb.: Cliff's Notes, 1972.

NOTES ON JAMES JOYCE'S *A PORTRAIT OF THE ARTIST AS A YOUNG MAN*.
London: Methuen Educational, 1971.

Quasha, George. JAMES JOYCE'S *DUBLINERS* AND *A PORTRAIT OF THE
ARTIST AS A YOUNG MAN*. New York: Monarch Press, 1965.

-----. JAMES JOYCE'S *ULYSSES:* A CRITICAL COMMENTARY. New York:
Monarch Press, 1965.

Staley, Thomas F. A CRITICAL STUDY GUIDE TO JOYCE'S *A PORTRAIT
OF THE ARTIST AS A YOUNG MAN*. Totowa, N.J.: Littlefield Adams,
1968.
    See K18.

INDEXES

This index includes all authors, compilers, editors, and trans-
lators of the works entered in this volume. Also included are
interviewers and interviewees, and contributors to collections
and panel discussions who are named in annotations, but whose
contributions are not otherwise entered and annotated in the
bibliography.

Borach, Georges F9, R4
Borel, Jacques S8
Borges, Jorge Luis Y11
Bornhauser, Fred M255
Botti, Lido F42
Bouchet, André du Y1
Bowen, Elizabeth H23
Bowen, Zack G13, G14, J96,
    K31, K36, M87, M284, M423,
    P9
Bowers, Fredson M244
Boyd, Elizabeth F. K37
Boyd, John D. J157
Boyd, Ruth A. J157
Boyle, Patrick H24
Boyle, Robert, S.J. G15,
    G27a, H25, J98, J105,
    J138, J145, M88–M91, M451,
    N66, N67
Bradbury, Malcolm M175
Brandabur, Edward J4, K38,
    P2
Brandt, Helmut X92
Brasil, Assis S9
Bredin, Hugh H26
Brennan, Joseph Gerard H27
Brewster, Dorothy K42, M98
Briand, Paul L., Jr. M92
Brick, Allan M410
Brion, Marcel N68
Briskin, Irene Orgel M363
Brito, Raúl Blengio-. See
    Blengio-Brito, Raúl
Brivic, Sheldon R. G16
Broch, Hermann M93, X5
Brodbar, Harold J106
Broes, Arthur T. N69–N72
Brooke, Jocelyn M94
Brooks, Cleanth J80, M95
Brophy, James D. H5, H143,
    H240, N206
Brower, Reuben A. J28
Brown, Carole L8

Brown, Homer O. J5, K3
Brown, Malcolm F10
Brown, Norman O. N12
Brown, Richard K. Appendix
Browne, Ray B. K38
Bruni, Alessandro Francini-.
    See Francini-Bruni, Ales-
    sandro
Bruns, Gerald L. M438
Bryer, Jackson R. M96
Buckalew, Ronald E. N73
Buckley, Jerome H. K39
Budgen, Frank F11–F14, F133,
    M8, N74–N76
Budnitskaya, R. Miller-. See
    Miller-Budnitskaya, R.
Burgauer, Arnold R5
Burgess, Anthony B20, G17,
    M9, N77
Burgum, Edwin B. M97, N78
Burke, Kenneth J158, K40,
    K41
Burrell, Angus K42, M98
Busi, Frederick N79
Butler, Christopher N79a
Butor, Michel G42
Byram, M.S. F72
Byrd, Don H28
Byrne, John Francis F15

Cage, John N13
Cahoon, Herbert E25, G57
Cambon, Glauco X30
Camerino, Aldo X31, X32
Campbell, John W. K4
Campbell, Joseph H29, M99,
    N14, N80
Campos, Augusto de N24, Y2,
    Y12
Campos, Haroldo de N81, Y2
Card, James Van Dyck M452,
    M453

Curry, Sister Martha   J25
Curtius, Ernst Róbert   M112,
   X6

D'Agostino, Nemi   T9, X34
Dahl, Liisa   H42, K48
Dahlberg, Edward   H43
Daiches, David   H44, H45,
   M113
Dalton, Jack P.   G42, M114,
   N16, N90
Daly, Leo   F25
Damon, S. Foster   M115
Daniel, George B.   H53
Daniel-Rops, Henry   M116,
   X35
Davies, Aneirin Talfan   S13
Davies, Stan Gebler   F26
Davis, Edward   K49
Davis, Joseph K.   J26
Davis, Richard B.   M218
Davis, William V.   J109
Day, Robert Adams   J99, M117,
   M118, M351, M352
Deakin, William   H46
de Almeida, Hermione.   See
   Almeida, Hermione de
Deane, Paul   J161
Deane, Seamus   M119
DeAngelis, Giulio   X7
Debenedetti, Giacomo   S14,
   T10
de Campos, Augusto.   See
   Campos, Augusto de
de Campos, Haroldo.   See
   Campos, Haroldo de
Decker, Heinz   X36
Delaney, Frank   F27
Delany, Paul   J27, J129
Delattre, Floris   T11
Delbaere-Garant, Jeanne   K50,
   M120

Delimata, Bozena Berta
   [Schaurek]   F28
Deming, Robert H.   E8, E9,
   G25
Deneau, Daniel P.   J116
den Haan, Jacques.   See Haan,
   Jacques den
Derwent, Lord   F47
Destéfano, José R.   T12
De Tuoni, Dario.   See Tuoni,
   Dario de
DiBernard, Barbara   M121, N17
Dibble, Brian   K51
DiGaetani, John Louis   H47
Dill, Wolfgang   F46
Dillon, John M.   N40
Dimes, Louis T.   M11
Döblin, Alfred   X37
Dobrée, Bonamy   N91
Doherty, James   K52
Dohmen, William T.   N92
Dolch, Martin   J89, J110,
   J126
Dolmatch, Theodore B.   N93
Dombrowski, Theo Q.   L11
Doody, Terrence A.   M122
Dorenkamp, John H.   J39
Doyle, Paul A.   D3, E10
Drachler, Jacob   N18
Drescher, Horst W.   T13
Drew, Elizabeth A.   K53, M123
Driver, Clive   B22
du Bouchet, André.   See
   Bouchet, André du
Duff, Charles   G27
Dujardin, Édouard   M12, M127,
   R8, X8
Duncan, Edward   M372
Duncan, Joseph E.   M124
Dundes, Alan   M125
Durant, Ariel   H48
Durant, Jack M.   M364
Durant, Will   H48

Jolas, Maria F74–F76, F90,
  F133, F145, G8, G45, H230,
  M93, N187, S6
Jones, David E. K83
Jones, William Powell G46
Jordan, John G23, H103
Jordan, Richard D. J36
Josipovici, Gabriel K94,
  M240
Joyce, Eva F133
Joyce, James. See Part I:
  Primary Bibliography
Joyce, John Stanislaus F77
Joyce, Stanislaus B5, F78–
  F82, F133, F148
Jung, Carl G. M180, X54

Kabish, Ernest Bernhardt-.
  See Bernhardt-Kabish,
  Ernest
Kahn, Ludwig W. V12
Kain, Richard M. B17, E17,
  E20, F83–F85, F101, F136,
  G58, H104, H105, J148, K12,
  K15, K84, K102, M35, M181–
  M187, M375, N144, P17
Kaiser, Gerhard R. X55
Kakabadse, Nodar X92
Kaplan, Harold J. M188
Karl, Frederick R. K85, M189
Kauvar, Elaine M. J149
Kavanagh, Patrick F86
Kaye, Julian B. H106, J73,
  J170, K86, M190
Kazemier, G. T6
Keen, William P. J37
Kelleher, John V. J171, K87,
  N1, N145
Kellogg, Robert H187, M376
Kelly, Robert G. H107
Kelly, Sean N28
Kennedy, Eileen J63

Kenner, Hugh G27a, G47, G48,
  H108–H110, K88, K89, M36,
  M191–M196, M428, N146
Kenny, Thomas J. F87
Kermode, Frank H111
Kerr, Alfred F88, R17
Kershner, R.B. K90, M377
Kestner, Joseph A. G44,
  H112, L17
Kettle, Arnold H113, M197
Khinkis, Victor E29
Kiasaschwili, Niko E29, X92
Kiely, Benedict F71, H114,
  H115
Kiely, Robert H116
Killham, John M198
Kimball, Jean M199, M200
Kimpel, Ben D. H117, M201
Kinkead, D. H150
Kinkead-Weekes, Mark H81
Kiralis, Karl N147
Klawitter, Robert H118
Klein, A.M. M346, M349, M419
Klein, James R. K91
Klein, Michael K92
Kloss, Robert J. J119
Klug, Michael A. M202
Knight, G. Wilson H119
Knox, George J172
Knuth, A.M. Leo G49, L8,
  M27, M203, M204, N27, N148
Koch, Ronald J. N27
Koegler, Horst X95
Köhler, Erich X98
Koljevic, Svetozar V13, X56
Kopper, Edward A. G50, M205,
  N149
Korg, Jacob H120, N150
Korninger, Siefried J64
Kreutzer, Eberhard X15
Kronegger, Maria Elisabeth
  G51
Kruse, Horst U4
Kumar, Shiv K. H121

M412, N1, N4, N22, N196, N197, R27, S44; U1, V5
Servotte, Herman   X79
Sessions, Roger   P3
Settanni, Ettore   Y9
Seward, Barbara   H195
Shapiro, Stephen A.   M289
Share, Bernard   H196
Sharpe, Garold   M384
Sharpless, F. Parvin   K133
Shattuck, Charles   J41
Shechner, Mark   G43, M57
Sheehy, Eugene   F137
Sheehy, Michael   F138
Shelley, Percy Bysshe   K15
Shloss, Carol   M290
Short, Clarice   J108
Sidnell, M.J.   H197
Sillanpoa, Wallace   H176
Silverman, Oscar A.   B6, P26
Silverstein, Norman   F70, M433–M436
Simon, Elliott, M.   L25
Simon, Irène   X80
Sisson, C.H.   P27
Slade, Carole   M291
Sloan, Barbara L.   J132
Slochower, Harry   H198
Slocum, John J.   E25, G57
Slomczynski, Maciej   G42
Smidt, Kristian   G74
Smith, Don N.   M292
Smith, John Bristow   K17
Smith, Paul Jordan   M58
Smith, Sydney G.   N204
Smith, Thomas F.   J183
Smyer, Richard I.   M293
Solberg, Sara M.   H199
Sollers, Philippe   H96, N24, N198, T26
Solomon, Albert J.   J92, J93, M294
Solomon, Margaret C.   M295, M398, N41, N199, N200

Somerville, Jane   J52
Sorensen, Dolf   P5
Sosnowski, James J.   G44, J82
Soupault, Philippe   F139, R28
Sozonova, I.   X81
Spears, Monroe K.   H200
Spencer, John   M296
Spencer, Theodore   B21, P28
Spender, Stephen   N201
Spiegel, Alan   H201
Spielberg, Peter   E26, J68, K134
Spilka, Mark   M297
Spivey, Ted R.   H202, N163
Splitter, Randolph   H203, N202
Spoerri, James F.   E27
Sporn, Paul   M429
Sprinchorn, Evert   K135
Squire, John C.   K136
Staley, Harry C.   H204
Staley, Thomas F.   E28, F140, F141, G75, H205, J1, J69, J124, K18, K19, K137, M59, M60, M298–M300, P29, P30, Appendix
Stanford, William B.   H206, M301, M302
Stanzl, Franz K.   J64, M303, X75, X82, X83
Staples, Hugh B.   F69, M408, N26, N203
Stark, Helmuth   R29
Starkie, Enid   H207
Stavrou, C.N.   M304, M305
Stein, Sol   M306
Stein, William B.   J86, J94, J112
Steinberg, Erwin R.   H208, K138, M61, M279
Steloff, Frances   F142
Stephens, James   F143, P3
Stern, Frederick C.   J141, M307, M350, M409

TITLE INDEX

This index includes the titles of all books, essay collections, monographs, and pamphlets entered in this guide, as well as of all Joyce's major publications. Article titles are omitted. In all cases of identical titles, the author's or editor's name has been place in parentheses after the title. The entry number(s) indicates the first, or, in a few cases, each complete listing of the title with full publishing data. An essay collection, therefore, will ordinarily have but one entry number, referring the user to the collection's full entry and its annotation where cross-reference numbers for its contents are provided.

ARTIST AS A YOUNG MAN, A
  K18, Appendix
CRITICAL WRITINGS OF JAMES
  JOYCE, THE B4
CRITICISM M221
CULT OF THE EGO, THE H79
CYCLICAL NIGHT, THE G68
CZAS W PROZIE STRUMIENIA
  SWIADOMOSCI X59

D'ANNUNZIO E IL SIMBOLISMO
  EUROPEO T34
DARK CONCEIT H94
DARK DOVE, THE H229
DAWN N7
"Day of the Rabblement, The"
  B4
"Dead, The" A2
DEAR MISS WEAVER F92
DECENTERED UNIVERSE OF
  FINNEGANS WAKE, THE N38
DEDALUS ON CRETE K8
DIONYSUS AND THE CITY H200
DIRECTIONS IN LITERARY CRIT-
  ICISM N55
DOCTOR LOOKS AT LITERATURE,
  THE M106
DOCUMENTARY AND IMAGINATIVE
  LITERATURE J159, K44
DUBLIN IN BLOOMTIME F120
DUBLIN IN THE AGE OF WILLIAM
  BUTLER YEATS AND JAMES
  JOYCE F83
DUBLIN MAGAZINE. "A James
  Joyce Number" G26
DUBLINERS A2, J23
DUBLINERS: TEXT, CRITICISM,
  AND NOTES J13
DUBLIN'S JOYCE G47
DZHEIMS DZHOIS R34
DZIELA WYBRANE R24

EARLY JAMES JOYCE, THE J8,
  K10
EARLY JOYCE, THE B5
"Ecce Puer" B3
EDWARDIANS AND LATE VICTORIANS
  K55
EGUZAILU NO BUNGAKU T39
EIGHT MODERN WRITERS H211
ELEMENTS OF FICTION J123
ELEVEN ESSAYS IN THE EUROPEAN
  NOVEL M85
EMINENT DOMAIN F32
"Encounter, An" A2
ENGLISCHE DICHTER DER MODERNE
  T31
ENGLISCHE KURZGESCHICHTE, DIE
  U4
ENGLISCHE ROMAN VON MITTEL-
  ALTER ZUR MODERNE, DER X75
ENGLISCHE UND AMERIKANISCHE
  LITERATUR-THEORIE T13
ENGLISH LITERATURE BETWEEN
  THE WARS H55
ENGLISH LITERATURE OF THE
  TWENTIETH CENTURY H35
ENGLISH NOVEL, THE (Dyson)
  E19
ENGLISH NOVEL, THE (Watts)
  H81
ENGLISH NOVEL, THE: A SHORT
  CRITICAL HISTORY M68
ENGLISH NOVEL, THE: FORM AND
  FUNCTION K141
ENGLISH NOVEL FROM DICKENS TO
  LAWRENCE, THE M339
ENGLISH NOVEL IN TRANSITION,
  THE H65
ENGLISH NOVEL OF TODAY, THE
  H80
ENGLISH NOVELISTS, THE H213
ENGLISH POETRY, 1900-1950
  P27

SUBJECT INDEX

This index includes all historical and literary figures, literary and mythological characters, and titles named or discussed in the entries and annotations in this bibliography.
Occasionally *implied* names and titles are also included (e.g.,
a discussion of the character Hamlet would be indexed under
both HAMLET and Shakespeare, whether or not title and author
are named). It also indexes literary and critical terms,
kinds of criticism, and prominent themes and topics in Joyce
criticism. Finally, it includes all references to cities and
nations, cultures and languages, places and institutions.

Joyce's works are indexed, by title, under his name. All remaining historical, literary, philosophic, or other titles are
indexed by title, with the author's name provided in parentheses. Stephen Dedalus' aesthetic theories and villanelle, both
subjects which have prompted considerable discussion, are indexed under the main entry for his character.

Allegory H94, J106, J145, L6, M371, P23
America: Culture and Literature F96, H205, J71, N222, N226, T13. Also see Boston, Broadway, Buffalo, Cornell, Gotham Book Mart, Hunter College, New York City, Yale University and individual American authors and figures, by name.
Anarchism G60
Anderson, Sherwood J25
AND QUIET FLOWS THE DON (Sholokhov) X81
Androgyny G66
Animals: Imagery and Symbolism J112, K29, K32, M148, M155, M282, N89, N197, X45
Annotations; Character Dictionaries, Directories, and Encyclopedias; Maps and topographical studies F17, G11, G13, G35, G41, J7, J13, K1, K9, K27, M20, M27, M35, M41, M51, M52, M55, M56, M64, M160, M167, M183, M237, M245, M257, M278, M291, M294, M341, M349, M383, M386, M416, M420, M437, M453, N1, N2, N9, N11, N15, N20, N21, N23, N34, N36, N37, N39, N40, N42, N45, N50, N60, N61, N69, N153, N217, N218, V5
Antheil, George F4, F149
Anthropology M325, N83, N94
Apocalypticism H210
Aquinas, St. Thomas G66, G69, H11, H26, H95, H140, H154, H220, K15, K83, M440, P5

Archaeology K60, M182, M193
Archetype. See Myth
Architecture. See Art
À REBOURS (Huysmans) M426
Aristotle G32, K83, M124, M198, M357, M448, N213, P1
Arnold, Matthew M328
ARS MEMORIAE (Bruno) M433
Art: Architecture, Drawing, Painting, and Sculpture E17, F56, F63, F147, G40, G79, G81, H130, H131, M16, M45, M64, M79, M93, N18. Also see below.
Art and literature G51, H99, H130, H131, K31, K79, M235, N79a, N103, N104, N106, N168, N188, N201. Also see art, and individual artists and art movements, by name.
Art Nouveau N104
Artifoni, Almidano F22
AS I LAY DYING (Faulkner) X59
Astronomy. See Science
Auden, W.H. F32
Augustine, St. G66, H139
Austen, Jane N182
Australia: Culture and Literature H192
Austria: Culture and Literature H69
Autobiographical fiction G35, G36, H71, H161, J77, J87, J143, K7, K12, K14, K15, K23, K114, K120, M19, M57, M168, M190, M310, M324, N6, N203, N208, P33, Z4
Autobiography K114, K120, M258

M354, M356, M358, M359,
M363, M372, M374, M380,
M381, M384, M389, M415,
M424, M428, M436, M448,
P1, P4, P24, V10, V15,
Z4
--. Aesthetic theory (in
   PAYM and STEPHEN HERO)
   G15, G69, G70, G72, G74,
   H8, H11, H13, H21, H26,
   H38, H59, H95, H138,
   H140, H145, H154, K6,
   K14, K15, K31, K38, K47,
   K49, K72, K73, K83, K97,
   K123, K127, M22, M108,
   M266, P1, P5
--. Shakespeare theory (in
   U) G20, G74, M22, M55,
   M57, M230, M280, M372,
   M375, M376, M377, M381,
   M384
--. Vilanelle (in PAYM)
   K33, K36, K65, K128,
   K131, P4
Defoe, Daniel K120, M51,
   M56, M258
DEHARBE CATECHISM H204
Derrida, Jacques N38
DeSassure, Fernand N146
Diaries. See Journals and
   diaries
Dickens, Charles B11, G48,
   H212, K39, M297, M339, X80
Dictionaries, Character.
   See Annotations
Directories, Character.
   See Annotations
DISSOCIATION OF A PERSON-
   ALITY, THE (Prince) N110
DIVINE COMEDY, THE (Dante)
   J20, J151, M15, M291, N53
Döblin, Alfred G1, M44,
   M222, X39

DON GIOVANNI (Mozart) M160,
   M264
DON JUAN (Byron) M2
DON QUIXOTE (Cervantes)
   M122
Döppelganger, The M111
Dos Passos, John X39
Dostoevsky, Feodor G77, T19
Double, The. See Döppel-
   ganger, The
Doyle, Arthur Conan H101
Drama and drama criticism
   A3, B4, B10, B13, B18, D2,
   G82, J15, J180, J181, M425,
   M428, P1, P18, P20, Y20.
   Also see EXILES and indi-
   vidual dramatists, by name.
Dramatic adaptations M421,
   N35, N108, N126. Also see
   Film and literature.
Drawing. See Art
Dualism N17
Dublin, Ireland A2, F15,
   F17, F19, F24, F27, F35,
   F56, F61, F67, F78, F83,
   F94, F106, F120, F126,
   F145, F150, F151, G10, G39,
   G47, G52, G73, G82, H103,
   H188, H196, H221, K84, M19,
   M27, M77, M225, M231, M260,
   M284, M291, M314, M408,
   N203, Y24. Also see Bel-
   vedere College, Clongowes
   Wood School, DUBLINERS,
   Phoenix Park, University
   College.
DU CÔTE DE CHEZ SWANN K106
Dujardin, Édouard G42, H19,
   H87, K48, M116, M127, R1,
   R8